Introduction

CW00985523

Underlying prin
Rationale
A suitable curricu
A single target
An ethos of succe
A choice of contra
Working well with
Recognition of all
Differentiation   16
Acceleration or fast tracking   18
Case studies   20
The vital link from identification to provision   22
Combating the underachievement of able pupils   24
The starting point and number of steps in a process   26
Finding time   28
Homework   30
Different working methods   32
Suitable reading   34

Thinking skills
Visual thinking   36
On the move   38
Length and style appropriate to the purpose   40
Question-and-answer sessions   42
Group-work   44
Problem solving   46
Classification   48
Evaluation   50
Prediction   52
Abstract thinking   54
Creativity   56
Numeracy   58
Lateral thinking problems   60
Logical thinking   62

Enrichment
Matrix problems   64
Detective work   66
Codes   68
Wordplay   70
Dictionary and thesaurus   72
Homonyms   74
Crosswords   76
Proverbs   78
Crossing subject boundaries   80
Poetry across the curriculum   82
Putting the fun into learning   84
Picture books   86

Final thoughts and answers
Putting on curriculum glasses   88
Going on from here   90
Answers   92

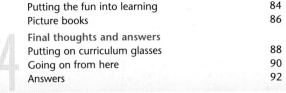

Underlying principles

Technique or Need

Rationale

☛ Teachers are very busy people. The level of paperwork has increased. Initiatives proliferate. To tackle anything with enthusiasm, rather than a token gesture, there has to be good reason.

☛ Until fairly recently there has been an apathetic approach to able pupils in many schools. Now, with government schemes and more attention from inspection reports, there has been a greater sense of purpose. In England, the White Paper of 2005 stressed the need for more lessons that are stretching and opportunities for gifted and talented pupils. Similar problems exist in other countries.

☛ There are three unhelpful attitudes that some teachers still need to combat:

1. Clever children look after themselves – they do not need attention.

2. Able children were born lucky. Attention should be directed to those with problems and difficulties.

3. A fear of able children; teachers sometimes worry that they cannot cope with very able pupils.

☛ The responses are clear. All children need and deserve attention, even if the help is provided in different ways. Training and materials are now widely available to learn how to deal with able pupils and how to improve provision for them.

Before teachers can get full benefit from teaching strategies and classroom activities with able and talented children, they need to take note of key principles. This section explains these key principles and how to apply them.

Application of Activities

Promoting the advantages

There are many extremely positive reasons for improving provision for able pupils.

✓ All children, and indeed all staff, have the right to reach their full potential.

✓ This is an equal opportunities issue. For some years teachers have accepted that no child should be discriminated against on the grounds of race, religion, gender or social background. Add ability to that list. Another way of viewing the same ideas is that of Inclusion.

✓ There are knock-on positive effects for other pupils. General expectations are lifted.

✓ Exciting teaching and learning opportunities are promoted. This lifts the morale of pupils and teachers.

✓ There is professional satisfaction for teachers in working in an enriched atmosphere. Being the facilitator for a child to succeed provides a real 'buzz'.

✓ It helps to reduce disaffection and bad behaviour because, when bored, some able pupils become mischievous.

✓ This is an important consideration in satisfying the needs of a sizeable group of parents.

✓ The welfare of the school is improved. Any school that does not look after its able pupils not only harms them but also every other pupil in the school.

✓ For teachers in comprehensive schools (and that includes primary schools), the welfare of the whole system is improved.

Put another way, quite simply:

**IT IS OUR JOB TO DO OUR BEST
FOR EVERY CHILD INCLUDING THE MOST ABLE.**

A suitable curriculum

☞ There are a number of problems with the daily diet of many able pupils. As a result some become bored and 'turned off'. Content has to be delivered, but it has to be presented in a challenging and interesting way.

Key situations
to avoid
include:

➡ Too many examples of the same level of difficulty when the pupil has already proved his or her competence.

➡ More steps in a process than is really needed just to be in line with pupils of lesser ability.

➡ Too early a starting point – one that would be appropriate for some children but that ignores what the able child already knows or can do.

➡ Too much 'spoon-feeding' in terms of teacher direction and instruction.

➡ Time gained by early completion of tasks being frittered away rather than allowing progression to more challenging activities.

➡ Too many prescribed or 'closed' tasks where the able pupil does not have the opportunity to develop the work.

Application or Activities

The use of appropriate Curriculum Tools avoids the problems.

Here are ELEVEN ENRICHERS

1. Presenting content in a challenging and interesting way.

2. The creative use of resources, including changing the purpose, moving the age and crossing subject boundaries.

3. Playing to individual preferred learning styles while maintaining challenge.

4. Using subject checklists not only to identify able pupils but also to inform the curriculum.

5. Looking at the common general needs of able pupils.

6. Using a taxonomy of thinking skills to place emphasis upon analysis, synthesis and evaluation.

7. Examining what makes a task more difficult and challenging, and incorporating those elements into the work programme.

8. Using the various forms of differentiation.

9. Employing a range of strategies for appropriate organization, and internal and external enrichment.

10. Learning from able children themselves, using questionnaires and surveys, and from the materials that 'turn them on'.

11. ENJOYMENT.

Note: these ideas are developed later in the book.

Technique or Need

A single target

☛ Targets and target-setting have come to dominate various aspects of public life in recent years, which is certainly true of education. The trouble is that when there are too many targets, efforts can be dissipated. Also it is easily measurable targets that tend to be used even if they are not the most important.

☛ The government identified a number of targets in connection with able pupils that teachers need to bear in mind – more setting, better test scores, early entry to examinations, participation in World Class Tests, and more children, in England, to enrol with the National Academy for Gifted and Talented Youth.

☛ A very important observation has been made as a result of school inspections and particular surveys. Since increased public awareness, there has been a substantial improvement in the provision of summer schools, special activities and enrichment courses. However, the provision for able pupils in normal lessons has not seen much improvement.

☛ This, then, has to be the single target:

Better provision in normal lessons, for that constitutes the bulk of the time for all able pupils and, without it, we are only looking at 'bolt-on' activities.

Application or Activities

Hitting the single target

There are a number of methods that can be employed to be in a position to evaluate whether there is improvement of provision for able pupils in normal lessons:

★ Examination of schemes of work and lesson plans to ensure that planning for able pupils is included.

★ Pupil tracking: following able pupils in different subjects and recording the type of challenge being offered and the levels of use of the various types of differentiation (see p16).

★ Classroom observation by teachers of their colleagues to witness the effects of changes.

★ Discussion about named pupils at regular intervals in staff meetings.

★ Interviews with a sample of able pupils to obtain their views on the provision available and whether it has improved.

★ Questionnaires for the parents of able pupils to fill in, including their views on provision in normal lessons.

★ Reviews of able pupils' progress as part of pupil target-setting or Individual Education Plans (see p23).

An ethos of success and achievement

☞ In England there is a pervading belief that it is not quite 'the done thing' to talk about success and achievement. Certainly one wants to avoid boasting and arrogance, but not celebrating success is a damaging practice.

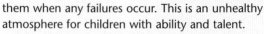

☞ The media seem to take delight in building people up prematurely and then destroying them when any failures occur. This is an unhealthy atmosphere for children with ability and talent.

☞ The greatest cause of underachievement in able pupils is peer pressure. There is a ridiculous notion that success is somehow not cool. As a consequence, pupils who do well, especially in academic work, are frowned upon and worse. There is an insidious form of bullying involving calling able children 'prof', 'boff' and so on.

☞ It is vital that schools work actively to promote a positive ethos. Otherwise able pupils will shy away from answering questions. They will deliberately stop performing at a high level.

☞ Every teacher is responsible for the atmosphere of his or her classroom. Ignoring the abuse of able pupils is, to put it bluntly, a dereliction of professional duty.

Application or Activities

Creating the right ethos

A whole-school approach is needed to create the right ethos. It could well include the following:

★ As well as a Code of Conduct in classrooms, a Code of Achievement should be displayed that encourages the shared celebration of success, rather than envy.

★ The adoption of a wide model of what constitutes ability (see p14). The more areas that are included, the greater the number of avenues to success and the larger percentage of children will be involved. What, then, is the point of abusing those who are good at English or mathematics?

★ Children already do value talent in some areas – modern dance routines, computer know-how and skateboarding, for example. All teachers need to work actively to show that success in, for instance, poetry is no different.

★ The display of appropriate messages on posters or notice boards and in social areas is helpful. Examples could be '**Success comes in cans not in can'ts**' and '**The only place where success comes before work is in the dictionary**'.

★ Photographic displays, newspaper cuttings and school awards should be in prominent view. One school had a gigantic display containing a photograph of every child and adult doing something well. The subliminal messages are clear – '**Success is cool**', '**Everybody can succeed**', '**We can celebrate success together**'.

★ School assemblies are also vital times to celebrate success. To overcome the tendency to become shyer as children get older, include staff. 'Can we applaud Mrs Jarvis who was a member of the winning quiz team at the Dog and Duck this weekend?'

A choice of contract

You stand with two contracts, rolled up neatly and tied with red ribbon, one in each hand and you offer them in turn to able children. You say:

Left hand (held out)

'In my left hand I have a contract that recognizes you as an able child. As a result, the contract requires that you work longer hours than other children, so that you can deliver your full ability.'

Right hand (held out)

'In my right hand I have another contract that also recognizes you as an able child. However, this contract does not require you to work longer hours but to work more smartly. You can deliver your full ability by making time through not repeating what you can already do and by missing out steps that you do not need, and then using that time to take on exciting and challenging tasks.'

Both hands (held out)

'Which contract do you want?'

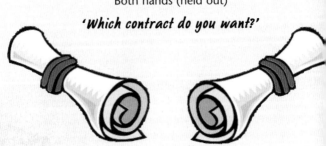

Application or Activities

What happens as a result?

Left-hand contract

Most able children will not want to work longer hours. This is an unattractive proposition. It seems punitive. Why should the fact that they are able mean that they have to work longer? This would take away leisure time. This contract makes some able children not want to be identified. 'Don't get mixed up with that as there goes your football or reading' is likely to be the response.

There are a few able children who will choose the left-hand contract, either because they are workaholics or because they gain credit with their parents, but they will be very much in the minority.

Right-hand contract

This contract has a much better chance of succeeding. It seems fairer. It allows time for other interests to be followed. This is not a bar to able children wanting to be identified. In fact it is quite the reverse because this way they are presented with more interesting work.

This contract does not, however, stop children with a particular talent or ability from spending extra hours in the art studio, on the sports field, in the drama studio, in the swimming pool, in the chemistry laboratory or, indeed, anywhere else if they volunteer to do so.

Working well with parents

☞ Some parents are unrealistic about the level of ability or the amount of time that can be spent on an individual pupil. However, the majority are not like that. They do possess information and experience about their able children that can be put to good use in a partnership with teachers.

☞ In England, the OFSTED report of December 2001, 'Providing for Gifted and Talented Pupils; an evaluation of Excellence in Cities and other grant-funded programmes', contains a very important comment: 'It was clear in the schools visited that, despite concerns about possible misunderstandings, teachers need to enlist the support of parents for their work with gifted and talented pupils if the provision for them is to be effective. Concerns about the reaction of parents – whether their children are included or otherwise – are not likely to be resolved by maintaining a discreet silence.'

☞ Consideration needs to be given to those parents of able pupils who love their children and wish to do their best by them, but they do not know what help to give. Teachers have a key role, here, in providing advice and pastoral support.

Application or Activities

Practical steps for parents

★ Hold a parents' meeting to discuss and explain the school's provision for able pupils. Put out a general invitation, rather than asking only certain parents.

★ Make available a school policy document on able pupils for parental perusal.

★ Explain the strategies on provision for able pupils in the school brochure.

★ Prepare a booklet for parents on ways in which they can help their able children.

★ Involve parents in the identification system. Invite them to write a letter detailing what they believe the child's abilities are and the evidence to support these comments. New information becomes available as a result of this process.

★ Keep parents well informed of any methods being employed to avoid any misunderstandings. If the level of difficulty of work is increased, parents need to know that so as to judge marks realistically.

★ Make clear the routes by which parents of able pupils can make comments and ask questions. The particular nature of homework is one example where concern might be expressed.

Technique or Need

Recognition of all types of ability

☞ The leading aim must be to make good provision for able children within good provision for all children. To achieve this, schools need to create an ethos of success and achievement (see p8) and to expand the pool of talent.

☞ Academically-able pupils are very important and their needs must be met, but they are only one part of the overall picture.

☞ The greatest cause of underachievement by able pupils is peer pressure and a belief that it is not cool to succeed. The wider the model of ability is, the more pathways to success there are available and the greater will be the number of pupils who achieve. This, in turn, produces an ethos of success and achievement, thus taking the pressure off those who are academically able.

☞ We need a wide model, not only to increase the number of children who have a stake in their school but also to satisfy the needs of society. In the many trouble spots of the world, do we need more physicists and engineers or more leaders and negotiators? The answer is that we need both.

Application or Activities

A wide and inclusive model

To improve provision for all able pupils, including those who are academically able, teachers and schools need to apply:

a wide and inclusive model.

This recognizes ability
across a wide range of activities.

1. High intellectual capacity.

2. Talent in the performing arts.

3. Mechanical, engineering and practical skills.

4. Sensitivity, especially carers and others with interpersonal intelligence.

5. Inspirational leadership.

6. Negotiating ability.

7. Physical prowess.

8. Presentational skills.

9. Creativity and imagination.

10. Problem-solving abilities.

11. Ability to work in teams and get the best from others.

12. Determination and perseverance.

13. Stamina, with the ability to concentrate over a long period.

14. Thinking 'outside the box'.

Differentiation

☞ Differentiation is one of the most important tools in good curriculum provision for able pupils.

☞ Successful differentiation involves a number of linked elements:

1. Recognizing that children show marked differences in ability and aptitude.

2. Accepting that those differences mean that children have contrasting needs.

3. Realizing that individual needs can only be met by variations in provision.

4. Planning programmes of work that take account of individual differences in terms of ability and, therefore, needs.

☞ The theory of differentiation has been around for a long time but reports and school inspections have shown that practice has not matched the theory.

☞ Recent government attention on improving the education of able pupils has included emphasis upon appropriate differentiation. 'Excellence in Cities', for example, asks for 'a distinct teaching and learning programme'.

Application or Activities

Forms of differentiation

**There are various forms of differentiation and
many can be applied at the same time.**

Differentiation by outcome or response
The same material or stimulus is used for all the children but the
work is set in such a way that able pupils can answer at a higher
level. Open-endedness is often a key feature.

Differentiation by resource or text
Able pupils are provided with more advanced resources to promote
more sophisticated responses.

Differentiation by task
Able pupils carry out tasks that are more challenging, even though
the subject is the same as for other children.

Differentiation by dialogue
Teachers use extended vocabulary, higher concepts and more
challenging questions in their spoken exchanges with able pupils.

Differentiation by support
Unnecessary instruction is omitted, but support is given in a
prompting, more sophisticated manner.

Differentiation by pace
Planning here refers to how many and how quickly tasks are to be
completed. Urgency and greater pace are employed for able pupils.

Differentiation by content
Time gained is used for able pupils to tackle material outside the
normal syllabus. This content produces a wider and deeper
understanding.

Differentiation by independence or responsibility
Able pupils are involved more in decisions about their own learning
programme. They help to decide where the work should go next.

Acceleration or fast tracking

- In documents such as 'Excellence in Cities', there has been support for acceleration.

- This is the practice of accelerating able pupils through a course ahead of other pupils. They cover work in advance of the normal chronological pattern. In examination courses this often results in early entry for the examination. There can also be co-operation with universities to include advanced material ahead of time.

- Some schools have, perhaps, adopted this approach without due consideration of the alternatives or the consequences of acceleration. This was certainly the view expressed in *Acceleration or Enrichment*, produced by the UK Mathematics Foundation, University of Birmingham School of Mathematics (2000), following a seminar held at the Royal Society.

- One obvious alternative to acceleration is enrichment, that is giving pupils suitably challenging material but within the normal organizational pattern.

Criteria to apply to acceleration

The following principles should be followed:

❖ In examination courses the results will be at least as good as they would have been if entry had been at the normal time.

❖ The course is not destroyed in terms of engagement and enjoyment by rushing through material.

❖ There is sensible follow-up planned in the time produced by acceleration.

❖ All partners in the child's education are part of the planning. Otherwise, for instance, acceleration in the primary school could produce repetition in the secondary school.

❖ The decision to accelerate is based not only upon the child's capacity to handle the more advanced work intellectually but also that social and emotional factors have been taken into account.

Case studies

☞ A case study is an example of a particular able child, normally with a message coming out of it on a potential problem and what would make good provision or suitable handling.

☞ Case studies can involve national figures, people from a particular locality or be restricted to a school itself.

☞ Pupils, past or present, from the school itself provide, perhaps, the most influential situations to consider, as teachers react well to cases close to their own experience.

☞ One major use of case studies is to assist the identification of able pupils. A collection of well-chosen case studies gives solid examples of the qualities required. Such a collection, by its inclusion of children of varied talents, stresses to teachers that there are many facets to being able and talented.

☞ A second major use of case studies is in staff training. Contrasting studies provide discussion opportunities for analysis of the case and the appropriate pastoral care and curricular provision.

Application or Activities

Anne

❖ Anne attended a series of enrichment sessions but the start was far from auspicious. On the first occasion, she made limited effort and appeared lazy.

❖ The one exception was a very fine contribution to a team verbal presentation, in which Anne excelled. She commandeered the flip chart and dominated proceedings.

❖ An honest report was given to the parents at the end of the course. Anne, a child of great self-confidence, bordering on arrogance, was present when the report was given.

❖ The tutor was delighted to see much greater all-round effort from Anne on subsequent courses. Her efforts on some tasks, especially written, were only moderate for a group of able children but whenever a verbal presentation was involved, she was a 'star'.

Points for discussion

1. Where do you place Anne within a model of what constitutes ability?

2. Why do you believe that she made a greater effort after the first course?

3. Are there any lessons for planning work in school or for constructing an enrichment course in your school?

Answers: p92)

Technique or Need

The vital link
from identification to provision

☞ We do not identify able children just to have a register or a list. If you said to an able child 'I have identified you as being able in a particular area but I am not going to do anything about it', the child would not be impressed and is likely to wonder 'Why bother?'

☞ The reason for identification is so that provision can be improved to meet the needs of the child. It is a starting point, not an end in itself.

☞ Ironically, the best form of identification is provision. You only know what somebody is capable of doing when the correct opportunity is presented. This places a premium upon lessons that are challenging, and that use varied inputs and outcomes. It is sad to reflect that many people might possess a talent of a high order but it is hidden as the opportunity to discover it has never occurred.

☞ School inspectors and internal evaluators look to see that the vital link is in place to take identification on to better provision. This can be the result of staff discussions, general pupil target-setting or the extension of the Individual Education Plan (IEP) system to able pupils.

Application or Activities

A sample Individual Education Plan

Name *Bernard Lamb*

Area(s) of the curriculum involved:
Tennis, mathematics

Background evidence (summary only):
Reports from the manager of the County Tennis Squad; a parental letter; teacher referral forms from the physical education and mathematics departments; a transition report from the primary school; very high CATs scores; internal mathematics examinations; outstanding performance during mathematics enrichment days.

Action to be taken:
Participation in specialist tennis coaching sessions.
Nomination for area tennis trials.
Enrichment and extension tasks in mathematics lessons.
Differentiated homeworks in mathematics.
Provision of wider resources in mathematics for interest and enjoyment, such as the books of Professor Ian Stewart and Tony Gardiner.
Entry to mathematics masterclasses at the local university.
Application to the National Academy for Gifted and Talented Youth.

Review:
Yearly from the date of this IEP.

Combating the underachievement of able pupils

☞ To some extent this is the most important area of all. Able pupils who are achieving can be assisted by work of a more challenging and exciting nature. There is great concern for those who are not delivering their talent.

☞ One step is to introduce an Underachieving Pupil Referral sheet. This asks about the present level of performance, the evidence for suggesting that the pupil can do better, the possible causes for the underachievement and suggestions to improve the situation.

☞ There are a number of possible causes to consider, including:

1. Peer pressure. It is not cool to succeed. Able pupils draw unfavourable attention to themselves. They might be bullied.

2. Laziness. Not all able children work hard and do their best.

3. Shyness. They may not want to be the centre of attention.

4. Poor working habits. There can be poor organization, a lack of stamina or a short span of concentration.

5. Boredom. If work is dull and repetitive, some able pupils give up.

6. An undiscovered disability. The pupil may have a hearing or visual problem, or be dyslexic.

7. Family background. If there is an absence of academic experience or support, then assistance and advice might be in short supply.

Application or Activities

Appropriate action depends upon the cause of the underachievement. These suggestions match the numbers on the opposite page.

1. A whole-school approach is required to promote an ethos of success and achievement (see p8). The bullying of able pupils needs to be tackled as an integral part of the whole-school policy on bullying. The first step is for all teachers to recognize that such abuse is unacceptable.

2. Sometimes a firm approach is needed. Just because you work to improve the provision for able pupils, does not mean that you 'go soft' on them.

3. Recognition of good work privately may well be the first step.

4. Advice on study skills will help those who are disorganized. Stamina and span of concentration have to be gradually built up by work of ever-increasing length and difficulty.

5. Work has to be presented in a lively, challenging way. Playing to the sense of humour of able pupils is also productive.

6. Professional help is required to uncover the problem and then to suggest remedial action.

7. Teachers need to step into the breach and provide more advice than would be needed in other cases. There may also be very practical steps, such as providing transport to sports trials.

The starting point and number of steps in a process

☞ For ease of organization, there is a tendency to start a group of children off from the same point. This can be a problem for the most able members of a group as the practice ignores previous knowledge and experience. Some able pupils are already 'some way down the road'.

☞ To repeat what one already knows can cause boredom and frustration. In some able children this can also lead to poor behaviour.

☞ Reading schemes for young children need to be reviewed in the light of this concern. If you start school already possessing some reading ability, it is soul-destroying going back to 'square one'.

☞ Consideration must also be given to the number of steps in a process. If it takes the average child six steps to achieve something, and the able child just three to achieve the same thing, why should the able child waste his or her time on steps that they do not need?

☞ The reward for adjusting the starting-point and the number of steps is the availability of more time. This time can then be used to challenge and excite the able pupils.

Application or Activities

➤ A group of able pupils came together with the author on a thinking-skills enrichment course. For some it was the first visit but others had attended earlier courses. This resulted in a mixture in terms of previous knowledge and experience. That same situation applies in the normal classroom when a 'new' topic is introduced.

➤ The particular piece of work involved a logic problem that could be solved by the matrix method (see p64).

➤ Children in the group, who had all been chosen for their ability, were given the choice of where they started and how they progressed.

1. Those who had never used the matrix method were advised to listen to an explanation of the technique.

2. Those who had used the method before were given the choice of listening to refresh their memories or to move on to the exercises.

3. The first exercise was called 'Case Histories'. The task was to match eight detective cases, known by names such as 'Brighton Blackmail' and 'Threatening Letter' with the year in which they were solved, by means of a series of clues. In 'Case Histories', therefore, there were two variables.

4. There was then a step-up in terms of difficulty to 'Detective Case Clues'. There were now three variables – the case titles from the previous exercise, the surnames of the detectives in charge and the vital clue that helped solve the case. The number of clues and the sophistication of language were increased to extend the challenge.

5. Participants were given the choice of doing 'Case Histories' first and then 'Detective Case Clues' or to go straight to the more difficult piece.

Note: these two pieces can be found in Barry Teare's *More Effective Resources for Able and Talented Children* (Network Educational Press).

Technique or Need

Finding time

☞ In an ever increasingly busy world, teachers and schools often make the plea 'Where do we find the time?'

☞ There are four main areas of need for time in terms of provision for able pupils:

1. Teachers are 'initiative fatigued'. They spend a great deal of time on paperwork. Even so, there is a need to plan good provision for the most able children in their classes.

2. There is a huge amount of prescribed content to cover. Heavy demands have been placed by the National Curriculum, the Literacy Framework, the Numeracy Framework and examination syllabuses. Time is required for able pupils to get involved in enrichment work.

3. The normal school timetable works on relatively short periods of time. However, activities that are more extensive are required for able pupils.

4. With large groups of children to teach, much time has to be devoted to those who are not the most able. The teacher still needs to find time to challenge the most able.

Application or Activities

Making time

These applications are matched, by number, to the needs on the opposite page:

1. Only the government of the day can really tackle problems concerning too much paperwork and too many initiatives. However, teachers can co-operate within the school, and across schools, to pool ideas and resources to use with able pupils. A website could be made available.

2. If able children are not asked to cover what they already know and are not required to use more steps than they personally require, time is freed up. Also, prescribed content can be covered in a more challenging way, at the same time as other members of the class are following more standard procedures.

3. Activities weeks and occasional suspension of the normal timetable can provide longer blocks of time. Some schools have used such a scheme in co-operation with the group called Creative Partnerships. Attendance at enrichment days, weekends or summer schools also gives able children the opportunity to tackle longer activities. Another technique is to use a group of homeworks, especially where the child has already mastered the content of the normal homework.

4. As difficult as it is, all children deserve a share of the teacher's time. For able children this will be spent differently. There is also a growing practice of enlisting the help of classroom assistants in making more contact available.

Homework

☞ The majority of purposes behind setting homework for pupils generally apply equally well to able children.

☞ Preparation for future lessons, research, working on their own, independent learning and organizational skills are all appropriate.

☞ Homework provides a good opportunity for diagnostic assessment by both pupils and teachers. It can also promote links with parents.

☞ The area of concern is where homework is used to consolidate basic skills. This is necessary for many children, but for able pupils, who have mastered the skill, it causes resentment because of the boring and repetitive nature of the tasks.

☞ Used properly, homework can assist able pupils by:

a) promoting choice

b) providing a chance to use the higher-order thinking skills

c) extending learning

d) stimulating reference to more advanced texts.

Application or Activities

The application here is by way of a case study.

Mary

- ❖ Mary is a perceptive, strong-minded girl who normally expresses her views clearly. She is an able child who demonstrates particular strength in mathematics.

- ❖ Recently there has been a growing problem over the non-completion of maths homework. Marks, once top-rate, have fallen. Mary has already served one detention after school, as punishment for non-completion, and she is threatened with another.

- ❖ Her parents, who have quite old-fashioned ideas about education, are both annoyed and mystified as there is no question about her ability to complete the homeworks – indeed it seems easy for Mary to do well.

Points for discussion

1. What are the possible reasons for this developing problem about maths homeworks?

2. Suggest solutions to improve the situation.

(Answers: p92)

以下。

Technique or Need

Different working methods

☞ Able pupils, the same as other children, have different preferred learning styles. Some enjoy physical activities and practical methods (kinesthetic learners); some benefit from visual inputs; others like learning by sound (auditory learners).

☞ These preferences need to be taken into account by using varied inputs and allowing varied types of response. However, preferred learning styles alone will not suffice. Whatever the style, there still needs to be real challenge or the provision will not be suitable for able pupils.

☞ Much work has been done on a range of learning conditions, which should be accommodated where possible. The optimum level of temperature varies for children. Some work best in silence, others benefit from a musical background. Being allowed to move around sensibly assists the work of some able pupils.

☞ Able pupils respond to a task in different ways. They should be encouraged to use the one that suits them best, so long as it is not ridiculously long-winded and time-consuming.

Three paths to the same answer

In some of the many courses with able children run by the author, a logic problem called 'Canine Avenue' (Barry Teare, *Enrichment Activities for Able and Talented Children*, Network Educational Press) was used.

The scenario used is an avenue with six houses, in five of which live a dog. Information enables the solver to link people with houses numbers 1–6 and where they were situated in relation to each other. From the introductory information and a number of linked clues, the task is to work out which dog belongs to which people and the number of the house where there is no dog.

❖ Some able children, who had a preference for mathematical-logical methods, employed the matrix method (see p64), with its system of ticks and crosses.

❖ Those who liked visual information drew a map of 'Canine Avenue', writing on the numbers, the people and the dogs, and crossing out alternatives as the clues were used.

❖ A third group cut up slips of paper and wrote upon them the names of the people, the numbers 1–6 and the breeds of dog, including 'no dog'. These kinesthetic learners then physically moved about the slips of paper to get to the solution.

All three methods proved effective and time-efficient. Allowing a choice of approach proved beneficial to all the children.

Technique or Need

Suitable reading

☞ It is good that able children read challenging literature. However, it is important to realize that they, as well as adults, sometimes like to relax with less demanding material.

☞ Able readers have the skills to read a book technically well ahead of their chronological age. The danger is that the book may have social and emotional elements far beyond the child's experience and understanding.

☞ A wide variety of reading books is advisable. Some boys prefer non-fiction. Poetry should be included.

☞ Features to look for in novels for able children include:

★ dealing with an important issue

★ being strong on wordplay and vocabulary extension

★ displaying a particular sense of humour

★ containing symbolism, second meanings, allegories, going beyond the literal

★ involving magic, mystery, fantasy, intrigue

★ displaying a mystical quality and strong sensitivity

★ exploring alternative ways of viewing the world

★ presenting a way of exploring the reader's own emotions

★ containing language that is haunting and beautiful

★ having strong characters who are believable

★ involving complicated plots that demand concentration

★ stimulating the imagination strongly.

☞ Above all, we need to pay heed to the words of Michael Morpurgo:

'The reason you put a book in front of a child is for the child to enjoy it, to learn to love reading. Books are not just there to be used as exercises.'

Application or Activities

Try these!

Some recent titles:

 Anthony Horowitz, *Raven's Gate*: new boy-hero Matt Freeman features in what is to be a series called 'The Power of Five'. A fast-moving adventure story with a sinister background; strange occurrences abound. Imaginative and creative writing.

 Geraldine McCaughrean, *Not the End of the World*: the author's treatment of Noah's Ark and the flood is spellbinding. It is a demanding and challenging text: strong on philosophical and moral issues. Much of the book describes loss, cruelty, squalor and brutality, but there is an underlying beauty and uplifting of the spirit.

 Terry Pratchett, *A Hat Full of Sky*: this is a very funny book but there are also beautiful passages of language. There is much symbolism and the book also deals with important themes. The climax is stupendous. It is, on the one hand, memorable nonsense and, on the other, a wonderful story of human relationships and true worth.

 David Almond, *Clay*: typical of this award-winning author, there is a mixture of magic and mystery together with stark realism. *Clay* has a strange beauty. You are left not quite knowing where the truth lies about the strange, living clay figure.

 Michael Morpurgo, *Private Peaceful*: the author has a deceptively simple style. He tells his stories very directly but there is a depth of emotion, humanity and understanding. The book concerns brothers Tommo and Charlie in the First World War but it also describes a picture of life in the Devon countryside that is touching despite its harshness. There is a clever time format. What food for thought there is in *Private Peaceful* for able children to contemplate!

Technique or Need

Visual thinking

- ☞ It is said that 29 per cent of people have a visual preference for their learning.

- ☞ To assist these children in particular, teachers are advised to make full use of posters, displays, maps, charts and graphs.

- ☞ Such learners benefit from keywords being displayed around the classroom.

- ☞ Visual preference learners enjoy presenting information in a pictorial format. They make good use of mind maps or topic webs. When problem solving, a useful route is to use a flow chart. Timelines, too, present data in an easily understood manner.

- ☞ Visual thinkers like to visualize scenes; they are observant. Such children are good at recognizing unfolded three-dimensional shapes. They appreciate presenting a story in a storyboard format.

- ☞ A very productive route is to encourage able pupils to make visual representations of concepts. One obvious method is that of cartoons. Science concept cartoons have become famous. The same idea can be used in all curriculum areas.

- ☞ Very successful with visually-able mathematicians has been to play 'Aerial Noughts and Crosses'. Having constructed a board in their heads, the nine spaces are completed by placing noughts and crosses alternately by giving their co-ordinates. Children say who has won the game and the co-ordinates of the three spaces through which the winning line passes.

Application or Activities

Stars in their eyes

In an attempt to see patterns and to organize their surroundings, humans have grouped stars into constellations. Most of the prominent constellations have names taken from ancient myths and legends. The star plans have been used as the basis for figures. A good deal of imagination is needed to convert the pattern of the stars into elaborate drawings, such as a scorpion or an archer.

your tasks

1. Study the made-up star plan below.

2. Make a copy of the star plan and then create a figure based upon the pattern of the stars. (You may find it helpful in visualizing a shape to draw connecting lines between the stars, in any way you find interesting.)

3. Write a short story centred on your figure.

THE STARS PLAN

xtension tasks

1. Make up patterns of stars of your own.

2. Create figures from these patterns or exchange plans with another pupil and design a suitable figure.

Technique or Need

On the move

☞ Able children have different learning styles (see p32). Kinesthetic learners tend to be active, enjoying movement and tackling tasks in a practical way. All children, in any case, respond to varied activities.

☞ Some materials can be dealt with in a stationary, standard way but they can be enhanced by creating a situation in which children move about. Treasure hunts have proved very popular with able pupils. In earlier books by the author (details on pp90–91) there have been a number of such pieces. '2 Across, 4 Down' requires pupils to collect clues on a treasure hunt, solve them and complete a crossword. In 'Passing Sentence' children visit 30 sites in an attempt to name 30 words. Coloured cards indicate whether the word is a noun, a verb, an adjective, an adverb or a preposition. 'Follow the Yellow Brick Road' is concerned with children's literature. 'The Mathematics Detectives' requires participants to locate ten general mathematical items and then solve 35 other sets of questions based upon a variety of elements, such as numbers, terminology, sequences, shapes and figures. 'Travellers in Time and Place' applies the treasure hunt format to the humanities subjects.

☞ Another scenario that works well and includes movement is a murder investigation. In 'Final Curtain' a circuit arrangement provides 'crime squads' with the opportunity to visit the scene of the crime, a theatre shop, a newspaper office, a theatre agency and the forensic laboratory to gather evidence.

Application or Activities

Knowing the victim

It is said by detectives that once you know the victim of a murder well you are assisted in the solution of the crime. Pupils are therefore asked to construct as detailed a picture as possible of the victim by studying evidence.

Various spaces are created to represent the rooms of the victim's house. The pupils, organized in crime squads, move around the locations on a circuit basis, viewing evidence and making notes. They then compile a report after discussion within the group.

The decisions on which 'rooms' to create and what evidence to place there are obviously flexible and capable of a variety of situations. Possibilities include:

- a study-type area housing documents, letters and an appointment book

- a bedroom with clothing and personal items

- a garage space, not used for a car but storing sports equipment and items concerned with DIY

- a lounge with bookcases and a newspaper rack containing magazines and periodicals.

Note: it is beneficial to provide evidence that is capable of a variety of interpretations to enable pupils to use higher-order thinking skills, creativity and imagination (while being realistic) in their discussions and report.

Technique or Need

Length and style appropriate to the purpose

☞ The way able pupils work varies considerably. Many of them, however, tend to cut corners, use their own shorthand and often do not show their own workings and reasoning. Their minds work very quickly and they want to solve a problem, or provide an answer, as speedily as possible. Setting down every detail becomes a tedious chore.

☞ Problems can therefore occur in test situations or in examinations. Without a proper explanation marks are lost. If the final answer is wrong, no credit can be given for the process.

☞ There is a danger that if able pupils are forced to set things out in the standard form all the time, they can become frustrated and bored.

☞ Fortunately, most able children are perceptive. They will appreciate 'doing a deal' whereas they do not respond well to 'flannel' about the wonderful qualities of SATs and other examinations.

★ The deal is:

a) On test days they answer in the required, detailed manner for everybody's sake, including their own.

b) Much of the time, in lessons and for homework, a shorter style is appropriate and will be accepted.

However 'the deal' does include enough practice of the standard format ready for test days.

Application or Activities

Terse Tom

During an enrichment course in Devon, the author was working with a group of able children from Year 6. The course was detective style and the pieces of work were chosen to challenge and to bring a number of thinking skills into play.

Take Any 5 From 52

There are five playing cards face down on the table. For this exercise the cards were given a points value (ace = 1, jack = 11, queen = 12, king = 13, others their actual number). Picture cards for this puzzle were aces, jacks, queens and kings. A series of seven clues were given about the positions, the suits, the number value of certain combinations and so on. (The full piece is published in Barry Teare, *More Effective Resources for Able and Talented Children*, Network Educational Press). The task was to identify the five cards and their positions.

Tom's answer

The full explanation, given that synthesis from the clues is required, takes up most of one side of A4. This was Tom's answer, completed at breakneck speed:

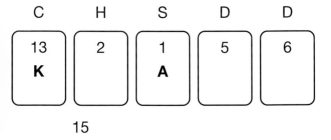

ABSOLUTELY CORRECT
Acceptable on the day but not in test conditions!

Technique or Need

Question-and-answer sessions

☞ Asking questions is a normal part of most lessons. It is a basic teaching skill that comes into use very frequently indeed. Getting the best value out of question-and-answer sessions is therefore very important.

☞ Able children have a particular need. They require a greater percentage of questions involving the higher-order thinking skills of synthesis, analysis and evaluation.

☞ Research has shown that, for all children, there is a preponderance of questions concerning knowledge and simple comprehension. Some years ago, Trevor Kerry in his book, *Effective Questioning* (Macmillan), found that 80 per cent of questions in the classroom were lower-order questions concerned with data recall or simple comprehension, 15 per cent of questions were to do with class management, discipline or administration, and a mere 5 per cent of the questions were higher-order. In separate research, Ted Wragg came up with similar findings. These studies were some time ago and techniques may well have improved, but not enough to answer the needs of able pupils.

☞ There is also a marked tendency to allow insufficient time for a child to respond. The teacher then asks somebody else or answers the question him/herself. If anybody responds to an important question instantly, it is probably true to say that not enough serious consideration has been given.

Application or Activities

★ Ask a colleague to observe one, or more, lessons and record the percentage of questions that fit the lower-order skills of knowledge and comprehension, the middle-order skill of application and the higher-order skills of synthesis, evaluation and analysis.

★ Ahead of lessons, deliberately plan sufficient questions to fit the higher-order thinking skills. Examples are: Synthesis – 'If the Germans had won the Battle of Britain, how do you think that the course of the Second World War would have changed?' Evaluation – 'What were the main factors that contributed to the success of the BBC television series "Bleak House" in 2005?' Analysis – 'How similar, or not, were the methods used in their work by Isaac Newton and Albert Einstein?'

★ Introduce a taxonomy of thinking skills, such as Bloom's, to pupils and get them to set questions at each level on subject matter currently under study.

★ Make a conscious effort to allow more time for an able pupil to make a considered response to a higher-order question.

★ Plan a sequence of questions on a topic being taught that probe deeper into understanding of the subject content.

Remember how important questioning skills are:

'A good question is like a candle in the dark, shedding light on both truth and mystery.'

'Robert Fisher, *Teaching Children to Learn*, Stanley Thornes, 1995, p17.)

Technique or Need

Group-work

☞ A very important aspect of provision for able pupils is how they fit into various groups.

☞ One element of group-work is the overall arrangement in terms of streaming, setting or mixed ability. As most able people are able in only particular areas rather than being equally able across the board (supported by the jagged profile most people have when analysing their multiple intelligences), streaming is not a sensible route.

☞ Setting has the advantage of grouping children by ability, subject by subject. A particular child can be in Set One for areas of strength but in lower groups where appropriate.

☞ Mixed ability groupings demand that planning be made to stretch and challenge the most able children.

☞ A second element of group-work is to examine the various types of small groups and then to see if they are beneficial to able pupils.

Application or Activities

Principles for setting

1. The top set is chosen on the basis of the essential ingredients of ability in the particular subject. For example, an over-emphasis upon computational skills will have the effect of omitting some really able mathematicians. Many of the world's greatest mathematicians have not been the strongest at calculation.

2. There is flexibility so that promotions and demotions occur where appropriate. Some pupils demonstrate their high ability later than others.

3. Especially in non-selective schools, the top set is not a homogeneous group. There will be a considerable gap between the top three or four children in the top set and the bottom three or four children in that same set. As a result there must be mixed-ability teaching within the top set.

Small groups: good or bad?

❖ Jigsaw groups are beneficial to able pupils. The children start in 'home groups' that are mixed ability. Members then go into ability groups to study particular aspects of the subject before returning to their 'home group' to share results.

❖ Pyramiding is not likely to be helpful to able pupils. In this system, individuals write down ideas before discussing them as a 'three'. Two 'threes' discuss again as a 'six' and then again as two 'sixes'. Pyramiding is also known as snowballing but the numbers increase from one to two to four to eight. Able pupils are likely to get very bored.

❖ Rolling activities involves a piece of work being divided into various stages. The stages are dealt with by different groups of children. As the higher-ability groups deal with the more difficult tasks, able pupils are properly challenged.

Technique or Need

Problem solving

☞ A number of overlapping skills are involved in problem solving – logical thinking, lateral thinking, synthesis, analysis, evaluation, organization of data, decision making, research and prediction.

☞ The English National Curriculum 1999 required every subject area to show where problem solving fitted into the programme of learning (the same would apply in other countries). That indicates just how fundamental problem solving is. It is also important to success in life, within personal relationships, at home and at work.

☞ Various problem-solving models have been suggested. A typical one is:

1. **Identification of the problem**. This may involve research.

2. **Defining the objective**. What would be a successful conclusion?

3. **Analyse the obstacles to success**. Which are the most serious? How can they be removed?

4. **Constructing courses of action**. Ideas are collected from many sources. Do past similar problems help?

5. **Evaluate the possible courses of action**. What would be the consequences? Cost them. How realistic are they?

6. **Decision making**. Having compared the various alternatives, decide which one seems the best solution when all factors are considered.

7. **Implementation**. Make a plan as to how the decision can be put into practice, including a timetable.

8. **Review**. Look back to see whether the problem has been solved.

Application or Activities

NO PROBLEM TOO SMALL

Odd-job companies and detective agencies in old novels used to advertise that no job was too small. Here we apply the same type of slogan to 'mini problems'.

1. During a murder case the shoes of a suspect were sent to the forensic laboratory. Tests showed that there were salt water marks on the soles of the shoes but not on the 'uppers'.

How did this information possibly help to solve the case?

2. Graham and Rob were on a journey. By the side of the motorway they saw a pig farm. The pigs were out grubbing about for food. The farmer had provided enough individual metal shelters to house the pigs.
Graham said he believed that a particular pig would always use the same shelter, whereas Rob thought that they would move about.

How could the argument be resolved?

3. Your school is going to host a sporting event for many schools in the area. There is only limited car parking space and many more cars than normal are going to arrive.

Use the problem-solving model to work out a solution.

4. You are helped by a stranger at the roadside when your car breaks down. You wish to repay their kindness with a small present. You want the present to be something that the stranger will want.

How do you find out what will be an appropriate present?

5. Two boys are caught fighting in the playground. Both accuse the other of starting it.

How can the truth be discovered?

Technique or Need

Classification

- Classification is about sorting objects or living things into suitable groups or classes.
- All children can classify but many able children can do it in a more sophisticated way. This often involves seeing alternative connections and, for that reason, the standard 'odd one out' questions, used in some test situations, are suspect if there is a single 'correct' answer in the marking scheme.
- Classification concerns a number of important elements – seeing connections, comparing, contrasting, recognizing similarities, recognizing differences.
- Exercises in classification often provide valuable information in the identification of able pupils as there is evidence of thinking beyond the 'standard', especially if pupils are asked to explain the basis of their classifications.
- Classification is particularly important in science but it has a much more general application as well.

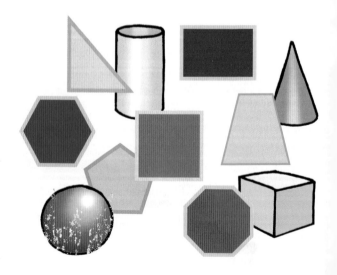

Application or Activities

1. Fill a large toy box with a great variety of toys. Ask young children to place them into groups and ask them the reasoning behind the groups.

2. For older children use a similar technique but fill the box with a variety of objects.

3. For each of the following three groups, ask pupils to find reasons for as many as possible of the components to be the odd one out:

(i)	paper	wood	iron	silk	cotton
(ii)	12	15	8	24	1
(iii)	file	trick	piece	check	light

4. Ask children to create some additional examples where more than one component could legitimately be the odd one out.

5. Create a range of made-up animals with detailed descriptions. Ask pupils to classify them into family groups and then to justify the classification scheme.

Technique or Need

Evaluation

- Evaluation is rightly regarded as one of the three higher-order thinking skills. Keywords include 'judge', 'criticize', 'recommend', 'form an opinion' and 'give your verdict'.

- Self-assessment or self-evaluation is an important area. It is part of what Howard Gardner refers to as intrapersonal intelligence. Looking critically at oneself is an essential step in making improvements in working methods and in making progress. School Inspection Reports have often commented that there is not enough pupil participation in their own learning.

- Seeing both sides of an argument is a vital ingredient in the successful discussion of issues within many subject areas, including English, science, history, geography, religious education, politics, law, philosophy and economics. Society will be benefited by able children with strong interpersonal intelligence influencing policy formulation, decision making and legislation.

- Evaluation of performance, by oneself and by others, is a key element of a number of areas, such as drama, dance, music and physical education.

- Evaluation is one of the mainstays of design and technology.

Application or Activities

the work is on course

Judgement is demanding in nearly all situations. When it takes place within personal relationships, the difficulties are increased.

your tasks

1. Read the scenario described below.

2. Answer the questions that follow the situation.

the scenario

Asif and Richard are very good friends. They have been together in the same classes throughout secondary school. They are now in Year 11 and taking GCSE examinations.

Asif is troubled by the fact that he knows for certain that Richard is cheating with his coursework in one particular subject. The cheating involves two pieces of malpractice. Richard's parents are giving more assistance than they should and, also, Richard is downloading material provided by other people on the internet and just copying it out. Asif is also aware that this subject is one that Richard wishes to study at Advanced Level and he must, therefore, secure a high grade.

the questions

1. What options are there for Asif to follow?

2. What are the advantages and disadvantages of each option?

3. In your opinion, what action should Asif take? Explain your reasoning.

Technique or Need

Prediction

☞ Predicting or hypothesizing is an important element of synthesis which is one of the three higher-order thinking skills, together with analysis and evaluation, which are vital in provision for able pupils.

☞ One rewarding route is to ask 'What if?' and 'What if not?' questions when working with able pupils. They often display sophistication in their responses.

☞ Prediction plays a key role in a number of curriculum areas, especially science, technology, mathematics, English, information and communication technology and geography.

☞ One essential stage of problem solving is to predict the effects of taking a particular course of action.

☞ Successful predictions are most likely to occur when careful analysis of existing data takes place first. There are likely to be influential pointers to future developments if there is close engagement with information already known.

Application or Activities

Predicting what will happen in a story from examination of an initial paragraph is just one of many applications.

your tasks

Complete the story started by the paragraph below. Look for clues in the title and in the opening passage.

A fateful choice

Sinead got off the bus at the terminus. She was very nervous but she tried to behave as normally as possible. No wonder she felt as she did. The telephone call had come like a bolt from the blue. Sinead had not expected to hear anything from Justin for some weeks yet. Still, this is what she had been trained to deal with and she was determined to give a good account of herself.

Sinead knew that there were two possible routes. Going via High Street and Monument Road was perhaps the safer but it was a long way around. After all, time was of the essence. Sinead decided on the more direct route. She stuck out her chin, put her best foot forward and entered Spider Alley

Technique or Need

Abstract thinking

☞ There is very little that can be said that applies accurately to all able children. However, one of the significant characteristics of a good percentage of them is the ability to succeed in situations that require abstract thinking.

☞ Going beyond the literal, the obvious or the concrete allows able pupils to demonstrate sophistication in thinking and understanding.

☞ There is a strong link with symbolism and allegory. The fact that often something stands for something else brings the whole area of codes into play.

☞ This type of thinking is evident in many areas of the curriculum, including algebra, signs and symbols in mathematics; proverbs, idioms, symbolism and second meanings in English; chemical notation and equations in science; musical notation; parables in religious education; and transferable terms in history and politics.

Application or Activities

PROFESSOR FIVESQUARE'S CODE

Professor Fivesquare likes to set problems to exercise the minds of his pupils, including codes. See how you would have fared in his class.

your tasks

Work out the meaning of the coded message by using the clues given by Professor Fivesquare.

PROFESSOR FIVESQUARE'S CLUES

1. There are two elements to the code.

2. My name is significant.

3. 5 is an odd number and so are the positions of 13 of the letters of the alphabet.

4. The treatment of the other 13 shares a characteristic with the London Underground stations Sloane, Russell and Leicester.

THE CODED MESSAGE

676 – 15 – 324 – 40   25 – 50

5 – 196 – 40 – 400 – 64 – 15 - 324

60 – 5 – 65   40 – 36

50 – 5 – 65 – 25 – 196 – 20

196 – 40 – 55 – 20 – 64 – 400

40 – 324

196 – 40 – 400 – 64 – 25 – 196 – 20

(Answers: p93)

Successful Provision for Able and Talented Children,
Network Continuum Education © 2006 Barry Teare

Technique or Need

Creativity

- Creativity is one of the most important elements in the wide model of ability. However, it does not have to go hand-in-hand with high intelligence. There can be overlap but many creative thinkers are not necessarily good at memory tests and other factors in academic success.

- Teachers need to create a climate in which creative thinking will thrive. It is vital to move away from a notion of there only being one way of doing things. There are very definite single answers to, for instance, a multiplication sum but, often, there will be more than one appropriate answer to questions and more than one way of getting to a solution.

- There are some misguided people in education who seem to believe that creativity is the bit that you fit in once you have done all the important work. They could not be more wrong. The biggest growth industry in the USA is the creative industry. In the UK, if creativity is not promoted in children, there will be serious economic difficulty. After all, the mines are closed, the shipyards are largely empty, farming has serious problems, the number of fish around our coasts is declining, very little is manufactured and even many call centres are abroad.

- Creativity is not just for the Arts. Able pupils need to work creatively in mathematics, design and technology, the sciences and right across the curriculum.

Application or Activities

Let your mind take flight

* Just imagine what might happen if a process was discovered to convert grass into plentiful energy.

* Update a detective story from the 1930s or 1940s, perhaps a Hercule Poirot novel written by Agatha Christie.

* Take the final paragraph of a story that you know and make it the first paragraph of a story of your own.

* Design one or more machine(s) to feed the birds (on the ground, on a bird table and from seed and peanut feeders) without having to set foot into the garden yourself.

* Explore the possibilities of swapping two characters from one book to another.

* Create an improved version of a game that you enjoy, describing the changes, showing their consequences and explaining why they could be considered an improvement.

* Consider what might have happened if Africans had colonized Europe rather than the other way around.

* Create a modern fable. It might help if you look at Jan Scieszka and Lane Smith's wonderful book *Squids Will Be Squids* (Viking, Penguin Books).

Successful Provision for Able and Talented Children,
Network Continuum Education © 2006 Barry Teare

Technique or Need

Numeracy

- Detailed guidance has been introduced on numeracy. Teachers need to pay attention to the framework. However, flexibility is needed in the provision for able pupils.

- The definition of numeracy, as used in the English Numeracy National Strategy, covers many areas. Problem solving is highlighted and this is a key area for able children. There is a danger if there is too much concentration upon computation. As previously mentioned, perhaps surprisingly, there are many able mathematicians for whom computation is not their strength.

- Advice on content and organization can help unsure teachers but there are dangers of rigid time constraints. Able pupils need the facility for continuing with an interesting area. Indeed, one of their strengths is being able to take the work on: differentiation by independence or responsibility.

- Algebraic ideas have been introduced earlier and this is a plus for able pupils as they will appreciate the abstract quality of the work.

- 'Talking mathematics' is also positive, providing that able pupils are not frustrated by the level of the talk. They need to bounce ideas off each other, and this can be organized in both the oral strategy and the plenary

- There needs to be avoidance of repetition and of too much direction. Challenging tasks are most easily organized in the main part of the lesson. Here curriculum compacting can take place. Able pairs can work together. Problem solving is likely to be assisted by the provision of appropriate puzzles.

- A very welcome emphasis is upon the correct use of mathematical language and symbols. There is encouragement to use a mathematical dictionary. These vary in difficulty and therefore differentiation by text or resource comes into play.

Application or Activities
The Final Number

How good is your knowledge of mathematical language? How well can you follow exact instructions?

your tasks

Follow all the operations listed below to arrive at a final number. You may need to do a little research.

The operations

1. Start with the eighth prime number.

2. Multiply by the number of units of the hypotenuse in a right-angled triangle where the other two sides were 3 units and 4 units.

3. Add on factorial 5 or 5!

4. Subtract the tenth number in the Fibonacci sequence.

5. Divide by the number of sides in a decagon.

6. Add on the second perfect number.

7. Divide by the number of chances in six of throwing a number less than five with one throw of the die.

8. Multiply by the fourth triangle or triangular number.

9. Subtract 2^6.

10. Add on half a century.

WHAT IS THE FINAL NUMBER?

(Answers: p93)

Successful Provision for Able and Talented Children,
Network Continuum Education © 2006 Barry Teare

Technique or Need

Lateral thinking problems

☞ Lateral thinking is a useful alternative to logical thinking or literal interpretation.

☞ There are a number of methods that can be employed with able pupils. The one used very successfully by the author on many courses is described below:

1. The problem is read out, once or twice. Children may make notes if they wish but this is not normally needed.

2. Groups discuss the problem. They are encouraged:

   a) not to contradict any facts in the story

   b) to make additions, if they wish, without negating the key points

   c) to look for more than one suitable answer

   d) to use their imagination without being unrealistic.

3. Answers are sought. Other groups consider the response and evaluate it for strengths and weaknesses.

4. While hearing another group's answer, other pupils are encouraged to listen carefully and to think critically about what they hear.

5. After hearing several possibilities, all the pupils take part in placing the answers in order of priority with the strongest at the top.

6. Pupils are reminded of the skills in use – lateral thinking, group discussion, referring exactly to data, fluency (looking for several answers), listening attentively and thinking critically. Links are also pointed out with the way these skills are required to solve problems in a number of subjects and a variety of situations.

Application or Activities

Abandoning Daisy

Alice Driver is very fond of her small car, which she has nicknamed Daisy. She uses the car on many occasions, travelling a variety of distances from as little as one mile to over 200 miles when visiting friends in another part of the country.

There is one notable exception to the pattern of Alice Driver's behaviour in relation to her car. On a weekly basis she visits her friend Tammy, who lives in an old-fashioned cottage near the very small village of Copseton. On these weekly visits, Alice leaves her car at home and walks the two miles to her friend's house.

★ What is the explanation for the exception to Alice's normal habit of driving everywhere in her beloved car? Why is the weekly trip to Tammy the only time she walks instead of going by car?

(Answers: p94)

uccessful Provision for Able and Talented Children.
etwork Continuum Education © 2003 Barry Teare

Technique or Need

Logical thinking

☞ The professor in C.S. Lewis' magical book, *The Lion, the Witch and the Wardrobe* (Lions) was dismayed by the children's inability to see the significance of pieces of information and how they fitted together.

'Logic!' said the professor half to himself.
'Why don't they teach logic at these schools?'
(p47)

☞ Logical thinking involves a number of really important areas – sequencing, reasoning clearly, close engagement with data, analysis, deduction and inference. Synthesis is often involved, for logical conclusions follow from studying information gathered from several, contrasting sources.

☞ It may well be that logical thought is most significant in the areas of mathematics, science and computer technology. However, it has relevance elsewhere. Piecing together the path of a story in English uses the same skills. A key component of history – cause and effect – is linked strongly to logical thinking. This also applies in geography and environmental studies when assessing, for example, the consequences of different possibilities for the production of energy or the location of a new town.

Application or Activities

Don't be Facetious

your tasks

1. Explain a very special feature of the word facetious.

2. From the clues below, work out the new order of letters once 'facetious' has been mixed up.

The clues

1. The sixth letter of the alphabet has an odd-numbered place in the rearranged word. It is neither first nor last.

2. Two letters that are next to each other in the alphabet are also side by side here, and in their correct alphabetical order.

3. Letter positions 7, 8 and 9 are occupied by three letters spelling out, in correct order, 'a fastening or bond'.

4. Three vowels follow each other in the rearranged word but in the reverse order to their alphabetical placings.

5. The 'a' has three letters to its left.

Answers: p94)

Successful Provision for Able and Talented Children,
Network Continuum Education © 2006 Barry Teare

Technique or Need

Matrix problems

Matrix problems ask the solver to bring together pairings from two variables through the use of clues. If the number of variables increases, the matrix grids are linked together. A number of important skills are used: logical thinking, careful use of data and synthesis. General matrix problems are good for thinking skills but curriculum content can also be added.

An example could be that five out of six children from this country are going on holiday to different destinations and one child is not going on holiday.

	Brighton	Florida	Newquay	Paris	London	None
Rita						
Lucy						
Sarah						
Dave						
Bill						
Bob						

- A clue stating that all the girls went on holiday, would place a cross for Lucy, Sarah and Rita against 'none'. A clue saying that the child with the longest name was travelling the furthest distance would place a tick for Sarah against Florida. Crosses could then be placed against all other destinations for Sarah and against Florida for all other children. There must eventually be one tick, and one tick only, in each row and column. Sometimes a tick can be placed by a process of elimination. In a more challenging matrix problem, the information from one or more clue has to be used at the same time to reach a solution (synthesis). Some clues leave more than one pairing as a possibility. Ticks should not be placed until a pairing is definite.

Application or Activities

In their Element

Six young scientists – **Natalie, Roger, Betty, Peter, David and Sophie** – were making a special study of one of six chemical elements. These were **gold, hydrogen, sodium, iron, potassium** and **copper**. Each child chose a different element.

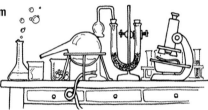

your tasks

Work out which element each young scientist was studying from the clues below.

The clues

1. Two boys studied the two elements whose symbol was made up of one letter only.

2. The child with the second longest name chose an element whose atomic number was between 20 and 30.

3. A boy whose name begins and ends with the same letter chose the element whose symbol is Au.

4. An element whose symbol contains the letter that starts the element's name was chosen by a girl whose name contains three vowels.

5. The element whose atomic number is 30 less than its atomic mass was chosen by a girl.

6. One child studied an element whose symbol was the same two letters that begins the child's name.

7. Roger chose the element with the lowest atomic number.

(Answers: p94)

Technique or Need

Detective work

☞ Detective mysteries have held great fascination and interest for both adults and children since their introduction into popular reading. Authors such as Agatha Christie, Ngaio Marsh and Dorothy L. Sayers have given way to a new generation of favourites, including Ruth Rendell, P.D. James, Reginald Hill and Elizabeth George. Many able pupils are intrigued by detective material: a good start to any learning situation.

☞ Detective materials employ a range of important thinking skills. Logical thinking is essential and they involve the critical areas of deduction and inference. There is an important place, too, for lateral thinking and considering evidence in a new way. Close engagement with data is vital. Synthesis is a key element as information from various sources has to be brought together. Analysis of data must be thorough and precise. Evaluation also plays a part, as a judgement is made about what is most relevant and important. 'Red herrings' have to be eliminated.

☞ The processes used in detective work are vital to success in many areas of the curriculum. The humanities subjects require the same skills but applied to a historical situation or geographical problem. Mathematical and scientific investigations also follow the same methods.

☞ Interest, motivation, challenge and transferable skills therefore make detective work very desirable to use with able pupils.

reading
the clues

In a murder investigation, the Lockinge Bay Crime Squad seem to have lost their way after a promising start. A number of clues and pieces of information had been assembled early on and a speedy conclusion to the enquiry was expected. The various leads had been followed up but progress had unexpectedly slowed.

It was at that point that Pat Laski came back to work after a short illness. He reviewed the evidence, which included:

❖ a right-handed golf glove

❖ a reference to a person in the case called Evelyn

❖ an appointment book entry for 'DROLIVER'

❖ an overheard telephone conversation that mentioned a house in Q.

Pat Laski caught up with the lines of investigation – the search for the right-handed woman called Evelyn, the unfruitful enquiries to find a place beginning with Q and a person or location called 'Droliver'. Gradually he saw the four critical mistakes that had been made and the investigation was back on track. He smiled especially at one misunderstanding, as it was familiar to him personally.

Your task

Work out the four misunderstandings that Pat Laski cleared up.

(Answers: p94)

Successful Provision for Able and Talented Children,
Network Continuum Education © 2006 Barry Teare

Codes

☞ Codes have an abstract quality in that something – a number, substitute letter, picture, punctuation mark, playing card, symbol – stands for something else. This plays to one of the strengths of many able pupils.

☞ Linked as they are to spies and detective stories, codes have a fascination for able children, so the interest element is present.

☞ Codes have had a particularly important part to play in various historical events.

☞ A general code can be used for thinking-skills purposes. Analysis, synthesis, deduction, inference, logical thinking, lateral thinking and close engagement with data all come into play. Codes linked to particular curriculum areas can also be used.

☞ Good working habits are encouraged, to avoid repetition of trying an idea for the solution, and careful use of data. They can be difficult to provide a real challenge. Some can be designed to take time to solve so as to develop intellectual stamina and span of concentration.

London Calling

You work in counter-espionage. For some time you and your colleagues have been trying to track down a cell of spies. There have been two major breakthroughs to help you. A coded message has been intercepted. Also, it has come to the notice of your team that the base for the spies is in London.

your task

Bearing in mind what has been said above, decode the secret message that has been intercepted. Explain your route to the solution.

$$20 - 2 - 2$$
$$20 - 11 - 10 - 1 - 23 - 5$$
$$7 - 13 - 5 - 23 \quad 14 - 20 - 2 - 2$$
$$2 - 17 - 1 - 25 - 17 - 1 \quad 9 - 1$$
$$17 - 6 - 25 - 10 - 6 \quad 23 - 17$$
$$2 - 10 - 20 - 6 - 1$$
$$23 - 26 - 10 - 9 - 6 \quad 1 - 10 - 22$$
$$14 - 17 - 1 - 23 - 20 - 14 - 23 - 5$$

(Answers: p95)

Successful Provision for Able and Talented Children,
Network Continuum Education © 2006 Barry Teare

Technique or Need

Wordplay

- Language is the key not only to English but also to many other curriculum areas.

- Many able children delight in wordplay. They love puns, nuances, alliteration, onomatopoeia and double meanings.

- Able pupils do not form a homogeneous group, but a characteristic many of them display is a very particular sense of humour. This is often manifested in pleasure in word humour.

- Vocabulary extension is a very important component of the English Literacy Framework.

- Subject-specific vocabulary is given prominence in every area of the curriculum.

- Wordplay can be the main target of an exercise or it can be a very important 'by-product'. Cryptic clues, for instance, are an essential ingredient in many logic problems.

- Let us indulge in 'paronomasia', a truly delicious word. It means 'a play on words'.

Camelot

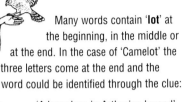

Many words contain '**lot**' at the beginning, in the middle or at the end. In the case of 'Camelot' the three letters come at the end and the word could be identified through the clue:

'A key place in Arthurian legend' (7), where (7) indicates the total number of letters.

your tasks

Identify ten words that contain 'lot' at the beginning, in the middle or at the end, from the following clues:

1. A trial scheme for the aeroplane   (5)
2. Apportioning a small piece of land   (9)
3. Place for inserting a coin or within the scheme   (4)
4. Good luck in this game of chance   (7)
5. A secret plan for the story   (4)
6. Wreckage from a ship   (7)
7. It is a stain on the paper or your character   (4)
8. A word to soothe   (6)
9. Vote for me   (6)
10. A feline mammal   (6)

extension task

Create suitable clues for ten words that have '**per**' at the beginning, in the middle or at the end.

(Answers: p95)

Successful Provision for Able and Talented Children,
Network Continuum Education © 2006 Barry Teare

Technique or Need

Dictionary and thesaurus

☞ Good use of the dictionary and the thesaurus is a specified area of work in curriculum guidelines and in the English Literacy Framework.

☞ This is a very obvious area where the quality of the tasks set can vary. Much dictionary work is dull and uninteresting. In fact it might deserve the comment that 'You can bore for England with a dictionary'. Treated correctly, the dictionary and the thesaurus can be a treasure chest of imaginative tasks.

☞ Most standard school dictionaries are small and contain a limited number of words. Able pupils should be making use of the substantial volumes published by companies such as Chambers, Oxford University Press and Collins. These give full explanations of the different meanings together with details of the derivation of the words.

☞ The range of sources involved here is wider than might be thought. Penguin and other companies publish dictionaries of quotations. The *Oxford Visual Dictionary* is a wonderful resource with its pictorial presentation and labels in English, French, German and Spanish. For English there are various dictionaries of riddles, idioms and so on. *The Oxford Dictionary of Nursery Rhymes*, edited by Iona and Peter Opie, is a classic collection of fascinating material. *Brewer's Dictionary of Phrase and Fable* has gone through many editions. There are entries on the meanings and origins of a vast range of colloquial words and expressions, on mythology and world religion, on folk customs, superstitions and beliefs, on historical figures and events and on famous literary characters.

☞ The English National Numeracy Strategy reminded us of the importance of using mathematical dictionaries. Subject-specific dictionaries are of great value across the curriculum.

'A' is for Absent

A challenging joint use of the dictionary and the thesaurus is to set a lipogram. Lipogram is the name given to a piece of writing, short or long, where a particular letter is banned.

your tasks

Rewrite the passage below, keeping as close to the meaning and style as possible, without using the letter 'a'.

the passage

All around there is hatred and fear. The new regulations have caused divisions among the inhabitants. Television news broadcasts have given details of the changes. This has not assisted the situation. The authorities anticipate demonstrations after today. The faces of the politicians are grave. All will remain worrying until an arrangement has been negotiated.

extension task

Which features of the passage cause most difficulty in removing the letter 'a'?

(Answers: p95)

Technique or Need

Homonyms

- Both homographs and homophones figure strongly in the English Literacy Framework. They constitute a good example of work that can be covered in a rather dull and routine way, or can be set in an exciting and challenging manner.

- Because of their nature, homographs and homophones play an important role in much wordplay and word humour. These appeal to a large number of able pupils.

- Homonyms is the general description of a group of words pronounced or spelled in the same way but having different meanings.

- Homographs are words that are spelled the same but have different meanings. An example is 'just', which can mean either 'fair or impartial' or it can mean 'at this very moment'.

- Homophones are words pronounced in the same way but differing in meaning or spelling or both. An example is 'bear' and 'bare', one the animal, the other being nude or unadorned.

Application or Activities

A Carefree Adventure for the Bird

The title refers to both the meanings of the word 'lark' (4), a homograph.

your tasks

Identify the following homographs from the 'double' clues.

1. A particular day for the fruit (4)
2. To equip the limb for war (3)
3. Sophisticated on a day free from heat (4)
4. A simple level stretch of country (5)
5. Sports equipment causes a noisy disturbance (6)
6. A drawn piece of clothing (3)
7. The berry-like fruit of the joint (3)
8. A balcony at the art exhibition (7)
9. The ships are swift (5)
10. The writing symbol shows the nature of the person (9)

extension task

Find ten more homographs and create 'double' cryptic clues for them.

(Answers: p96)

Successful Provision for Able and Talented Children,
Network Continuum Education © 2006 Barry Teare

Technique or Need

Crosswords

☞ Crosswords have a number of benefits when used with able pupils – they challenge, wordplay is involved, lateral thinking is required and there is precise engagement with data.

☞ There is a plentiful supply of material with examples, at all levels, readily available in newspapers.

☞ Teaching particular types of clues provides intellectual challenge:

1. An anagram is normally indicated by words such as 'confused', 'jumbled', 'afresh', 'anew' or 'disorganized'.

2. Indicators such as 'within', 'in' or 'some' mean that the letters of the solution are to be found running consecutively elsewhere in the clue.

3. Some clues are based upon homographs, where there are two meanings of the same word.

4. 'Outside' leads the solver to place the solution to one part of the clue at either end of the solution to another part of the clue, together giving the overall definition.

5. Charades involves miming the individual parts of a word. In crosswords, the solution is made up from the clues to the component bits.

6. Homophones in clues are indicated by phrases like 'we hear' or 'sounds like'.

7. Reversals ask the solver to place some letters backwards. Indicators include 'returning', 'back', 'backwards'.

Application or Activities

Clued Up

your tasks

Solve the following crossword clues. There is one each of the seven types explained previously, although not in the same order.

1. Make a rush at the price set (6)
2. Serious enclosed ground near church (9)
3. Returning artist gets profit (6)
4. Relaxed by disorganized side rule (8)
5. The provider is seen in stolen derrick (6)
6. The boxing match outside the cattle sound causes the tyre to burst (7)
7. Be appreciative that the Victorian exhibition, we hear, was almost at capacity (8)

extension task

Write seven more clues of your own to fit the types already used.

(Answers: p96)

Successful Provision for Able and Talented Children,
Network Continuum Education © 2006 Barry Teare

Proverbs

☞ A proverb is a short traditional saying that gives advice. In a proverb, a generalization is given a specific, often metaphorical, expression.

☞ It is the two levels of meaning that makes proverbs particularly valuable in the teaching of able pupils. They are more likely to understand the symbolism involved and that there is a more general application to comprehend. This gives proverbs an abstract thinking quality.

☞ Proverbs are also of interest in provision for able pupils because they are wonderful examples of wordplay and they present ideas in such an imaginative, succinct and economical way. Rhyming and alliteration are often used.

☞ There is a historical facet, too, in that proverbial sayings were popular from the Middle Ages onwards, and they have altered with time. *The Oxford Companion to the English Language*, edited by Tom McArthur (Oxford University Press), tells us that 'Do not spoil the ship for a halfpennyworth of tar' originated with 'hog' rather than 'ship'.

☞ Work on proverbs was common in schools up to the 1960s but then went out of fashion. Fortunately, the English Literacy Framework put proverbs back on the map. Even so, when doing such work, it is helpful to have a list of proverbs available for children to refer to

Every Why has a Wherefore

your tasks

1. Find two proverbs that seem to contradict one another.

2. Which proverb is described cryptically as 'Watch carefully before you emulate Kermit or Jeremy Fisher'?

3. Write your own cryptic clues for other proverbs.

4. Create some modern proverbs of your own. An example might be 'All that threatens is not a weapon of mass destruction'.

5. Decide which proverb is being described in this short story:

   'During the Second World War there were frequent air-raids on cities and towns by the Luftwaffe. Blackout precautions were put into force so as not to guide the German bombers. This included switching off street-lighting. Unfortunately many car crashes resulted, with heavy casualties. This is when the catseye® was invented – a system of small reflectors set in the middle of the road to help motorists.'

6. Choose a different proverb and write a short story, fact or fiction, to illustrate it.

(Answers: p90)

Successful Provision for Able and Talented Children,
Network Continuum Education © 2006 Barry Teare

Crossing subject boundaries

- Primary school teachers are used to dealing with all subjects in the curriculum. This makes them more likely to see links in terms of content, techniques and resources. Secondary school teachers are more likely to concentrate on what immediately appears in their own subject specialism.

- Curriculum mapping is a useful device to show the overlap and connections between various areas of the curriculum.

- Some really exciting enrichment courses for able children have involved co-operation between specialists. The Kilve Residential Centre in Somerset has gone 'MAD' with a course linking activities from mathematics, art and drama.

- One particular aspect of crossing subject boundaries is to see if resources designed for one area can be successfully used in other areas. After all, a good idea is a good idea, and many of them can be transferred into other contexts. This was one of the features referred to in 'Eleven Enrichers' (p5).

Coming out of the box

Always look to see if a resource with interest and challenge can be applied elsewhere.

'Four bidden playing cards'

A pack of cards has been produced by the Association of Teachers of Mathematics (www.atm.org.uk). On one half of the card is a mathematical term such as 'vertical', 'cuboid', 'circle' or 'rotation'. On the other half of the card there are four words. Children are asked to define the term without using the four forbidden words. This is difficult as these words have been chosen because they refer to essential qualities of the term.

The playing cards can be used directly. Others can be designed to meet the needs of children of different ages. Pupils can be asked to write their own. Also, the idea can be transferred into other areas of the curriculum. In history, the terms could be 'entente', 'alliance' or 'demilitarized zone'; in geography, 'meander', 'oxbow lake' or 'erosion', and so on.

'True, false and 'iffy'

Tony Gardiner, in his 'Maths Challenge' books for Oxford University Press, uses a splendid idea. He gives a group of statements about a number or shape. Children copy these onto paper and cut them into individual slips. Then they place them into three columns depending upon whether they think they are definitely true, definitely false or 'iffy'. This third column is the most interesting. The exercise provides a kinesthetic method. It can be extended to various levels of difficulty in mathematics. It can equally be applied to other subject areas. Statements about characters and/or the plot of a book being studied in English would be appropriate. Parts of a scientific investigation could be treated in the same way, and so on.

Technique or Need

Poetry across the curriculum

☛ Poetry is an important area to include in books to be read and enjoyed in English. It is a very powerful area of literature. Andrew Motion describes 'its power to engross and move us, to its ability to challenge and brace us, and to its exultation' (quoted in *Staying Alive: real poems for unreal times*, edited by Neil Astley, Bloodaxe).

☛ There are long narrative poems but most poetry is short. This succinctness is an important skill for able children to develop; a distillation of essential elements, ideas and concepts takes place. There is also an exactness about the choice of words. Coleridge's verdict was 'Poetry; the best words in the best order' (*Table Talk*, 12 July 1827).

☛ Abstract thinking (p54) plays an important part in much poetry. The symbolism, allegories and double meanings make poetry of great significance to able pupils.

☛ Able children are required to make use of the higher-order thinking skills of synthesis, evaluation and analysis when reading quality poetry.

☛ To maintain interest and engagement, curriculum delivery needs to be as varied as possible. One of many routes is to involve poetry, not only in English but also across the curriculum.

Shelley

Application or Activities

Well versed

★ The study of history opens up many opportunities to use appropriate poems. The second and third verses of 'The Mask of Anarchy' by Shelley are:

I met Murder on the way –
He had a mask like Castlereagh –
Very smooth he looked, yet grim;
Seven bloodhounds followed him:

All were fat; and well they might
Be in admirable plight,
For one by one, and two by two,
He tossed them human hearts to chew
Which from his wide cloak he drew.

In this powerful piece of work, Shelley goes on to attack other members of Lord Liverpool's government, in power at the time of the Peterloo Massacre in Manchester.

★ Michael Rosen, well-known children's author, was commissioned by the STAR group (Science, Technology and Reading), made up of the Royal Society of Chemistry, Institute of Physics, Esso UK and the Design Council, to write 100 poems about chemistry, physics, the environment, and design and technology. Able children delight in the resulting book – *Centrally Heated Knickers* (Puffin Books).

★ In *Math Talk* by Theoni Pappas (Wide World Publishing/Tetra), a number of mathematical ideas are expressed as poems for two voices. From this book, mathematics can be performed – a lovely idea.

★ Open-access competitions can be organized for poems on any area of the curriculum, thus providing a different and interesting activity.

Putting the fun into learning

- Most people learn best when the methods used are interesting and enjoyable. This is certainly true of most able pupils.

- In recent years, with so much stress placed upon test scores and league table positions, some teachers feel that there is a choice between rather dull and straight teaching that produces good results or having a more enjoyable curriculum that does not give as high results. This is not true and schools employing creative learning methods have also done very well in terms of results.

- One of the characteristics of many able children is a particular sense of humour. It does, on some occasions, get them into trouble.

- Many able pupils delight especially in word humour – puns, nuances, double meanings, alliteration, amusing images and so on.

- One of our greatest living mathematicians, Professor Ian Stewart, in *Math Hysteria* (Oxford University Press) explains that his love for mathematics partly stemmed from Martin Gardner's games column as 'it kept me interested and made it clear that there was plenty of room for new ideas and creative thinking' (pvii). In other words, maths can be fun; and so can all school subjects.

Application or Activities

Sounds like charades

This is a verbal game that explores important areas of literacy such as antonyms, synonyms, rhymes, spoonerisms, homographs and homophones. Pupils are reminded of the meaning of those terms. They then identify book titles by means of a list of component elements and amended titles.

1. 'a head of boo large towns'

(comprising an antonym (that is also a homophone), a rhyme and a synonym)

Answer: *A Tale of Two Cities*

2. 'the level of lacy mug'

(comprising a synonym of a homophone, a rhyme and a synonym)

Answer: *The Story of Tracy Beaker*

3. 'pester hurry and the foblet of gire'

(comprising a synonym, an antonym and a spoonerism)

Answer: *Harry Potter and the Goblet of Fire*

★ Also ask pupils to create their own examples.

Picture books

☞ Many people would assume that picture books are only of value with young children. This is not true. They have produced fantastic results with children of all ages when used in an imaginative and creative way.

☞ Detailed illustrations allow the setting of logic problems – 'Which of these sheep is the oldest?' – solved from a series of clues. They are suitable for higher-order thinking skills questions.

☞ For able readers one would expect to provide, perhaps, lengthy and challenging texts with an extended vocabulary. There is, however, an important role for picture books, especially those with no words at all. Because there is no text, the reader can interpret what is going on at any level they wish. The imagination is stimulated as the viewer has to play a more active role.

☞ This also works well in modern foreign languages. As there is no text, the reader can provide words not only at any level but also in any language.

Application or Activities

Picture this

Quentin Blake, *Tell Me a Picture*

In *Tell Me a Picture* (National Gallery Company), the author has chosen 26 paintings and drawings. Children create their own stories, stimulated by the pictures. On separate pages, Quentin Blake has drawn characters pointing out details and asking questions. You can, of course, also assemble pictures of your own to do a similar job.

David Macauley, *Rome Antics*

In this wonderful book (Dorling Kindersley), the reader accompanies a homing pigeon as it takes a scenic route, rather than the most direct way, over the city of Rome. The pigeon passes some of Rome's most magnificent architecture before finally delivering a message to a man in his room. Children can interpret the mystery behind the one-word message.

Felicia Law and Phillipe Dupasquier, *Old Farm, New Farm*

This old book (1980) from Octopus Books is quoted as an example of what can be done to change the challenge in a picture book. At the start the reader sees a picture of battered, run-down Old Farm. At the end there is a fantastic transformation to New Farm. In between, the farmer carries out a series of tasks. Many higher-order thinking skills questions can be posed – 'Would you have bought Old Farm?' 'Is this a realistic view of a farm?' 'In what order would you have carried out the jobs?' 'Why?' 'Can you see an example of pathetic fallacy?' (The sun shines on New Farm while for Old Farm the sky is dark and threatening.) This is typical of what can be done with a simple picture book.

Technique or Need

Putting on curriculum glasses

★ Imagine that you have a pair of curriculum glasses, decorated and somewhat eccentric in design, but magical in use; when you put them on you see how to present material in a challenging and enjoyable way, taking advantage of the Eleven Enrichers (page 5).

★ By understanding the curriculum tools that work for able children, you are no longer restricted by the availability of purpose-designed materials. Resources are now infinite because you can see new uses for all sorts of things.

★ Tide tables, for example, are invaluable when on holiday but they can also be used for detective scenarios and mathematical problems.

★ Jigsaws also provide a mathematical resource, especially the ones that have a number of rectangles one inside each other, thus giving the opportunity for questions on the number of straight sides and the number of corners. Remember, too, that interest in jigsaws is a well-known identifier of mathematical ability in young children. Some jigsaws lead to observation exercises and logic problems. Others have subjects that are ideal for history and geography.

★ Specialist playing cards provide a variety of opportunities. A 'Famous Women' pack leads to classification tasks and a discussion on the criteria for inclusion. A map of the London Underground, in sections, has wonderful geographical possibilities.

Application or Activities

All wrapped up

Sheets of wrapping paper provide a brilliant resource. Not all wrapping paper – you need to put on your curriculum glasses to understand the possibilities. They include the following examples (something similar works without having the exact sheet):

★ Under the sea

This is a single picture of various forms of life at various depths from the ocean bed up to the surface of the sea. The illustrator has used artistic licence. Can you see anachorisms? Yes, there are items out of place, as not all the creatures would be found in the same location. Working on scale, are the creatures the correct size relative to each other and, therefore, how deep is the water?

★ Beach huts

There are rows of beach huts underneath each other, filling the sheet, and all slightly different. A logic problem can be created. From clues, decide which one is Hannah's hut. If all the beach huts comply with building regulations, what are those building regulations? Classify the huts into groups, explaining the reasons for the divisions.

★ A single complicated picture

With one design, a piece of creative writing can be set. Advanced-level art examination papers used to provide candidates with a poem or small piece of prose and ask them to create a painting based upon the passage. Reverse the process. This sheet is the finished product of the artist. Write the poem or piece of prose that stimulated the painting.

The possibilities are endless –
but only for appropriate examples – so put
your curriculum glasses on!

Going on from here

Using the Pocket PAL as a springboard

Even though this Pocket PAL is compact, a great deal of information has been included together with many themes, much advice, plentiful details of teaching techniques and a substantial number of pieces of work to use with able pupils. As such, the Pocket PAL is aimed to be very helpful to all those responsible for able children. Even so, ideas can be developed further and it is impossible to include long pieces of work here due to the limited space and format.

The able and talented children series

Readers are advised that there is much more to read and use in other books by Barry Teare, published by Network Educational Press.

1. *Effective Provision for Able and Talented Children*. This is mainly a book for teachers on how to provide successfully for able children in the wide sense. It includes sections on school policy, identification, under-achievement, pastoral issues, personnel matters, classroom practice and management, and monitoring and evaluation.

2. *Effective Resources for Able and Talented Children*. The book starts with a section on the curriculum principles behind good provision for able children. The huge majority of the book consists of challenging and exciting materials divided into 11 themes.

3. *More Effective Resources for Able and Talented Children*. Sixty-five new materials appear in this book, with fresh themes as well as new pieces in the many sections similar to the previous book.

4. *Challenging Resources for Able and Talented Children*. All the 62 activities are brand new – most are based around entirely new topics, while some take a fresh approach to revisited topics from previous books.

Going on from here

5. *Enrichment Activities for Able and Talented Children*. Based upon a very large number of courses run by the author for able children in various parts of the country, this book starts with the theory behind successful enrichment activities including aims and objectives, the selection of participants, creating an encouraging atmosphere, the role of the teacher, pastoral issues, the key curriculum elements and how to judge the success of the event. The huge majority of the book is a treasure trove of brand new resources.

6. *Parents' and Carers' Guide for Able and Talented Children*. The book's prime target is that of parents and carers. However, teachers and schools have also been enthusiastic about the contents. There are three main sections:

   ★ a discussion of issues and practices

   ★ advice on all curriculum areas about places to go, resources to use, activities to do, websites to visit and how to provide beneficial support

   ★ the question 'What makes a novel suitable reading for able and talented children?' is examined. There is also a detailed and lengthy list of recommended authors and titles, with comments and explanations as to their inclusion.

7. *Problem-solving and Thinking Skills Resources for Able and Talented Children*. The book has a wealth of resources to deliver exciting and challenging learning that has at its core transferable thinking skills and problem solving. Many of the materials have strong curriculum links. Others prepare able children in more general ways to tackle situations across the curriculum.

Other contacts

1. NACE: The National Association for Able Children in Education (www.nace.co.uk).

2. NAGC: The National Association for Gifted Children (www.nagcbritain.org.uk).

3. The DfES has a dedicated Gifted and Talented Unit (www.standards.dfes.gov.uk/giftedandtalented).

Answers

'Anne' (p21)

Among several possible factors, the following are certainly worthy of consideration:

1. Anne undoubtedly has ability and she is particularly good where presentational skills are concerned. She is in danger of being left out of an identified cohort if written work dominates the criteria too much.

2. She was, perhaps, not used to being assessed so honestly. In a strange way, the tutor won her respect and therefore she responded better on subsequent occasions.

3. If the qualities of all the able pupils are to be seen, a variety of opportunities and styles of working is required both in lessons and in enrichment sessions. Anne's oral skills, and working with a team, could only be demonstrated through an appropriate opportunity.

'Mary' (p31)

1. The most likely reason for Mary's growing disenchantment is the nature of the homeworks. They may well repeat the level of work already set in the lesson. Mary, as an able mathematician, will have mastered the skills quickly. She is then being asked to consolidate what does not need consolidation. As a result she has become bored and frustrated. Being a strong-minded girl, she has taken the law into her own hands.

2. The number of examples at the same level of difficulty needs to be reduced for Mary, even if other pupils in the class need more practice. For homework there are a number of opportunities. Mary could be asked to solve problems on the same topic but at a much higher level of difficulty. An alternative is to set questions on completely different material that are challenging for Mary. These will work best if they are set in unusual and amusing ways.

Answers

'Professor Fivesquare's Code' (p55)

The 13 oddly positioned letters of the alphabet are ascending multiples of 5. The 13 evenly positioned letters of the alphabet are given a value that is a square of their position. As a result, the letters are coded thus:

LETTER	A	B	C	D	E	F	G	H	I
POSITION:	1	2	3	4	5	6	7	8	9
CODE:	5	4	10	16	15	36	20	64	25

LETTER:	J	K	L	M	N	O	P	Q	R
POSITION:	10	11	12	13	14	15	16	17	18
CODE:	100	30	144	35	196	40	256	45	324

LETTER:	S	T	U	V	W	X	Y	Z
POSITION:	19	20	21	22	23	24	25	26
CODE:	50	400	55	484	60	576	65	676

The message therefore says:
'Zero is another way of saying nought or nothing.'

The Final Number' (p59)

1. 19
2. 19 x 5 = 95
3. 95 + 120 = 215
4. 215 - 55 = 160
5. 160 ÷ 10 = 16
6. 16 + 28 = 44
7. 44 ÷ 4 = 11
8. 11 x 10 = 110
9. 110 – 64 = 46
0. 46 + 50 = 96

he final number is 96.

Answers

'Abandoning Daisy' (p61)

Among a number of possible answers, can be included:

★ Alice uses the weekly walk to get some exercise.

★ There is no available parking space at Tammy's cottage.

★ Access to Tammy's cottage is very rough and/or difficult and Alice does not want to risk damaging Daisy.

★ Tammy is a keen environmentalist and Alice does not take the car to please her friend.

'Don't be Facetious' (p63)

1. The five vowels appear once, and once only, in their alphabetical order.

2. C U O A F S T I E

'In their Element (p65)

	GOLD	HYDROGEN	SODIUM	IRON	POTASSIUM	COPPER
NATALIE	X	X	✓	X	X	X
ROGER	X	✓	X	X	X	X
BETTY	X	X	X	✓	X	X
PETER	X	X	X	X	✓	X
DAVID	✓	X	X	X	X	X
SOPHIE	X	X	X	X	X	✓

'Reading the Clues' (p67)

1. A golf glove is worn on the opposite hand to the one you use for writing.

2. Evelyn is both a man's and a woman's name (as indeed is Pat).

3. 'DROLIVER' was actually Dr (doctor) Oliver.

4. Overhearing, the place was not Q... but Kew.

Therefore the search was now concentrated in Kew for a left-handed man and enquiries were made about Dr Oliver

Answers

'London Calling' (p69)

London is in the message as might be expected. These letters can then be used throughout the message. 'All', 'call', 'in' and 'to' are now very obvious. Common sense works after that.

The message says:

'All agents must call London in order to learn their new contacts.'

'Camelot' (p71)

1. pilot
2. allotment
3. slot
4. lottery
5. plot
6. flotsam
7. blot
8. lotion
9. ballot
10. ocelot

'A Is for Absent' (p73)

An answer is:

Everywhere there is intense dislike, deep concern too. The new rules resulted in divisions between the residents. Television news bulletins itemized the differences. This did not help the position. The people in office expect protests from tomorrow on. Those in politics show concern in their expressions. Everything will continue to be worrying until discussions produce some form of settlement.'

❖ Particular problems include the two-letter word 'an', the link word 'and' and tenses of verbs.

Answers

'A Carefree Adventure for the Bird' (p75)

1. date
2. arm
3. cool
4. plain
5. racket
6. tie
7. hip
8. gallery
9. fleet
10. character

'Clued Up' (p77)

1. charge (double meaning, homograph)
2. graveyard (charades)
3. reward (artist = 'drawer', reversal)
4. leisured (anagram)
5. lender (within 'stolen derrick')
6. blowout ('bout' outside 'low')
7. grateful (homophone, 'great' → 'grate'; 'full' almost)

'Every Why has a Wherefore' (p79)

1. One pair is certainly 'Too many cooks spoil the broth' and 'Many hands make light work'.
2. 'Look before you leap.'
5. 'Necessity is the mother of invention.' Are there others?

Beat those win
perfect roman

En

Smoke Gets in Your Eyes,

a blazing debut novel from Louise Marley
in the magnificent and elegant
Tinakilly Country House Hotel

Tinakilly

WIN A ROMANTIC WEEKEND FOR TWO BY
ANSWERING THE FOLLOWING QUESTION:
Q. IN WHICH COUNTY IN IRELAND IS TINAKILLY HOUSE?

A. _____

ANSWERS ON A POSTCARD CLEARLY MARKED
SMOKE GETS IN YOUR EYES COMPETITION TO:
Poolbeg Press, 123 Grange Hill, Baldoyle, Dublin 13

Closing date for all entries 2nd April 2002
The draw will take place on the 8th of April 2002
The first correct entry drawn will win the prize of
2 nights B&B and one evening meal (subject to availability)
The judge's decision is final

A SMALL LUXURY FOR LOVERS OF THE FINER THINGS IN LIFE

TINAKILLY COUNTRY HOUSE AND RESTAURANT,
RATHNEW, COUNTY WICKLOW, IRELAND

Smoke gets in your eyes

LOUISE
MARLEY

POOLBEG

Published 2002
by Poolbeg Press Ltd
123 Grange Hill, Baldoyle
Dublin 13, Ireland
E-mail: poolbeg@poolbeg.com
www.poolbeg.com

The moral right of the author has been asserted.

Typesetting, layout, design © Poolbeg Group Services Ltd.

1 3 5 7 9 10 8 6 4 2

A catalogue record for this book is available from the British Library.

ISBN 1 84223 053 0

Cover Design by Slatter-Anderson
Typeset by Patricia Hope in Palatino 10/14
Printed by
Omnia Books Ltd, Glasgow

About the Author

Louise Marley was born in Southampton and previously worked as a civilian administrator for the police. After several years spent working out in gyms and health clubs, she now finds it far more relaxing to write books about them instead.

She currently lives in Hampshire with her husband, their two children and five goldfish.

The goldfish live in a tank.

For more information about Louise Marley visit her website
www.louisemarley.co.uk

This book is dedicated to
Andy, Jodie and Luke
with love

Chapter One

March

The day Caitlin learnt she was pregnant, her husband Hugh cracked open a bottle of champagne. Not supermarket plonk but the very best vintage, stored for posterity in the cellars of his family's hotel. Caitlin would have been impressed – if she had not discovered him, twenty minutes later, pouring it over his half-naked mistress.

Caitlin had known something was up as soon as she returned from her doctor's appointment. Her staff were unusually pleasant, keen to discuss the arrangements for Hugh's birthday party that evening, but vague as to his actual whereabouts. So she was not at all surprised to find him in bed with another woman. After all, it could have been worse. It could have been another man.

Amanda de Havilland lay across Caitlin's four-poster bed, her dress casually rucked down to her hips, her blonde hair framing her face like an undeserved

1

Louise Marley

halo. "Be careful, Hugh!" she giggled, as he shook up the bottle once more. "I'll drown!"

"Funny," said Caitlin acidly, "I would have thought silicone floated."

Amanda sat up and shrieked, pulling the bedsheets protectively against her. Despite the perfect DD breasts, she looked like a schoolgirl in her pale pink dress. All that was missing were the pigtails and lollipop. Caitlin wondered if Amanda had dressed that way on purpose. Everyone knew Hugh liked his women young. Which was why he had married her.

Hugh, quite unperturbed by the arrival of his wife in the middle of entertaining his mistress, lit a cigarette. "But, Caitlin," he smiled sardonically, "I thought you'd enjoy a night off."

Calmly he picked up his clothes, strewn around the room in a fit of romantic passion. His socks went on first, then his boxer shorts and jeans – taking the utmost care not to trap his disappointed cock in the zip.

Caitlin, infuriated by his apparent indifference, looked for something to throw. As their suite was crammed with family antiques, mostly hers, she had to make do with the champagne bottle. It smashed beautifully against the carved oak headboard and showered glass and alcohol across the green patchwork quilt, embroidered in 1915 by Hugh's great-grandmother, ruining it forever.

Amanda screamed and threw herself under the bed.

Hugh didn't even blink. "Why don't you have a drink, Caitlin? It might improve your aim."

2

Caitlin stared at the broken glass and, feeling the shock wash over her, sat abruptly on the window seat before her legs went AWOL. The whole scene was like an action replay of her childhood. An endless succession of stepfathers in bed with the maid, the nanny, her teenage friends . . . She remembered her distraught mother, the violent screaming matches, slammed doors. And now Hugh was behaving in exactly the same way. Just as her mother had said he would.

Involuntarily Caitlin's eyes met his. The blue irises were rimmed pink from late nights and early drinking. Deep lines of discontent ran tracks from his nose to his mouth and fanned out from his eyes across his cheeks. His hair was grey, his lips mean and spiteful. He looked far older than his forty years. Amanda could have been his daughter. It was obscene.

Through a plume of cigarette smoke, Hugh was studying her equally carefully. He took another long, slow drag, the tip glowing orange, then removed the cigarette from his mouth, tapping his fingers against the tip, carelessly showering ash across the threadbare Axminster. "So you *have* been drinking . . ."

"Yes." Caitlin blinked back the tears as she remembered how happy she had been, not thirty minutes previously. After the doctor had told her the news, she had planted a huge lipsticked kiss on his cheek and virtually danced out of the surgery, swinging around lampposts and jumping in puddles like a manic Gene Kelly. "That's what you're supposed to do with champagne," she said. *Celebrate . . .*

3

He gave a wry smile and dropped his cigarette into a discarded glass, still half-full of flat champagne, where it fizzed and went out. "True – but it's not as much fun."

She watched the cigarette bob up and down, slowly turning the alcohol grey, vaguely symbolic of her love life. It was his audacity that hurt her most. He didn't care how she felt – perhaps he just assumed their life would carry on as it always had, that she would forgive him, yet again, and that a bunch of flowers would make everything all right.

But perhaps not this time. As her heart grew another coat of armour-plating, she picked up one of his elegantly handmade shoes and hurled it at him.

"Missed," laughed Hugh, just before its mate clobbered him across the ear.

Caitlin looked frantically around for more ammunition.

Believing a ceasefire to be in progress, Amanda slid surreptitiously from beneath the bed to retrieve her bra, still clutching her dress to hide her nakedness. Although it pained Caitlin to admit it, Amanda was by far the most attractive of her husband's many indiscretions. Her Barbie doll looks contrasted perfectly with the dark green William Morris wallpaper – far better than a pasty-faced brunette. If Hugh decided to move his little tart in on a permanent basis, at least he would not have to redecorate.

Amanda's purple lace bra had somehow become hooked over a Tiffany lamp. There was an undignified scramble but Caitlin got there first.

4

Triumphantly she pulled out the padding. "Silicone *and* Wonderbras? Is anything about you real?"

Amanda prettily burst into tears and was gallantly rescued by Hugh. "Now then, girls," he smiled, placing himself between them, "I'm quite willing to be shared."

"I bet you are," snarled Caitlin, launching a convenient bowl of potpourri in his direction. The porcelain clanged to the floor, amazingly not breaking; the dried petals showered over him like confetti. "You bloody pervert!"

"Actually," Amanda's voice wavered bravely as she peeped out from behind Caitlin's husband, "Hugh and I are going to get married."

"Married!" Caitlin spluttered.

Hugh shrugged. "I'm so conventional."

"But not conventional enough to get divorced first?" Caitlin looked at Amanda, the fairytale princess who always got her man, even if he belonged to someone else. It wasn't difficult to calculate how she had won Hugh's cheating heart.

"Let me guess," began Caitlin slowly. "You're pregnant? It's amazing what one can achieve with a packet of condoms and a pin. Well, I'm sorry to wreck your happy ending but I'm having a baby myself. A legitimate one."

"You're *what*?" Hugh seemed genuinely shocked.

"Preg-nant," Caitlin repeated, with some irritation. "You know, bun in the oven, with child, up the duff, about to drop one . . ."

"Are you sure it's mine?"

Bastard. "Oh definitely," she replied, hoping he could

not hear the tremor in her voice. "I haven't had a vision of the Archangel Gabriel since I gave up on the tequilas."

Amanda was frantically doing sums on her fingers. "But Hugh said he hadn't slept with you since Bonfire Night."

"Then he's a lying toerag." As her life turned into a West End farce, Caitlin realised she sounded more hysterical by the minute, but was quite unable to do anything about it. "The baby was conceived on Christmas Eve. It's surprising what one can do with a bit of mistletoe and tinsel. I got out my stockings and guess what? Santa wasn't the only one who came."

"Well," said Hugh, slowly smiling. "I suppose that does change things . . ."

Amanda regarded him warily. "What sort of 'things'?"

He ruffled her hair. "Well, can't dump the old girl now, can I?"

"But Hugh!" she whispered. "You told me you loved me!"

Hugh lit another cigarette. His hand trembled faintly. "A man will tell a girl anything to get her into bed, darling. Surely you can't be that naïve?"

Caitlin, taken aback by his abrupt change of mind, could almost hear Amanda's heart breaking.

"Please, Caitlin," the girl appealed. "Please . . . make him change his mind. You know you don't love him."

How do you know how I feel? thought Caitlin. When I'm not even sure myself . . .

* * *

Kirkwood Manor Hotel was a Gothic Victorian house pretending to be a Jacobean mansion. Built of red brick in 1860, it had projecting bay windows, four rows of spindly chimneys, and a gabled roof edged by elegant stone balustrades. There were many themed gardens but Caitlin's favourite was the Elizabethan Garden, which opened out from one of the hotel drawing-rooms. It was always deserted, due to a dubious-looking pond stretching its entire length; even the ducks refused to swim in its melancholy depths. But she liked the peace and quiet. Its bleakness matched her mood and she was guaranteed never to be disturbed.

So there Caitlin sat, with her head in her hands, trying desperately not to cry, in case a guest wandered past and saw her. She hoped she was successfully hidden behind a moss-covered statue of Venus but guests had a habit of turning up in the most unlikely places and always became dyslexic when faced with signs saying, 'Private' and 'Keep Out'.

Why had everything gone so horribly wrong? She had been so pleased to learn about the baby, now her happiness had disintegrated like sugar in the rain. Had she really been surprised to find Amanda in her bed? Hugh had been persistently unfaithful for the first five years of their marriage. Did she really expect the baby to make a difference?

Hunting through her pockets for a handkerchief, the only one she could find was white linen with an 'H' embroidered upon it. Disdainfully, she dropped it into

7

the nearest lavender bush. She would rather use her sleeve.

She sniffed. On the other hand . . . Caitlin snatched up the handkerchief and blew her nose noisily. Sitting back on the little stone seat, she regarded the hotel through a mist of tears, wondering if he was looking down from their bedroom window. And if he was, why didn't he come into the garden and make it up to her?

"Hi, Mrs Kirkwood!" said Fabian, the fitness instructor, as he jogged around the statue. "What are you doing out here in the cold?"

Caitlin shoved the handkerchief in her pocket and looked up into Fabian's friendly, blue-eyed gaze. She could not help but smile. Why was the boy always so cheerful – and so full of energy?

"I thought you'd be getting ready," added Fabian, jogging on the spot.

He looked like an advert for breakfast cereal, thought Caitlin, feeling fat, frumpy and as healthy as a chain-smoking asthmatic. His handsome, boyish face did not have a single drop of sweat running off it. He was as bouncy as Tigger, probably hell first thing in the morning, and she bet he'd never had a vitamin tablet in his life.

"Ready?" she repeated eventually, realising he expected an answer. "What for?"

Fabian threw a few mock punches at Venus. "Have you forgotten what day it is?"

"Friday?" Caitlin felt too weary to halt the sarcasm creeping into her voice. "I'm only covering reception and that's not until seven o'clock."

Fabian grinned. "No, you're not. It's Mr Kirkwood's birthday party. Had you forgotten? Princess Victoria is arriving in less than an hour and the hotel is crawling with cops searching for bombs. Didn't you notice the sniffer dogs?"

Caitlin screamed and, leaping up, began to sprint around the pond, hurdling the lavender borders and box hedging.

Fabian chuckled. Crazy Mrs Kirkwood – always good for a laugh. Tucking a few loose strands of hair back into his ponytail, he ran a lap around the pond and exited through the stone archway at the far end. The whole of two thousand acres of parkland lay before him. And beyond that, the King's Forest, stretching all the way down to the sea. He switched on his personal stereo, took a deep breath and bounded forward.

In his enthusiasm he narrowly missed leap-frogging a couple of chubby female guests, shell-suited bottoms up in the air, as they bent to admire a clump of wild daffodils. "Sorry!" he called cheerfully. As he sprinted off across the park he turned, ran backwards, and waved merrily to them. After some hesitation, they dutifully waved back.

Fabian headed towards the woodland path, scattering the fallow deer sheltering under the rhododendrons. It was unlike Mrs Kirkwood to forget things, he reflected, but then, she was getting on a bit.

After all, she must be at least twenty-four.

* * *

9

When Caitlin burst back into her bedroom, all trace of Hugh's romp with Amanda had vanished and he was sitting primly on the edge of the four-poster bed, like a vestal virgin in black tie, fastening his silver cufflinks.

He looked up disapprovingly. "Where the hell have you been? I've had one gormless idiot after another barging in to pester me about the arrangements for this stupid party." He stood up and took his dinner jacket off the back of a chair. "What's the point of employing a manager when I have to do everything myself?"

Caitlin sighed and, picking up her hairbrush, sat down at her dressingtable. Studiously avoiding Hugh's reflection in the dusty looking-glass, she tugged the brush through her tangled, windswept hair. "You didn't employ me. I came free with the wedding certificate."

"Free! You're the most expensive bloody mistake I ever made!"

"Expensive? And how did you run the hotel before you married me?"

"No problem," said Hugh. "I had a *manager*."

Before Caitlin could think of a suitably sarcastic retort he had gone, slamming the door after him. Caitlin put down her hairbrush and grimaced at her reflection. Her long black hair had already started falling out in clumps due to stress, her once emerald eyes had lost their sparkle and were now the colour of pond sludge. Why did she have this horrendous feeling that she was making a terrible mistake? Did love truly conquer all – or was she really staying with Hugh to give her baby the father and home life she never had?

Miserably, she started on her make-up. Endless cleansing, toning and moisturising, in the manner the beauty books demanded, was enough to turn anyone into a mindless zombie. She blended in her foundation and reached for her spot-cover stick. Lately it was becoming a case of join-the-dots. So much for pregnancy making a woman bloom. And that was another problem, she realised, as her waistband dug into her tummy. What the hell was she going to wear that wouldn't make her resemble a circus tent?

Half-heartedly Caitlin wandered over to her wardrobe. Her clothes reflected the misery eating of the last five years and were every size from 12 to 16, including an over-optimistic 10. She thumbed dispiritedly along the rail.

At the very end was a full-length, white lace gown. She dragged it out. Simultaneously demure and sexy, the plunging neckline would take attention away from her plunging waistline.

She pulled off her clothes and slid the dress over her head. It was perfect, although slightly too tight, but the short train at the back hid the bulges and, provided she did not eat dinner, she would be fine. And, who knows, she might finally win Hugh back.

Even Hugh could not fail to recognise her wedding gown.

Chapter Two

Every January, Marina Theodopoulou made three New Year resolutions. (1) To save money, (2) To lose weight, and (3) To get laid. By December 31st she would have failed each one. But at least it saved having to think up three more.

This year, Marina vowed, would be different. By supreme effort, in the two months since Christmas, she had lost just over a stone. Last autumn she had sold the rights to her latest slushy 'Marina Grey' novel to a film production company and, to the amazement of her bank manager, still had most of the money left. And tonight, *tonight* she was most definitely going to get her man.

Marina wondered if she was the only author of 'bodice-rippers' writing the raunchiest of sex scenes purely from imagination. If her fans ever found out . . . Marina shuddered. It would be the equivalent of discovering Barbara Cartland had ghosted *Lady Chatterley's Lover*.

Marina hauled her compact from the depths of her handbag and flicked it open. The battery-operated lights inside were too dim to do anything other than touch up her make-up and Marina had no intention of asking the chauffeur to switch on the interior lights of the borrowed Jag. She did not want him to think her vain.

Even in twilight she thought she looked pretty good. Tumbling black, pre-Raphaelite curls, held firmly onto the top of her head by two antique jewelled combs, large brown eyes, heavily outlined in kohl, smokily mysterious. Observing that she had eaten her crimson lipstick, Marina hastily touched it up just as the chauffeur manoeuvred the Jaguar through the crumbling gateway to Kirkwood Manor Hotel and down the long drive.

The chauffeur swung expertly around a large stone fountain, with Cupid pissing in the centre, and glided smoothly to a halt outside the imposing entrance. Marina snapped her compact shut and hastily shoved both it and the lipstick into her handbag just as he opened her door.

Marina smiled happily at him. With his chiselled jaw, penetrating brown eyes and smooth olive skin, he could have stepped straight from the pages of one of her books, *Love in the Sun*, or maybe *Desert Lover* (which had had to be pulped following a minor title misprint, causing a flood of furious telephone calls from cookery shops – but lots of lovely publicity and, eventually, quadruple sales).

Although Marina earned an absolute fortune from her writing, and spent it just as quickly, she had actually 'borrowed' both the chauffeur and the car from her neighbour, Lady Richmond. He came highly recommended by Lady Richmond's seventeen-year-old daughter, Belinda, who had assured Marina that he was a dream in bed (or a 'fabulous fuck' as she had so indelicately put it). Anyway, Marina had decided to have him lined up as first reserve in case tonight's date failed to show. Marina, being of Greek descent, believed in giving fate a helping hand – if not a downright shove.

After several minutes of exchanging steamy eye-meets with the chauffeur, Marina eventually alighted from the car and tugged her short, tight, red velvet dress over her rather chubby bottom. Her unfamiliar high heels scrunched the short distance across the gravel and wobbled up the steps to the front door. Before she could raise one elegantly manicured hand to the wrought-iron bell pull, the heavy oak door creaked open like a scene from Hammer House of Horror.

At the other side stood a beautiful young man, trussed up in a suit that did not belong to him. His dark blond hair was brushed back from his face and gathered at the back of his neck by a thin velvet ribbon. With his great long legs he towered threateningly over Marina but his haughty expression deteriorated into a wide smile as he recognised her.

"Hullo Marina – I mean, good evening, Miss Grey. May I take your coat?"

Marina grinned. "I'm not wearing one, Fabian."

"Eh? Oh yeah . . ." He laughed self-depreciatingly. "You can see I'm no butler."

"Butler?" Marina regarded his ponytail in awe. "You look like a highwayman."

"It was Mr Kirkwood's idea," Fabian grimaced. "You know, grand country house, servants, butler. It's all to impress Princess Victoria."

"I thought you were an aerobics instructor? You ought to look at your job description."

Marina, still wrestling with erotic thoughts of Fabian as a highwayman, stepped quickly into the hallway, admiring the huge banks of red roses arranged at intervals along the oak-panelled walls. She gently touched the velvet petals. They were real too. All these flowers must have cost a fortune. No wonder Hugh Kirkwood could not afford to hire a genuine butler. She hoped poor Caitlin was not doubling up as a waitress.

"Job description?" scowled Fabian. "What job description? I wouldn't mind but Mr Kirkwood lets Amanda prance round the ballroom like bloody Ginger Rogers while I'm stuck as Jeeves. Why doesn't anyone appreciate me, Marina? Even Cinderella had a fairy godmother."

Marina had a ghastly vision of Hugh Kirkwood in a pink tutu and spangly tights and hurriedly changed the subject. "Has Princess Victoria arrived yet?"

Fabian was not paying attention. "Oh my God . . ."

Marina peered over his broad shoulders. Descending the elaborately carved oak staircase was

15

Caitlin Kirkwood, dressed entirely in white, as though she were the avenging ghost of Miss Haversham.

"She's wearing a wedding dress!" he said. "Romantic or what!"

Normally Marina would have agreed with him but, as Caitlin's best friend, she was well aware her marriage had more rocks than the British Geological Museum. She watched in horror as Caitlin launched herself, rather unsteadily, from the bottom step and glided across the hall, her arms outstretched in genuine welcome. Hell, how much had she had to drink tonight?

"Marina!" Caitlin beamed, giving her friend a hug. "You look fantastic."

Marina caught her first whiff of alcohol fumes and smiled dubiously. "That's a beautiful dress. Didn't you wear it to your wedding?"

"Yes." Caitlin's headlamp green eyes were slightly off-focus. "See, even after five years, I can still get into it."

"I bet Hugh was touched?" Marina inwardly groaned. An unfortunate choice of words. Any touching-up was inevitably done by Hugh – Mr Tactile himself.

Caitlin steered Marina on a slightly off-course journey towards the ballroom. "He doesn't know yet. It's a surprise."

Marina, expecting a frantic society bash and looking forward to being treated appallingly by some upper-class English cad, was bitterly disappointed at the frumpy couples shuffling half-heartedly around the dance floor. The middle-aged DJ was playing 'Lady In Red'; some women were even dancing together. Didn't Hugh have any young, glamorous friends?

"Damn," she said out loud. "Why are all the women wearing red?"

"Left over from the Hunt's Valentine's Day Ball, I guess," replied Caitlin, idly tapping her foot to the music. She helped herself to a couple of glasses of champagne and, downing them both, leant back against the wall and gazed round in search of another waiter.

As the Valentine Ball, less than a month previously, was precisely when Marina had last worn her gown, she blushed furiously and vowed to splurge her next advance on a complete new wardrobe from Versace. And, if one of their fantastic backless, strapless, held-together-with-safety-pins creations failed to land her a man, she would bloody well ask for her money back.

As she scanned the room for any likely conquests, Marina became gradually aware that Hugh Kirkwood was glaring thunderously at his wife from the opposite side of the ballroom, despite dangling a couple of the local totty from his arm. Marina glanced at Caitlin knocking back yet another glass of champagne and realised drastic action was called for. But how to get her off the drink? Deciding she would have to make a supreme sacrifice, Marina stepped back into the corridor and caught Fabian's arm as he drifted past the doorway, trailing fake-fur coats across the dusty flagstones, on his way to the cloakroom.

"Fabian, will you dance with Caitlin?"

Fabian, only too willing to be distracted and join the party, tossed the coats into a corner and regarded his boss doubtfully. "What happens when she moves away from the wall?"

"Please, Fabian, you have to help me keep her off the alcohol until the Princess arrives."

Fabian gave her a devastating smile, blithely unaware of the effect it was having on Marina's knees. "You know I'd do anything for Mrs Kirkwood. She was responsible for getting me this job." He paused, pushing his floppy blond fringe from his eyes in embarrassment. "But she's had too much to drink. Look at the way she's swaying."

"She's swaying in time to the music," protested Marina.

"She is not at all in time to the music!"

"Please, Fabian? You'd drink too much if you were married to that bastard."

"You can say that again." Fabian watched Hugh Kirkwood surreptitiously stroke the bottom of one of the waiters, while staring dreamily at the besotted Amanda, and shuddered. "If I were married to him I'd bloody well shoot myself."

* * *

Caitlin had always been amazed that a man so patently horrible as her husband should have quite so many friends. From little old ladies to the dizzy heights of royalty, everyone liked Hugh Kirkwood.

His greatest friend was Douglas Oakes whom he had known since Harrow. Hugh had cold-heartedly set out to become his friend because Douglas was the Marquis of Pennington and a Marquis was just one step down from a Duke. Douglas, however, had such a good-natured, easy-going personality that it was impossible not to like him. And Hugh had liked him a whole lot more after he married a genuine royal princess – the granddaughter of the Queen of England.

The Marquis and Marchioness of Pennington finally arrived just before eleven, in Douglas's favourite gold Aston Martin, escorted by a fleet of unmarked police cars. Douglas wore his family's green and mustard tartan; Princess Victoria was unusually resplendent in floor-length gold lamé. Like most of the Royal Family, she was happiest in jodhpurs and co-ordinating mud.

As Victoria and Douglas entered the ballroom a sudden quiet came over the guests. Hugh disdainfully disposed of Amanda like a ten-day-old curry and tried unsuccessfully to battle a route through the crowded dance floor. Victoria, however, had caught sight of Caitlin attempting to blend in with an extravagant flower arrangement, and waved enthusiastically.

"Yoo-hoo! Caitlin!"

Caitlin felt the unrelenting glare of two hundred pairs of jealous eyes swivel in her direction. Much as she liked the young Princess, she would far rather crawl into a dark corner and hibernate. But she took a fortifying gulp of champagne and made an effort to

19

appear more cheerful, hindered as Hugh suddenly materialised beside her.

"Your Royal Highness!" he beamed. "How wonderful that you could make it. What a terrific gown. Givenchy?"

"Haven't the foggiest," grinned Victoria. "Douglas bought it. Sometimes I think he only married me to make the perfect accessory to his car."

The DJ, having been primed by Hugh, whipped off 'Lady In Red' and placed a rather scratchy 'Goldfinger' on the turntable. Douglas's absolute hero, apart from his cricket captain at school almost thirty years ago, was James Bond.

Douglas was delighted. "My favourite song!" He offered Caitlin his arm. "Care to dance, my dear?"

Oh God, her worst nightmare. Although Caitlin had once danced professionally in the West End, the last time she had performed in public, at a charity concert before the Prince of Wales no less, she had accidentally floored the male lead and stuck her foot through the high-tech scenery. Enough embarrassment to make anyone take up alternative employment.

Muttering about twisted knee ligaments, with all the accuracy of someone who watched *ER* repeats purely to drool over George Clooney, she attempted to go into reverse. She only succeeded in crunching Hugh's foot with her stiletto heel.

He pushed her back onto Douglas's welcoming arm and relieved her of her champagne glass. "Enjoy yourself, darling," he said with tangible sarcasm. "And *do* try to stay upright," he stage-whispered. "There's a dear."

Victoria watched her husband depart onto the crowded dance floor, then looked hopefully at Hugh. But Hugh, having to repay several favours, started to manoeuvre her in the direction of the bar.

"Let me get you a drink, Your Royal Highness. And introduce you to some people I know you would love to meet."

"Super," said Victoria, glancing sadly back at the dance floor. She turned towards the bar but her way was blocked by a tall, handsome young man with blond hair flowing well past his shoulders.

"Your Majesty," he hiccuped, bowing so low his nose almost scraped the floor. "Would you care to dance?"

"Fabian!" bellowed Hugh.

"Why, that would be lovely." Victoria smiled and, taking his proffered arm, quickly steered him into the centre of the dance floor without giving either Hugh, or her outraged bodyguards, so much as a backwards glance. "Thank you very much for asking me."

* * *

Hugh watched Princess Victoria doing The Doop with Fabian and wondered if he ought to cut in. Fabian did not seem to be treating Victoria with the reverence one should accord a royal princess. Unfortunately Hugh could hardly Twist let alone Doop – which appeared to be some sort of drug-induced Charleston. Belatedly he wondered where the DJ had obtained the dreadful music from. He would not put it past Caitlin to hand over Fabian's CD collection, purely to irritate him. She knew dance music gave him migraines.

Despite Marina's best efforts, Caitlin had consumed numerous glasses of champagne, shedding most of it (and her inhibitions) carelessly across the ballroom floor, as she danced with every man present except her husband. Hugh regarded her progress with disdain. After his one duty dance with Lady Richmond, wife of the Lord Lieutenant, he merely propped up the bar with Amanda on one arm and matching teenage blonde, Belinda Richmond, on the other.

He knew he should feel remorse as Amanda tried desperately to win him back but, to be perfectly honest, he had grown bored with the entire subject hours ago. As her pleadings became incoherent, bordering on hysterical, he did not bother to hide his yawns and, sliding one hand beneath Belinda's short pink skirt, he distracted himself by caressing her bottom, dispassionately watching her squirm in ecstasy. At least someone appreciates me, he thought, and ordered another bottle of wine.

Directly opposite his point of view was Marina, sitting happily on Douglas's knee, one hand burrowing beneath his shirt, the other disappearing up his kilt. Hugh smiled faintly. Nanny had always said the respectable ones were the worst. Briefly he wondered what Marina would be like in bed. Grateful, probably –

like some slobbering Labrador puppy. He shuddered and wondered if he ought to rescue Douglas.

The Marquis, having consumed as many glasses of whisky as Caitlin had champagne, did not seem unduly worried. Marriage into the Royal Family had probably cured him of any hang-ups. Although the two Special Branch officers flanking him, wearing identical dark suits, looked distinctly frosty at the prospective breach of security.

After persuading one of the local plod (easily distinguishable in a pale grey suit from M & S) to take his place, one Special Branch officer strolled off through the terrace windows to light up a cigarette. Lucky him, thought Hugh enviously. Time off for good behaviour.

He stirred the bowl of peanuts on the bar before him with the cocktail stick from Amanda's pina colada and, cutting her off in mid-whinge, said loudly, "I'm bored."

Amanda was shocked. "But this is your birthday. How can you be bored? All your friends are here, you've had loads of expensive presents and you've even got a real live princess as a guest."

"And my wife providing the cabaret."

From his other side, Belinda Richmond giggled. Hugh smiled lazily at her. In appearance, Belinda and Amanda were very similar. Long, golden hair, deep blue eyes, large bouncing breasts. Standing on each side of him they could have been bookends. Hugh's imagination transported them to Caitlin's four-poster. He sighed. After this afternoon's fiasco, that would be asking for trouble.

"Isn't it hot in here?" commented Belinda, vigorously fanning her face with one slim hand, causing a minor turbulence in her Wonderbra.

Playtex must use incredibly strong underwiring to tolerate that much strain, thought Hugh, completely hypnotised by all the jiggling flesh.

"Yes," agreed Amanda. She linked her arm firmly through Hugh's. "Perhaps you'd like a walk in the garden, darling? I'm sure you'd feel happier away from this noisy crowd."

Something in Hugh's brain clanked into place. "What I'd really like is a swim."

"What a terrific idea," said Belinda. "Let's go and play in the pool. With the Princess here no one will miss us. I don't have a swimsuit but well, as it's just you and me . . ."

"And me," interrupted Amanda grimly.

"Three's a crowd," snapped Belinda.

"Safety in numbers."

Belinda regarded Hugh from beneath her mascara-encrusted lashes. "Ah, but I like to live dangerously . . ."

"It is true that two is company," injected Hugh smoothly. "But I have always found that three can open up all sorts of possibilities . . ."

The two girls glanced doubtfully at each other.

Amanda made her decision first. "OK, let's go. If we leave now, while everyone is dancing, we'll not be missed."

"Has . . . er, has the indoor pool got a lock?" asked Belinda.

"So much for living dangerously!" scorned Amanda. "Why would anyone want to come and gawp at you when they could be gawping at a royal princess?"

"Yes, the pool has got a lock," said Hugh. "And a bar, and music, and satellite TV . . ." And closed circuit TV, he added to himself. He could make a recording to cheer himself up on rainy days. Things were most definitely looking up.

They fought their way around the crowds, who were massing on the edge of the ballroom and desperate for a glimpse of the Princess. Then out though the French windows and onto the terrace. Hugh had forgotten the Special Branch officer standing there, his features masked by a haze of cigarette smoke, the raindrops incongruously sparkling in his short, military-style hair.

"Evening," said Hugh, sidling past, each arm entwined around the waist of a teenage blonde.

The officer merely nodded, his navy-blue eyes indifferent.

"I bet he's a bundle of laughs in bed," muttered Belinda, when they were almost, but not quite, out of earshot.

Hugh glanced back. The officer blew out another cloud of smoke and leant on the stone balustrade, watching their progress across the lawn, towards the west wing of the house. Deliberately, Hugh took the girls the long way round, past the barbecue and through the shrubbery. Even as a child he had hated to share his toys – unless it was to his advantage.

The old thatched barn housing the indoor pool was unlocked. Hugh switched on the main lights but ensured the blinds were drawn across the windows so no one would know they were inside.

Although the barn was older than the house, the pool had been built in the 1980s, when the fitness craze first swept the country. There was also a huge bubbling jacuzzi, just right for intimate parties, as well as a steam room, sauna, and solarium, for those who liked it hot. For those less physically inclined, there was a bar, and loungers were grouped around the pool and arranged on the sundeck outside.

Amanda and Belinda stripped off their clothes, scattering them carelessly around the pool edge, and dived in. Hugh entered the staff office, loaded his favourite Kenny G album into the CD player and inserted a fresh videotape for the CCTV monitor. By the time he came out, the two girls were splashing around, having called a reluctant truce, and were generally showing off.

"Happy birthday to me," he hummed to himself, watching the lush female flesh bouncing and wobbling about in the turquoise water. "Mmm . . . Happy birthday to me!" He dived into the pool fully clothed.

Belinda and Amanda squealed as a huge wash of chlorinated water showered over their bleached blonde heads. Hugh surfaced next to Amanda and pulled her into his arms, lifting her up out of the water and sitting her up on the side. The water clung to her skin, shimmering like diamonds.

"Venus rising from the foam," Hugh sighed, flicking droplets from her hardened pink nipples.

"Blame Fabian," giggled Amanda. "He's worked here eighteen months and he still can't get the chemical balance of the water right."

"The poor boy is so easily distracted. How many times have you slept with him?"

"Twice," lied Amanda, blushing. "And believe me, 'sleep' was the operative word."

Jealously, Belinda watched from the other side of the pool as Hugh lowered his head, lifting one of Amanda's firm white breasts into his mouth.

Slowly Belinda swam over and stood behind him, curving her body against his, fumbling for the fastening of his trousers. As she struggled with the fly buttons, Hugh was finally distracted from Amanda's glorious breasts long enough to turn around laughing.

"I was coming to you in a moment," he chided and kissed her, sliding one hand over her hip and between her thighs.

Amanda hauled him back by the tails of his shirt and wound her legs tightly around his waist.

Hugh began to laugh. "Girls, why fight when you can both have me?"

"But I want you to have me!" implored Belinda.

"Darling, as we have all night, we can all have each other! And, as it's my birthday, I think I ought to go first. So tell me, Belinda, how long can you hold your breath under water?"

Chapter Three

Through a haze of alcohol, Caitlin realised everyone was laughing at her. But it was not the drink that had made such a fool of her; it was her husband. So much for his promises; he had disappeared with that bloody Amanda. Stuff the sympathy vote – she should have kicked her out, bag and baggage, when she had had the chance.

Maybe it was not too late. Before she changed her mind, Caitlin put down her champagne glass and staggered across the dance floor. Weaving in and out of equally inebriated couples, she eventually made it to the hallway. She narrowly missed colliding with Lord and Lady Richmond, who were having an argument over who had last seen their daughter Belinda.

"Try your chauffeur," hiccuped Caitlin as she passed, swinging around the elegantly carved banister and clambering up the oak staircase on all fours. "Driving girls wild is his speciality."

Caitlin headed for her bedroom, on the second floor, as this was Hugh's natural habitat. She had no idea what she was going to say when she finally found Hugh and Amanda, but had the idea that it was going to start, "Now listen, you bastard . . ." Solemnly Caitlin practised it a few times before throwing open the bedroom door.

The door swung back, slamming so hard against the wall the bare floorboards trembled beneath her feet. The room was in darkness; unusual, for Hugh was certainly not shy. Caitlin clicked on the electric lights. The four-poster was empty and so was the bedroom. For a moment she remained in the corridor, unable to believe her eyes. She was so sure she was going to encounter an action-replay of this afternoon, it was almost disappointing to find the room completely deserted.

Caitlin swayed across the threshold and sat miserably on the bed. *"Romeo, Romeo, wherefore art thou, Romeo?"*

Really there were not that many places for a fornicating couple to hide. Caitlin hitched up the petticoats of her gown, then the quilt cover, and bent double to peer beneath the bed. Nope, not under there either.

As the alcohol began to clear she realised she was right beside Hugh's enormous wardrobe. "Ah hah!" she cried. "Gotcha!" and pulled open the door. Nothing. Just rows and rows of Hugh's precious Armani suits. He loved Armani. Yet he had never bought her so much as a pair of tights from his favourite designer. Idly Caitlin flicked through them. She had not realised he had so many. There were dozens and dozens. They must be worth a fortune. So this was where all their money went . . .

A gleam of an idea began to filter through. She zigzagged across to the chest of drawers beside the bed, collected a pair of scissors and zigzagged back, snipping at the air experimentally. The perfect revenge for the rejected wife. But she was not going to cut off the sleeves. Oh no, that was far too easy to fix. Caitlin grabbed the first pair of trousers to hand and began to hack out the crotch.

After massacring the trousers she started on the jackets and shirts, neatly clipping out large round holes just where the nipples would be. Not satisfied with that, she used bright red lipstick to draw little Mary Quant flowers around the holes. Half an hour later and Hugh's suits resembled the costumes for a Paul Raymond revue.

Taking the scissors and a handful of fresh lipsticks, Caitlin staggered out the door, into the corridor and along a few doors to Amanda's room. Like most of the hotel employees, Amanda's room overlooked the front of the house. It was locked but Caitlin had a pass key.

Hugh allowed his employees to decorate their quarters in any way they wished, provided they paid for the materials, the work was done professionally and the colour scheme was tasteful. Most of the staff could not be bothered but Amanda, boosted by the allowance from her wealthy father, had transformed her room until it resembled something from Arabian Nights.

It was white throughout. Amanda had draped muslin over the windows and from the ceiling to form curtains around the wrought-iron bed – like a mosquito net, thought Caitlin. There were posters from old black and white movies on the walls, white fairy lights entwined around the bed and lots of coloured glass bottles jammed with candles, which had half-dripped wax down the sides. With all the muslin, Caitlin decided it was a miracle the room had not gone up in flames long ago.

Again Caitlin had theatrically thrown open the door but did not really expect to discover the happy couple. She peered under the bed just to check but there was nothing – just suitcases – and they were empty too. Obviously Amanda had no intention of leaving. Caitlin could not resist a quick prowl around but there did not appear to be much to look at. Amanda's father lived in a large house on the other side of Calahurst; she only used her hotel room when she wanted a leg over.

Caitlin opened the wardrobe. Baby blues and pinks hit her straight between the eye. Essex girl strikes again. And then Caitlin recognised some of the designer labels. There was no way Amanda could afford these clothes on her salary and unlikely that Daddy dearest had bought them. Even Caitlin would find it difficult to afford a fraction of them and she owned the hotel. Brandishing her scissors like Norman Bates, Caitlin slashed her rival's clothes to ribbons.

After that, she scrawled the lipstick over them, then opened the window and began to hurl out the contents of Amanda's underwear drawer. A suspender-belt caught on Lord Richmond's Rolls and a mint-green bra swung from the ear of Cupid in the fountain. Caitlin giggled. It was like playing hoopla. She tried again with some French knickers but they didn't fly very well, landing forlornly in the rhododendron bushes. The thongs and G-strings were much better, a bit like catapults.

Caitlin was having so much fun that she didn't notice she had an audience until there was a yell of indignation from below. Leaning out as far as she dared she spotted Lord Richmond directly beneath her. He had sneaked out of the house only moments before, hoping to light up one of his cigars without being caught by his wife. Now he was wearing a fluffy pink thong over his bald head. Appalled, Caitlin pulled her head in and hastily shut the window before he saw her.

She began to feel sick. Maybe some fresh air would make her feel better. And she ought to beat a retreat before some hero decided to discover where the artillery had originated from. She gathered up the evidence and ran.

Downstairs, every beat of the dance music crashed against her forehead like an iron bar. The route through the front door was blocked by Lord Richmond and his equally sozzled cronies, laughing like schoolboys, as they collected Amanda's underwear and began to drape it across the parked cars and then over each other. Caitlin recognised a minor aristo parading in a lace bra, the MP for Norchester wearing another like earmuffs and a High Court Judge with French knickers on his head. What wouldn't *The Sun* pay for a snapshot of that lot?

The only other escape route was into the ballroom – the last place Caitlin wanted to be but the champagne sitting in her stomach was fizzing so alarmingly it felt like Mount Vesuvius.

Fearing an eruption, Caitlin shoved and pushed her way across the crowded ballroom to the French windows, which led out onto the terrace. She knew everyone was staring, whispering and pointing but right at this moment she was in too much of a hurry to be fussy. Making an entrance was one thing – a spectacular exit quite another.

Barging between a romantically entwined couple, Caitlin threw open the French windows, hurtled across the terrace and jumped the short flight of steps to the lawn. She made directly for the herbaceous border but when she got there she found she no longer felt sick, just faint. Abruptly, she flopped onto the damp grass and rested her forehead against her knees until the dizziness subsided – leaving overwhelming guilt instead. First thing tomorrow, she'd go out and buy Amanda a whole new wardrobe of clothes. But in more suitable colours. Grey perhaps, and navy-blue . . .

"Can I help?" asked a deep male voice.

Horrified that anyone could have witnessed her making such an idiot of herself, Caitlin slowly raised her head. An extremely handsome man was standing in front of her, gingerly holding a woman's stiletto shoe by the heel.

"Hello," said Caitlin reluctantly, hoping he was one of Hugh's dissolute chums and not a hotel guest.

"Hello." He held out the shoe. "I think this belongs to you."

"Does it?" Caitlin hitched up her skirt and many lace petticoats in search of her feet. Her sheer tights were laddered and distinctly grubby and, sure enough, only one cream satin shoe remained on her foot.

The man knelt on the grass. "May I?"

Caitlin nodded, hoping her feet were not sweaty from all that dancing. The shoe slid on with ease.

"There you are, Cinderella!"

Caitlin stared into blue eyes so dark they appeared almost black. Her heart gave a jolt. Prince Charming – five years too late.

"My name is Caitlin," she said, scrambling to her feet and holding out her hand.

He shook it solemnly. "That's an unusual name. Dylan Thomas' wife was called Caitlin."

Caitlin, who had not the faintest idea who Dylan Thomas was, remained silent. Instead she smiled up at this tall, dark, handsome stranger and attempted to appear enigmatic.

"Can I get you a drink?" he suggested.

"A glass of mineral water would be very nice," she said, frantic to sober up.

"OK, I won't be long." He disappeared up the steps to the ballroom.

Finding her heels were rapidly sinking into the soggy lawn, Caitlin tiptoed the few yards back to the terrace and decoratively arranged herself on the bottom step. Dodging the rain-clouds was a beautiful full moon, which she hoped was showing her cleavage to advantage and camouflaging her spots at the same time.

Belatedly she remembered her search for Hugh. It would be typical of him to turn up now, just when she was beginning to have fun. Fun? She was behaving disgracefully. Hugh's bad habits were obviously rubbing off. She stood up, about to flee into the night, when Prince Charming reappeared at her side and handed her a glass of mineral water. On top was a wilted slice of lemon, floating like a dead albino goldfish. She would definitely have to have words with the bar staff.

"The party is still going strong," he said and smiled that devastating smile.

Caitlin felt her legs go and sat down. It wouldn't hurt just to stay and chat, would it? She realised his accent was not quite English enough. Was he American? Australian? It occurred to her that she did not even know his name.

"Are you a friend of Hugh Kirkwood?" he added.

She laughed hollowly. "Certainly not!"

"A friend of the family?"

Her lips twitched. "I know his wife very well."

The man stared up at the sky. The moonlight silhouetted his high cheekbones and aquiline nose. The nose had a bump halfway down. Perhaps he had broken it sometime. Caitlin wondered how.

"This is a gorgeous house," he was saying. "I know it looks Jacobean but it's Victorian, isn't it? The Victorians built such wonderfully Gothic mansions. Has it been a hotel long?"

The house? Who the hell wanted to talk about the house? She had been hoping for more romantic conversation. Frantically she tried to remember what Hugh had composed for the hotel brochure.

"It's been a hotel since the seventies," she said at last. "It was built by Hugh's – er, Mr Kirkwood's great-great-grandfather. He made a fortune in shipbuilding but his family spent it all. Every time they ran out of money they lopped down a copse and built another boat. It's a miracle there's any forest left."

"So when the boatbuilding dried up they diversified into the leisure industry?"

"Uh huh. The house was originally named after the mistletoe growing in the forest. A lot of the Victorian mansions around Calahurst are. Lord Richmond's pad is called Ilex House – the posh name for holly. Hugh changed the name to Kirkwood Manor. The Americans like that sort of thing."

Caitlin realised she had finished her drink and carefully balanced the empty glass on the stone balustrade. Her feet had gone to sleep; she wriggled them experimentally.

"Would you like to dance?" suggested the man.

"No, thanks." It came out far more brutally than she

had intended. Anxious to make amends she quickly added, "But we could go for a walk if you like." No way was she going to let him disappear into the sunset.

He seemed rather taken aback by the suggestion though. "A walk?"

Anyone would have thought she had suggested a quick romp in the bushes. "Just around the garden," said Caitlin, hoping it was too dark for him to notice her flaming cheeks. "The moon is so bright now we'll be able to see quite clearly. The River Hurst flows through the edge of the woods, just past the rose garden. There's a boathouse on the banks. It's over a hundred years old."

He appeared amused. "Come up and see my boathouse, huh?"

Caitlin's face felt as though it was being chargrilled. "You'll be perfectly safe," she muttered testily. "You'll be within shouting distance of the house. Not to mention all those police officers prowling the place because of the Princess." Hell, was it really this difficult to pick up a man these days, or was she just out of practice?

He offered his hand to help her up. "But will you be safe from me?"

Caitlin smiled irrepressibly as a little voice inside her head said, *I do hope not . . .*

* * *

Marina danced with Fabian. As the DJ was playing a romantic number, Marina had her arms wound tightly around Fabian's neck. She had discarded her high heels some time ago so he had to stoop to avoid being throttled. Marina attempted to squint at her watch but it had become tangled up in his blond hair. Eventually she gave up and looked at his.

"I haven't seen Caitlin for a long time," she said.

"Yeah, it is dark in here."

Marina decided it would take too long to explain. "I wonder where Hugh has gone? It's a quarter past twelve. Weren't the fireworks supposed to have been set off at midnight?"

"Were they?" he commented disinterestedly, before bending to kiss her neck.

Marina, hardly daring to believe her luck, danced to another chorus. They shuffled past the Richmonds' table. "Look," giggled Marina, "Douglas has fallen asleep on Lady Richmond's shoulder."

Fabian eyed Lady Richmond's large expanse of plump, white, comfortable shoulder. "Seems like a good idea to me."

"The Princess looks pretty fed up. Shouldn't she have left by now?"

"My Dad says all the Royals look fed up. It's their bone structure. You only have to see the way the Queen looks on a five-pound note."

Marina sighed and untangled herself. "We'd better go and find Caitlin and Hugh."

"Maybe they've gone off for a bonk."

"Maybe they have – but not with each other, that's for certain. In fact, I bet that bastard's making up to some teenage strumpet right now." Marina untangled herself from Fabian's embrace. "Still, I suppose we ought to make the effort to find them. You go and search the garden. I'll check upstairs."

Fabian grinned. "And whoever finds the most fornicating couples wins!"

* * *

Caitlin sat on the river bank, dangling her bare feet in the water. She had abandoned her shoes somewhere behind her on the lawn. The water was inky black with only the reflection of the moon to create ripples of silver across its surface. In the daytime the river was so clear the gravelly bottom could be easily seen, as well as occasional fish.

Oblivious to the damp grass soaking through her skirts, Caitlin stared across the water, deep in thought. On the opposite bank were the pastures which Hugh rented out to a local farmer. There ought to be a herd of cows in there at the moment but Caitlin could not see them. Maybe cows went home to bed at night like everyone else. Like she ought to do. Just a few hours ago she was all for playing happy families with Hugh, and now she was falling in love with a perfect stranger.

The man had rolled up his trousers and was swishing his feet back and forth in the water. His socks had been screwed up into little balls and stuffed into his shoes which were abandoned beside him. The moonlight shone on his short, 'Caesar' style hair. Caitlin wanted to run her fingers through it and ruffle it up. But, she reminded herself firmly, she was a married woman. To make certain she sat on her hands. He certainly was the most perfect stranger.

It occurred to her that if she was planning on committing adultery she really ought to ask his name. But just as she turned to ask, his face moved, blotting out that treacherous moon, and his mouth landed firmly on hers. She was so surprised she froze.

He kissed her gently, as though fearing rejection. Then more confidently, his tongue dipping and diving between her lips, dancing the lambada with her tongue, until she got quite carried away and joined in, in a most immoral fashion, wrapping her arms around his neck and pulling him closer. Then his mouth began to slide down her neck, the tip of his tongue curling around the little hollows of her collarbone. Caitlin sighed and melted into him.

Vaguely she realised that this was the bit where she was supposed to put up a fight, in case he thought she was completely without virtue, but she wasn't stupid. Just as the stranger's hand crept around to caress the back of her neck, sliding into the top of her dress, while her mind slipped into oblivion, a familiar voice broke her concentration.

"Mrs Kirkwood . . . er, hem . . . Mrs Kirk . . . wood . . ."

"Mrs Kirkwood?" her new friend whispered softly in her ear.

"I can explain," said Caitlin, knowing full well she couldn't.

"Mrs Kirkwood," repeated Fabian patiently, "may I have a couple of words?"

Caitlin grit her teeth. "Sure, piss off."

"That's three," muttered the voice in her ear.

Caitlin giggled.

"Mrs Kirkwood," continued Fabian relentlessly, "it is *urgent*."

The man released her.

Caitlin scrambled to her feet, grabbed Fabian and hauled him away from the riverbank. "What's so urgent? Has something awful happened?"

"The fireworks that were supposed to go off at midnight? Didn't."

"Oh hell! Has anyone noticed?"

"Only Marina and I suppose she doesn't count. Most people have dropped off to sleep in the Residents' Lounge."

"Drawing-room," corrected Caitlin automatically. "But I can still hear music."

"The DJ refuses to go until he gets paid."

"God, there goes our entertainment licence. Oh well, Hugh can sort him out when he decides to turn up. Now, how are you at lighting fireworks?"

"Dunno, but I've got a cigarette-lighter here somewhere." Fabian tugged it out of his trouser pocket. The silver glimmered in the moonlight as he flipped the lid off and tried to light it. Nothing happened.

"Terrific!"

"Sorry, I've never needed to use it. Dad bought it for my twenty-first – he doesn't know I don't smoke and I didn't want to hurt his feelings."

Like he always hurts yours, thought Caitlin, but

41

didn't say anything. Poor Fabian. She knew how he hero-worshipped his father.

"Here, try mine," suggested the stranger, having heard every word. Another silver cigarette-lighter flew through the air.

Fabian neatly caught it. "Thanks!" he called. "I'll bring it straight back."

"*I'll* bring it straight back," said Caitlin. She smiled up at her new friend. "I'll return just as soon as I've sorted out these fireworks."

"Don't be too long," said the stranger, "or I might turn into a handsome frog."

Caitlin hitched up her wedding dress and followed Fabian in the direction of the barbecue. The stranger sighed and took out another cigarette – before he remembered his missing lighter. Slightly peeved, he flicked the cigarette into the fast-moving water and looked around for his shoes.

* * *

Caitlin left Fabian with a torch, a list of instructions and the stranger's cigarette-lighter. She gathered up a box of sparklers for the guests and set off back towards the house, taking the route past the indoor pool to save her bare feet. The huge chestnut trees, just coming into bud, cast long, sinister shadows across the barn but she could see her way by the lights streaming through the open door.

Caitlin slowed down. That was not right. The

poolside was washed down every evening by the caretaker, who then locked the barn-door at ten o'clock promptly. Caitlin tiptoed across the flagstone path, pausing as she reached the open doorway. Every light in the building blazed.

The sensible thing would be to call security, or one of those bored Special Branch officers. But Caitlin could hear laughter and lots of splashing, hardly the behaviour of a terrorist. Most likely it was a gang of Hugh's dreadful friends.

Caitlin entered the barn.

Chapter Four

"I've never had an older woman before," sighed Fabian, sleepwalking his fingers across Marina's plump breasts. "You were fantastic!"

"Practice," lied Marina. It was amazing what one could learn just from reading books. Then, as Fabian's words sunk in, "What do you mean *old*? How old are you?"

"Twenty-one." He picked up one of Marina's long black curls and pretended to make a moustache with it.

"A real babe in arms," grumbled Marina. "I'm only four years older than you."

"Don't get angry. It was supposed to be a compliment. Can we do it again?"

"Do what?" enquired Marina testily.

"Mmm," Fabian pulled her closer. "Anything you like . . . what's your favourite position?"

Marina swallowed. "My . . . er . . . what?"

He snuggled against her warm golden skin. "Or

44

fantasy. What's your favourite fantasy? I'll tell you mine if you tell me yours."

Marina was saved, literally, by the bell. The doorbell. Clutching her Laura Ashley bedsheets against her naked body, she attempted to slide out of bed without revealing her cellulite.

"Where are you going?" complained Fabian.

"Someone's at the door."

"So let the maid answer it."

"It's Sunday. It's the maid's day off." Maid? What maid? She wasn't royalty.

"Well, let them wait," said Fabian, snuggling under the bedclothes. "Fancy someone calling on you first thing Sunday morning. You could be at church."

"I don't think they'd have me." Marina tugged at the bedclothes. Fabian suddenly released them and laughed as she almost went over backwards. She wrapped the bedclothes firmly around herself and grabbed her pink satin wrap off the back of the bedroom door.

Fabian yawned and rolled over. Marina sighed, unable to believe her luck. He did have a gorgeous body, long, lean and muscular from all those workouts. It seemed a pity to let him go cold. Slowly she draped the bedclothes back over him and struggled into her dressinggown before he could open his eyes.

But Fabian had fallen asleep.

Marina slipped into her high-heeled, fluffy pink slippers and wobbled down the staircase into her sitting-room. Her cottage had been built in the seventeenth century with an abundance of oak beams, exposed brickwork and inadequately roaring fires. The first thing she had done on moving in was to install central heating and double glazing. Luckily the council had not yet found out. Marina's cottage, like most of Calahurst village, was a listed building.

Through the small glass pane in her front door Marina could see the back of a man's head, distorted by the bull's-eye glass. He looked like the Elephant Man. With some trepidation she opened the door. The man turned – what a revelation. Towering above her was Apollo. Marina blinked. This was Calahurst not Delphi.

The man waved a little black wallet before her eyes. Fastened to one side was a plastic-looking silver crest. On the other, enclosed in scratched perspex, was a minuscule colour photograph.

Realising she was staring at him, she muttered, "The electricity meter is in that little cupboard behind you," and attempted to shut the door. The man's foot slid in the gap. Marina glared up at him. "What do you think you are doing?"

The man glared back. "I'm not actually here to read your electricity meter."

"Then what do you want? I warn you, I've got a big, strong man upstairs."

His mouth twitched. "That wasn't quite what I had in mind either. I'm DCI Hunter and I'm looking for Mrs Caitlin Kirkwood."

"DCI?" queried Marina, inexplicably thinking of paint.

"Detective Chief Inspector."

"Oh." Marina fumbled in her pocket for her tortoiseshell spectacles and shoved them onto the end of her nose. DCI Hunter's face swum into focus. He had dark brown hair, hazel eyes and finely sculptured features. An ageing Cary Grant. He was undoubtedly good-looking, by anyone's score-chart but, as he must be at least forty, maybe a little too old for her. He wore a very nice suit though. An Armani copy.

She hurriedly stuck the spectacles back into her pocket. "What do you want with Caitlin?" she asked, as he obviously had no intention of going away. If it hadn't been for Fabian upstairs, Marina would have been sorely tempted to invite him in for coffee. Or something.

DCI Hunter sighed. "Is she here?"

"Caitlin? Of course not. She lives at the hotel down the road. You must have passed it to get here. Kirkwood Manor Hotel? It's a great big Victorian mansion. Her husband owns it and she's the manager. It's been in his family for over a hundred and fifty years."

"Really." DCI Hunter did not appear to be impressed. "I do have reason to believe Mrs Kirkwood is here."

Marina frowned. The man was obviously an idiot. "Why?"

DCI Hunter stepped to one side and pointed behind him. "Well, that for a start!"

Marina stared incredulously at the gold Aston

Martin parked half on her driveway, half in her beloved rosebed. "Good gracious, that's Douglas's car!"

"Yes, madam."

"But Douglas is not here – at least, I don't think he is." She put her hand to her forehead. This was all a bit much to comprehend on a Sunday morning. Especially before she'd had lunch. Or breakfast come to think of it.

"It is possible Mrs Kirkwood er . . . 'borrowed' the car, madam?"

"What for?"

"I don't know. If you tell me where I can find her I will ensure I ask her!"

"But I've told you," Marina spoke very slowly and clearly. "She isn't here!"

"Yes, I am," said a tired voice behind her.

Marina turned in astonishment. Still wearing her white wedding dress, decidedly crumpled and covered in river mud and grass-stains, was Caitlin.

"Mrs Caitlin Kirkwood?" enquired DCI Hunter politely, waving his warrant card in front of her nose as though attempting hypnosis.

"Yes, that's me." Caitlin slumped despondently back onto one of Marina's chintzy sofas – where she must have spent the night. "But not for much longer. I'm going to divorce the sleazy bastard." She wrenched off her wedding ring and aimed it at the coal scuttle. It missed. She massaged her forehead. "Have I got a headache! Sorry, Marina, I broke in last night while you were at the party. You really ought to get that back window fixed."

Marina was trying desperately to keep up with the conversation. "Why break in? I'd have given you a key."

"I couldn't find you," shrugged Caitlin. "And I had to leave in a hurry. I've left him, Marina. I couldn't wait a second longer. Do you know what I caught the bastard doing this time?"

Marina was reluctant to make suggestions with a police officer in attendance.

"I caught him having an orgy in the pool!" Caitlin put her head in her hands. "The bastard, the mean rotten bastard. He was having an orgy in the pool with Amanda de Havilland and Belinda Richmond and, worst of all, he was having fun."

Marina blinked. "An orgy? What sort of an orgy?"

Caitlin peered through her fingers with some irritation. "You're the one that writes the soft porn. What do you think?" Slowly she raised her head and looked at DCI Hunter, hovering determinedly on the doorstep like a double-glazing salesman. "I suppose you've come for the car?" she said sadly. "I hope I didn't cause some huge security scare? I didn't think Douglas would mind me borrowing it. He's a friend of my husband but quite nice."

"It wasn't really the car I came about, madam," DCI Hunter looked meaningfully at Marina. "If I could come in?"

Marina begrudgingly stood aside.

"Oh God," said Caitlin. "Has there's been an accident?"

DCI Hunter shifted uncomfortably. "There's been a fire at the hotel."

"A fire?" Caitlin paled. "Was anybody hurt?"

"An adjacent barn housing the leisure complex was set alight by a stray firework."

"Thank goodness no one was in it," said Marina.

"But Hugh was in there," said Caitlin, her face crumpling. "That's what you've come to tell me, isn't it? He's dead . . ."

* * *

After calling the police station on his mobile phone, to request someone collect Douglas's Aston Martin, DCI Hunter drove Caitlin back to Kirkwood Manor in his own car. Marina went too, completely forgetting about Fabian asleep in her bed.

The hotel was only a couple of minutes' drive from Marina's cottage, at the Calahurst end of Mistletoe Lane. As DCI Hunter clumsily manoeuvred his Cavalier through the narrow stone gateway and down the long curved drive, Caitlin stared blankly out of the window across the parkland. She was hoping to see some signs of the fire but the old barn had been around the other side of the house and was hidden from the drive by the chestnut trees.

The sun had burnt off the early morning mist and she could clearly see the manor sprawling at the end of the drive. The red brick glowed almost pink and the sunlight glinted on the old, warped glass of the mullion and transom windows.

DCI Hunter drove up to the front of the house. Amanda's underwear festooned the shrubs and flowerbeds on either side of the door and Cupid, in the fountain, was beautifully dressed in a pink fur bikini. Distracted, DCI Hunter accidentally scraped the side of his car against the wall of the pond.

While Marina worriedly checked the fountain for damage, DCI Hunter just sat and stared at the multi-coloured silks and satins paraded before him. "That must have been some party you had last night . . ."

He was talking to air. Caitlin had jumped out of the car and run up the steps to the front door. She found it jammed.

Locked? She shook it again. But the front door was never locked. Maybe it was stuck? As she kicked it the door swung open. On the other side was a fair-haired, freckly man whom she recognised from the party last night. He had a neat, conservative hairstyle, an immaculate grey suit and black shoes so highly polished she could see her reflection. The only jarring note was a flamboyant red tie with a cartoon cat capering across. It must have been a present from his wife.

Caitlin stared at him in astonishment. "Who the hell are you?"

He met her accusing stare with steady blue eyes. "Detective Inspector Clive Reynolds, ma'am."

Caitlin rounded on DCI Hunter, who hadn't managed to reach the door quickly enough. "What is this? A police officers' convention?"

Before DCI Hunter could reply, DI Reynolds said, "I'm here to preserve the crime scene, ma'am."

"Crime scene?" Caitlin's voice went up an octave. "What crime scene?"

"Well, the fire . . ." began DI Reynolds, then caught sight of his boss's face and lapsed into red-faced silence.

Caitlin glanced accusingly at the DCI. "You said the fire was caused by a stray firework."

"Well –"

Caitlin pushed between them. "Out of my way!"

DI Reynolds made a grab for her but missed.

Caitlin ran through reception, along to the ballroom. She fumbled with the window latch and sprinted across the terrace, down the steps and into the garden.

A smell of bonfires pervaded the air. Across the lawn was the ruined pool house. The timber frame had collapsed like a house of cards, the thatched roof was mere ashes. The aqua tiling around the pool could be glimpsed through the wreckage, though the tiles were now blackened and cracked. Even the surrounding chestnut trees were scorched as thin columns of smoke weaved up between their burnt branches.

The ruins still smouldered and firemen were carefully poking about in the rubble. The lawn had been churned up by a fleet of fire engines and cars. Two uniformed police officers, slumped against a patrol car, hurriedly stood to attention as DCI Hunter ran past in an all-out effort to catch Caitlin before she reached the pool house. Marina and DI Reynolds were in pursuit.

Caitlin skidded to a halt on the edge of the ruins,

horrified by the utter devastation, and bit on the back of her hand to prevent herself from crying out. She remembered last night, Hugh and the girls splashing about, and moved like a sleepwalker into the debris, plucking at the blackened rubble with her bare hands.

The firefighters saw her and shouted a warning but DI Reynolds, being younger and fitter, grabbed her first and hauled her back.

"Ma'am, you cannot go in there."

Aware the tears were pouring down her face, she scrubbed at her eyes with her hands, smearing her face with soot. "But Hugh's under there!"

"It's too dangerous. You'll be hurt."

"I don't care!" Caitlin kicked him in the shins, forcing him to release her. "It's my hotel! I can do what I bloody like!"

"Caitlin," pleaded Marina, putting her arm around her friend's shoulder. "Calm down! You can't do anything here. Come back to my house and have a nice drink."

"*Drink?* Why the hell should I want a drink?" She pushed Marina away but came up against DCI Hunter.

He caught her arm, forcing her to look up at him, trying to make her understand. His hazel eyes were compassionate. "Mrs Kirkwood, you must remain calm. There is nothing you can do. The bodies have been removed to the mortuary. No one is there now."

Again Caitlin chewed on the back of her hand – anything to avoid breaking down – unaware she had drawn faint pinpricks of blood. "How did it happen?

You said something about a crime scene? That means you think the fire was deliberate. Some *bastard* tried to burn down my hotel on purpose! My husband was *murdered*!"

"The Fire Investigation Unit are sifting through the wreckage. It could take weeks to discover the cause. As soon as they find anything you will be the first to know."

"*Weeks?* I want to know now!"

"Caitlin," Marina slipped an arm around her shoulders, "you're in shock. Come back to my house for a cup of tea. You can't do anything here."

"I don't want a cup of tea!" screamed Caitlin, pushing her away. She put her hands over her eyes. "My husband's dead. Why are you all just standing around? Why doesn't someone *do* something?"

Embarrassed, Marina looked away and her eyes met DCI Hunter. "Was anyone else hurt?"

"We found two bodies," admitted DCI Hunter reluctantly. "Mr Kirkwood was formally identified by Detective Superintendent de Havilland – an old friend of the family I believe? We're still working on the other one."

Marina shuddered. "How horrible."

"But there were *three* people in the pool house," said Caitlin. "I saw *three* people."

"We only found two bodies," said DCI Hunter. "I'm very sorry, Mrs Kirkwood, but your husband is most definitely dead."

Caitlin did not appear to hear him. She just stared

blankly at the ruined pool house. "Three people," she whispered. "Two bodies."

DCI Hunter followed her gaze. "The third person must have left before the blaze. The firemen have been all over the ruins. There was no one else there, I can assure you."

"I'll take Mrs Kirkwood back to the house," volunteered DI Reynolds. "And make her coffee."

Marina waited until Caitlin had sleepwalked her way across the lawn, before asking in an undertone. "Could someone have survived?"

"Are you crazy?" muttered DCI Hunter. "Look at it. The building has been totally destroyed. The roof was thatched. There were flammable chemicals stored in the loft area. The fire could have been caused by a firework going off-course. It could have been started by an electrical fault. But, as one of the firefighters found a charred cigarette-lighter amongst the debris, at the moment the fire looks deliberate. *No one* could have survived. Witnesses heard an explosion and saw the barn suddenly collapse inwards. We only recognised the male victim because he was found floating face down in what remained of the pool. The other body will have to be identified by alternative means."

Marina stared at the ruined barn. The charcoal embers still glowed. "I know Hugh was an evil bastard but who would hate him enough to kill him?"

DCI Hunter said nothing.

Chapter Five

Caitlin had hired a Victorian funeral carriage to convey Hugh's coffin from the hotel to the church in the village. It had not been her idea; Hugh, flamboyant to the last, had it written into his will.

The hearse was black and gilt and had huge glass panels in the sides. It was drawn by four black horses, each with feathered plumes nodding on the top of their heads. One of the undertakers, in a Victorian frockcoat, walked solemnly in front of the carriage; Caitlin and Marina walked behind, their high heels skidding on the gravel drive.

The hearse was piled high with flowers and there were more when they reached the seventeenth century Church of St Peter – the patron saint of fishermen. Caitlin had requested simple arrangements of white lilies but the Marquis of Pennington had taken it upon himself to help out. He had hired an expensive florist, who had bedecked the whole church in white flowers –

in front of the stained-glass windows and hooked on the end of the oak pews. There were even floral archways over the aisle. It was more like a wedding than a funeral. Caitlin cringed at the bad taste.

As they arrived at the church, the heavens opened and the rain, which had been threatening for the past two hours, came thundering down, accompanied by violent streaks of lightning. Caitlin shivered into her coat. As a child she had been terrified of thunderstorms. She hoped it wasn't a bad omen.

The undertakers entered through the porch, Hugh's coffin weighing heavily on their shoulders. The organist began the first hymn. Caitlin tried desperately to quell the panic rising up within her, urging her to flee out into the storm, as far away from the church – and the coffin – as possible.

As though reading her mind, Marina firmly took hold of her arm, accidentally knocking Caitlin's bag to the floor, disgorging its contents in a six-foot radius. Caitlin swiftly dropped to her knees and scrabbled about, scraping everything back into the bag but still a lipstick and three pound coins rattled down through a grill in the flagstoned floor.

Hugh had no family, apart from a younger brother in America, who had not even bothered to reply to the frenzied letters and faxes Caitlin had sent. And Caitlin had deliberately not informed her estranged family – they had never liked Hugh anyway. So it was a very small procession that the vicar led down the aisle to the front of the church. Just Caitlin, Marina and the Marquis.

Douglas stared firmly ahead, Marina stared firmly at the floor but Caitlin smiled nervously at the congregation, thrilled to see so many people had cared about Hugh. All she received back were stony glares.

After an eternity they reached the end of the aisle; waiting patiently while the undertakers lifted the coffin from their shoulders and precariously balanced it on a wooden stand just beneath the altar. Marina pushed Caitlin into the front pew and she found herself thigh to thigh with a kilted Douglas, his wide-apart hairy knees emerging from the green and gold tartan. Douglas gave her a watery smile and patted her shoulder. Maybe it was meant to be a fatherly gesture but Caitlin wriggled closer to Marina, squashing her up against the end of the pew. The Vicar opened his prayer book and cleared his throat.

Caitlin stared at the coffin. Until now, it was as though Hugh had been somewhere else. She could not believe that he was dead. She had drifted through the last week in a daze, expecting him to walk in the door at any moment, but now she had the evidence before her. He was inside that coffin. Dead. She would never see him again.

Frantically Caitlin searched for a handkerchief and found both Marina and Douglas offering theirs. Douglas's had lace around the edge. It would be so awful to ruin it, so she took Marina's instead, chewing hard on the edge to stop herself from crying, and sliding slowly down the seat so that no one could see her.

Why was it considered so dreadful to cry at funerals? Damn the British and their stiff upper lip. The organist started on another hymn. *'The Lord's My Shepherd'*. Why had she chosen that tune? Hugh hated it. She should have got them to play something by Kenny G. Oh God, why had she been such a useless wife?

The organist finished. Douglas got up to deliver the eulogy. He had the stiff upper lip down pat. In a strong, clear, very English voice he told the congregation of their schooldays, how Hugh had taken over his family's ailing hotel and transformed it into a huge success, how much he had loved his beautiful wife and longed for a child to make his life complete.

Caitlin bit harder on the handkerchief, overwhelmed by guilt. She appreciated Douglas had to bend the truth a little to make them sound like the perfect couple, but did he have to tell such out-and-out whoppers? Or maybe it had never been Hugh at fault but her? Perhaps she was to blame that theirs had been such a miserable marriage. She ought to have tried harder. Yet she and Hugh had been such total opposites their union had been doomed to failure. He should have married the glamorous Annelise Fitzpatrick as his mother had wished.

She did not realise the service had ended until Marina kicked her ankle. Again she, Douglas and Marina made up the little procession behind the coffin and out into the churchyard, with the other mourners behind them. They stood silently around the graveside as the coffin was lowered into the cold, stony earth and the vicar said another prayer. The rain still poured unrelentingly but Caitlin's hat had the effect of a large golfing umbrella. Marina, typically, had a minuscule umbrella in the depths of her handbag which metamorphosed into a virtual marquee.

The coffin disappeared from view. If Caitlin craned forward she could see it snugly wedged at the bottom of the grave. She felt sick and again tried to distance her thoughts away from its contents. It was the only way she could cope. She might have hated Hugh's infidelity with a passion, but not enough to want him to end up like this. Marina clutched at her arm, obviously fearing she was about to faint. It struck Caitlin that she had not told anyone, apart from Hugh and Amanda, that she was pregnant.

The vicar handed around a little box of earth for everyone to throw in a handful, which thoroughly turned Caitlin's stomach. But, even worse, she realised she was more concerned about getting soil up inside her newly manicured nails.

As the vicar finished, a woman wearing dark glasses stepped forwards and dramatically threw a daffodil onto the coffin. Caitlin, teetering on the edge of hysteria, nearly burst out laughing. A daffodil! But she turned away from the grave, having no wish to meet the mystery woman. She had long since given up trying to keep track of Hugh's many mistresses, although the gleam of red beneath the woman's hat suggested it was Annelise.

As she picked her way through the graves towards the gate, hampered by her totally unsuitable shoes, Caitlin thought people might stop and talk to her, say how much Hugh was missed, but no one did. People gathered in little groups and just watched silently as she stumbled every now and then, clutching at Marina for support. After what seemed an eternity, she walked through the gate, the chauffeur of the funeral car opened the door and she got in, Marina beside her. Douglas was behind in his own black Bentley.

Caitlin took off her hat and attempted a bright, if wobbly, smile. "Thank God that's over."

Marina regarded her worriedly. "You've still got the wake."

Caitlin, watching the churchyard disappear in fine drizzle behind them, was not listening. "There must have been over a hundred people in that church," she murmured, "and not a single person spoke to me."

* * *

The funeral cars pulled up outside the front of the house. Caitlin jammed on her hat and scrambled out. She could hear the rest of the village swarming up the drive in their cars. No one ever obeyed the 15 mph signs. The pea shingle would end up all over the park.

She ran up the stone steps and into the hall. The honey-coloured oak created a gloomy atmosphere, matching her mood. There were hundreds of sprays of white gladioli shoved into glass vases, rising like skeleton's fingers, stark against the wood. The kitchen staff had prepared a magnificent buffet in the ballroom, set up on tables covered in the fine white linen reserved for weddings. Waiters, bearing silver trays laden with varying shades of sherry, stood to attention in each corner. They alternated with more explosions of spiky white flower arrangements, balanced on huge curly black stands, the same ones that had been used for Hugh's party. Caitlin shivered.

When she returned to the hall, the villagers were queued right back from the reception desk and down the stone steps onto the drive. Steeling herself, Caitlin moved forward to greet Lady Richmond, the wife of the Lord Lieutenant, who eventually extended a cold hand. Caitlin wondered if she was supposed to shake it or kiss it. Lord Richmond, his bald head gleaming under the electric lights, his cigar clamped firmly between his teeth, slipped his arm about Caitlin's shoulder, showering ash down the front of her dress.

"Sad loss to the community," he said, breathing smoke into her face. "Very unfortunate indeed." He just had the chance to squeeze her before his wife hauled him off towards the buffet.

Caitlin rubbed her shoulder where his fingers had touched her, wishing she could take a bath. Why was she only fancied by the old, ugly and bisexual? Then she found her hand being vigorously shaken by Raj Patel, a local businessman. His heavy gold rings dug painfully into her fingers and she had trouble concentrating on what he was saying.

"Poor Hugh," he said, in his sing-song accent. "I shall miss him very much. He was a good friend to Sanjay and myself when we first arrived here from India."

"He was? Er, was he?"

"Oh yes. He introduced me to many influential people. My idea for a nightclub on the quayside would have come to nothing if I had not had his excellent advice."

"Really?" Caitlin wondered if Raj was getting Hugh muddled with someone else. Apart from Douglas, did Hugh actually know any influential people? And he had never done anything to help anyone other than himself.

After Raj's younger brother, Sanjay, had solemnly shaken her hand while simultaneously patting her bottom, Paul de Havilland, Amanda's father, materialised before her, like a rather depressed ghost. Caitlin had always thought him a rather cold-hearted, remote sort of man but he seemed genuinely distressed by Hugh's death. He had been great friends with Hugh's father.

She took Paul's hand, wondering what explanation Amanda had given him for being fired from her job so abruptly. She certainly could not look him in the eye, so she studied his tie instead. Embroidered upon it was the crest of the county constabulary. It was quite pretty.

"You have my deepest sympathy, Mrs Kirkwood," he said, his face an inscrutable mask. "You have a difficult time ahead."

Caitlin shuddered and pulled her hand back. It was

almost as though he was telling her fortune. He gave
her the creeps. She watched uneasily as he followed the
Patel brothers into the ballroom, like their shadow in
his grey Armani suit. He had no need for a cheap M
& S copy. Paul de Havilland was a wealthy man.

It took an hour for Caitlin to greet everyone. Vainly
hoping to see Princess Victoria, the entire village had
shown up to pay their respects. Caitlin wished she
could escape. Their insincere sympathy was stifling;
their sneering faces more than she could bear. But with
Dungeon Master Marina permanently superglued to
her side, she was not going anywhere. Boy, did she
need a drink! If only a waiter would walk this way. It
was almost as though an exclusion zone had been placed
around her.

As the last mourner trickled into the ballroom
Caitlin wriggled her numb fingers. "Now I know how
the Queen feels." She attempted to inch towards a
handsome blond waiter but found Marina hauling her
along to the ballroom.

Marina parked her next to the buffet table. "Here,"
she said, thrusting a plate of sausage rolls under
Caitlin's nose. "Have something to eat. It will cheer
you up. It always works for me."

Like she was supposed to be happy at her husband's
funeral? Caitlin shook her head in disbelief. Sometimes
Marina's logic could be difficult to fathom.

The smell of rancid sausage meat, combined with
Marina's overpowering perfume, made Caitlin want to
throw up. Sending the tray of rolls flying, she clapped

her hand over her mouth and bolted for the French windows.

Marina sighed and knelt on the floor to clear up the debris.

"What's the matter with Mrs Kirkwood?" asked Lord Richmond, who had nearly been knocked over. "Is it all getting too much for her?"

"Touch of food poisoning," muttered Marina, without thinking.

Lord Richmond abruptly replaced the sausage roll he had been sidling up to his mouth and waddled off to discuss the lack of police officers on the beat with a wearied Paul de Havilland.

Marina grit her teeth. "The amount of time that girl spends being sick," she muttered to herself, "anyone would think she was pregnant."

* * *

After ten minutes spent nose-to-nose with the shrubs in the herbaceous border, Caitlin felt a whole lot better and sat back on her heels. One day, she vowed, she might actually have the opportunity to be sick in a toilet.

"This is getting to be a habit, Mrs Kirkwood," drawled a male voice.

Caitlin leapt up, attempting to brush the mud from her black dress. She plucked up the courage to look up and recognised the stranger she had fallen in lust with last week.

"We've got to stop meeting like this," she said, wishing she could think of something more original.

"Why? At least I always know where to find you." He smiled. "Can I fetch you a drink? Mineral water?"

"Bugger mineral water," said Caitlin with feeling. "I'll have a large sherry, please."

"Have mine," he offered. "I haven't touched it. Sherry is not really my thing but a waiter forced it on me."

"Some people have all the luck." Caitlin took the sherry, unwilling to gulp it down with him watching. She fiddled with the stem of the glass. "It was nice of you to come," she said at last.

His humorous expression at once sobered. "I was sorry to learn of your husband's death."

"I know," said Caitlin grimly. "Everybody was."

He seemed to be searching for something tactful to say. Eventually he settled on, "How will you cope – running this huge hotel by yourself?"

"Pretty much as I did before," retorted Caitlin. "Besides, I need the money if I want to eat." She forgot herself and took a large gulp of her drink. The alcohol stung the back of her throat, causing her eyes to water.

The man mistook her tears. "I'm sorry. That came out wrong. This must be terrible for you, burying a husband at your young age."

As though I dug the grave myself, thought Caitlin hysterically, taking another slug of sherry and finding she had polished it off. God, she was becoming an alcoholic.

She glanced back at the ballroom. She could see faces at the mullion windows, pretending they were not watching her, talking about her. Well, sod them! Why didn't she give them something to get their teeth into?

She secretly stole another look at him. The weak sunlight caught the auburn glints in his dark brown hair. Then she felt ashamed of herself. She had been a widow for barely a week. What of poor Hugh, lying in that miserable churchyard?

Hugh was a womanising bastard, she told her conscience firmly. And he never cared a damn for me.

But I loved him . . .

She shivered.

"Are you cold?" asked the man. "Would you like to borrow my coat?"

Before she could reply, she saw the French doors onto the terrace had opened. Oh bugger, Marina checking up on her again?

Instead two men stepped through the door, almost identically dressed in dark suits, like the Blues Brothers without the sunglasses. At first Caitlin thought they were waiters, then, as they strode determinedly across the lawn towards her, she recognised DCI Hunter and his chum DI Reynolds.

The man followed her gaze. "Trouble? I'll leave you in peace."

"Oh – you don't have to!"

"I ought to be going anyway."

Damn, damn, damn. "When will I see you again?"

Oh hell, what kind of woman was she? To chat up a man at her husband's funeral?

"No doubt you'll see me around," he replied. "I live just down the road."

No he didn't, or surely they would have met before? Caitlin looked miserably at him. Why couldn't men ever tell the truth? Why should the presence of a 'Y' chromosome make such a difference?

The police officers drew closer. Frantically Caitlin tried to think of something to say that would make him stay. Unfortunately the word which came out was, "Goodbye."

"Bye," said the man, turning back towards the terrace. "Call me. I'm in the book. My name is Granger. Marc Granger."

And he walked out of her life, nodding to the police officers as he passed.

"Granger," muttered Caitlin under her breath, desperate to commit it to memory. "Marc Granger."

"Mrs Kirkwood?" said DCI Hunter.

No, Little Red Riding Hood, she thought sarcastically but kept her mouth shut. It was never wise to antagonise the police.

She smiled tentatively, feeling she couldn't take any more bad news. "Hello, Chief Inspector. How are you? Have you found out what caused the fire?"

DI Reynolds took a deep breath. "Caitlin Mary Kirkwood, I am here to arrest you for the murder of Hugh Francis Kirkwood —"

"Murder Hugh?" Caitlin felt herself go cold. "Me?"

She watched in a daze as Inspector Reynolds snapped a pair of cuffs on her wrists. Did they think she was about to run off into the woods? "But I haven't *done* anything."

But DCI Hunter just talked over the top of her voice. "And your former employee, Miss Amanda Jane de Havilland –"

Caitlin stared at him in shock. "Amanda? She's *dead?*"

"You have the right to remain silent –"

"I don't understand . . ." Over the DCI's shoulder she could see the curious faces of the villagers, still watching everything through the windows, soaking up every moment of her discomfort. She could have been the chief exhibit at a freak show. How they must hate her.

"I haven't done anything," her voice came out as a whisper. "I don't . . . but I haven't . . ." Her brain knew what it wanted to say but her mouth was having difficulty forming the words. Her tongue seemed too big for her mouth and she had an overwhelming desire to throw up – but she mustn't, not over the DCI's smart black suit. It would be so embarrassing. She gagged, feeling the bile rising up the throat. Why the hell had she drunk that sherry?

Weird though, DCI Hunter seemed to be swaying from side to side too. She wished he'd stop. It was like being on board ship.

Caitlin made a huge effort to concentrate. "Why are you saying this to me?"

The DCI was regarding her with concern. "Mrs Kirkwood, are you all right?"

"Fine," she snapped. "But stop . . . stop shifting about. You're making me feel . . . sick." She took a deep breath. It was no good. She couldn't hide it any longer. "Got to sit down, going to faint," she gasped. She made a grab for his arm, as her legs buckled, taking him by surprise as he staggered under her sudden weight. "Got to . . . sit down . . ."

There was a buzzing in her ears, like an angry wasp, and the trees began to close in, black and threatening.

And Caitlin was vaguely aware, as though watching an old black and white movie, of DCI Hunter trying to keep a hold of her as she slipped through his arms, of DI Reynolds vainly leaning forwards to help, as the ground rose up and slapped her in the face and everything just faded away.

Chapter Six

Marc Granger owned a seventeenth-century cottage on the edge of Calahurst, where its cobbled streets disappeared into the depths of the King's Forest. The cottage had been bequeathed by his grandmother and, even after ten years, her chintz and Wedgewood were still in evidence. Though the roses around the front door were long since dead and the thatched roof had more green stuff growing in it than the whole of the half-acre garden.

Detective Superintendent Paul de Havilland walked gingerly down the garden path towards the door. He knew there were ancient flagstones somewhere beneath the rotting leaves he was walking on; he just hoped there was nothing else. The little gate had already come off in his hand as he opened it, and thorns from the overgrown roses constantly caught on his expensive suit trousers. Needless to say, when he finally did reach the front door, he was not in the best of tempers.

Ordinarily Paul would have admired the old-fashioned brass bell pull but not when he had to fight his way through a forest of dead brambles to find it. The bloody house was like Sleeping Beauty's Palace – and not at all the sort of place where he expected Marc Granger to live. But then, how much did he know about the man anyway?

Paul's eldest daughter had dated Marc for a whole year. Paul, despite feeling Marc was totally wrong for the impulsive, hot-headed Georgia, had liked him immensely. Although notoriously reserved, Marc was sincere, forthright and so totally honest his colleagues in Special Branch had nicknamed him 'The Last Boy Scout'.

Georgia had told her father that Marc's parents had emigrated to Canada when he was six, then had been killed in a car accident when he was fifteen. Marc had been sent back to England to live with his grandparents, now also deceased, in this very cottage. Paul shivered. Any other young man would have sold up, moved on to the bright lights of Norchester, bought a flashy apartment – but not Marc. Marc had stayed put – and not altered a thing.

For a moment Paul paused on the doorstep, wondering if he was about to make a mistake asking Marc for his help. Perhaps, but one thing *was* for certain, Marc was the only person Paul could trust, implicitly, to do the right thing.

The bell pull had rusted and Paul had to knock on the solid oak door, receiving a fist full of splinters. Marc Granger opened the door while he was still cursing. He was dressed in baggy shorts (of an indeterminate colour) over black lycra cycling shorts and a blue T-shirt which had been bleached by the sun.

"Mr de Havilland," said Marc slowly, obviously surprised, and not terribly thrilled, to find him on his doorstep at seven-thirty on a Sunday morning. "I was just going out for a run."

Paul suppressed a smile. "How very noble of you. May I come in?"

"Sure." Marc begrudgingly held open the door.

"Don't worry. I'll wipe my feet. I must have five years' worth of dead leaves stuck to my shoes, not to mention half a decomposed hedgehog."

Marc smiled despite himself. "I think that's a sweet chestnut, sir."

Paul scraped his shoes on the doorstep, then wiped away any remainder on the hairless coir mat. "So you do know something about gardening?"

"Oh yeah, I just haven't had the time . . . er, sir."

Paul handed Marc his overcoat. "I trust you have the time to make me a cup of tea and for Christ's sake, stop the yes sir, no sir, crap. It's not as though it comes naturally to you."

"Yes – er, sure thing." Marc flung the overcoat carelessly across the staircase banister and led the way through to the pretty little sitting-room. Both men had to duck as they passed under each blackened oak beam.

Although Marc obviously intended Paul to wait in the sitting-room, Paul followed him through to the kitchen. Despite the fall-out from last night's dinner, it resembled something out of *Homes And Gardens*. Paul's housekeeper would die for that Aga and the rows of beautiful antique china, arranged on the pine dresser beneath several layers of dust.

Paul was a bit put out when Marc made the tea in two chipped Nescafé mugs and tried not to look shocked as Marc dunked a teabag into each one and then squeezed it out with his fingers. The cottage really was wasted on the man. Marc ought to live in some bachelor flat with black MFI furniture, wall-to-wall hi-fi speakers and Avedon nudes sneering down from grey rag-rolled walls.

"KitKat?" offered Marc, flourishing a dusty biscuit tin with *Views From The Lake District* emblazoned on the sides.

Paul doubted whether he'd been further north than Oxford. As his stomach churned, he tried to remember the last time he had eaten. Yesterday lunchtime? Of course, Hugh's funeral. What a fiasco that had turned out to be.

He helped himself to two. "Thank you," he sighed and, ducking through the narrow doorway, went back into the sitting-room.

Marc followed, absent-mindedly stirring his tea with a KitKat finger.

Paul sank down into one of the chintzy sofas, his knees almost hitting his chin, and gratefully sipped his tea. "I'm aware you're on leave, Granger," he said. "I suppose you're wondering why I'm here?"

Marc smiled and bit into his KitKat, unaware that the end had dropped off in his tea.

"You were at Hugh Kirkwood's funeral on Saturday?" continued Paul.

Marc's smile faded but he remained silent.

"You were in deep conversation with his widow?"

Marc's smile disappeared altogether. "Is that a crime?"

"I presume you met Mrs Kirkwood while you were on protection duty at the hotel a week ago?"

"That is correct." Marc looked grim. "Although I was under the impression that my private life is my own affair."

"So it is, Granger." Paul could not help the animosity revealing itself in his voice. "Except that last Saturday you were on duty, supposedly protecting Her Royal Highness, the Princess Victoria of Clarence. Not attempting to get your leg over the hostess."

"Is this a discipline?" asked Marc furiously. "Because if so, I want it done properly, with a Federation rep present."

To ensure he kept tight control over his volatile temper, Paul concentrated on carefully peeling the red wrapper from the KitKat, sliding his thumbnail along the silver paper and breaking the bar in two. "Are you aware that Mrs Kirkwood has been arrested for the murder of her husband?"

Marc only hesitated for a second. "Has she been charged?"

"No. There is a slight problem over the lack of evidence."

"DI Reynolds firing off prematurely again?"

Paul bit into the KitKat and said nothing.

"She's innocent," said Marc.

"If she were that innocent," snapped Paul, with some irritation, "we would not have arrested her."

"So what evidence *have* you got?"

"Not much. Hugh took out a rather large insurance policy almost a year ago, for both himself and his wife, each to benefit if the other died. There is also a brother, Leo Kirkwood, in America who would inherit if they both died together."

"And let me guess," sighed Marc. "The Kirkwoods are broke?"

"In hock up to their perfectly capped teeth. Fraud squad have been keeping themselves amused by dredging through the hotel accounts and were thrilled at the whopping great discrepancies they found. You know the sort of thing – £5,000 spent on pens and pencils, £3,000 spent on paperclips – very amateurish."

"I don't mean to sound rude but what has any of this got to do with me? If you have a complaint about my behaviour last weekend, you should bring it up with my commanding officer."

"From midnight last night I *am* your commanding officer. Since your transfer from Special Branch came through."

Marc sighed. "Well, let me assure you, there is no relationship between myself and Mrs Kirkwood. I won't be meeting her again."

"I'm afraid you'll have to. We've set up a murder squad. Detective Superintendent Drysdale from 'A' Division is in charge. Seb Hunter is responsible on a day-to-day basis." He paused. "I've recommended that you be part of the team."

Marc's eyes narrowed. "Why?"

Paul smiled thinly. Granger made no pretension to honouring rank. It was another of the reasons he had selected him for the task.

"Because of the lack of evidence, we'll have to release Mrs Kirkwood without charging her. But I need someone to keep a close eye on her."

"But why me?"

"You cannot have looked in a mirror lately."

"You're not seriously suggesting that I –"

"Just romance the girl a little," said Paul blithely. "Think upon it as widening your circle of friends." He attempted another bleak smile. "Did you know, less than 1% of couples meet at a health club?"

"You think I'm going to be surprised?" Marc's scorn was tangible. "I know what health clubs are like. Narcissistic misfits searching for fast love. Honour and commitment don't come into it."

Paul took another sip of tea. Not so thirsty now, it tasted like stewed hedge-cuttings. He realised his hand had started to shake and so put it down again. Apparently the doctor's drugs were wearing off.

"What's the problem, Granger?" he asked nastily. "Can't be ethics – you're ex-Special Branch." He reached into his breast pocket and pulled out a small plastic bag. "Perhaps this will help you reach a decision?"

Marc smoothed the creases from the bag. The plastic was clear, enabling him to view the contents, and around the neck was an orange property label. There was something small, square and black inside. Marc shuddered. Although half-melted from the intense heat it had been subjected to, it was easily identifiable as a cigarette-lighter.

"Do you recognise it?"

Marc's fingers closed over the charred metal. "Yeah, it belonged to my grandfather – but I guess you knew that already. What is this? Blackmail?"

Paul said nothing.

"I lent it to Mrs Kirkwood."

"How very ungallant of you to tell me."

"You can prove that it was used to start the fire?"

"Oh yes."

"So she is guilty . . ."

Paul leant back into the sofa, half-closing his eyes. He felt very old. All this play-acting grated on him. "I'm asking you to find out the truth," he sighed. "I want someone I can trust. I want my own spy in the camp."

Marc frowned. "Why are you not heading this squad yourself? Why have they brought in Detective Superintendent Drysdale?"

"Because the Chief won't let me become involved."

"But the murder took place on your own patch."

For a moment Paul found it difficult to form a reply. "It's just been confirmed," he began slowly, "the woman who died with Hugh Kirkwood was my daughter, Amanda."

* * *

Caitlin sat on a hard wooden bench in Cell Number 5, Calahurst Police Station. She had been seen by a doctor, who had proclaimed her fit and healthily pregnant – so now everyone was going to find out her business – then had been given a mattress and blankets and been left to stew in a cell overnight. The mattress was stained and torn, so she leant it against the wall, sat on the bench and huddled miserably beneath the blanket until dawn. She had no watch. The only way to tell the time was by observing the navy-blue sky gradually lighten to grey through the inch-thick tiny windowpanes.

With dawn came breakfast. As Caitlin was female, legislation demanded she be looked after by a police matron rather than the male gaoler. Calahurst nick was only a small station so it had no matron – a WPC was commandeered instead. The woman sulkily brought Caitlin some toast, cereal and coffee, and a copy of *The Sun* and asked if she wanted to use the shower facilities. Caitlin declined. When WPC 297 collected the tray thirty minutes later, she left behind a toothbrush and comb. The toothbrush was made from rubber and had just enough paste on it for one brushing. Caitlin felt as though she was staying in some surreal hotel.

After breakfast DCI Hunter and DI Reynolds collected Caitlin for interview. They were clean-shaven, dressed smartly in neatly pressed suits and both ponged of Obsession For Men. Caitlin felt dirty and smelly. She felt even worse when she was introduced to her solicitor. A glamorous redhead in a lavender suit, she could have been Annelise Fitzpatrick's twin sister. Both officers surreptitiously admired her long legs. Being taken seriously was evidently not high on the solicitor's list of priorities.

The interview room was still within the cell complex, although they had to pass through a locked door to get to it. The room was empty except for a table and four chairs. On the table was a tray of steaming coffees and a large tape recorder.

DI Reynolds plugged it in and switched it on as they all sat down. Carefully he peeled the cellophane from three audio-cassettes, placed them all in the tape deck and pressed 'Record'.

DCI Hunter cleared his throat. "This interview is being recorded. I am Detective Chief Inspector Hunter. The other police officer present is Detective Inspector Reynolds. I am interviewing Caitlin Mary Kirkwood. Also present is Mrs Kirkwood's solicitor, Miss Olivia Greenwich. The date is the 15th of March. The time is 1000 hours.

"This interview is being conducted in the interview room at Calahurst Police Station. Mrs Kirkwood, at the conclusion of the interview I will give you a notice explaining what will happen to the tapes."

DI Reynolds read out the caution and then asked Caitlin if she understood what had been said.

"Yes." Her voice sounded like a rusting gate. The last few hours had held a dream-like quality but now everything seemed horribly real. There was no way she was going to blag her way out of this one.

"Would you please tell me your name, address and date of birth."

"Um, Caitlin Mary Kirkwood. I live at Kirkwood Manor Hotel, Mistletoe Lane, Calahurst. I'll be twenty-five years old on 28th August."

The door crashed open and in walked a fat, red-faced man, grimly clutching a tray of coffees, a bulging file wedged underneath his arm and a ring doughnut clamped between his teeth.

"Pete!" exploded DCI Hunter. "Can't you bloody read?"

"Oh my God! You're recording?" The fat man dropped the doughnut and then found he had no free hand to pick it up. "I'm sorry – the sign wasn't up on the door." He played footie with the doughnut, attempting to kick it into the bin.

With exaggerated politeness, DI Reynolds picked it up between his thumb and forefinger and put it on the tray.

"Thanks," muttered Pete. "I'll go and use the room across the corridor."

"That would be nice," said DCI Hunter.

As Pete backed towards the door, DI Reynolds politely held it open for him.

Unfortunately as Pete retreated, another police officer and a young man, wearing a dishevelled suit, walked in. The coffee went everywhere.

"Shit!" said the youth, as the coffee soaked his suit. "That's my deposit down the sewer. When I get out of here, I'll sue you lot for so much money –"

"Fabian!" Caitlin stood up, sending her chair crashing onto the tiled floor and turned on DCI Hunter in absolute rage. "Why is he here? He didn't do anything. Don't tell me you seriously believe Fabian killed my husband? The whole idea's a joke!"

"You're telling me." DCI Hunter looked at his watch. "The interview concluded at 1005 hours. I am now switching off the tape." He pressed the 'Stop' button. "Take them back to the cells. This is a complete waste of time. "

"What? But I've spent all night in there!" Caitlin, all bravado vanished, looked beseechingly towards her solicitor who merely shrugged and looked bored. "Surely they have to charge me or something?"

"My dear, this is not *The Bill*." The DCI seemed to be in danger of losing his habitual cool. "We have to go through the preliminaries. This takes time."

The solicitor stood up, smoothing imaginary creases from her lavender suit until she had everyone's attention. "May I respectfully remind you that you are obliged by law to release my client, charge her, or obtain an extension from a magistrate."

The DCI coldly ignored her and turned to his colleague. "DI Reynolds, kindly escort Mrs Kirkwood to the cells. Miss Greenwich may remain with her or sit in the waiting area. I shall resume this interview in twenty minutes. When the interview has been concluded I will make a decision on how to proceed. Now, is everyone happy with that – or shall we take a vote?"

Chapter Seven

Olivia Greenwich, exchanging hot and sticky meaningful glances with DI Reynolds, elected to remain in the waiting area. Caitlin couldn't blame her. If Caitlin had the choice, that's where she would sit too.

She huddled on the bench, her knees close to her chest, and shivered. The blanket and mattress had been taken away during her interview. She counted the tiny window-panes for something to do, and the tiles on the floor, then read all the graffiti, scratched into the brown paintwork of the metal door. Perhaps she ought to add her name too, except there didn't seem to be anything to write with. The police were hardly going to leave cans of spray-paint lying around.

Caitlin thought she was entitled to a phone call – but whom would she contact? Her only friend was Marina Theodopoulou, who knew exactly where she was – and was probably writing an indignant letter to *The Times* at this very moment. There was, of course, her family . . .

although remembering the horrible things she had said to her mother when they last met, perhaps she had better wait until a real disaster presented itself. Going by the events of the last week, she would not have long to wait.

The cell door opened, clanging against the wall, the rusted metal hinges squealing. WPC 297 had brought in the coffee Caitlin should have had in the interview room. It was no longer steaming.

"Thanks," said Caitlin, pathetically grateful to see someone.

The WPC threw it in Caitlin's face. "It was a pity to see it go to waste."

Caitlin felt as though she was on someone else's bad trip. The cold coffee dripped gently off her chin and descended in tiny rivulets into her cleavage. Her hand shaking, she dabbed at her wet neck with the sleeve of her dress and wondered what she was supposed to do next. Surely the police were supposed to be the good guys?

The WPC leant back against the wall, arms folded. Caitlin flinched at the hatred clear in her blue-grey eyes. What had she done to cause the WPC to despise her so much? Although – she did appear vaguely familiar . . . was she another of Hugh's harem? One of the many who waited for hours in the hotel bar, desperate to hear him mutter those sweet and meaningful lies.

The policewoman looked his type. Even in the gloom of the cell, Caitlin could see she was very attractive, despite the butchness of the navy-blue uniform, thick tights and clumpy shoes. Her make-up was air-hostess perfect, although her long golden curls had been brushed flat to her head and beaten into submission with Kirby grips.

The WPC walked slowly towards her. "Why don't you admit it, Mrs Kirkwood? We know you murdered your husband. It won't take our DCI long to prove it." She bent down, her face only inches from Caitlin's. "You might as well confess now."

Caitlin, although her heart was frantically break-dancing against her ribs, refused to be intimidated. "Three *Hail Marys* for penance and I'm out of here, right?"

"Why did you kill her?" The WPC was so close, Caitlin could smell her perfume. Ralph Lauren's Safari. Ironically it was the same fragrance Caitlin used herself.

"I didn't kill Hugh or Amanda," Caitlin slumped back on the bench in utter defeat. "Why won't any of you believe me?"

"Amanda was my sister."

"Your *sister*?" Hell, so *that* was why she looked so familiar. "I'm sorry," said Caitlin sincerely. "I'm really very sorry. But you've got it all wrong. I'm innocent. Her death wasn't anything to do with me. I wasn't even there when the fire started."

The WPC regarded her consideringly for a moment, her blue-grey eyes completely devoid of emotion. "Have you ever been trapped inside a burning building?"

The question seemed innocent enough. "No . . ."

"Have thick black smoke flood into your lungs, forcing out the oxygen, choking the very life out of you?"

"What?"

"Do you *know* what it feels like?" The WPC grabbed Caitlin's hair and yanked her up. She tugged a cheap, plastic cigarette-lighter from the pocket of her skirt. A *snap* and the flame shot upwards.

"Help!" screamed Caitlin, frantically trying to get free. She felt the cold metal of the cell door pressing against her cheek and thumped it with her free hand. "Somebody help me!" But all she could hear was drunken laughter from the adjoining cell.

The cigarette-lighter seemed to float through the air of its own accord, the flame singeing the ends of Caitlin's long black hair. The smell was revolting. She felt the heat against her skin. The ends of her hair starting to smoulder.

"Do you know what it feels like?" repeated the WPC jerking Caitlin's head back.

Caitlin felt clumps of hair being literally torn from her head. It was incredibly painful. "Yes," she moaned. "Yes . . . just leave me alone . . ."

The WPC pushed Caitlin away from her so that she fell onto her knees. It hurt. Beneath the sludgy brown tiles was a concrete floor. Caitlin bent over double, feeling the tears finally trickling down her cheeks, expecting the blows to come raining down at any moment.

"God, you're a wimp," she heard the WPC say contemptuously, then her sensible shoes clumped across to the door. There was a clunk as the huge deadlock slid back into the door.

Caitlin raised her head, unable to believe the torture was over. Yet, without another glance in her direction, the WPC was casually walking out of the cell and back to her life, as though nothing had happened.

And then the WPC paused. DI Reynolds was already standing there. He took one look at Caitlin, cowering on the floor, and said, "WPC de Havilland, I think you had better come with me."

* * *

Seb Hunter drank the remains of his black, sugarless coffee, picked up his already bulging file on Caitlin Kirkwood and left Detective Superintendent de Havilland's office just as DI Reynolds escorted WPC de Havilland through the open door.

"Hi, Georgia," said Seb, standing aside for them. He smiled kindly at her. "I thought you were going up to the Lakes for a few weeks."

But Georgia merely marched through the door with her nose in the air. He could almost see the permafrost forming in her wake.

Like father, like daughter, thought Seb wearily. He closed the door behind them and walked back to his office, scattering curling post-it notes in his wake.

Detective Superintendent de Havilland was surprised to see his daughter too. Particularly as she was not actually based on his Division.

"Hello, Georgia. I thought you were still in the Lake District."

"No, I arrived home yesterday." She sat on the edge of her father's desk with a nonchalance which infuriated Clive Reynolds, who had not intended this to deteriorate into a social occasion. "You know I can't stand the place," she added. "Far too quiet. Though you always used to drag us there as kids."

"The natural rugged beauty of the Lakes is completely wasted on you, Georgia." Paul very nearly managed a genuine smile. "Strange though, Amanda used to love going there – and she was a real townie."

"Amanda lied through her teeth to keep you happy."

Paul winced. "And you've always said what you thought. So why are you here? Who have you upset now?"

"Sir," interrupted Clive, unable to wait his turn any longer. "I have just prevented WPC de Havilland from setting fire to Mrs Kirkwood's hair."

He said it so pompously Georgia laughed. "It was a joke, Clive! Did you lose your sense of humour along with your sergeant's stripes?"

"The poor woman was terrified! She was cowering on the floor, crying her heart out."

Georgia regarded him with dislike. He thought he was such an elegant creature, with his silk ties and matching handkerchiefs – yet the suit was shiny and his fingernails were dirty. The man was such a prat. And she bet he had been the school snitch.

"Poor woman?" she mocked. "The cow murdered my sister! If that was a man down in the cells you would be screwing a confession out of him, not coming over all delicate on me."

"Even if we had arrested a man for the murders, I certainly would not have put a match to his hair."

"Wimp," muttered Georgia, under her breath. "It was a cigarette-lighter," she said out loud, "if we're going to get picky." She deliberately yawned widely. "You shouldn't take everything so seriously."

"This is serious. The police get a bad enough press without you trying to bump off the prime suspect. What if the media should find out? We've had hordes of journalists camped outside since we sent out the press release about her arrest."

Georgia fidgeted. "Give me a break! I was only trying to intimidate her."

"You succeeded."

Paul de Havilland slammed his fist onto the table. "I can hardly believe what I am hearing. You sound like squabbling children." His cold grey eyes settled on Clive. "Are you trying to tell me, in a very roundabout fashion, that WPC de Havilland tried to set fire to Mrs Kirkwood's hair, with a cigarette-lighter, to elicit a confession?"

Clive, patently unable to meet his boss's fury, stared at the orchid on the desk instead. "That is correct, sir."

Paul looked at his daughter. "WPC de Havilland?"

"Yes, Dad – er, sir." Under her father's scrutiny, Georgia slid off his desk and sidled to attention.

"I cannot believe you would be so stupid, Georgia.

Apart from being guilty of GBH, you know a confession signed under duress is not legal. Didn't you learn about the perils of basing a case on a confession with no hard evidence to back it up? Haven't you heard of the Guildford Four, for Christ's sake?"

Georgia smirked. "The Calahurst Two?"

Clive felt the fury crackling from his boss and cringed, dropping his gaze to the carpet. Even Georgia realised she had gone too far. It was several moments before Paul could trust himself to speak.

"Georgia," he said eventually, "I understand how distraught you are about your sister's death. We were all hit badly. I was hoping a holiday would help you to heal the wounds."

"A holiday!" spat Georgia. "Amanda's dead and a trip to Lake Windemere is going to make it all right?"

"I understand how you feel –"

"Bollocks! You're so fucking repressed, so deeply *frozen* you never feel anything! No wonder they call you the Snow King. Amanda was my *sister!* Not another of your bloody statistical returns. You don't care about Amanda. You don't even care about me. You only care about this bloody job. And the fact that none of your golden boys can instantaneously solve the only crime that directly affects *you*."

Clive shifted his weight from one foot to the other, crimson with embarrassment, but by now Paul and Georgia had forgotten his existence.

Paul put his head in his hands. "She was my *daughter*."

"So you *do* remember?"

"Georgia –" His voice was wretched.

"Yes, *Daddy*?"

Paul swung his chair around and stared out across the grey slate roofs of Calahurst. "Georgia, if it was anyone else standing before me on such a charge –"

Back to business, thought Georgia, scowling at his back. Let's just shove all that nasty emotional stuff under the carpet.

"They'd be kicked out of the force so fast their feet wouldn't touch the ground," she completed the sentence for him. "I know. Don't think you owe me any favours just because we're related."

Paul glanced back at Clive, still rather pink about the ears, who he guessed was storing all this up for future reference. "Georgia, as you're not one of my officers, strictly speaking it's not up to me but your Divisional Superintendent, Jimmy Campbell, to discipline you."

"Actually it's Detective Superintendent Drysdale," she said bitterly. "I've been promoted to CID Aide on his Division. Nice to see you follow my career –"

"What career?" snapped Paul. "Don't you see, if DI Reynolds makes his complaint, there will be a full-scale investigation and you'll finish up before the Chief Constable."

"And be summarily dismissed. I get the picture, *Daddy*. I suppose even you cannot whitewash this amount of crap."

He regarded her in despair. "Did you expect me to?"

"No," she allowed herself a tiny, bitter smile. "DIY never was your strong point."

Paul grit his teeth and looked back to Clive. "Thank you for bringing this matter to my attention. You can be sure it will be dealt with in the proper manner."

"Yes, sir."

Georgia watched Clive leave, convinced he would linger outside to listen. Dirty, rotten sneak.

Paul waited until the door had closed. "Georgia, I was so proud of you when you joined the force."

"Really?" she said, unable to hide her sarcasm. "You've never mentioned it before."

"While Amanda took after your mother, with all those dance classes and acting lessons, I always thought you were like me."

Perhaps he did sound sincere . . . Georgia began to feel herself melt. "I've ruined everything, haven't I?" she muttered.

"You've never learnt to control your temper –"

"It's just like yours . . ."

His voice became harsh. "Which is why I advise you to keep it in check."

She scuffed one sensible shoe against the pile of the carpet. "All I wanted to do was find Amanda's killer. I know she was a vain, selfish, silly creature – but I loved her and now she's dead." She felt the tears slide down her cheeks and blinked frantically.. "We've got to find out who did it, Father. It doesn't matter what happens to me . . ."

She thought her father might take her into his arms and reassure her. But he remained resolutely seated in his high-backed chair, like Caesar without the laurels.

Looking faintly embarrassed at such an emotional display, he handed her his handkerchief. She didn't use it, merely twisted the cool fabric in her fingers, sniffing defiantly, feeling ten-years-old once more.

"Why do you think Clive brought you to my office, instead of taking you directly to Detective Superintendent Drysdale?"

Georgia shrugged. "Your office is nearer?"

"He wants promotion."

"That's no secret. He bet Marc Granger he'd make Chief by the time he was forty-five. What has that to do with me?"

"He'll say what I want him to say. There is an alternative to a formal discipline. I want you to put in a request for a career break."

"A career break?" sneered Georgia. "Only civvies take career breaks."

"So start a trend," sighed Paul.

He meant it too. "How long for?" she asked sullenly, winding the handkerchief around her fingers.

"Two years ought to allow the dust to settle. By then Mrs Kirkwood will be serving a long term in prison and even the most indefatigable gossip-monger will have forgotten she ever existed."

"*Two years!* You can stuff that! I've just made CID Aide. I'm going places."

"You don't have a choice, Georgia." His words lashed like a whip. "Either you take a career break or you'll find your career broken for you."

Chapter Eight

Caitlin was released from the police station an hour later, following a half-hearted tape-recorded interview with DCI Hunter. When she attempted to make an official complaint to the Station Sergeant regarding her treatment, she was given a form to complete. No one was interested, least of all her solicitor, who had vanished – presumably to The Stables pub opposite with DI Reynolds.

The gaoler returned the few possessions she had on her when arrested. Caitlin signed for them and was allowed out, via the back door. She almost fell over the stacks of rubbish piled up outside for the refuse collectors.

The tradesmen's entrance, she thought sourly, determined to complete the complaint form as soon as she got home. If she ever got home. It was a two-mile walk and, judging from the dark sky, about to tip it down at any moment. Quelling the impulse to scrape her diamond engagement ring down the side of a parked patrol car, Caitlin pulled her jacket over her head and ran round the side of the station to the front. If she hurried she could catch the Number 5 bus to Norchester, which went straight past Kirkwood Manor.

As she pushed open the side door, leading from the car park to the pavement out front, she realised why she had been let out the back way. The police had actually been trying to do her a favour. Camped outside the front entrance were hordes of journalists and press photographers, even a cameraman from the local television. Caitlin froze. Surely this wasn't all for her?

One of the journalists saw her trembling by the gate and, grabbing his photographer, tried to steal away from the rest of the group. He was unsuccessful. The cry went up, "There she is!" and the whole lot of them charged. Caitlin tried to escape back into the station yard but the journalist slammed the gate in her face. He had a dark, sardonic face, with a cruel twist to his lips. He looked so much like her late husband she almost blacked out. Then he had the effrontery to calmly light a cigarette.

At the sight of the flame, Caitlin felt sick and very afraid. Aware that she had started to shake uncontrollably, she tried to back away, to run, to hide, but a spotty youth clutched hold of her arm and thrust a microphone underneath her nose.

"Why did the police arrest you, Mrs Kirkwood?"

"Leave me alone!" croaked Caitlin, hypnotised by the acne bobbing about in front of her eyes. "Why can't you leave me alone?"

"C'mon, Mrs Kirkwood. Tell me everything," leered the sardonic journalist, shaking his match until it went out. "We'll make it worth your while."

Caitlin watched him casually drop the match on the pavement, where it landed in a puddle, a pathetic sliver of soggy wood. She dragged her eyes back up to his face. "What do you mean?"

The journalist nudged the youth, who obediently clicked off his tape recorder. "How much?" he asked briskly.

"Money?" queried Caitlin, completely perplexed.

"10K?" suggested the Journalist.

"Ten thousand pounds!" Caitlin was incredulous. "You'll give *me* ten thousand pounds? Whatever for?"

"To tell all, sweetheart." His eyes roamed insolently over her body. "Anything else would be illegal."

"But there's nothing to tell."

His black eyebrows furrowed and joined together. "Now don't get coy. Word is you killed him because he beat you up."

Caitlin felt suddenly cold. "Who told you that?"

The youth shifted uncomfortably. "Loads of people. Everybody knows."

Everybody knows . . . the one secret she had been desperate to hide. And now 'everybody knows'. Her shame and humiliation slowly burnt into a fury, annihilating the last fragment of fear.

"Everybody knows?"

The youth took a swift step backwards at the unadulterated rage sparking from her green eyes.

"No one knows the truth except me. And I'm not talking. If you print any lies I'll sue the pants off you."

"Lies?" mocked the journalist. He pulled a sheaf of paper from his pocket. "Sworn affidavits, sweetheart."

Caitlin snatched wildly at them but he held them too high, way out of her reach. She vented her rage by prodding him violently in the chest. "And how much did you pay for those, you bloody sewer-rat? How much cash did it take for my friends and neighbours to betray me?"

Thrown off balance, the journalist crashed backwards onto the pavement. And as he sprawled in the gutter, his own photographer took his picture. Caitlin could only watch in amazement. The whole scene was starting to take on elements of a circus. This was crazy – yet, had the prat fallen on purpose? To look a fool on the front page of his own paper just to get a half-baked story on her?

Caitlin could not believe it. Aghast at what she had done, albeit by accident, she would have apologised and helped him up but the other journalists surged around her. She felt like a cornered fox about to be torn apart by slathering, ravenous hounds.

"Have you been charged with your husband's murder, Mrs Kirkwood?" asked a glamorous redhead – Annelise Fitzpatrick and Olivia Greenwich rolled into one.

"Of course not!" snapped Caitlin. "I'm innocent."

"Then why did the police arrest you?" enquired the redhead blithely.

"They have to arrest someone," replied Caitlin without thinking, "or else they look stupid."

"Really?"

Caitlin realised a scrawny teenage girl beside the redhead was carefully writing down every word said. How could she be so dense? These were journalists, for Christ's sake. This was no time to be making a confession. Why couldn't she keep her big mouth shut?

"So why did you kill your husband?" asked another hack, elbowing the teenager aside and almost poking out the redhead's eye with the cigarette wedged in his mouth.

"I didn't!"

"He beat you up, didn't he?"

Caitlin put her hands over her ears. "Why does everyone keep saying that? It's not true!"

"He blacked your eye last Christmas?"

Yes, but she was not going to admit to that. Where the hell did they get their information? "No comment," she said, unable to lie at short notice.

"Weren't Hugh Kirkwood and Amanda de Havilland having an affair?" asked the spotty youth, making his comeback.

"No comment."

"Isn't it true they were both found naked, floating in the swimming-pool?" taunted the first journalist, who looked so much like Hugh. "After a wild, no-holds-barred orgy?"

This was obviously news to the redhead. "Was the Princess at the orgy too?"

"Did she ask you to hold her tiara?" grinned the sardonic journalist. "I hope you didn't frighten the corgis."

Everyone burst out laughing.

Caitlin found herself recovering some of that towering rage. "No bloody comment!" She hit out, blindly. The journalist stepped neatly aside and this time it was the spotty youth who found himself in the gutter.

"Ten thousand pounds, Mrs Kirkwood," said the sardonic journalist, waving a cheque in front of her eyes. "Just sign a contract and I'll make all these nasty reporters go away."

Ten thousand pounds to tell a journalist what she had told the police for free. Yes, it was tempting – but would it end there? Would they ever leave her alone? She had seen what the press did to people like her. Perhaps she would be seen as the innocent victim at first, then, as they built her up, they could just as easily tear her down. There would be a backlash. She would become notorious, a figure of hate . . . an outcast.

Slowly, deliberately, Caitlin took the cheque. And, as the journalist smirked in his triumph, she ripped it into shreds, throwing the pieces into his face. "And you know where you can stick it!"

"Bitch!"

"Caitlin!" yelled a woman's voice, as a Jaguar drew up at the pavement.

Lady Richmond. Caitlin would have got into a car with the devil himself if it meant rescue from this mob.

She wrenched open the door of the Jag and clambered into the back seat, locking the door behind her.

"Drive!" she cried to the chauffeur, ignoring protocol. "Just drive anywhere!"

The chauffeur obediently released the handbrake, put his foot on the accelerator and screeched away from the kerb. The press, deprived of their prey, furiously ran after the car, banging on the roof and trying to pull open the doors.

Caitlin slunk down in the seat, flashbulbs lighting up against the stormy sky. She hoped Lady Richmond's car would not be damaged. The insurance would not cover the cost and Caitlin certainly could not afford it. But the journalists were soon left behind. After a few moments Caitlin bobbed up to check out of the back window but they were now driving through the Forest.

She sat back in the seat and sighed. "Thanks, Lady Richmond. You saved my life."

"Lady Richmond!" spluttered Marina. "I've got a good mind to make you walk home."

Caitlin was abashed. "Sorry, Marina. It's very good of Lady Richmond to keep lending you her car. Does she know you're using it to collect me?"

"It's my car," beamed Marina. "It was delivered this morning. I bought it with the money I made from the film rights to *A Midsummer Kiss*."

Caitlin smiled faintly. "Bang goes New Year's Resolution Number 2."

"I deserved a treat," protested Marina. "Look at all that weight I lost."

"Yes, you can't eat a car. What about the Lotus you bought with the proceeds from *Love Under The Stars*? Is it still rotting in your garage?"

"I couldn't work the clutch."

"I hope this is an automatic."

"I did better than that! I bought a chauffeur too!"

Caitlin stared at the man driving. "That's Lady Richmond's chauffeur."

"I know. He comes highly recommended."

"I bet he does," said Caitlin, catching sight of the chauffeur smouldering at her in the rear-view mirror. "But can you afford his wages?"

"I'll just have to write six books a year instead of four," said Marina complacently. "But if it doesn't work out, he's promised to teach me to drive for free."

"All over the back seat, no doubt," muttered Caitlin.

Reflected in the rear-view mirror she could clearly see the chauffeur glance back at her – and brazenly wink.

* * *

In the reception of Kirkwood Manor Hotel was a large blackboard, propped up on an easel, upon which someone had chalked in pink bubble-writing, '*All Aerobic Classes Cancelled*'. Caitlin used the sleeve of her dress to carefully rub out each word.

"Why did you do that?" grumbled Marina, who had spent the best part of the morning writing out the sign and colouring in each letter.

"The aerobics classes are now uncancelled."

"Who's going to take them? One of your fitness instructors is dead and poor, darling Fabian has been arrested for her murder."

"I shall be taking the classes."

"You?" Marina was incredulous. "But you haven't instructed an aerobics class for almost five years."

"Someone has to do it and it might as well be me. This hotel is losing money faster than Linford Christie on knicker-elastic. If it goes bankrupt, so do I. And I'll never be able to get another job. Who would hire a hotel manager without a single qualification?" She glanced down at her expanding stomach, and bottled out of telling Marina the complete truth. "And who would hire an overweight aerobics instructor?"

"Caitlin, about the guests . . ."

"What's the problem with the guests?"

"There's no problem. There are no guests."

Caitlin paled. "But there were at least four doubles and a single room booked the day before Hugh's funeral."

It was as though the information had to be dragged out of Marina. "They all checked out," she admitted at length, amidst much shuffling of her feet. "And . . . er, moved into the Richmond Arms . . ."

Caitlin's temper, still smouldering from her encounter with the reporters, sparked again and she brutally kicked the easel, making Marina jump.

The easel flipped over and smacked onto the floor. "Well, sod them!" said Caitlin bitterly. "I hope they get salmonella poisoning. How am I supposed to pay the staff?"

"That won't be a problem," assured Marina, moving a small occasional table out of her friend's range. "You have no staff either."

* * *

It was a long time since Caitlin had worn her leotard. She eventually found it, along with her cycling shorts and Reeboks, screwed up at the bottom of her wardrobe, beneath some thigh-high boots bought to excite Hugh when he had still cared.

She was aware her kit was hopelessly out of date but that was the least of her worries. How could she possibly compete with the blatant sex appeal of Fabian, even if he was thicker than a Yorkie Bar? Perhaps a nice relaxing glass of French brandy would help? She dismissed the thought abruptly. Alcohol would cause more problems than it would help. And not only that, she couldn't afford the fees of a drying-out clinic.

Caitlin pulled on a baggy T-shirt to disguise her rounded tummy and, avoiding her reflection in the mirror, headed towards reception to see how many people were booked into the step-aerobics class.

As she flipped through the diary, awash with Tipp-ex and crude crossings-out, there was a sudden crash of thunder and Fabian fell through the door, accompanied by a shower of hail and a blast of frozen air.

What an entrance, thought Caitlin, admiring the

way his soaked jeans clung to his long legs, his massive shoulders silhouetted against the storm like some Viking god. Fabian wrung out his long blond hair, his pride and joy, which was now plastered around his face like cold spaghetti. It was a while before he realised he had an audience.

"Sorry I'm late, Mrs Kirkwood . . ." He pulled a soggy handkerchief from his pocket and noisily blew his nose. "I'll make the time up."

Caitlin closed the diary and glanced at her watch. "Have you been at the police station all day?"

"Yeah, they let me go when my solicitor threatened to cause a stink." He grinned. "But I'm not allowed to leave the country."

As he stood there shivering, Caitlin felt desperately sorry for him. Despite his humour there was something bleak behind those cornflower-blue eyes. Fabian had finally lost his bounce.

"For heaven's sake, Fabe," she said brightly, "come and stand by the fire. You'll catch your death."

Fabian let Caitlin bully him out of his jacket and shirt, watching her drape them over the furniture to allow them to dry. She tugged a red cloth from a nearby table and wrapped it around his shoulders to warm him up.

"I had to walk all the way from the police station," grumbled Fabian, steaming gently. "I hadn't got any money for a bus."

"You should have telephoned." Caitlin pulled his towering frame down to her level and rubbed his head with the ends of the tablecloth. "You could have reversed the charges."

"It beats me why I was arrested in the first place. Do I look like a mass murderer?"

"Don't take it personally – I expect the police think that because Hugh was bonking Amanda, you were jealous and killed them both."

"So that DCI was telling the truth," frowned Fabian. "I thought he was just winding me up. Poor Amanda."

That was one way of looking at it, thought Caitlin, wishing she'd kept her big mouth shut. She dumped his jacket into his arms and gave him a shove towards the stairs. "Go upstairs and take the rest of your clothes off, before you catch cold."

"Is this a private orgy or can anyone join in?"

Caitlin almost went through the ceiling. Standing nonchalantly against the reception desk was a sun-tanned, long-limbed man, dreadlocks well past his shoulders, oval, metal-rimmed sunglasses balanced on his beaky nose. He was dressed from head to foot in tattered black leather, had a motorcycle helmet over his arm, a dirty rucksack over one shoulder and a large paint-splattered ghetto-blaster in his hand. It was quietly chuntering out Bob Marley and the Wailers, but sounded as though the batteries were about to conk out at any moment.

"We're closed," said Caitlin, trying not to giggle as a half-naked Fabian sprinted up the staircase, trailing tablecloth and mud behind him. "I mean, we're full."

She was sorely tempted to rent the man a room but,

although she was desperate for a guest, she didn't dare, in case he scared other prospective clientele away. And frankly she doubted he had the means to pay.

"Sorry," she added, and meant it.

"Full?" enquired the man, laughter twitching at his lips.

Caitlin followed his gaze to the board behind the desk. Every room key, labelled from one to thirty, hung on a row of brass hooks.

"Yes," she replied. "Absolutely full. Jam-packed. Couldn't get another single person in."

"How about a married one?" The man raised his eyebrows above his sunglasses. "You think I would bring your hotel into disrepute? I promise not to hold any wild parties, at least not until after 9.00 am. And I don't do drugs, or smoke, but I must admit to a certain fondness for Guinness and reggae. But then, nobody's perfect."

Caitlin regarded him blankly.

"I'm even house-trained." He sighed. "You know, it's very quiet here, for a full hotel."

Caitlin felt her cheeks warm. "The guests are out on an excursion."

"Really?" He perked up. "Where to?"

"Sites of important archaeological significance."

"In the King's Forest?" He laughed. "That won't take long."

Caitlin strode over to the door and held it open. The rain began to dot the dusty floor.

The man lazily leant back against the reception desk

and grinned, revealing perfect white teeth. "You're not very hospitable, are you?"

Heck, was she never going to be rid of him? "You could try the Richmond Arms in town," she suggested, ultra-politely. "They always have rooms."

"For riff-raff like me?" The man sighed and picked up his belongings. The ghetto-blaster left a smear of yellow paint behind and finally clunked off. "To the Richmond Arms it is," he said, pausing on the doorstep and looking up at the purple-black sky. "But be assured, I shall be writing to Mother to tell her how you treat your only brother when he came to support you in your hour of need." And he stepped out into the torrential rain.

Her *brother?* Caitlin stared at the man's retreating back. Then again, there was something very familiar in that lolloping walk. She ran after him, catching hold of his arm, and hauled him back; her other hand whipping off his sunglasses. Two beautiful, black-fringed, very familiar, emerald eyes stared back. They ought to be familiar. They were identical to her own.

"Jack?" she cried, flinging her arms around his waist, squeezing all the breath out of him, and getting soaking wet in the process. "Is it really you?"

The man gazed fondly at the top of her head. "Of course! I'm very hurt that you didn't recognise me."

"Even Mother would not recognise you." She blinked back the tears and, to distract him, tweaked his dreadlocks. "Are these real?"

"Ow! Of course they're real! It took me five years to grow them."

She frowned. "Is it really that long since I saw you?"

"Yep. It was in this very hall. There were more flowers then and you wore a white dress –"

"My wedding day . . ."

"You do remember?" His eyes clouded over. "You stood over by the desk and told Mother and me that you never wanted to see us again because we were such an embarrassment to you."

Caitlin cringed at the memory – but she had been only nineteen. Everyone did stupid things when they were young – and in love. "Mother accused me of marrying Hugh for his money," she said defensively. "That the marriage would never work and that Hugh was only marrying to have children and to hide the fact that he was bisexual." All of which turned out to be true, she realised guilty.

"Oh yeah," grinned Jack. "It's all coming back to me now. He pinched our stepfather's bottom and tried to grope him in the shrubbery."

Caitlin attempted a smile but it came out rather twisted. "It was the worst day of my life . . . until now. Is that why you're here?" She regarded him uncertainly. "Have you come to gloat?"

He pulled her into an all-enveloping hug, crushing her cheekbones against his ribcage. "Why, hush your mouth, Caitlin! I'm ashamed of you for even thinking such a thing!"

Caitlin managed to wriggle free. Being cuddled by her big brother was akin to being slobbered over by a St Bernard. "So why are you here?"

"I've run away from home."

"You're twenty-six years old."

"So I'm a late developer."

Caitlin laughed. "Liar, you came to see if I was all right."

Jack looked sheepish. "Well, we're such a close family."

A sudden, alarming thought popped into Caitlin's head. "Mother isn't about to turn up too, is she?"

Jack snorted. "Are you kidding? She's in California, staking out some phoney Spanish marquis. Poor guy doesn't stand a chance. Mind you, as he was interrogating me about the size of *our* family fortune, ha ha, I think they probably deserve each other."

Caitlin grimaced. "I don't really fancy another stepfather."

"I didn't fancy any of them. Tell you what I do fancy, though. Nice steak and chips, hot bath and perhaps a massage to finish?"

In five years Jack hadn't changed a bit. "Sorry," said Caitlin, "my one and only masseuse sloped off while I was helping the local police with their enquiries. As far as dinner is concerned, I can just about manage beans on toast, or takeaway pizza if you'd rather, but you're welcome to a room for the night. You can stay all week if you like." She indicated the rows of keys behind her. "Take your pick."

He beamed. "A double en-suite with four-poster, jacuzzi and view of the park, please."

"You've just described the bridal suite."

"I'll take it," said Jack. "Do I get the bride too?"

Chapter Nine

The very same day that Caitlin was released from custody, Marc decided to call into Calahurst Police Station. He intended to visit the murder squad in the incident room, read up on the statements, listen to some interview tapes and generally do his homework. He was still officially on leave but felt restless.

He missed Caitlin by ten minutes.

It had not been Marc's idea to swap Special Branch for CID. He had enjoyed helping to provide protection duty for visiting royalty, the element of risk that made life that little bit more exciting. It got him out and about and away from those petty station politics he hated so much, the pointless IT courses, the repetitive paperwork. In fact, apart from pounding the beat as a uniformed officer he could not think of a more boring job than the CID at Calahurst, where the only crime was allowing tourists free range to tramp wantonly throughout the Forest.

As he drove his dusty Mondeo towards the busy station car park, he saw his ex-girlfriend's distinctive MGF sports car abandoned outside The Stables pub opposite. The soft top was down and the drizzle gleefully splattered the red-leather seats. Either she couldn't find anywhere to park in the tiny station yard, or she was working her way through the pub's famous fruit wines.

Marc sighed, drove past the station and pulled his car in next to the MGF. He had to park crookedly to fit in the available space. It was typical of Georgia to treat her possessions so carelessly. She had blown the equivalent of two years' wages buying the car and then left it uncovered in the rain, the keys glinting temptingly in the ignition.

Rover promised its customers that the roof could be put up in five seconds. Unfamiliar with the mechanism, it took Marc five minutes, by which time he was drenched. Swearing profusely, he pocketed the keys, cast a nervous glance towards the police station and entered the gloom of the pub.

The Stables public house had acquired its name thirty years before when it had been converted from a barn. It had once housed the horses of the Lord of the Manor, whose derelict mansion had been demolished to make room for the new police station. The landlord had kept the original stalls and iron mangers, although they were now stuffed with plastic foliage rather than hay. Bridles, stirrups and spurs hung from large brass hooks which, with the red velvet curtains, gave the overall appearance of a whore's games room.

Seats and tables had been hacked from large wooden barrels and some wag had stuck a stuffed barn owl on one of the oak beams above. At least, Marc presumed it was stuffed. It had not moved for a very long time.

The pub was deserted apart from Georgia de Havilland, slumped on a bar stool, still in her WPC uniform, surrounded by a dozen empty glasses. Even the bartender had left, presumably in search of more scintillating conversation.

Marc dropped the keys to the MGF into Georgia's wineglass. What looked like Ribena splashed in a ten-inch radius. "Have you gone stark raving mad, George, darling? Or do you just have PMT?"

"Bloody chauvinist!" Georgia swung out with her fist.

Marc ducked, catching hold of her wrist and pressing it ruthlessly back until he held her in a half nelson. "You know it's against force regulations to drink on duty, the barman knows it too. Yet you're sitting in a pub, right opposite the police station, wearing uniform. Do you have a death wish?"

"Let me go!" Georgia twisted violently, attempting a karate kick, but fell off the bar stool and slithered to a heap on the flagstone floor, long legs sprawling, her skirt riding up to reveal a ladder in her thick black tights. She looked up, dazed and confused. "What happened to the bar?"

Marc dragged her to her feet. "You'll never be a Vegas showgirl."

She regarded him with cross eyes. "Marc? Is that you?"

"Who were you expecting? A six-foot invisible white rabbit?" He sighed. "Come on, George. I'll take you home so you can sleep it off. You're going to have one hell of a hangover tomorrow. Have you paid your bill?"

She glanced up, hopefully. "Were you offering to pay it?"

"Spoken like a true die-hard feminist."

"Oh, drop dead. I don't need your sermonising. I can get it every day from my father." Georgia shook him free and resumed her seat, swaying slightly, fishing her keys out of the glass and shaking them dry. "God, Marc, they're all sticky. What did you think you were doing?"

"I'm trying to prevent you from sabotaging your career."

"What career?" hiccuped Georgia.

He frowned. "Your career was fine yesterday. You had just made CID Aide and it was drinks all round. What did you do overnight? Kiss the Chief Constable and turn him into a frog?"

Georgia stared glumly at her wine glass. "Worse, I set fire to Caitlin Kirkwood's hair."

"*You did what?*" It was with supreme effort that Marc kept a hold of his temper. She had always had an unfailing ability to infuriate him to the absolute limit of his control, then sit back and laugh at the consequences. "You're joking, surely?"

Georgia idly ran her finger around the rim of her glass. "Remember, remember, the Fifth of November . . ."

"It's the 15th of March." He resisted the temptation to slap her.

"Beware the Ides of March." Georgia raised the glass to her lips.

Marc dashed it from her hand. The glass fell to the flagstoned floor, smashing into zillions of pieces, the spilt strawberry wine trickling over the stones like blood.

"Thanks," said Georgia. "That cost me £1.80."

"What the hell is the matter with you?" Marc demanded furiously. "You're a grown woman, a police officer – don't you have any pride? Getting drunk – on duty – at the first sign of trouble, setting light to the main suspect in a murder investigation. I appreciate you have problems, George – what I can't understand is why can't you take Prozac like everyone else. You sure are making a fool of yourself."

"Who to?" Georgia airily waved her hand. "The place is empty. The barman keeps trying to close up but I won't let him. Come on, relax. Let me buy you a beer or something. What are you drinking?"

"Vomit," snapped Marc. "You make me want to throw up."

She grimaced. "Ugh! Do you have to be so graphic?"

When she was in this mood it was hopeless to attempt reason. Marc placed her arm around his neck, put his own around her waist and attempted to help her across the flagstoned floor to the exit.

Georgia hardly put up a fight. "Are you trying to take advantage?" she giggled.

"No," said Marc firmly. God, for such a skinny creature she sure was heavy. "Why did you have to get so drunk? Do you think alcohol is going to solve all your problems?"

"Why not? Doesn't make you fat like chocolate or give you spots."

He smiled, despite himself. "True – but I can see your liver waving a white flag from here."

"Can you?" Georgia plucked at her navy-blue sweater. "Where?"

After over-shooting the exit three times, Marc managed to turn her sideways and crab-walk through the door. The barman appeared from the shadows, gave Marc a smile of gratitude and bolted the door behind them.

Marc propped Georgia up against the passenger side of his black Ford Mondeo while he scrabbled in the pocket of his raincoat for his keys. Half a packet of Polos tumbled out, rolling into the gutter, but he could not be bothered to pick them up. Besides, if he left Georgia leaning drunkenly against his car too long she was likely to end up next to them.

As he moved around to the driver's side, he glanced anxiously up at the smoked-glass windows of the police station and prayed no one was watching. It was a strict policy of the Chief Constable that neither police officers nor civilians were allowed to drink alcohol while on duty. 'The law is not above the law' was one of his favourite sayings. If Georgia was caught it would mean instant dismissal. And it would be too much to hope that they would not be recognised by their colleagues. Georgia's racy sports car was far too distinctive – and the only one of its type in Calahurst. Her uniform did not exactly help her blend into the background either.

At last he found his keys, unlocked the car, and opened the passenger door.

"This is not my car," said Georgia, digging in her heels.

Marc gave her a shove. "Tough. I'm not letting you drive home in your condition. Even if you didn't run some poor sod over, you would probably end up in Wales."

"I'm going to be sick!"

Marc hauled her out by the scruff of her neck. "Not in *my* car."

Georgia fell onto her hands and knees, her nose about an inch from the pavement. "I feel so ill!"

"Hurry up or you'll attract a crowd." Marc leant back against his car and lit a cigarette. At least no one could see her while she was crouched on the ground. But as she began to cough and splutter into the gutter he finally took pity on her, rubbing her back and all the while keeping a watchful eye on the police station.

After a few moments Georgia raised her head. She was white-faced and wan. "I feel better now." She crawled onto the back seat, flopping across its full length. "Oh Marc," she murmured, looking distinctly green. "I'm never going to drink again."

"Yeah, and I'm the Sugar Plum Fairy."

Then as he climbed into the driver's seat, adjusting the rear-view mirror, he saw that she had fallen asleep with her mouth still open, snoring gently.

* * *

Apart from a disastrous fortnight living in sin at Marc's cottage, and the time spent at college, Georgia had always lived with her father, Paul de Havilland. He owned a large, art-deco style house, situated outside Calahurst on the far side of the King's Forest, overlooking the sea. The locals nicknamed it 'The Snow King's Palace', both for its abundance of glass and crystal, and Paul's cold, aloof nature.

Named Orion House, it had been built for Paul's maternal grandfather, the younger son of a baronet, who had also been an enthusiastic astronomer. There was a long, sweeping gravel drive and a front garden consisting of manicured lawn and enormous cedar trees. Along the edge of the drive were hosts of decaying daffodils and huge banks of rhododendrons, the massive chrysalis buds peeping between dark leaves. Paul could not see the point of extensive gardening. As long as everything was neat and tidy, that was enough for him.

The drive led to the stables, converted by Georgia's grandfather into a large double garage and mostly unused workshop. Paul did not see the point of DIY either. Why trouble oneself, if one had the money to pay someone else?

As Georgia was seemingly comatose, Marc had to carry her the last few feet from the car, along a winding stone path, to the front door. He knocked. No one answered so he went in. The door was never locked. Who would be fool enough to rob the Head of Calahurst CID? Particularly when he owned three large Dobermans.

As Marc entered the hall the dogs came rushing up to him, skidding on the tiled floor, barking their heads off. But once they had had a good sniff and accepted Marc as a friend, they wagged their tails and happily trotted back to the kitchen.

The entrance hall· had the appearance of a conservatory, with a domed glass roof some thirty feet above. The floor comprised alternating black and white stone tiles, there was a veritable forest of potted palms and orange-trees around the walls and in the centre of the room was an ornate marble fountain, gushing excitedly into little pools of pink alabaster water-lilies. Even eighty years ago they had been considered tacky.

As Marc staggered towards the huge curving staircase, straight out of an old Ginger Rogers movie, the housekeeper emerged from behind a pillar, looking distinctly unimpressed.

"Good afternoon, Mr Granger," she said, chilly enough to freeze the fountain.

His heart sank. Euphemia Barnaby – who could have given Mrs Danvers a run for her money. Ebony hair scraped back from her pale, bitter face, she was dressed in her usual black suit, white silk blouse and dazzling array of antique brooches, making her resemble a manically depressed magpie. Marc knew she had never liked him, since she had caught him canoodling in the orangery with Georgia's younger sister on Christmas Eve. But then, apart from her unrequited passion for the bloodless Paul de Havilland, did Euphemia like anyone?

Marc made the effort to be nice. It can't have been easy, slaving away the best years of her life in the forlorn hope she might one day be upgraded to be the second Mrs de Havilland.

"Good afternoon, Mrs Barnaby," he smiled. "Beautiful weather we're having this time of year."

"It's raining," said the housekeeper pointedly.

Marc fixed a polite smile to his face and refused to bite. After a few frosty seconds, she flourished a duster and disappeared into a sitting-room. Marc stared helplessly at the staircase. To hell with this, Georgia weighed a ton. He put her down on the bottom step and gently slapped her face.

"George! Wake up!"

She lazily opened one eye. "And I thought you were going to slay Dragon Barnaby and carry me off to your castle in the clouds."

"Dream on."

Georgia pouted. "Don't you like me any more?"

Marc shivered. It was uncanny how much she resembled Amanda. Bleached-blonde hair, large blue-grey eyes, dark eyebrows and lashes. He always felt that, if somehow the looks and vulnerability of Amanda could have been combined with Georgia's humour and intelligence, one would have had the perfect woman. That was another reason their relationship had failed. He had never been able to decide between the two.

Marc felt that old, familiar longing rising within him and was forced to turn away, lest she read it in his eyes. Their relationship had already limped well into injury time. This was no time to start on penalties.

"As you appear to have made a miraculous recovery, I'm out of here," he said.

"My knight in rusting armour."

Her flip comments brought another damsel in distress to mind. "You didn't really set light to Mrs Kirkwood, did you?"

"Sure did!" she mimicked his Canadian accent effortlessly.

"God, George. How could you? Was she hurt?"

Her merriment evaporated. "Unfortunately not." She sat abruptly on the bottom step. "I didn't even get the chance to singe her eyelashes. Bloody Clive Reynolds charged to the rescue like the 7th Cavalry. He hauled me up to see Dad."

Marc could not believe what he was hearing. No wonder she had set out to get drunk. It seemed her career as a police officer was over before it had begun.

"Your father knows about this?"

"Yeah, I even lived to tell the tale."

"Cut the crap."

"I was fired."

Marc was incredulous. "Just like that? Without a Discipline? You behaved appallingly but he can't just kick you out."

"Daddy knows best. He called it a career break."

"I should have known you were exaggerating. You got off lightly."

"Only civvies have career breaks. It's as good as the sack."

Marc sat next to her and draped his arm over her shoulders, hoping to placate her. "Sounds like a great idea to me. You could study art, history, English –"

"Bor-ing!"

He shrugged. "Or anything else you wanted."

Georgia regarded him through half-closed eyes. "I want you."

Marc blinked. "Sorry?"

She slid her hands under his raincoat and across his white shirt. He could feel their chill through the fabric.

"Let's go to bed."

He wanted to. He desperately wanted to. Falling out of love took far longer than falling into it. But, he realised, she was too drunk to consider the consequences. His heart would be happy to pick up the crumbs of their relationship. His head was smarter.

So he attempted to let her down gently. "Go to bed? But it's lunchtime."

"Live a little."

He tapped her nose. "That's a very sweet offer, George, but I guess I'll have to turn you down. You know you'll regret it in the morning."

Georgia pointedly removed her hands. *"You'll* be the one doing the regretting."

"Aw, come off it, George. You were the one that dumped me – for that baby-faced DC from fraud squad. You can't just turn me on, turn me off, like I'm the standby switch on your TV."

Georgia stood up and brushed down her skirt, her cheeks flushed, her eyes glittering dangerously. "I hate you, Marc Granger." She turned on her heel and walked slowly up the stairs. "Why don't you just piss off and leave me alone?"

Marc watched her leave and felt an absolute bastard. "I'm sorry, George!" he called after her.

Georgia did not reply.

Marc sighed and started up the stairs, aware that Mrs Barnaby was watching his progress, her beady black eyes boring neat round holes into his back, every step of the way.

Georgia's bedroom overlooked the sea and was decorated in swirls of green and aquamarine to match the view. One wall was completely glass and led out onto an enormous balcony. It was decorated in much the same way as it had been three months ago, when Marc had last seen it. Involuntarily he glanced towards her bed. Georgia, an art-school drop-out, had designed it herself, a wrought-iron monstrosity, painted gold, twisted and contorted by the local blacksmith to recreate a galaxy of stars and crescent moons. He dragged his eyes away. Had another man lain there since?

Georgia stood on the wide balcony, seemingly without a care in the world, peeling off her uniform and hurtling it into the garden below.

Marc made a dive for the window, then forced himself to step more slowly, in case she decided to throw herself over. She had recently lost her sister after all. Grief could wreak havoc on the fragile balance of the mind.

"For Christ's sake, George. Come back inside."

Georgia glanced disdainfully over one shoulder. Betty Grable in sensible shoes.

"Come for the floor show?" she enquired icily. She kicked off one lace-up and, after dangling it tormentingly for a moment or two, casually dropped it over the railings.

"I came to apologise," he said quickly, hoping to keep her talking and not jumping.

"So apologise." The second shoe followed its mate. She tugged out her hairgrips and her long blonde curls spiralled down over her shoulders. The fine drizzle had given her skin an ethereal sheen. She looked like a flat-chested Barbie doll left out in the rain.

"I'm sorry," said Marc, edging all the while towards the balcony, realising he had now run out of conversation. How the hell was he going to distract her?

"Thank you," said Georgia. "Now you can get lost." She sat down on a wooden sun-lounger to remove her thick black tights. When she stood up the slats had stamped railroad tracks across her pale thighs.

"Come inside, George," pleaded Marc. "It's damn near freezing."

"I thought you'd gone." She tried, unsuccessfully, to unhook her bra. "Stayed for the grand finale, eh?"

"You'll frighten the neighbours," he joked half-heartedly.

Georgia was scornful. "This is middle-class suburbia – more wife-swapping, soft drugs and organised adultery than a weekend of satellite television."

As she struggled with the catch on her bra, Marc pulled the dark green duvet off the bed and, before she had time to put up a fight, bundled it around her cold, wet body, dragged her inside and shut the sliding window. He locked it, shoving the key in his pocket.

"Spoilsport," she pouted, and began to grope at his pocket in the most disconcerting manner.

"Don't do something you're going to regret in the morning. It isn't fair." Valiantly he fought her off. "You're drunk. You don't know what you're doing."

"So you keep saying. What's *your* excuse."

As he stared into her silver-blue eyes, now stone-cold sober, Marc found he was unable to let her go. Georgia undid his raincoat and snuggled against him, the damp of her hair seeping into his shirt. He groaned softly. Pure, exquisite torture. How had he allowed himself to get this far? Her shoulder gleamed invitingly between blonde curls and duvet. Involuntarily he smoothed her hair to one side and slid the back of his hand down her neck. That beautiful creamy white skin . . .

Georgia, her eyes closed, purred into his chest. It was as though she had his mouth on traction beam. Gently he slid his lips over her bare neck. She smelt faintly of the perfume he had given her for Christmas. Jasmine and roses . . .

The duvet slipped to the floor. Marc fought silently with his conscience.

"Well, will you look at that," said Georgia, feigning disgust. "All my clothes just fell off!"

"Not all of them," said Marc. And unhooked her bra.

Chapter Ten

Caitlin reluctantly left Jack in charge of reception while she had her lunch. With his dreadlocks and Sidestreet Raybans he was likely to terrify any prospective guest and, after discovering that one of his eyebrows was pierced and had two little slices shaved out of it, Caitlin had insisted he kept his sunglasses on.

Jack had tuned the television into MTV, taken the phone off the hook and had his feet up on the reception desk. Balancing his sketch pad on his lap, he was attempting to draw his hero, Bob Marley, from an old music video. The sunglasses began to slide down his nose.

"Hi there!"

Jack's pencil shot across the page, snapping the lead. He whipped his feet off the desk, nearly knocking over his coffee, and shoved his Raybans back over his eyes.

On the other side of the desk the Harrison Ford look-alike (circa 1977) grinned. "Do you think someone could show me round the gym? I want to take up membership of your Leisure Club."

"I'll get Rick for you," Jack replied. "He's our gym instructor."

"How about Mrs Kirkwood?"

"Mrs Kirkwood?" Jack's heart spiralled into his shabby trainers. Another sick ghoul. Since Caitlin's arrest had been splashed throughout the tabloids, their only customers had been bespectacled 'anoraks' who would troop mud into reception, 'ooh' and 'ahh' at the dark Gothic decor and ask, in breathless excitement, if this was where the *murder* had taken place.

"My name is Marc Granger," added 'Harrison'. "I'm a friend of hers."

Jack's eyes, the colour of frosted crème de menthe, appeared over the top of the Raybans. "Yeah, right!"

The temperature in reception dropped several degrees.

"I want to see Mrs Kirkwood," said the man, pronouncing each word slowly and very clearly, as though English was Jack's second language. "Please call her for me."

Jack was unable to think up a valid excuse. Besides, there would be no end of trouble from Caitlin if he let a real *bona fide* punter escape.

"OK," he said. "Wait here. I'll see if I can find her."

"Try real hard."

Jack found Caitlin alone in the magnificent dining-room, watched over by glowering family portraits that Hugh had not been able to sell. The tables were set for fifty – as though a coach party was imminent. Caitlin was dejectedly pushing a piece of soggy cauliflower around her plate, perhaps wondering how much it would take to lure Chef back. Jack remembered that cooking had never been her strong point. And it had taken him all morning to fathom the tin-opener.

"What's the matter?" she grumbled. "Can't you cope with the stress?"

Chomping hard on the retort about to come freewheeling out of his mouth, Jack said, "There's a guy in reception with a dodgy American accent. He reckons to be a friend of yours."

"I don't have any friends. Not even American ones."

"He says his name is Stewart Granger."

Caitlin's lips begrudgingly smiled. "Do you mean *Marc* Granger?"

So the guy had been telling the truth. "Something like that. He wants to look round the gym." Jack studied her reaction carefully. "He asked for you personally."

"Yes!" Caitlin punched the air.

Jack sighed. His sister had always been transparently predictable when it came to men. He hoped it wouldn't end in tears. "Let me guess. Your Prince has finally come?"

"You bet – and not a fairy godmother in sight."

* * *

Marc had assumed the gym would be deserted but Rick was languidly polishing the large mirrors, and, lying flat out on a workbench, swinging dumbbells up and down like a manic gull, was local celebrity Marina Grey, impossible to miss in her fuchsia leotard and yellow lycra shorts.

"Hello," said Rick, somehow managing to get four syllables out of the word. He was a tall, swarthy, handsome hunk. The sort that kicks sand in your face in Mediterranean resorts, shortly before bonking your girlfriend under a tamarisk tree. There was also something about that dark, macho beauty that made Marc think that if Rick was not gay, he was seriously bi-sexual.

Rick was wearing the tiniest of purple vests, designed to reveal the maximum amount of rippling muscles, 'lunch-box' shorts and a black baseball cap. He must think the hat made him look young and trendy, decided Marc, and refrained from enquiring if the roof leaked. At least Rick was wearing it the right way round.

"Hi," said Marc, deciding it wouldn't hurt to be polite.

"And what can I do for you?" asked Rick, eyeing him up and down in much the same manner as a stray dog would regard raw steak.

"Just a workout. Mrs Kirkwood is meeting me here for a fitness test."

"*Just* a workout?"

Where *did* Caitlin get her staff? thought Marc

wearily. He was about to utter an icy put-down when Marina dropped a dumbbell.

Rick's bravado vanished and he frantically polished at the dent visible in the maple floor. "Mrs Kirkwood will kill me," he muttered in despair. "She's just looking for an excuse. In fifty years' time someone will find me buried underneath the terrace with a stake through my heart."

He swiftly pulled a bench over the dent in the floor just as Caitlin made an appearance. Considering she was supposed to be an aerobics instructor, thought Marc, she could certainly do with losing a few pounds. That was quite a tum she had cunningly disguised under a red basketball vest.

"Sorry to keep you waiting, Marc," said Caitlin. "If you'd like to hop onto the bike, I'll give you a fitness test."

Marc was almost knocked sideways by the scent of Thierry Mugler's Angel and the not-so-celestial fire of passion in her green eyes. *What the hell was he letting himself in for?* He swung himself up onto the bike. Attached to the front was a digital panel which resembled something salvaged from a spaceship. As he began to pedal, it lit up like the Fourth of July.

Caitlin took his pulse and wrote down the result on a pre-printed sheet attached to the clipboard. Carefully she printed his name at the top. "Do you smoke?"

"In moderation."

"How many a day?"

"Twenty," lied Marc.

"And do you drink?"

"A pint with the lads, Sunday lunchtimes, when we're not working."

"You work Sundays? Poor thing. What do you do?"

"Engineer," muttered Marc, hoping she wouldn't ask him to elaborate.

"How often do you exercise?"

"Um, a bit of running, occasional game of soccer with the lads. I used to play a lot of ice hockey." In *Canada*, he thought, inwardly groaning. Like Brits were really keen on that particular sport! Two seconds into his undercover work and he had already blown it. James Bond he wasn't.

Caitlin, however, had not appeared to notice his gaffe. "But not now?"

It was like the Spanish Inquisition. "There are no ice rinks around here." *The truth at last!* "Field hockey is too slow for me."

On the opposite wall, above the mirrors, was a TV screen tuned to Sky Sports, though the sound was switched off. A glamorous instructor was leaping about in front of a step aerobics class of professional dancers. The gym's music system was blaring techno rock. The TV instructor was completely out of synch.

He remembered why he was here. "Do you take step aerobics classes too?"

"And aerobics, boxercise, body-conditioning, circuit-training –" She reeled them off without even looking up from her clipboard. "There's a step class starting in fifteen minutes. You'll be able to watch. I'll give you a timetable later. Either Fabian or myself take several classes a day. They're very popular, particularly in the evenings. You have to book a week in advance."

Yet the rest of the hotel is going downhill faster than an elephant on in-line skates, thought Marc. He glanced back at the clock on the bike. He had only been cycling a couple of minutes and he was already out of puff. He sneaked a look at Caitlin's reflection in the mirror opposite. Even at thirty feet she looked smug. Maybe a gym was not the best place to seduce a confession out of her.

Seduce. Hell, was he crazy? The poor girl's emotions were already stir-fried. She didn't deserve another bastard to rot up her life. Besides, after jump-starting his relationship with Georgia, to dally with Caitlin would be practically suicide. Not to mention damned exhausting.

With her raven curls and sparkling Irish eyes Caitlin was certainly attractive, if slightly overweight. *The Black Widow.* The thought popped involuntarily into his head. He had to admit though, she didn't look like a murderer.

Caitlin took his pulse again, her cold fingers pressing against his neck. He had to force himself to concentrate on Marina, wheezing away on the running machine, instead. At least he would not have to feign sexual attraction. Maybe this job would not be as difficult as he had imagined.

As he noticed Caitlin frown, he joked, "Am I dead?"

"How old are you?"

"Thirty," he said, automatically knocking two years

off for courtship purposes. According to the file Paul de Havilland had prepared for him, Caitlin Kirkwood was only twenty-four. Yet Hugh Kirkwood had been forty. Perhaps she liked old men. Perhaps she only liked *rich* old men.

"Your heart rate is much higher than it should be for a man of your age," Caitlin was saying disapprovingly.

She sounded just like his old schoolteacher. She'd be muttering about smoking behind the bike sheds next.

"You are extremely unfit. If you want to make any progress you'll have to give up smoking. Giving up alcohol would be a bonus too."

He forced himself to pay attention. "Pity, I was about to ask you for a drink."

Caitlin was still doing her calculations. "Nothing to stop you drinking cola. Diet cola."

"Hell, I'm really in for a fun time. Are you telling me I'm fat too?"

She grinned and brandished an enormous pair of plastic pinchers. "Soon find out. This calculates the percentage of body-fat. We pinch the skin over your biceps and triceps, over the shoulder blades and across the hip-bones."

Quaint, thought Marc. At the police training college they used the latest computer technology, calculating fat weight, lean weight, the amount of water in the body . . . Mrs Kirkwood's gym needed one helluva kick up the ass to see it into the twenty-first century.

The bike beeped and all the lights flicked off the screen. Caitlin took his pulse again and inserted a

series of dots on a small graph. She waited a few
moments then took his pulse again, turning the chart
around to show him.

"That's where you should be," she said, indicating a
blue shaded area in the centre. "And that's where you
are."

"In the red," sighed Marc. "You sound like my bank
manager. Have I got long to live?"

"Your recovery rate is a disaster. You have the fitness
level of a fifty-year-old man."

It was a wonder he could get it up at all. "Diet cola
here I come," he joked feebly.

"I'll just get Rick to test your body-fat first. And
then your strength and suppleness."

Marc felt put out. Was he losing his touch? "Why
can't you test me?"

"I'm only allowed to test women's body-fat." Her
eyes twinkled mischievously. "It involves a fair
amount of groping you see. Rick!" she yelled over the
loud funky music. "Victim for you."

Rick dropped the blonde as obediently as a pedigree
retriever. The guy must have been listening to every
word. Calvin Klein fought silently with Thierry Mugler
as Rick sauntered over, bronzed shoulders glistening in
the artificial light.

"Maybe I'll skip the fat test," said Marc.

"It won't take long." Caitlin walked towards the exit.
"I'll meet you in the bar after my step class. Why don't you
try out the sauna or the steam room? Great for getting
toxins out of the body and making the skin feel really soft."

"Perhaps he's 'dry-clean only'?" said Rick.

Marc smiled tightly.

* * *

The hotel bar was not difficult to find – it was adjacent to the gym, in what had once been the library. The books were still there but locked behind glass doors. They were very old but looked immaculate, as though they had never been read. The room was panelled like the hall, with the same moulded plaster ceilings. The French windows led out onto the terrace, just above the rose garden and there was a portrait of a teenage Hugh Kirkwood over the fireplace. The eyes seemed to watch Marc's every move.

The bar was empty apart from a grey-haired man seated in a high-backed chair close to the stone fireplace. His raincoat was folded carefully on the chair beside him, a briefcase as big as a suitcase sat next to his feet like an obedient dog. He was so engrossed in The *Financial Times*, a tumbler of whisky by his side, he did not appear to realise he had company. All Marc could see was the top of his head.

Marc chose a table by the French windows – easy romantic getaway through to the terrace and as far from Mr *Financial Times* as possible. He glanced at his watch. Caitlin's aerobic class should have just finished. Just time enough to have a drink to help him forget what he was about to do. He slung his jacket over one of the chairs and approached the bar.

Jack appeared, as though by magic, and poured him a pint of Guinness with more froth than a Page 3 Girl's bubble bath.

"How did you know I wanted a Guinness?" asked Marc, aware that guilt was making him disagreeable.

"There isn't anything else," shrugged Jack. "It's Guinness or Babycham."

Marc thumbed back to the man by the fire. "That guy's got whisky."

"Mr de Havilland brought a number of cases from old Mr Kirkwood," replied Jack. "We keep them for him in our cellar."

"Mr de Havilland!"

"Yeah. Do you know him? Hey!" he called, as Marc picked up the Guinness and stalked across the bar. "You haven't paid for that drink!"

"Put it on my tab."

Jack looked as though he wanted to debate this further but the telephone ringing in reception sent him sprinting out the door.

Marc marched over to the grey-haired man and pulled down his newspaper. "Detective Superintendent de Havilland, I presume?"

"Granger, what a nice surprise."

"Checking up on me, *sir*?"

"Not at all. I often come here for a drink when I'm off duty. Hugh's father was an old friend of mine." Paul carefully folded his newspaper, placed it inside his briefcase and stood up. "If my presence disturbs you I shall be on my way."

Silently, Marc stood back to allow him to pass. Paul paused in front of him, appearing to study his face. Marc could see the slivers of blue in the man's steely-grey eyes. Like fragments of ice.

"I've never met an officer quite like you, Granger," said Paul at length. "Working with you should be an interesting experience."

Marc watched him leave, then sank into the armchair Paul had just vacated. Without realising what he was doing, he reached out for the remainder of Paul's whisky and downed it in one go. The alcohol caught the back of his throat, causing him to cough. An interesting experience? Detective Superintendent de Havilland was on another planet. An encounter with him was comparable to opening the freezer in a heatwave. Marc tried to remember if Paul had always behaved this way or if Amanda's death had sent him over the edge.

He was not aware of time passing but when Marc next glanced at his watch, he was astonished to find almost an hour had gone by since Caitlin's step class had finished. Even allowing for her to shower and tart herself up, Caitlin was late. Could it be . . . was he *actually* being stood up?

"Hey!" he called to Jack, who was sitting behind the bar, thoughtfully drinking Guinness and sketching Marc as a sour-faced Red Indian.

Jack looked about in exaggerated confusion before finally glaring at Marc. "Are you addressing me, perchance?"

"Yes. What's the time?"

"Time you had a watch." Jack returned to his drawing, emphasising Marc's broken nose, turning it into a mini Mount Rushmore.

"Jesus!" exclaimed Marc, storming out. "No wonder you have no guests!"

Jack laughed, finished his Guinness and, tucking his sketchbook under his arm, strolled back into reception. It was eerily quiet. He looked at his watch. Caitlin's class had finished ages ago. He'd seen the women troop through reception, some still in their leotards, resembling brightly coloured dragonflies.

He put his sketch pad down and wandered off down the corridor to put his head around the entrance to the aerobics studio. It was deserted. Opposite were the women's changing rooms. He hesitated, then rapped determinedly on the door and opened it. No one screamed. The place was empty – although the showers were still running at the far end. The room was full of steam.

"Caitlin! Are you there?"

The white stone tiles were wet and slippery as he walked through, stopping to check the changing cubicles on the left, tugging back the rose-coloured curtains to make certain they were empty. Then on, past the pink lockers, stacked like mini filing cabinets, and finally the sauna. That was empty too.

"Caitlin! It's me, Jack!" he called, approaching the showers.

Silence.

The steam dripped down his face. Irritably he

wiped it with his sleeve. Some cow must have left the shower going and flooded the whole floor. Wading through a pool of water, he entered the showers and fumbled along the cubicles, searching for the one with the water left running.

He found it and switched it off, thoroughly soaking himself in the process. His foot kicked against a discarded towel and he bent to pick it up, finding he was groping a body instead. Horrified, he dropped to his knees. It was a young woman, still in her swimming costume, curled up into a tight ball, her inky black hair moving against the tiles like seaweed.

"Caitlin!" His voice choked in his throat. He attempted to pick her up but she was dead weight and just slithered from his grasp, emitting a tiny moan.

"Christ, Caitlin! What's the matter with you? Are you drunk?"

Caitlin's head lolled against her shoulder. Jack grabbed her under her arms and began to drag her back out of the shower. Her foot caught under one of the cubicle panels and he had to lay her back on the floor to release it. It was as he bent towards the white tiles he noticed the dark stain leading from the shower to Caitlin's body and the crimson bubbles swirling around and down the plug-hole.

Blood.

"Oh my God! Somebody help me!"

Chapter Eleven

Caitlin opened her eyes and, instead of Heaven, saw rows of yellowing polystyrene ceiling tiles. She turned her head sideways. Silhouetted against the blue and turquoise stripy curtains hanging around her bed was a spindly metal tripod. It was about six feet tall and had a small, plastic bag hanging from it. Thick, gooey, purple-red liquid dripped hypnotically into a narrow tube, spiralling down into the back of her hand.

"Blood," she said.

The curtain swished back and a nurse materialised. "Good morning, Caitlin. How are you?"

Caitlin opened her mouth to reply and a thermometer was shoved into it. The nurse picked up her wrist and timed her pulse, checking it against the little silver watch pinned upside down on her chest. She then examined the bag hanging from the tripod.

"Hmm, this isn't going through very quickly, is it?" And she squeezed the bag.

"Ow!" Caitlin felt a sharp stabbing pain shoot up her arm and her eyes watered.

"I'm sorry. Did that hurt?"

Caitlin could not be bothered to reply.

The nurse flicked through her medical notes, tucked into a blue folder. "I see you are down for painkillers. Would you like some now?"

Like Smarties, thought Caitlin. A junkie's paradise. But why were they offering a pregnant woman drugs?

"Have I lost the baby?"

The nurse hesitated, like a rabbit caught in the headlamps of an oncoming car. "The consultant will be doing his rounds in a moment. You can discuss –"

"Have I lost my baby?"

"Well . . . um . . . yes, I'm afraid you have."

The room darkened. Caitlin felt as though she had just been pushed off a cliff. She was falling, falling . . . like Alice down the rabbit-hole. She closed her eyes. This was just a bad dream. She would wake up in a moment. Just a couple of seconds more. She would close her eyes and when she woke up she would be back in her GP's surgery, where he would be congratulating her on her pregnancy. She would drive home to Hugh, he would take her in his arms and tell her how much he loved her, how proud he was of her. The previous few weeks never happened.

Caitlin opened her eyes and reality hit. A NHS hospital bed in a dingy side ward, an excruciating pain centred in her lower belly, old bloodstains on the sheets and a needle taped to her bruised and swollen hand.

She had lost her husband and now she had lost her longed-for baby. Everyone she had loved, the family she had struggled so hard to achieve, was gone, wiped out in an instant. She wanted to rip out all these clear plastic tubes invading her body. Why prolong the agony? What was the point of continuing with this life when she had nothing left, when even hope had gone?

The nurse's mouth was rapidly opening and closing two inches from her face but she couldn't hear the words that were coming out, which seemed a bit pointless. Caitlin picked at the tape on her hand and ripped it off, pulling out the catheter inserted into her skin beneath, tearing it. Blood, still seeping down the plastic tube, suddenly spurted across the bedsheets.

"Great," muttered the nurse, and pressed the emergency buzzer beside the bed.

Caitlin turned her head towards the wall and closed her eyes, wishing she were dead.

* * *

The consultant discharged her from hospital a week later with a goody bag of pills and an appointment to see a psychiatric nurse. There was no reason why she should not carry another baby to full term, he had said. Her miscarriage had just been 'one of those things'.

Marina brought her home in her Jaguar but, despite churning out an 80,000-word novel every three months, could not think of anything to say in comfort. So the journey back to Calahurst was spent in silence, Marina squirming in misery that she was unable to say anything to help her friend, Caitlin staring through the window, her expression totally blank.

Marina, Jack and Fabian had decked reception in flowers and *Welcome Home Caitlin* banners, and had arranged a wonderful celebration dinner imported from the local Thai restaurant. But Caitlin just walked past everything without saying a word, straight upstairs to the room she had once shared with Hugh, closing the door quietly behind her and closing the heavy velvet curtains on the world outside.

She took a long time carefully arranging the little brown bottles of pills on her dressingtable. Picking up her appointment card to see the psychiatric nurse, she tore it into minute fragments and flushed it down the loo. Then she changed into her pyjamas, climbed into bed and stayed there.

* * *

April

"She just lies in bed and stares at the wall," sighed Jack. "I don't know what to do."

Marina sat opposite him, placing the large bouquet of red tulips she had bought for Caitlin on the dining-table between them. Jack hardly glanced at them. He had his head in his hands, the ebony dreadlocks falling over his face unable to disguise his pale, drawn features and the purple smudges beneath those beautiful jade eyes.

143

Marina struggled to find something to say. The jaunty spring flowers seemed inappropriate, incongruous even. Births, marriages and deaths, somehow there would always be flowers. She ought to put them in water; the bright green leaves were already starting to shrivel.

"Is Caitlin eating OK?" asked Marina. It was the best she could do.

Jack fiddled with the elegant silver cutlery set out before him. "I kept taking food up on a tray," he admitted eventually, "but the cleaners found it all underneath her bed and now they refuse to go in."

"Sack them."

Jack glared at her. "Which would leave the cleaning to me and Fabian! Don't you think we have enough to do?"

"I'll put you in touch with the agency I use. They're not so picky." Marina took a pack of salmon and cucumber sandwiches from a large leather satchel which doubled as her handbag. She unwrapped them carefully, removing every last piece of salmon from the clingfilm. "But promise me you will contact her doctor? Caitlin can't go on like this."

"*I* can't go on like this! And I *did* contact her doctor. Do you think I don't care about my sister? This old codger came all the way out here especially and she refused to see him. He was furious. I don't think he likes making house calls."

"He doesn't. He'd far rather spend his afternoons on the golf course. You should have asked for his partner. The young, sexy one." Marina noticed Jack hungrily eyeing her salmon sandwiches and offered him one. He wolfed it down, in a matter of seconds, including the cucumber slices.

"You don't mind me bringing my own food, do you?"

Jack patted his stomach. "Not at all. Feel free to bring as much as you like."

Before tipping out what was left of her lunch, Marina ran a finger over the plate in front of her. "This has dust on it!"

He shrugged. "It's been there for at least a fortnight."

Perhaps it was as well Caitlin had retired to her bed. Marina re-wrapped her sandwiches. "Jack, this is absolutely disgraceful. It's no way to run a hotel. The place will go bankrupt – that's if you're not closed down by the Health Inspector."

The green eyes flashed dangerously. "I know. So I thought I'd close it first."

"You can't do that! What will Caitlin say?"

"Nothing," snapped Jack, slamming his fist so hard against the table the crockery rattled. "Like she's said all week."

Marina stared at him. Jack the gentle giant? She had never seen him this way. "But it's imperative the hotel keeps going," she said compassionately. "Caitlin needs the money. Hugh left nothing but debts. This place means everything to her."

He didn't raise his eyes from his coffee cup. "Not enough to get her out of bed."

She tried again. "Caitlin's lost her husband and a

145

baby in less than a month *and* been arrested on suspicion of murder. She's about to have a complete breakdown. You have to give her time to get over it. Can't you run the hotel until she recovers?"

"That's a joke! What do I know about hotels?"

Marina, rather belatedly, attempted damage limitation. "You're doing a splendid job."

"Of course I am. I have no staff and no guests. How can I possibly fail?"

Fabian skidded breathlessly into the dining-room. "Mr O'Neill! Mr O'Neill!" He was still wearing his bright purple gym-kit from the morning's aerobics class.

Jack did not even glance in his direction. "Fabe, you and I will get along much better if you call me by my first name. I keep thinking my father's come back from the dead."

"We've got a guest, Jack! A real live guest!"

"A *guest*?" Jack stared at Marina in horror. "What should I do?"

Marina put her sandwiches back into her handbag. "Perhaps they're lost and have just stopped to ask for directions."

"With a complete set of Louis Vuittan luggage?" asked Fabian dryly.

Seeing Jack's complexion blanch completely, Marina patted him reassuringly on his elbow – she couldn't reach his shoulder. "Relax, don't panic."

"Panic?" He stood up so abruptly his chair was knocked sideways. "Of course I'm going to bloody panic!"

"This is not a problem. It's an opportunity."

"Well, here comes that opportunity right now," muttered Fabian from the corner of his mouth.

Marina had just enough time to pick up Jack's chair as an impossibly thin, terrifyingly glamorous woman glided into the dining-room. She was aged somewhere between forty and fifty, wore a floor-length mink and her shiny black hair was styled into a very elegant chignon. Her eyes were hidden by dark glasses, her lips and nails had been painted a glossy red.

That had better be a fake fur, thought Marina with distaste. A couple of Dalmatians and she would have been a dead ringer for Cruella de Vil.

"Without doubt," the woman said, in an icy, upper-class accent, "this is the worst hotel I have ever set eyes upon. How you expect to make a profit is totally beyond my comprehension."

Marina glanced anxiously at Jack, praying he was not about to say something rude in return. But Jack looked as though someone had just smacked him around the face with a large wet fish.

"Mother," he said, "it's you!"

She slowly removed the sunglasses. Her large brown eyes, heavily outlined in kohl, softened. "Of course it's me!"

"It's very nice to see you . . . er, what brings you all the way out here?"

His mother airily waved her heavily jewelled hand. "I was just passing . . ."

There was a glimmer of a smile across Jack's face. "To or from California?"

His mother frowned. "Don't be sarcastic, darling.

You sound just like your father. I was in London, visiting my friends, when I heard the terrible news." She paused and eyed him beadily. "It's a fine state of affairs to learn of family problems through the newspapers. And *The Sun* at that."

Marina could tell Jack was desperately trying to calculate his defence strategy and said quickly, "Let me take you to see Caitlin."

"That is why I'm here," said Jack's mother coolly.

"Mother," said Jack firmly, "I don't think Caitlin will see you. Remember the fiasco at the wedding?"

"Nonsense. That was five years ago. Of course she'll see me. I'm her mother."

"Mrs O'Neill . . ." began Marina.

"Lady Howard," muttered Jack helpfully.

"Actually I'm now the Marchesa del Lisle de Monterez," corrected his mother. "You're a husband out." She turned to Marina and smiled. "But you may call me Elena."

Jack paled. "You *married* that phoney Spaniard?"

"He's worth five hundred million."

"Sure he is."

"I've seen his portfolio."

"I'm glad to hear it."

"Elena," Marina began again, "Caitlin is not herself at the moment. She refuses to see anyone."

"Hardly surprising when you read the rubbish that's been written about her in the newspapers!"

"There's a bit more to it than that." Marina glanced helplessly at Jack.

"Caitlin was pregnant," he admitted reluctantly. "She lost the baby. Now she's having some kind of breakdown. All she does is stare at the wall. She refuses to eat –" His voice broke. "I don't know what to do . . ."

Elena gently patted his shoulder. "I'm here now, darling. Just show me the way to her room."

But it was Marina who led Elena back out into the hall and up the main staircase as Jack, relieved someone else had shouldered the burden, headed off towards the bar.

Caitlin's bedroom was in complete darkness. The heavy velvet curtains and green decor conspired to block out all light. As Marina hovered nervously on the threshold, Elena strode through the twilight zone and dragged back the curtains. Caitlin, a lump under the green velvet counterpane, did not move or even make a sound.

Elena pulled back the quilt. "Darling? Are you awake?"

Caitlin did not reply. By bending down Elena could ascertain that her eyes were wide open. As the sunlight fell on Caitlin's face, Elena was shocked at the transformation of the daughter she had last seen five years ago. Her pale, Celtic skin was sallow, her cheeks now sunken and dark smudged circles were under her eyes. Her glossy, black hair was lank and matted.

How the hell had Caitlin allowed things to slide this far? If she wanted help, all she had to do was ask! Elena would have been there like a shot – interfering again . . . she admitted honestly. She tried so hard to have a conventional relationship with her daughter yet somehow always antagonised her even more.

Caitlin had definitely been Daddy's girl, having more in common with her hapless, feckless, ultimately *useless* father than just his Irish colouring. But Patrick was long since dead. Elena shivered. It seemed to be the curse of the O'Neills that they always fell victim to tragedies of their own creation.

Elena smoothed a greasy lock from Caitlin's forehead. "Oh my poor, poor darling . . ."

Caitlin turned her head, confused. "Mother?"

Elena struggled to get a grip. "When did you last eat, darling?" The words came out rather more bossily that she had intended. Here we go again, she thought resignedly. Let battle commence.

But Caitlin merely closed her eyes. "I don't know . . . what day is it?"

"I'll get something sent up." Marina scurried away, obviously pleased to be useful.

"Would you like a glass of water?" asked Elena. *Come on, Caitlin, say something!* Tell me to get lost. Tell me you never want to see me again. Tell me what an interfering old hag I am! *Please,* Caitlin . . .

There was no reply. Elena went to the bathroom anyway and filled a tooth-mug from the sink. En route back to her daughter she passed the dressingtable, stacked high with assorted bottles of drugs and paused to read some of the labels. No wonder Caitlin didn't know what day it was. It was amazing that she even responded to her own name. Wretched doctors. They offered a lifeboat, then cut it adrift and let you get on with it.

Elena dropped the tablets down the toilet, threw in a pack of razor blades as an afterthought (one could never be *too* careful) and flushed the chain. The razors, because they were in a plastic container, floated determinedly to the surface; the tablets got stuck somewhere in the U-bend. Elena put the lid down on the rapidly overflowing bowl and returned to the bed. Caitlin had not moved.

"Come along, darling," she said, in the same voice she had used when her daughter had been a child. "Sit up and drink this water. You don't want to become dehydrated."

Caitlin obediently rolled onto her back and struggled up. She was wearing a pair of red satin pyjamas with teddy bears pirouetting across her chest. The teddy bears looked distinctly grubby.

Elena wrinkled her nose. "Why don't you have a nice bath before lunch?"

Caitlin regarded her mother over her glass. "Are you attempting to organise my life again?"

Eureka! Welcome back, Caitlin!

Elena struggled to hide a triumphant grin. "Someone has to." She went to run the bath water, emptying a dusty bottle of Safari bubble bath into it. When she returned, Caitlin had finished her drink. Elena retrieved the glass before it rolled off onto the floorboards and helped Caitlin out of bed and into the bathroom, disdainfully dropping her pyjamas into the bin instead of the laundry basket. Caitlin clambered into the scented bubbles without a word.

Relieved, Elena left her to it and moved back into the bedroom, tidying it up as she went. It was lucky her fifth husband couldn't see her now, she thought ruefully. He had kicked up such a stink about paying all that alimony when she insisted that she couldn't survive without a maid, a butler, a chauffeur, a gardener, a chef . . . Elena began to laugh.

Marina was pushing the door open with her bottom and manoeuvring a tray through into the bedroom. On the tray was a plate of rather squashed salmon and cucumber sandwiches, a crumpled linen napkin and a glass vase with a bowed red tulip stuck into it.

Deciding to be helpful, Elena took the tray from her. "Don't you have any other staff?"

"Two cleaners and a caretaker," replied Marina frostily. "I'm not 'staff'. I'm Caitlin's friend. My name is Marina Theodopoulou."

"I remember. You attended the wedding." Elena glanced disparagingly at the tray. "So who made the sandwiches? The caretaker?"

"Tesco," snapped Marina, indignant that Elena did not appreciate the sacrifice she was making in giving Caitlin her own lunch, even if it had been around. "They just got a bit squashed in my bag."

Elena rested the tray on the dressingtable, hiding the little rings in the dust where Caitlin's tranquillisers had sat. "This is no way to run a hotel."

"I'm not running it. In the absence of Caitlin, Jack is managing the hotel. If you wish to speak with him, he is in the bar – er, stocktaking. I am going home."

Elena was unused to being spoken to in such a manner, even by her ex-husbands. So, the little Greek pudding had tenacity – and loyalty too. Elena knew exactly what Jack was up to in the bar. He was his father's son after all.

"Thank you for all your help, Miss Theodopou . . . lopu . . . opu . . ."

Marina cut her short. "No problem."

"Tell me, Miss Theo . . . er, Marina. Does Calahurst possess a hairdressing or beauty salon?"

Marina was taken aback. "Well, there's Kayleigh's in the High Street but I think Nirvana on the quayside would be more 'you'." She appeared to be struggling not to say something.

"You wonder how I can think of my hair at a time like this?" smiled Elena. "It's for Caitlin. It will be a nice treat and will hopefully take her mind off this unpleasant business."

"You think a makeover is going to help Caitlin forget her miscarriage? You're crazy! She's on the edge of a nervous breakdown. Have you seen the array of pill bottles the doctor prescribed? It was a virtual drug-store of uppers, downers, tranquillisers and sleeping pills. Caitlin needs a shrink not a hairdresser."

"Have you suggested she visits a psychiatrist?"

Marina sat miserably on the window seat. "Yes. Caitlin does not have a very high opinion of them. She

153

had an appointment to see a psychiatric nurse but didn't go. The nurse phones here every couple of days. It's embarrassing but I can't *make* Caitlin attend. It's up to her to decide whether she wants treatment. I found her the name of a counsellor specialising in miscarriages but Caitlin would not see her either. She just lies in bed and stares at the wall. The hotel once meant so much to her. Now she doesn't give a damn."

"So a visit to the hairdresser would not really do any harm?"

"I suppose not . . ."

"If you're feeling down, don't you find a visit to the hairdresser cheers you up? If your make-up takes ten years off you, you're wearing a sexy black dress and you have a dinner date with a handsome young man, doesn't it make you feel terrific?"

Marina smiled reluctantly. "I get the same effect from a box of Belgian chocolates." She sighed. "Would you like me to book you an appointment at Nirvana?"

"Yes, please. Tell them I would like their top stylist. I don't care how much it costs."

"Nirvana is owned by Raj Patel, an old friend of Hugh's. Caitlin could probably get a discount."

"And over-familiarity and sloppy service too, no doubt. Book the appointment in my name – the Marchesa del Lisle de Monterez. I find that usually does the trick."

"Er, yes, of course." Marina paused. "Um . . . how do you spell that?"

Chapter Twelve

To Caitlin, it felt as though she was slowly emerging from fog. Waking up from a dream in which she had no responsibility for her actions. She was surprised to find herself at Nirvana for she had no recollection of ever travelling there. What day was it? What was her mother doing here? And why was the pale, little face staring back from the mirror not her own?

She leant forward and examined her reflection, as all around her smiled delightedly. It *was* her – yet she looked completely different. The hairdresser had drastically hacked six inches off her hair, leaving her with a shoulder-length bob, parted down the middle, swept behind her ears revealing her fine Irish bone structure, with a front section sliding sexily over one eye. Somehow she seemed to have lost about three stone, her spots had cleared up and, while by no stretch of the imagination did she have a perfect complexion, someone had done a very good repair job with tinted foundation and heavy-duty concealer stick.

She appeared to have had a manicure too. A complete set of false, blood-red nails were now stuck over her own short, stubby ones. Caitlin wiggled her fingers experimentally, feeling like Morticia Addams. She wondered how long it would take them to drop off. Scratching simply wouldn't be the same.

As they drove back to Kirkwood Manor from Nirvana, Elena said, "I'll arrange for some clothes to be sent from London for you. There's this wonderful new designer I'm encouraging – he's become quite a protégé of mine."

"I've a wardrobe full of clothes," muttered Caitlin, watching Calahurst flash past in a blur of red brick and grey cobblestones. *In every size from ten to sixteen.*

"Not the *right* clothes, darling." Elena bit her lip. "Why don't you come back to California with me. Lovely weather – but unfortunately no men."

My mother is running my life again, thought Caitlin despairingly. And I'm practically twenty-five. She knew Elena had a huge guilt complex about the endless procession of stepfathers, in her search for a financially secure family environment. To Elena, eternal happiness came in the shape of a gold wedding band and an account at Fortnum & Mason's. Caitlin sighed. Her mother meant well but, if she didn't watch out, she would find herself married to some chinless stockbroker, living in the green-wellie belt of the home sweet Home Counties.

But what other choices were there? Running a crumbling hotel, which was fast gaining a more dubious reputation than the Bates Motel, or back to the chorus line? A haggard twenty-something, competing against gorgeous teenage nymphettes, fresh out of stage school.

Her fingers stole around to smooth her rounded belly. It felt just the same but there was no spark of life there now. She shut her eyes. She could not even bear to think what might have been. Her feelings were far too raw. Far better to try and forget she had ever been pregnant. *I loved you so much, yet I never even had a chance to meet you.* She dropped her hands into her lap.

"Sorry?" said her mother. "Did you say something?"

"No, nothing." She began to chew on her thumbnail, a habit her mother hoped she had grown out of, distractedly peeling away a long strip of red varnish. It was quite therapeutic.

The car swung into the driveway of Kirkwood Manor. Caitlin began to wonder if the place was cursed. Her life was like a game of Snakes and Ladders. Whatever happened, she always ended back here. If she was superstitious she might start thinking the house had some hold upon her.

I think I'd just shoot myself, she thought miserably. If it wouldn't mean the waste of a perfectly good bullet.

The car swung around the fountain and parked up against the front door, sending a spray of shingle across the steps and into the hall. I'll have to sweep that up later, she realised, climbing lethargically out of the car. When she had first seen this house, over five years ago, she had so longed to be 'Lady of the Manor'. What a ridiculous juvenile dream. Hugh had been so handsome, just like one of Marina's romantic heroes; Caitlin had truly believed she'd won Prince Charming. The reality was King Rat.

"Oh, what beautiful flowers," gasped Elena, from somewhere inside the dark, gloomy hallway. "Come and look, Caitlin. I think you have an Admirer."

Caitlin trudged wearily up the steps. Why did her mother have to be so enthusiastic about everything? It was like living with Vic Reeves.

Elena stood by the reception desk, tearing into a little florist's envelope. Beside her was an enormous bouquet of pink and white roses. "Raj Patel," she said at length, a tiny frown marring her otherwise perfect complexion. "Who's he?"

"He owns Nirvana," replied Caitlin, ignoring the flowers and retreating into the manager's office, ostensibly to make herself a cup of coffee, "and the nightclub on the quayside."

"An Admirer with a steady income," said Elena approvingly.

"Can somebody move these flowers?" growled Jack, "They're dripping all over my sketchpad."

"What shall I do with your roses, Caitlin?" asked Elena.

"Stick them in the bin for all I care," sighed Caitlin, feeling the tears well up in her eyes. She blinked them away. How many years since a man had bought her flowers? For one glorious moment she had thought they were from Marc.

Forget him, she told herself firmly. And peeled away another lengthy sliver of nail varnish.

"I'll put them in her room," confided Elena to Jack. "For when she's cheered up."

"I think this is as cheered up as it gets." Jack watched his sister pull a clump of paper tissues from the box on the manager's desk and bury her face in them. "What shall I do with him?"

"Him who?"

"Raj Patel. He's waiting for Caitlin in the bar."

Elena followed Jack's gaze. Caitlin had up-ended the tissue box on the desk and was frantically scrabbling around the drawers for a fresh supply.

"Perhaps you had better ask him to leave," she replied. "This does not seem to be a good time."

"Why me?" protested Jack.

"Because you're the man."

"The sexual revolution has completely passed you by."

"I'm your mother. Do as you're told."

Caitlin emerged from the office, pink-eyed and red-nosed. "Oh, stop bickering. It goes right through my head. And stop talking about me as though I wasn't capable of making the smallest decision for myself. I've had a breakdown, not a lobotomy. My brain still functions. *I'm still here!*"

She tore the top sheet off Jack's sketch pad and noisily blew her nose. "*I'll* go and talk to Raj, and if *I* want to chuck him out I shall." And she stalked off in the direction of the library.

Jack looked at his mother, worried that she, too, was about to burst into tears.

By supreme control, Elena blinked back the tears hovering on her feathery false eyelashes. "You'd think Caitlin would be pleased that a nice man was showing some interest in her and sending her flowers. A nice *rich* man too."

"Ah," grinned Jack, "so she hasn't told you about her crush on Stewart Granger?"

"What *are* you talking about?" Elena regarded him irritably. "Stewart Granger's been dead for *years*."

* * *

Raj Patel was standing by one of the French windows, admiring the view across the rose gardens, though the shrubs were little more than thorned stalks. He turned as Caitlin approached, his matinee-idol grin and capped teeth outshining his heavy jewellery. He looked as though he had just stepped out of an ancient Hollywood movie. Valentino, eat your heart out, thought Caitlin.

Raj, with his love of thick gold neck-chains and ID bracelets had always held a squirming fascination for Caitlin. Too young to remember the seventies, she was unused to seeing men wearing such loud jewellery, although Raj, with his regal exotic looks, could get away with it. It was easy to see why the women of Calahurst found him so attractive. He had a good body, black eyes and a narrow, hooked nose and, although she hated herself for it, Caitlin always wondered what he was like in bed.

"Thank you for the flowers, Raj," she said begrudgingly.

He beamed, taking hold of her hands in his. "You're welcome, Mrs Kirkwood. How well you are looking! That hairstyle really suits you."

Caitlin smiled tightly, hopeless at accepting compliments. Besides, she knew Raj of old. He was a vulture. He was only being nice because he wanted something. And if he didn't want her, it must be her hotel.

"I did not realise the Marchesa was your mother. Do you have a courtesy title?"

"No. My father was plain Mr O'Neill. My mother always made a point of trading up. From impoverished Irish artist to wealthy Spanish aristocrat in seven easy steps." She realised she sounded hysterical, and not at all loyal to her long-suffering mother, and lapsed into embarrassed silence, wishing he would just go away and leave her alone.

Raj seemed to read her mind. "Forgive my intrusion. I realise now you are still . . . er, unwell."

"Not that unwell."

"You should take a holiday, Caitlin. A nice rest in one of those wonderful spa towns that are to be found in this beautiful country. I can recommend a fabulous health resort in Staffordshire. My sister stayed there last year; she came back a completely new woman."

He was a devious devil, she had to give him that.

"Are you suggesting that running this hotel is too much for me?"

"Not at all. Let us say you have had more pressures and stresses in these last few weeks than most people face in a lifetime."

"True. And?"

Under Caitlin's direct headlamp gaze, Raj began to appear uncomfortable. She had the idea that, despite his many years in this country, he was still not used to the English direct manner of speaking. And she *was* being unpardonably rude.

"I would like to make you an offer," he admitted at last.

"Oh yes?" She bit back the sarcastic comment hovering on her lips.

He frowned. "For the house. I wish to buy it."

"'It' is a hotel and 'it' is not for sale."

"Why not? I will pay more than it is worth."

"It's worth quite a lot."

"How much?"

She smiled at his exasperation. "More than you could afford."

"How would you know if you will not let me bid?"

Caitlin stared out of the window. Until now she had thought of nothing but the baby. She felt guilty that she could care about anything else – and an inanimate object at that. But if the hotel went, what would she have left?

"You have no guests," Raj goaded. "No money. How do you expect to survive?"

It was like being back at the hospital. *'This blood isn't going through very quickly, is it?'* Squeeze, squeeze.

Caitlin dug her new fingernails into the palm of her hands to prevent herself raking them down Raj's perfectly smooth cheek. "I'll manage."

"Who would want to spend a holiday in a house with such a gruesome past?"

"What is so gruesome about it?" retorted Caitlin, feeling one of her fingernails snap off and flutter to the floor. It gleamed against the brown carpet like a solitary drop of blood.

"Your husband and his mistress being burnt alive is pretty ghastly."

She noticed how he emphasised 'mistress', almost licking his lips around the word. "They did not burn alive!" She choked back a sob. "They were killed by falling masonry. And I consider it very tactless of you to bring the subject up. In fact, I find you very tactless altogether. So why don't you just leave my hotel or I'll throw you out!"

"You?" He regarded her disparagingly. "*You* could not throw me out." He gazed around at the library, at the dust, at the cobwebs. "And you have no staff, no husband. No one to look after your interests."

"And what, pray, am I?" asked Jack from behind the bar. "A hologram?" He unfolded himself from his barstool to give Raj the benefit of his lanky six-foot-three-inch frame and two-foot dreadlocks.

Raj appeared unruffled. "Family loyalty. I admire that."

"Oh yes," said Jack. "We're a really *close* family."

Raj picked up his overcoat and briefcase from a nearby chair and handed a glossy white folder to Caitlin. "Read this at your leisure," he said smoothly. "And call me."

After he had left, Caitlin collapsed onto a bar stool, her legs shaking too badly to hold her up. She looked longingly up at the bottles arrayed against the wall but knew they were only there for show. The only alcohol left on the premises was her late father-in-law's vintage hoard in the cellars. And if she started drinking that, she might not be able to stop.

Jack clumsily put an arm around her shoulder. "Are you all right?"

"I'm fine," she lied – not terribly successfully.

"What did he want?"

"To buy the hotel."

"Brilliant! How much?"

"I don't know." Caitlin gazed down at the folder. "I suppose this is a proposal."

Jack snatched it out of her hand and opened it. On top was a letter with Raj's company logo, a little oak tree, and written beneath, *Greenwood Development*. Jack gave it a cursory glance and let it slip unchecked to the floor. Next was a shiny hotel brochure which he tossed aside. Then he came upon a list of figures.

"Wow!" he said, his eyes glittering. "Guess how much he's willing to pay for this dump?"

"I haven't the slightest idea." The brochure Jack had dropped caught Caitlin's eye. She bent and picked it up. The photo on the cover was of an old house, not dissimilar to Kirkwood Manor – mock redbrick Jacobean but in reality Victorian. She turned over to the first page. This must be the health spa that Raj had recommended.

"Three point five million," sighed Jack. "Oh Caitlin, I could come just thinking about it. Three point five million. We're going to be so *rich*."

Caitlin smiled at his naïveté. "The park and farmland alone is worth ten times that with planning permission."

"This is the King's Forest," pointed out Jack. "William the Conqueror's personal hunting ground. No way could you get planning permission. Even if it wasn't for all of those damn trees, you're likely to be sitting on the site of some medieval castle."

"If the council can authorise themselves to construct a distributor road through the Forest, I can build a housing estate."

But Jack was not paying attention. "Sell up. Cut loose. It's not as though it's your family seat you're selling. You have no ties."

"I love this house."

"You can't love a house. It's only bricks and cement. You're not Scarlett O'Hara for Christ's sake! Let's have a little realism, please. Did Raj leave a contact number?"

Caitlin looked her brother straight in the eyes. "Let's get one thing straight. I am not selling this house. This is my home. Don't you realise we've never had a home? We spent our entire childhood in hotel suites and other people's guest bedrooms. Don't you ever feel that you want to settle down?"

Jack shuddered. "Settling down means being responsible."

Caitlin slowly gathered up the paperwork Raj had left and arranged it into a neat little pile. "I'll never understand you."

"And I'll never understand you. You can buy a dozen homes with the money this Patel guy is offering. A home of your own, not your late husband's."

"I'm not going to turn Kirkwood Manor over to Raj Patel so that he can turn it into another wretched nightclub."

"A nightclub?" Jack stared down at the proposal. "*'The Pleasure Dome' – Exclusive nightclub, casino and themed restaurant'*. Does Calahurst, retirement capital of the world, really need another nightclub? Most of the residents have one foot in the grave."

"With the new road, the yobs from Norchester will be able to reach Calahurst in under fifteen minutes. He does a roaring trade at Last Days already." She carefully slid the literature back into its shiny folder. "Just because Raj says he is transforming the hotel into a nightclub does not mean he will. That's the way he operates. Nothing is straightforward. I bet if I were to sell up to him, he'd raze this house down to the ground within the fortnight and jam in a couple of hundred houses."

"But it's a listed building."

"No doubt the house would turn out to be structurally unsafe and have to be knocked down. There

are ways around rules and regulations in the building
and redevelopment business, Jack. Don't be so naïve."

"Why not take the money and run? Who cares?"

"I care. I have a plan of my own." She handed Jack
the brochure advertising the health farm. "How about
Kirkwood Manor – no, Mistletoe House Health Spa?"

"A health spa?" He laughed. "What the hell do *you*
know about health spas?"

"Nothing – but I know an awful lot about the leisure
industry. The hotel already has a thriving leisure
membership, which has stuck with us through thick
and thin. All I need to do is expand the beauty side and
hire a couple of hairdressers."

"Simple! And how many beauticians and hairdressers
do you know?"

"I'm going to pinch Raj's head beautician from
Nirvana. Poetic revenge."

Jack smiled. "I think you mean poetic justice."

"Whatever."

"What makes you think the girl will want to bury
herself in this dump?"

"Because I'm going to pay her lots of money."

"And where are you going to get the money from?
You're broke, remember?"

Elena poked her head around the door. "Oh, has
that nice man gone? I hope you thanked him for his
flowers, darling."

"Mother," said Caitlin, smiling sweetly, "could I
possibly borrow some money?"

"Of course, darling." Elena took her cheque book

from her handbag. "How much would you like? A couple of hundred?"

"I suppose a million would do to start with."

Elena did not bat an eyelid. "I'll call the bank in the morning."

Jack was outraged. "You're not actually going to lend her the money?"

"Why not?" hissed Elena. "If it makes her happy? She's my daughter."

"And I'm your son," he retorted, unimpressed. "So, what do I get? A Lear jet?"

* * *

June

"Mr de Havilland would like to see you in his office."

Marc groaned and, tugging off the earphones he was wearing, looked up at the blonde WDC loitering next to his desk.

"Right away," she added, with a discernible smirk.

"Oh goody," said Marc.

"Have you been a bad boy?"

"You wish." Marc pushed aside the interview tapes he had been wading through and stood up, his chair scraping the wooden floorboards. The CID general office did not run to carpet.

DI Reynolds, in discussion with DCI Hunter, looked meaningfully at his watch. "Lunch already, Granger?"

"No, I'm off to take a piss. Would you like to come too?"

DI Reynolds stepped furiously forwards but DCI Hunter forestalled him. Marc scowled. He didn't need Seb to protect him.

The CID general office was on the ground floor of Calahurst Police Station. All senior staff had their offices on the first floor. The class system was rife in the police force. Detective Superintendent de Havilland's office was smaller than the station Superintendent's but it was more tastefully furnished. It had a dark-blue carpet, lots of grey filing cabinets, some comfortable squashy blue chairs and a beautiful old oak desk which had once belonged to the Chief Constable.

On the desk was an exotic-looking plant and a spanking new computer hidden under an immaculate white cover. So far Detective Superintendent de Havilland had managed to avoid being sent on any IT courses.

As Marc walked in, Paul was seated at his desk, flipping through a sheaf of expense claims, scrawling his signature on each one with a cheap constabulary biro. Marc couldn't help a smile. Both DCI Hunter and DI Reynolds used fancy, gold-plated pens – the sort that write upside down at fifty thousand feet.

"I don't know why you're looking so cheerful," said Paul, authenticating his signatures with a worn ink-stamp. "Boy George would make a more effective undercover officer than you."

"Thank you, sir." Marc turned to leave.

"I do not remember dismissing you." Paul looked up, his grey eyes frostier than usual. "How did you make

Sergeant, Granger? It cannot have been your bedside manner."

"No, sir."

"You appear to have upset Seb Hunter too and he gets on with everyone."

"Yes, sir."

"For God's sake, Granger, you were once almost my son-in-law. Cut the crap and tell me what's really going on in that head of yours."

Marc looked blank.

"That busy?" Paul actually smiled. "Honestly, Marc, do you want to stay a Sergeant all your life? That prat Clive Reynolds made Inspector over a year ago and he joined the same time as you. I don't understand it. Don't you like being a police officer?"

"Twenty years and counting, sir."

"Until retirement? You will have earned every penny of that pension. I could make it easier and fire you."

Marc smiled wryly. "Thank you, sir."

Paul pulled open the top drawer of his desk and took out a thick, white envelope. His name and address were neatly inscribed on the front in calligraphic writing. He looked at it thoughtfully, then passed it across to Marc.

"I've been invited to a party, Granger, and I want you to go in my place."

Marc opened the envelope. Inside was a small white card with an unfamiliar silver crest. Underneath was a drawing of Kirkwood Manor.

"The Grand Opening of Mistletoe House Health Spa," he read out loud. *"Saturday 16th June."*

"The event of the year," said Paul sarcastically. "Clever idea to change the name though. Mrs Kirkwood has dug the Princess Victoria of Clarence out of mothballs and the villagers are squabbling amongst themselves for an invitation. Apparently there will be live music, dancing, rivers of champagne, a cabaret and probably a bloody circus too. Detective Chief Superintendent Nicholson is tearing out what little hair he has left over the security arrangements for the Princess and I've arranged a weekend break for myself in Paris."

Marc looked down at the invitation.

"Yes, you do have to go," said Paul. "I would be very interested to know where Mrs Kirkwood found the money to carry out a complete refit of her hotel."

"I believe her mother is married to an American millionaire with a dubious Spanish title."

"How fortunate."

"I thought we were winding down the scale of the murder investigation due to lack of funding?" said Marc pointedly.

"We have one last shot before the inquiry folds due to lack of interest. And, while I would hate you to feel under any kind of pressure to bring in a result, the whole case depends on you."

Marc regarded his boss with beady dislike. "Does DCI Hunter know what you have planned?"

Paul smiled faintly. "No. I shall tell him you are doing a little job for me."

"Teacher's pet," muttered Marc.

"Look at it this way. It gets you out of the office."

Chapter Thirteen

There were so many cars parked outside Kirkwood
Manor, the night of Caitlin's Launch Party, that Marc
had to abandon his Mondeo in Mistletoe Lane and
stumble up the drive in the dark. As he rounded the
final bend, he was almost flattened by the Marquis of
Pennington's Aston Martin, wantonly spraying shingle
across the grass like bullets from a machine gun, as it
belted back towards Calahurst.

The Marquis was closely followed by two unmarked
police cars – a third had driven in front. Idly Marc
wondered which of his Special Branch colleagues was
on protection duty tonight and wished it had could
have been him. Anything was preferable to this idiotic
subterfuge.

From the outside, Kirkwood Manor, or Mistletoe
House as it had been renamed, looked much the same.
And, even from the inside, it was hard to spot exactly
where the Marchesa's £800,000 had been spent. The bar

still resembled a gentleman's club, the dining-room a works canteen and reception a Victorian psychiatric hospital.

Marc followed the music into the garden, pausing only to knock back a couple of whiskies in the bar. As he had only cleaned his teeth fifteen minutes before, in anticipation of corrupting Mrs Kirkwood, the alcohol tasted disgusting. Grimacing, he stepped through the French windows onto the terrace, then caught his breath. There, sitting with her back to him on the balustrade of the terrace, was his prey, chatting happily with her friend, romance novelist Marina Grey.

Marc slunk down the side steps and into the shrubbery before he was seen. He needed time to formulate a plan of attack. He ducked past the crowd on the dance-floor, behind the stage where some dreadful reggae band were murdering the Beach Boys' 'Surfin' Safari', and emerged by the path to the tennis courts. As a sexy little waitress flounced past, he appropriated a glass of champagne and drank it back so fast that the bubbles exploded up his nose.

He noticed Caitlin had cut her hair and lost a substantial amount of weight, revealing a heart-shaped face and cheekbones on which you could skate. Her dress was obviously couture – full-length silver-grey satin, with embroidered georgette side panels and shoestring straps. Low cut at the front and back, tight around the bodice and hips, it swirled out into mini-pleats and plunged towards the garden like a shaft of moonlight.

She was gazing wistfully at the couples shuffling

around to the music. He decided she must want to dance. It was such an enchanted evening, what woman wouldn't? As he turned to discard his fluted glass in the privet hedge, he was shocked to realise he was looking forward to seducing the beautiful Mrs Kirkwood.

And hated himself for it.

* * *

Caitlin sipped her champagne and felt the warm glow invade her body. "This is the best party I've ever been to," she sighed, "and it's mine."

Marina, who had been at the pina coladas, agreed as together they watched the pink and orange sunset. They were seated on the balustrade that edged the terrace, their ballgowns inelegantly hitched up to their knees, their feet dangling over the herbaceous border. Caitlin had lost her shoes somewhere in the blue haze of the ceanothus but had not appeared to notice.

Between them was a large bottle of lukewarm champagne and a half-empty bowl of peanuts. Marina was eating the peanuts, Caitlin was flicking them at Annelise Fitzpatrick, who was flirting outrageously with Jack. Considering Annelise was an easy target in a stupid pink and white crinoline, like a giant inside-out mushroom, Caitlin's aim was deplorable. She had hit Jack twice and Marina once and the nearest she had got to Annelise was a direct hit into her fluted champagne glass. No mean achievement – if she had actually been aiming at it.

Caitlin gave up. "So, Marina, who have you got off with tonight?"

"Only Fabian. I don't suppose he counts?"

"Not your *own* boyfriend, no."

"What about you?" Marina swirled the depths of her drink with a cocktail stick, stabbed a cherry and popped it into her mouth.

"William Fitzpatrick French-kissed me in the conservatory."

"He doesn't count either," said Marina. "He's an MP. They're all up for it."

Caitlin poured herself out another drink and topped up Marina's pina colada, drowning the miniature floral arrangement.

Marina fished it out and dropped it into the ceanothus bush before Caitlin could use it as an offensive weapon. "Lovely champers," she sighed, picking up the bottle and reading the label. "Vintage Krug? But that must have cost you a fortune!"

"Not a penny. We're drinking the contents of Hugh's precious wine cellar – all 30,000 bottles."

Marina giggled. "At least you're not likely to run out." She took another swig. "Oh look," she said. "There's a man over there, waving to you."

"Really?" Caitlin perked up. "Where?"

"Over there, on the other side of the dance-floor, next to the stage."

"Good grief," exclaimed Caitlin, almost toppling off the wall. "It's Marc Granger!"

"Who's he?"

"I met him at Hugh's birthday party."

"Did you?" sighed Marina enviously. "He's very good-looking. How did I miss him?"

"You were having far more fun with a blond."

"He's waving again!" Marina nudged her. "Wave back! He's gorgeous!"

Caitlin raised her hand, paused, then frowned. "Come to think of it, I don't remember inviting him. We had a date, the day of my – accident – and I never heard from him again."

"Perhaps he thought he had been stood up?"

"He never phoned."

"So you dented his pride. This is no time to play hard to get." Marina, growing irritated with her friend, waved to Marc.

"Marina!" Caitlin slapped her hand down.

"Well, someone has to take the initiative." Marina watched in satisfaction as Marc waved back and headed their way. She struggled, inelegantly, to swing her legs back over the balustrade and onto the terrace. Her scarlet dress, shimmering with sequins, was moulded closely to her body, making it almost impossible to move.

"Don't do anything I wouldn't do!" she beamed and, taking her drink with the bowl of peanuts balanced on top, trotted off across the terrace towards the garden. As she passed Marc on the steps, she surreptitiously give him the thumbs up.

Caitlin, cringing with embarrassment, debated jumping into the ceanothus.

"Hello," said Marc smoothly. He leant against the lichen-stained balustrade.

"Hello," said Caitlin, staring at her feet, aware of a huge crimson blush spreading over her entire body. She suddenly realised she had lost her new shoes and peered down into the herbaceous border.

"Cinderella Rockerfella?"

Caitlin looked up blankly. "Sorry?"

"Never mind," he smiled. "That's a beautiful dress. You look as though you've fallen out of a fairytale yourself."

"Thank you. It was a present from my mother."

"The Marchesa del Lisle de something or other?"

"Yes," Caitlin smiled ruefully. "She appears to have moved in."

"And your brother Jack, the out-of-work artist?"

"News travels fast." Caitlin poured herself another drink.

He gazed out at the dance-floor set up in the middle of the lawn. "You do know how to hold a party. Where's the Princess?"

Which was the one question everyone seemed to be asking her tonight. Is that the only reason he came?

"She came; she cut the ribbon; she left," Caitlin replied wearily. "Princess Victoria is very nice but I think the Palace views me as an embarrassment. It was kind of her to turn up when you think of all the bad publicity I've had. I think it's only because her husband was an old friend of Hugh's. They were at school together."

He shifted his weight from one foot to the other. "Would you like to dance?"

Caitlin hesitated. The band, friends of Jack's, named The Surfaris, were now playing a reggae version of 'Surfin' USA', a song not really conducive to romance – or dancing for that matter. Perhaps they did requests. As she watched the band she suddenly noticed Fabian on stage with a microphone in one hand and a can of beer in the other. He appeared to be providing backing vocals.

Marc followed her gaze. "He's good, isn't he? You used to be a singer too, didn't you? In the West End."

Caitlin stared at him in astonishment. What was he, a detective or something? Although if he had gone to all the trouble of finding out . . . "Not quite," she admitted. "Yes, I appeared in several West End shows – however, the chorus was the pinnacle of my success."

"If you don't want to dance, how about that romantic walk you keep promising me?" He grinned. "You could show me your boathouse . . ."

Caitlin gazed at the dying embers of the sunset. The boathouse was off the beaten track. It was growing a bit too dark for a jaunt in the woods. They always became spooky after dark. The villagers were convinced the forest was haunted by the ghosts of the cavaliers slaughtered in the Civil War.

Idly she watched Annelise making eyes at Marc over Jack's shoulder and had a sudden desire to do mischief. "OK," she said and slid her legs back over the balustrade. Marc lifted her down. Thank God she had lost some weight. She would hate to put his back out.

Marc led her down the steps and into the garden, pausing only to extract her shoes from the herbaceous border. Embarrassed, Caitlin quickly thrust her grubby feet inside, leaning on him for support. As they walked around the dance-floor in the middle of the lawn, she realised he was still holding her hand. She didn't remove it, hoping he was not one of those awful tactile people that would even hold hands with Jack the Ripper.

She took Marc the long way round, past the rose garden, the exotic scent of the overblown blooms trailing them into the woods. As they walked through the whispering birch trees, the path became overgrown, the brambles catching against her gown, until they had to walk single file. As they came out of the woods, onto the edge of the river, Caitlin pointed to a dark mass looming next to the water.

"There it is. That's the boathouse."

The boathouse was little more than a low-slung, wooden shed, straddling a small stream which flowed lethargically into the deeper, faster waters of the River Hurst. It was old but sturdy, in good repair, and had recently acquired a new coat of creosote.

Caitlin had done her homework. "I know it doesn't look much but it's over a hundred years old. Hugh's family used to take boats up and down the river on pleasure cruises and have amazing picnics. A complete dinner party on the banks of the river. A bit more up-market than today's sandwiches, crisps and diet cola, don't you think?"

"I think you were born in the wrong century."

"Unfortunately there wasn't much call for step aerobics a hundred years ago."

But Marc had gone on ahead and was picking his way through the long grass and stinging nettles to the door. It was locked with a shiny, new padlock. He peered through the window. Caitlin wished she had remembered to bring the key. She rubbed the goose-pimples on her arms and wondered why men were always fascinated by water and boats. When she had suggested a trip to the boathouse, a trip to the boathouse was not actually what she had in mind.

"Is there anything inside?" asked Marc.

"Oh yes, several punts that the guests used to float up and down during last summer. Hugh kept them in good repair and always made sure guests signed a disclaimer. No one ever did capsize but he had no wish to be sued."

He glanced mischievously over his shoulder. "Would you like to go on a picnic?"

Caitlin was rather taken aback. "Now?"

"Perhaps one day next week if the weather remains fine. I'll double-check my shifts and get back to you. I can't promise smoked salmon and champagne though!"

"Oh," said Caitlin, unable to believe her luck. "Oh yes please!"

Marc struggled back onto the footpath. "Where does this lead?"

"Just along the river. It's a public footpath and is very popular with ramblers in the summer. They used to drive Hugh crazy. Their litter blows all over our land. The route tracks through Calahurst and the Forest, all the way to the sea.

"I wasn't planning on walking *that* far!" He put his arm around her shoulders. "Shall we?"

Caitlin cuddled up to him. He was nice and warm. Her dress only had the tiniest of straps to hold up the bodice. Now the sun had set, the breeze was becoming chilly. They walked along the dusty path of the riverbank, the party just a hum in the distance, the water lapping rhythmically against the bank. The moon was reflected in the water. It looked as though someone had swirled a tin of silver paint upstream. She glanced up at Marc's profile. He too was gazing at the fast-flowing river. She wondered what he was thinking but knew better than to ask.

They came to an old wooden seat the foresters had made from bits of left-over tree and sat down. Caitlin wondered if she ought to say something but decided to remain quiet. It was a long time since she had flirted and she was out of practice. Hugh had been her first serious boyfriend and he'd been the one to do most of the running. Not that she'd tried too hard to get away, she remembered ruefully.

Marc still had his arm around her shoulder. He started to stroke her hair. Perhaps he had preferred it long. She tried to recall when she'd last cleaned her teeth and if she'd eaten any garlic at the buffet dinner.

"Do you miss your husband unbearably?" he asked, taking her by surprise.

Down to earth with a bump. "All the time," she lied. "Time is a great healer though," she added, lest he take it the wrong way.

"If you ever feel the need to, you know, talk, you can always phone me. My parents died in an auto accident so I know what a shock sudden death is." His hand moved down to the nape of her neck, his thumb rotating slowly over her skin.

"God, how awful. Did it happen recently?"

"I was fifteen. We had emigrated to Canada when I was six. When they were killed I came back to England to live with my grandmother. She was great – but she died several years ago as well. Now there's only me."

That explained his not-quite-English accent. "My father is dead too," she volunteered, "Although my mother married again." *And again, and again, and again . . .*

His hand had dropped to her shoulder, playing with the sliver of fabric that held up her dress. Caitlin stared up into his face, hidden by the shadows. She knew if she moved a fraction of an inch towards him he would kiss her. But she hadn't got the nerve. He made the decision for her, turning towards her and lifting his other hand to trail one finger down her nose to land on her mouth. His face moved closer, blotting out the silver moon. Instinctively she shut her eyes and held her breath. His hand slid round to cup the back of her head as he kissed her. Caitlin felt the tension melt away; his lips moved on hers, tongue gently probing her mouth, tasting of toothpaste and champagne.

"Oh, Caitlin," he groaned.

She happily wound her arms about his neck and kissed him back with enthusiasm. He must feel something for her to sound like that.

As his kiss became more possessive, a sudden rush of warmth raced through her veins, like the aftermath of an explosion. His hands had moved to caress her shoulders, thumbs caught up beneath the straps of her dress, twisting and turning the slivers of fabric around his fingers, the merest touch against her skin sending her pulse sprinting off the scale.

She tentatively slid her hand between the tiny buttons of his shirt, spreading her fingers across his heart, feeling the warmth of his skin burn against the palm of her hand.

"Hell," he said, and broke abruptly away from her.

She stared at him in shock. The breeze cooled her burning cheeks but it took her a while to focus. She ached with disappointment, yet still he played with the strap of her dress. Confused, she glanced down and found one of the straps had broken in two.

"I'm terribly sorry," he was muttering. "I've ripped your dress."

She giggled at the horror in his voice. "It's come loose from the buckle, that's all." She took the strap from him and threaded the end of the fabric through the little round disc attached to the bodice of the dress. "See? No problem!"

Marc grinned, hugely relieved. "Thank God for that. I certainly could not afford to buy a new one!" He leant back against the seat and lit a cigarette.

She waited a few minutes in silence, unwilling to break the spell, hoping he would make the next move, feeling like a schoolgirl on a first date. What had she done wrong? Why didn't he kiss her again? *Because he didn't want to.*

She had been a widow a matter of months, yet she would have leapt into bed with Marc without giving her husband a second thought. Miserably she stared at the swirling water. She should just jump in and have done with it.

From the corner of her eye, she watched as Marc raised the cigarette to his lips. His hand seemed to shake. Perhaps he was not as cool and calm as he made out to be.

Marc took three long drags on his cigarette then discarded it, viciously grinding it into the earth with his heel. This was not the time to remind him about litter. He stood up and held out his hand. Caitlin took it wordlessly. She felt like crying from disappointment.

"We're going back to the party," he said, without a trace of emotion. "Before someone realises you're missing."

Who? she thought dolefully and trailed behind him, back along the path towards the house. As they emerged from the shrubbery, the party was much as they had left it. Fabian had progressed from backing vocals to lead singer but the band was still playing reggae covers of The Beach Boys. The guests had thinned slightly, as it was quite late, but those remaining were still dancing enthusiastically.

She stared unseeingly at the band, unwilling to let Marc witness the easy tears. She should not have had so much to drink.

As though realising she had gone quiet, he gently turned her to face him. "I'm sorry if I'm behaving strangely," he said. "I'm just not used to – er, used to chatting up widows. If you don't want to see me again I'll understand. I'll find another gym."

"No!"

He smiled crookedly. "You think you might like me then?"

Caitlin looked at him uncertainly. Was he still teasing her?

"Would you like to dance?"

She nervously ran her tongue across her dry lips. "Do you think we could have another drink first?" She needed time to sort out her jumbled emotions.

"Champagne?"

She smiled wryly. "I think I'd better stick to mineral water."

"Don't go away." And he headed off towards the hotel.

Caitlin turned to watch the dancing and collided with her mother. Elena, wearing a voluminous black lace gown, like Marie Antoinette in mourning, served up with lashings of diamonds, should not have been that easy to overlook.

"I have a surprise for you, darling," she beamed. "Look who's turned up. All the way from America!"

Her new stepfather?

"He heard about your problems and jumped straight on a plane. Wasn't that amazing?" Elena stepped backward to allow the man through the crowd. He had jet black hair, a tanned complexion and deep brown eyes.

Caitlin felt frozen in time. The party whirled around behind her, leaving just the two of them in a barren, silent vacuum. His face was unfamiliar, yet she felt there was something in that cruel, mocking smile . . .

"It's your brother-in-law, Leo Kirkwood!" cried Elena delightedly. "Don't you recognise him? He was Hugh's best man at your wedding."

"No," whispered Caitlin. Her voice sounded a long way off, as though it belonged to someone else. "It's *impossible* . . ."

The man smiled, although it did not reach his eyes. "Caitlin, darling! How lovely to see you again. You're looking well."

"*Hugh* . . ."

As the ground came up beneath her, he pulled her into a cold embrace, pressing his dead, passionless lips to the warmth of her cheek. And he said, so softly that only she could hear, "And all this time I thought I'd killed you."

Chapter Fourteen

Caitlin woke up in her own bed and knew from the black pit in her stomach that she had not been dreaming. It was the same primeval fear she had felt when her baby had been lost. The fear she could still reach out and touch whenever she closed her eyes.

She switched on her bedside lamp and reached out for her bottle of pills. Then remembered Elena had flushed them down the loo weeks ago. She bit into the back of her hand to stop herself from screaming out loud and Elena materialised by her side.

"Darling, you gave us such a shock! I didn't realise Leo resembled his brother so closely. You must have thought you were seeing a ghost."

"He's not Leo! He's *Hugh*!"

"No, darling, he's *Leo* – you remember? Your husband's younger brother?" Elena began to ramble. "He fell out with Hugh just after your wedding and went to live in the USA. Please, Caitlin. You've got to remember?"

"He is Hugh!" repeated Caitlin hysterically. "I was married to him for five years. Don't you think I would be able to tell?" She clutched at her hair. "Hell, who have I buried in the churchyard?"

Elena pushed her daughter's tangled hair back from her forehead. "Caitlin, calm down! What's got into you?"

"I think she's been drinking," drawled Hugh. "The bar staff saw her take at least three bottles of champagne. Vintage champagne," he added caustically.

Caitlin threw herself at him, clawing at his face. "You bastard! How could you leave me like that? I loved you! Why didn't you let me know you were still alive?" As he caught her wrists and firmly held her at arm's length, she began to cry, hot bitter tears. "Where have you been all this time? Everyone thinks I killed you! Don't you read the papers? Didn't you know I was arrested for your murder? Even if you hate me, you could have come forward and said you were still alive."

As he failed to reply, she found herself staring into his new brown eyes. Chocolate brown, with a tiny blue line around the edge. She stiffened. He was wearing contact lenses!

Hugh blinked and turned away, thrusting her into the arms of her mother, as though he could no longer bear her near him. Caitlin realised he was trembling. Was it compassion, guilt – or just plain indifference she had seen behind his carefully constructed facade?

"Hugh?" she pleaded. "Why don't you say something? Tell them the truth!"

A figure in a smart black suit emerged from the shadows and Caitlin felt a needle prick her arm. "No," she cried, flailing her arms wildly. "I'm not mad! Why won't any of you believe me!" The room swam out of focus, until all she could see were the three pairs of eyes watching her, curiously, as though she was some new specimen of the insect world squirming on a pin. "I don't want to die. Please Hugh, I don't *want* to die . . ."

* * *

The next time Caitlin opened her eyes it was morning. The green velvet curtains had been drawn back and daylight flooded the bedroom, catching on the motes of dust gently spiralling towards the floor. Slowly she sat up. She had a headache pulsing behind her left eye and her tongue felt as though it was wearing a puffa jacket. Gradually, in tantalising fragments, the events of the previous night came back to her. It was like watching a chewed-up videotape.

Insects, pins, formaldehyde. What an awful nightmare, she thought, and resolved never to drink again.

She swung her legs out of the bed and caught sight of her reflection in the dressingtable mirror. Her hair stood on end like Dennis the Menace and her make-up was smeared all over her face. Retribution. She deserved every spot and wrinkle she got.

She stood up and stretched, feeling quite stiff, and went over to sit at the dressingtable. Her arm was sore where the needle had entered and she noticed her skin was slightly red. Picking up the pearl-backed brush, that had been a wedding present from Hugh, she began to tug it through her unruly hair.

If it had all been a dream, why did her arm hurt?

With growing unease, she stared at her image in the mirror. "I am not mad," she said, desperately trying to calm the wild, fluttering panic. "I am not going mad. If I was mad I would not know I was going mad because I would be."

"I'm glad to hear it," said Hugh, amused. "It makes my life so much easier."

Caitlin screamed and dropped the brush. She stared incredulously as Hugh casually folded up his newspaper, placed it on the armchair where he had been sitting, and walked over to stand behind her. He picked up her hairbrush and held it out to her.

She dashed it from his hand. "What the hell are you doing here?"

"It's my bedroom too."

"That's not what I meant. You're supposed to be dead. Six foot underground."

"Strange," he said bitterly. "I thought you'd be pleased to see me." He paused. "Don't you remember *anything* that happened last night?"

Caitlin rubbed her arm. "I remember absolutely everything. With complete distinction and clarity."

"Good, I hate having to repeat myself."

She stared at his reflection in the mirror. It was his face, but there was something not quite right. Perfect white teeth, perfect brown skin. What had happened to the lines and wrinkles? His hair was styled differently and no longer grey. He looked years younger; the way he had on their wedding day. She recognised the slow-burning sex appeal, the half-apologetic smile, the same mischievous twinkle in his blue eyes that had made her fall in love with him all those years ago.

Except now he had *brown* eyes.

"You've lost weight," he said. "It suits you." He reached out as though to stroke her cheek and she flinched away. "I am real, you know. I'm not a ghost!"

"Bully for you!"

His hand dropped to his side. "You certainly know how to make a man feel wanted."

"You let them think I was mad! You let them drug me! Why didn't you tell them the truth!"

He studied his beautifully manicured fingernails. "There are several . . . let us say, pressing reasons . . ."

"If you're pretending to be Leo, he must have been the man found in the wreckage of the pool."

"Well done, darling." The corner of his mouth lifted. "Who do you think you buried? There aren't that many corpses wandering around Calahurst."

"But what was Leo doing here? Did you invite him?"

"Oh, yes."

She shook her head, bewildered. "You two can't stand each other."

"I did have to offer him money." Hugh sighed. "Sad, really, that it had to come to that."

Caitlin frowned. "What was he doing in the pool

house anyway? Why didn't he come and say hello to us, introduce himself?"

"The pool house was where he had been told to go and collect his money."

"And instead he died in a fire. What a horrible accident."

He gave her an old-fashioned look. "It wasn't an accident, Caitlin."

"You set fire to the pool house? *Deliberately*? But Leo and Amanda –"

He shrugged carelessly. "Something had to be done to destroy the evidence."

"What evidence?"

"That they had been murdered."

For a moment she could only stare at him in icy shock as the full horror washed over her. "You murdered your own brother? How *could* you?"

"Easy. With a five-pound hammer. Just like knocking the top from a hard-boiled egg."

Caitlin felt sick. "And Amanda?"

"Was supposed to have been you," he admitted casually. "Blonde hair looks dark when it's wet. My friend made a mistake. Pity really. I'm going to miss her. She was terrific in bed. *Crazy* imagination."

Caitlin began to edge towards the door – yet at the same time, she had an almost suicidal desire to know the truth. "But why go to all this trouble if you just wanted to disappear? Couldn't you have found another false identity to use? Like they do on TV – using old birth certificates?"

"And give this all up?" He gestured around the room. "To *you*? Oh, no. Taking on Leo's identity was the only way to insure my future. I never liked him any way. Irritating little twerp. He cared more about horses than he did about anyone or anything else." Hugh paused, reflectively. "A bit like Papa really."

Caitlin was still trying to get her head round this surreal information. "But the house was already yours."

"And the debts too. Six months ago I had this brilliant idea. I would murder you, murder me, burn down this hideous, money-eating house and collect on the insurance as my own younger brother." His smile was twisted. "Funny how it always works in films.

"So, I almost bankrupted myself paying the premiums, I go to all the trouble of luring Leo back from the States for my birthday party, suffer some extremely painful and expensive plastic surgery in some Third World hellhole and, when I finally make it back to this country, what do I find? All that's been burnt down is some poxy barn, my wife is alive and well, and the insurance company won't pay up because they think the fire was started deliberately by my wife to murder me."

Caitlin's hand groped behind her back. *An insurance policy?* Her fingers closed around the cold yet welcome metal of the door handle. *So that's why the police thought she was guilty. Put it together with Hugh's string of infidelities and there was motive with a capital M.*

Slowly, praying it wouldn't squeak, she turned the

handle. It slid effortlessly around a quarter turn and stopped. Locked? The door was *locked*? Utterly frustrated, she kicked it with the back of her heel.

Hugh smiled and held up a key. "Leaving so soon?"

There was no use pretending. "I'm going to call the police." Her voice wavered and she took a breath to strengthen it. "Now you're back, they'll *have* to believe I'm innocent."

He walked slowly towards her, murder in his eyes. It was too late, there was nowhere to run. She shrank back against the door, her nails digging into the wood as she closed her eyes and waited for the first blow. As she felt his breath, cool against her cheek she wondered how she could have ever loved him. If there had been a knife in her hand she would have thrust it straight between his ribcage and twisted. It wasn't so long ago that she would have given anything to have been held in his arms but now all she felt was revulsion – and fear.

"You've wrecked months of planning and lost me a fortune," he said, his fingers closing around her throat. He began to increase the pressure. "Why couldn't you have just died, like you were supposed to?"

Deprived of oxygen, she found his words blurring into each other as she was forced to concentrate on achieving each new breath. As she finally began to feel the descent into unconsciousness, he wrenched her away from the door, throwing her onto the floor, watching her struggling to inhale.

"I have in my possession a videotape," he said, "of

you interrupting my fun with Amanda and Belinda. And a friend of mine has the cigarette-lighter you dropped, which has your fingerprints all over it. Although, for some curious reason, the police are under the impression they already have it."

Marc's cigarette-lighter. Or perhaps Fabian's? She had forgotten all about them. She must have dropped the two lighters, and the sparklers, when she caught Hugh in the pool with Amanda and Belinda.

"Still want to go to the police?" Hugh derided.

Checkmate. She shook her head in defeat. Even if she did admit the truth to the police, she was just as likely to land either Marc or Fabian in trouble in her place.

"What do you want me to do?" she asked sadly.

"Nothing. Things can go on pretty much as they have before. I like the work you've done on the Manor. I suppose your mother paid for it? Well, more fool her. I certainly don't intend to pay her back." Hugh smiled maliciously. "You're still the manager; I want you here where I can keep an eye on you – but I don't really want you back as my wife. I quite like being the young, free and single Leo Kirkwood." He glanced at her stomach. "You don't look very pregnant?"

"I lost the baby."

"Are you sure you were even having a baby? That it wasn't just a figment of your imagination?"

"Contact the doctor if you don't believe me. I lost four pints of blood, spent two weeks in hospital and had a nervous breakdown. Is it any wonder I'm not terribly happy to see you?"

"You don't have to be happy, Caitlin," was his weary reply. "You just have to do as you're told."

* * *

It infuriated Caitlin that everyone believed Hugh to be his own younger brother and accepted him as the rightful heir to the family estate with the minimal amount of fuss.

Hugh, for his part, was impressed by the miracle Caitlin had achieved in transforming an old-fashioned, almost dowdy hotel into an exclusive health resort – although he would never have dreamt of telling her, or even expressing an interest in the changes she had made.

Instead, he spent the next week prowling round, finding things out for himself. He was not so impressed to find his prized possessions had been donated to Oxfam and that someone had been making serious inroads into his father's irreplaceable wine cellar. Worse still, that his wife had only taken three months to get over his 'death' and, as everyone was only too delighted to inform him, had acquired a handsome, chain-smoking stud by the name of Stewart.

* * *

Three days after the launch party, Hugh sat in the hotel manager's office with his feet up on Caitlin's new, and very expensive, mahogany desk and read through the files of accounts and the last few bank statements. There were hundreds of pounds going out but thousands of pounds coming in. Since the party, every room and suite, apart from those his damned in-laws had commandeered, was booked until October. If it carried on 'til Christmas he would have made as much profit in six months as he had during the last five years. He couldn't understand it. Why did a mere lick of paint make such a difference?

Feeling bored, Hugh was about to buzz Kimmie – Caitlin's pretty but dim secretary – for a bit of bimbo-baiting, when there was a knock on the door and Jack strode in without bothering to wait for an answer. They glared at each other in mutual dislike.

"There's a Ms Kelly in reception," Jack said.

"You're covering reception?"

"It wasn't my idea. The new girl went sick."

"Sick of this place no doubt." Hugh's finger hovered over his buzzer. Why did Jack feel the need to bother him with petty details?

"Ms Kelly has come to see Caitlin for a job interview."

"So?"

"So Caitlin seems to have disappeared."

Hugh watched the luscious Kimmie teeter past his window on her way to lunch, waving a cheery goodbye, her long brown legs displayed to perfection in the tiniest of red skirts. He thumped the desk in frustration. "Christ, do I have to do *everything*?"

Jack was offended. "I would interview her myself but I know bugger all about aerobics."

"Aerobics?"

"Yeah. Caitlin was thinking about hiring another fitness instructor. She's interviewed four candidates this week but didn't like any of them."

"I suppose they were all too sexy?"

Jack clenched his fists but remained calm. "Ms Kelly is a late entry."

"What does she look like?"

"A butch Meg Ryan, the morning after a night on the tiles."

"My type."

Jack regarded him stonily. "Any woman is your type."

"You have no sense of humour," sighed Hugh. "Just send in coffee and bickies in five minutes in case I need rescuing."

Ms Kelly was nothing special and bore little resemblance to Meg Ryan. Jack must need his eyes tested as well as his dreadlocks cut.

The girl had light brown hair, styled very short in an Audrey Hepburn urchin crop, blue-grey eyes and over-plucked eyebrows. She wore a lime-green tunic and matching Capri pants, had an authoritative air about her but a distinctly flat chest. However, once her eyebrows grew back, and if she grew her hair, bleached it blonde and donned a cleavage enhancing bra, there could be possibilities.

Hugh gave her a very languid tour of the hotel, escorted her along to the Fitness Studio, surreptitiously locked the door behind them and asked her to pretend she was taking an aerobics class. Without batting an eyelid, she stripped down to tight, black lycra shorts and matching high-necked leotard, slotted a cassette into the tape deck and went at it gung-ho. Hugh sat back to watch, lazily speculating whether he could get away with advertising topless aerobics classes and if that would encourage more men. Probably. And probably the vice squad too.

After ten minutes of horrendous thump, thump, thump 'music', Hugh had to ask her to stop before he developed a migraine. Ms Kelly had hardly built up a sweat. She packed up her Reebok step, climbed down from the little stage, and patiently awaited his verdict. He leisurely ran his eyes over her body. She had very long legs, he noticed, which gave her the overall appearance of a rather prim greyhound. It should be fun to seduce her. He made her wait a few more moments for his decision. She didn't even fidget.

"OK," he said at length, having run out of delaying tactics. "You're hired. When can you start?"

She shrugged. "Whenever you like?"

"Tomorrow?"

"Sure."

She didn't even look enthusiastic. But he wasn't disappointed. He liked women that were particularly hard to get.

"Shall we have a celebratory drink at the bar?" he suggested.

She looked wary. "Sorry, I can't."

"It's not a problem. Let's go back to the office and sort out the paperwork?"

"OK."

A woman of few words. It just got better and better. Hugh placed one arm around her shoulders, smiled and held out his other hand. "Well, congratulations, er . . ." he glanced down at her CV on the chair, " . . . Georgia. Welcome to Kirkwood – I mean, Mistletoe House. I hope you enjoy working here."

Georgia de Havilland forced an enthusiastic smile. "I'm looking forward to it already."

Chapter Fifteen

Fabian's mouth dropped open. "He did *what*?"

Georgia calmly poured Fabian another glass of Pimms. "He took me into the aerobics studio, locked the door, and asked me to audition."

"On your own?" Fabian took a hefty gulp of Pimms without realising he was doing it. "Without a class?"

"That's right." Georgia refilled her own tumbler but was careful to ensure it was mostly fruit and chunks of ice.

"What a complete pervert!" exclaimed Fabian, helping himself to fifths. "When I tried for the job, Caitlin asked me to take one of her classes while she stood at the back to see how I got on. Then, afterwards, she went round asking everyone what they had thought."

"That is how you're supposed to do it."

"Why didn't you scream or something? Kick him in the balls?"

"He didn't try anything," admitted Georgia. "Or I

would have done. Perhaps he didn't fancy me. Anyway, I put my worst step tape on, one I knew he would hate, then did my most exhausting routine. After ten minutes he couldn't take any more. He's so old he probably thinks dance music is something you play to teach five-year-olds ballet."

"And garage is where one stores the Bentley," grinned Fabian, mimicking Leo's public-school accent perfectly.

"The creep asked me out for a drink though," added Georgia, "to discuss my role in the future of Mistletoe House."

"Bastard! Talk about sexual harassment! He sounds as bad as his brother. Did you know, Hugh Kirkwood and Rick used to keep a running tally sheet of who had slept with the most customers? They used to like middle-aged housewives best because they – quote, unquote – 'used to try the hardest and were the most desperate'."

"Hugh Kirkwood sounds like a perfect monster." Georgia fished a slice of cucumber out of her drink and began to nibble around the edges. "Tell me more."

"Oh, well . . ." Fabian glanced nervously around. "I don't want to sound bitchy . . ."

"I *love* it when you're bitchy."

Fabian stared into her huge blue-grey eyes, so very like Amanda's, and quite lost his heart. "Well," he began confidingly.

Georgia moved closer.

They were sitting under one of the pool umbrellas,

having helped themselves to the wine bar back at the house, safe in the knowledge that Caitlin and Elena had gone shopping, Jack was painting and Leo Kirkwood was out attending to some mysterious business with the ubiquitous Raj Patel.

"Well," repeated Fabian, so quietly Georgia had to lean forward to catch what he was saying, "he's dead."

"Yes, Fabian, I do know that!"

"And people shouldn't speak ill of the dead. It's bad luck."

Georgia ignored her overwhelming desire to dunk his head in the Pimms and asked instead, "How did Hugh die?"

"In a fire in the old pool house – next to where the tennis courts are now. Caitlin had the ruins turfed over. She didn't want anything left to remember. So sad, don't you think?"

"Very," agreed Georgia, who really couldn't give a shit. Her whole life boiled down to the simple obsession of catching her sister's murderer. Nothing else mattered.

"Anyway, it was the night of Hugh's fortieth birthday party . . ."

"Yes . . ."

Fabian swished his fruit around his glass with his swizzle-stick. "Fancy dying on your own birthday. Cosmic, eh?"

Georgia could have howled with frustration. She wished she had picked whisky or vodka or gin or anything other than Pimms. Although famous for its innocuous taste and high alcohol content, the Pimms did not appear to be getting Fabian drunk quickly enough. She managed to squeeze another couple of inches into his glass while he was preoccupied with twirling the swizzle-stick around his fingers like a cheerleader's baton.

Fabian took another swig from his glass. A slice of lemon batted him on the nose. He picked it out and bit into it, pith, peel, the lot. Maybe the Pimms was working after all.

"Mr Kirkwood was a right bastard," he added.

"Runs in the family," muttered Georgia, taking a swig of her own drink to cheer herself up. She was supposed to be taking a step class in two hours, which should make for an interesting experience. Drunk in charge of a Reebok step.

"He was screwing my girlfriend."

Georgia started. At last! "Oh yes?" she prompted. "Did she work here too?"

"Yeah. She was gorgeous," Fabian sighed. "Blonde hair and a terrific figure."

"It helps," agreed Georgia. *Men.* So predictable.

"I loved her. She was absolutely gorgeous . . ."

And to Georgia's horror he began to cry great big splashy tears into his Pimms.

Feeling more than a twinge of guilt at having brought the subject up, she put her arm around his shoulders, "Don't upset yourself, Fabe. She wasn't worth it."

Fabian shoved her away. "She was! I wanted to marry her. I'd picked out a ring at Samuel's, arranged the finance and – and he took her away from me. How could I compete with designer clothes, jewellery from Asprey's, weekend trips down the coast on his mate's yacht? Her Dad was rich. It was what she was used to. My Dad lives in a council house on The Oaks estate."

What could she say? Georgia felt an absolute cow for having brought the subject up.

"And she used to laugh at me," muttered Fabian, "Telling me Hugh was much better in bed, that he used his imagination. They used play these wild sexual games apparently. On their own and with other people." For a moment there was a glimmer of a smile hovering around the sullen mouth. "What did she expect me to do? Go out and buy glove puppets?"

Georgia grinned. Six years of working alongside a shift of red-blooded males, who quite happily treated her as one of the lads, meant she was way beyond feeling embarrassed discussing someone else's sex life. In fact, if only she had the time and inclination, she could tell Fabian a few stories to make his hair curl.

"Sounds like a right cold-hearted bitch to me," she commented. "You're well rid of her."

Fabian gave a wry smile. "But the *really* weird thing is, I'd do anything to get her back. Hopeless case, I guess."

The guy was a regular doormat, thought Georgia irritably. "Now Hugh's dead perhaps she'll come back."

"No, she won't."

"Yes, she will, trust me. That type always do. Just like bloody boomerangs." *Until something better came along, of course . . .*

"You don't understand. She can't come back. She's dead!"

Georgia was instantly contrite. "Oh God, I'm sorry! Me and my big mouth! Was it sudden? Car accident?" *Please God, don't let it have been terminal cancer . . .*

Fabian regarded her strangely. "She died with Hugh in the fire. I thought . . . I thought everyone knew." He smiled faintly. "I wondered why you didn't change the subject the moment I mentioned her. Everyone else does. It's as though the poor girl never existed."

Georgia was still trying to get a grip on what he was telling her. One minute he was rambling on about irrelevancies, the next he suddenly dropped this bombshell. "But I thought only two people died in the fire?"

"That's right, Hugh and my girlfriend – Amanda de Havilland."

* * *

Georgia had moved into Mistletoe House the day after her interview, with two suitcases crammed full of newly purchased aerobic wear. She didn't want those rich, pampered bitches getting one over on her. She was given a room on the second floor, where the rest of the live-in staff resided, including Leo Kirkwood – although he had three rooms knocked into one. Georgia's room was clean and tidy, and had a nice view of the river – provided one stood on a chair – so she was not too inconvenienced. Although it did give her a depressing glimpse into how the lowly paid lived.

Two days later, Jack O'Neill, Caitlin's elder brother, asked her out on a date.

He was not her type. She liked her men mean and moody, with fast cars and fast lives. Jack was far too placid and laid back, and she was itching to give him a short back and sides. But she accepted anyway. She had squeezed all the information she could out of Fabian. It was time for a new challenge.

Jack suggested a drink at The Stables, followed by Raj Patel's nightclub Last Days, neither of which, luckily, were on Georgia's list of regular haunts. She wore a black A-line miniskirt, lime-green cropped T-shirt and black boots. It had been 85 degrees during the day but Georgia had a tendency to be a fashion victim. It was the only personality trait she had ever had in common with her sister Amanda.

At The Stables Georgia drank three fruit wines to give her courage and then swayed down the cobblestoned street towards the quayside. The seventeenth century buildings along the quayside had the highest rates along the South Coast and were rented by nautical shops, restaurants and designer boutiques, separated from the water's edge by elegant black railings. At the end of the quay was Raj's nightclub, Last Days, in the remains of a large and rather ugly Victorian church.

Last Days was a play on the owner's name and decorated in glorious reds and golds, exuberant Indian fashion. The interior was a fibreglass 'ruined' temple, with vine-strewn statues doing rather naughty things to each other. It was only as Georgia looked closer she realised the statues were living, breathing people, posing absolutely motionless.

There were three bars – one wine bar, one cocktail bar, and one that served juice and mineral water. The young, beautiful bar staff all wore glittering Indian and Colonial costumes. The focal point was a waterfall spilling into an artificial lake. It was heavily surrounded by bouncers, presumably in the event some prat got drunk and dived in.

Jack and Georgia were the only ones buying alcohol, which gave away their age. Everyone else was in a scrum at the juice bar, frantically buying little bottles of mineral water, two at a time. Their average age was nineteen. Georgia felt like an OAP.

She was rather embarrassed to be standing next to the totally untrendy Jack, who was still wearing his sunglasses, despite the gloom, and looked exactly like a white Bob Marley. In fact, after the DJ spotted him, a few reggae records pounded through the Club. Jack was delighted. Georgia began to edge away. She managed to edge so far away that someone else bought drinks between them not realising they were together.

As she stared forlornly at her reflection in the mirror behind the bar, a man on her other side said, "Hello."

Georgia turned, about to tell him to drop dead, when she came face-to-face with Leo Kirkwood. Jackpot!

"And what's a girl like you doing in a place like this?" he said, moving nearer, invading her personal space.

And this was supposed to be a chat-up line? Or was he taking the piss?

Georgia reminded herself she was working and attempted to look seductive. "I'm looking for a man like you."

He seemed rather surprised by the blatant come-on but, obviously not one to miss out on an opportunity to score, moved even closer. She could see the grey roots growing through his jet-black hair. He was older than he looked, although he took care to disguise it well. Georgia found it slightly creepy.

"Can I buy you a drink?" he asked.

Georgia elbowed her untouched drink out of sight. "Yes, please. Peach wine."

Leo Kirkwood waved a tenner in the direction of the barman. "Peach wine and the same again for me," he muttered, turning back to smile lazily at Georgia, "I do like a girl who can hold her alcohol."

Girl? *Girl?* His hand slid along the bar and began to stroke her upper arm. Out of the corner of her eye, Georgia could see Jack frantically searching for her. If she wanted to move in on Leo Kirkwood she had better act fast.

"Would you like to dance?" she said.

This had the opposite effort to that intended. He visibly paled. Of course, she remembered, he didn't like modern dance music. So what was he doing here? *Picking up women, stupid!*

"We could always wander upstairs and watch everyone else?" she suggested.

Leo relaxed. "Fabulous idea." He slipped his arm around her waist, his hand smooth and warm against her bare skin, and led her towards the spiral staircase.

Georgia tried not to shudder. There were certain men that women did not like to 'get stuck in lifts with' and Leo Kirkwood was one of them. She closed her eyes and thought of Amanda. It seemed to give her a cold, dispassionate strength. At least she didn't have to worry that Leo was the murderer, as he had been out of the country at the time.

Jack watched in disbelief as his date walked off with someone else. Georgia felt sorry for him. She felt extremely sorry for herself as Leo followed her up the spiral staircase, She could feel his eyes looking up her skirt, and was convinced she could feel his hot breath on the back of her thighs. What the hell was she letting herself in for?

Georgia glanced back at Jack and saw him sarcastically raise his glass to her. She grimaced, quite aware she was behaving like a bitch. Jack might be a buffoon but he was also kind and good-natured. He did not deserve to be treated like this.

Leo walked along the edge of the balcony until they came to a deserted spot in a dark corner, directly over the top of the waterfall. If he gets fresh, I can always chuck him in, thought Georgia. They balanced their glasses on the balcony and peered down at the dancers gyrating below. They were just one heaving mass of sweating bodies.

"Why don't you like to dance?" she asked him.

"Because I'm not very good at it. Besides, I left my handbag and white stilettos at home."

She laughed. "Dancing's not difficult. You just sway about and wave your arms in time to the bass."

"And look a total prat."

"Yes, but so does everyone else."

He tucked a stray curl behind her ear. "I'm not everyone else."

She took a step backwards and stepped on the toe of a young man behind. She turned to apologise but found she was talking to his back. He was more interested in putting his tongue down the throat of a mini-skirted granny.

Perhaps she wasn't so old, thought Georgia, trying to not stare. She turned back to Leo. Talk about mismatched couples. Perhaps they ought to swop. But Leo obviously went for younger women, just like his brother Hugh.

"Why so shy?" asked Leo, taking one hand in his.

Georgia smiled limply and quelled the impulse to hurl him over the balcony. To take her mind off it, she glanced back down to the bar, hoping to see Jack. With his distinctive hair he was not difficult to spot. He was leaning back against the bar, chatting up a teenage blonde. That hadn't taken him long. Piqued, she turned back to Leo.

He had moved in on her midriff. "Aren't you cold?" he asked, running a leisurely finger across her brown tummy.

She couldn't believe the nerve of this guy. Had he

never heard of sexual harassment? What was she supposed to do? Say, '*You* can warm me up any time?' and other assorted crap. Over her dead body. Was this what dating older men was really like? Where *did* they get their chat-up lines? From a Christmas cracker?

She decided to try the hard-to-get approach. That was one tactic at which she was guaranteed success. So she ignored Leo's hand and sadly watched Jack, laughing with the teenage blonde. At least someone was having fun.

She had made her bed, so she could hardly complain if someone else wanted to lie in it.

* * *

Jack had been about to cut his losses when a perky little blonde in a tight blue dress had sauntered up to him and said, "Hello, I'm the Honourable Belinda Richmond, my father's the Lord Lieutenant."

He burst out laughing, thinking this was her standard witty chat-up line, and shook her outstretched hand. "Hello, I'm the Dishonourable Jack, out-of-work artist, down-and-out painter. Are you here on your own?"

"No, I came with some girlfriends but they were all asked to dance and I wasn't."

Jack held grimly onto his glass and purposefully missed the hint. He frequented nightclubs because he adored listening to loud music, guzzling Guinness and meeting stimulating people that he could later paint. Like most men, he hated dancing.

"This is the first time I've been here," he said, sipping at his Guinness and leaving a white moustache on his upper lip. "It's great, isn't it?"

Belinda regarded him with amusement. "It's all right." She leant towards him and wiped his lip with her finger, then put it in her rosebud mouth.

Jack flattened himself against the bar.

She raised her eyebrows. "Are you gay?"

He spluttered into his drink. "Certainly not!"

"I don't mind if you are." She fluttered her eyelashes at him.

Jack glared at her. "I can assure you, I am most definitely not gay!"

"Good, so why are we wasting time? Let's just break the ice and go to bed. Get rid of all these sexual tensions. Your place or mine?"

Jack was speechless. That he found her attractive was not in question. Left to his own devices he would have bought her a Guinness, worked his way through his limited repertoire of poetry, offered to paint her nude and taken advantage. He was a bit taken aback to be propositioned himself. If his newly found drinking chums from The Stables could see him now . . .

Belinda lost patience. "Come on," she said, grabbing his arm and hauling him away from the bar. "Let's dance while you think it over."

Jack let himself be hauled. He must be getting old, he decided. In his day it was the men who made the first move. He wasn't used to lying back and enjoying it.

However, he could learn to adjust.

Belinda wrapped her arms around his neck, no easy achievement as she was only five-foot-two. She was a pretty little thing, he decided, with her turned-up nose and wide blue eyes, bouncing curls and jiggling breasts – currently pressing against his lower ribs.

They slowly moved around the dance floor, swaying completely out of time to the repetitive drum 'n' bass music. She was nuzzling into his dreadlocks. As he was so tall, he had to stoop to prevent himself swinging her off her feet. It was beginning to give him backache.

"Shall we sit the next one out?" he suggested.

Belinda's face fell. "Don't you like me?"

"Of course I do," he said hastily. "Would you like a walk along the quayside? We could get a breath of fresh air, perhaps get a drink at The Parson's Collar?"

"OK, I'll get my bag," said Belinda and skipped off, returning with a minuscule quilted blue handbag, suspended on a silver chain, which she slung around her neck. She put Jack's arm around her waist and grinned up at him. "I'm ready," she beamed.

Jack smiled back. Well, she was kind of cute . . .

* * *

Georgia, fighting a losing battle against Leo's wandering hands, watched Jack leave with the little blonde and was irritated to realise she was jealous. She was further annoyed when Jack, spotting her surveillance, grinned and waved up at her. She stepped back from the balcony, into the shadows and Leo's arms.

He pulled her against him. "There, isn't that better?"

Georgia resisted the temptation to knee him in the groin. "So, Leo," she smiled, "why are you chatting up the hired help?"

He moved back slightly. "I don't consider you the hired help," he said, sounding offended. "At Mistletoe House we all work together as a team."

How sweet – and what utter bollocks. "How are you adjusting to life as a hotelier?"

"It's certainly different from show-jumping but I'm enjoying the challenge."

"Bet Caitlin's nose was put out of joint when you turned up out of the blue."

His eyes narrowed. "My sister-in-law is a terrific manager. I don't know what I would do without her."

"So you don't hold her responsible for your brother's death?"

Leo abruptly pushed her away from him. "Are you a journalist?"

She had gone too far. She had as much tact and diplomacy as Attila the Hun on a trip to Northern Italy. This was probably why it had taken her forever just to become a CID Aide. Slowly, hating herself, she lifted one hand and smoothed the frown lines from his brow.

"I'm sorry, darling. I was just curious as to how you got on with each other. You don't seem to like her very much. It's a very strange relationship, you have to admit."

He caught hold of her hand and gripped it tightly. "What's your game, Georgia?"

She laughed nervously and played the bimbo. "Tennis, cricket, anything you like really."

He didn't laugh, merely smiled maliciously. "I know," he said. "Why don't we talk about you?"

"Me?" squeaked Georgia.

"Mmm. When I hired you I thought you seemed familiar. Yet your CV says you lived in Norchester."

"All my life," lied Georgia.

"And prior to working at Mistletoe House you did a stint at the gym in Norchester?"

"Yes, three years."

"The manager has never heard of you."

They stared at each other. Georgia felt cold. His warm chocolate-brown eyes had just hardened and his nails were digging into her hand. She tried to pull it back.

"I lied," she said, looking at her feet. "I needed the job."

"That much?"

She raised her face to his and attempted to look appealing. "I was desperate. I'm sorry. I know you're quite within your rights to fire me . . . but please don't."

"Why shouldn't I? Fitness instructors are not difficult to find."

"Good fitness instructors are," she retorted.

"And are you good?"

She attempted humour. "What do I have to do to convince you? Sleep with the boss?"

He grinned, showing very even, very white, teeth. "That can be arranged."

* * *

Jack and Belinda walked hand in hand along the boardwalk which surrounded the large U-shaped quay. They admired the many yachts and cruisers, window-shopped and paused for a drink at The Parson's Collar wine bar. Then, as the reflection of the moon painted silver streaks across the black river, they meandered along the shore to the sailing club. There were smartly painted white railings around the club compound but that wouldn't keep Jack out. To him, they were virtually an enticement to clamber over.

Laughing playfully, Belinda ducked and dived through the racing dinghies, playing hide and seek, while Jack followed more sedately, feeling a lot like someone's decrepit old uncle. They sat on an old upturned boat, abandoned on a grassy bank, and flipped stones across the water, trying to make them bounce, watching the river flow endlessly to the sea.

Jack had his arm around Belinda's shoulders, worried that she might get cold, and she snuggled against him like a little kitten. He felt very protective until she suddenly raised her hand and shoved him away. Taken by surprise, he overbalanced and slid off the boat, landing on the grass, winded. Swearing loudly, he sat up and Belinda jumped on top of him.

Giggling, she straddled his hips. "I've got you now."

"So you have," he acknowledged. "Would you mind shifting? You're sitting on my dinner."

She leant back and whipped her blue slip dress off over her head. Slowly she ran her fingers through her hair, pulling it up towards the stars. It caught fire in their ghostly light before falling back onto her pale naked skin. Diana, Goddess of the Moon.

"Belinda!" he rasped. "What the hell are you doing?"

"Seducing you," said Belinda complacently. "I don't think you're gay; I think you're inexperienced."

"*What?* Now listen, Belinda –"

Quickly she undid the silver buttons on his black shirt and began to fumble with the zip on his jeans.

"Belinda!" he implored, trying to pull her hands away. "You don't know what you're doing!"

"Yes, I do," she said, slipping her little warm hands inside his jeans. "See," she added triumphantly, "I knew you liked me!"

Jack groaned, admitting defeat, and flopped back against the sand. "I don't have any condoms," he lied.

"That's OK," said Belinda smugly. She dangled her handbag two inches from his nose. "I do."

Chapter Sixteen

The following day Caitlin watered the geraniums and citrus-trees growing in the pots around the new outdoor pool as she had nothing better to do. It also helped her steady her nerves and start to think her problems through. As she reached the far end she had to tug on the hosepipe to stretch it to its limit. It wouldn't budge. Irritably she looked to see if it had become entangled with a shrub and found Hugh standing on it.

"I know it comes naturally to you, Hugh darling," she said wearily, "but don't be a bastard."

Hugh stepped to one side. "You're right," he agreed, shrugging his hands into the pockets of his jeans and walking casually over to stand beside her. "I *should* make the effort to be a nicer person. Particularly as everything is going so well."

He obviously got laid last night, she thought sourly. Perhaps by his new fitness instructor – who was so

219

terrified of Caitlin she would leave the room the moment she came in.

Trying to pretend that Hugh's presence had no effect on her, Caitlin concentrated on filling each terracotta pot to the brim, twice, before moving on to the next one. From the corner of her eye, she noticed his expensive trainers following closely behind the hosepipe and paused. She had not realised he owned a pair of trainers. Surely he had not taken up aerobics? Without realising it, she flooded one of the containers with so much water the little citrus-tree bobbed up to the surface, still restrained in its root ball.

"So, your mother's millions don't run to employing a gardener?" he enquired blithely.

"Yes, they do," replied Caitlin, though gritted teeth. "Five mornings a week. But I felt like doing this. It gets me out of the house. And away from you."

"Now who's being nasty?" He put both his arms around her waist and playfully hugged her back against him.

His body was warm and he smelt of Polo Sport. Flustered, Caitlin dropped the hosepipe and it showered them both with water. Laughing, Hugh kicked it aside but still he did not let her go. Caitlin began to feel that horribly squirming sensation of lust which had attracted her to him in the first place. She struggled but he held her too closely.

"How about a nice romp in the bushes?" he asked softly.

Caitlin elbowed him in the ribs. He groaned and let her go.

"Bitch," he grunted, rubbing his torso, and grabbed for her again.

She gave him a hefty shove and he tumbled backwards into the pool. Just for a second she worried that perhaps Fabian had drained it, but no, there was an massive splash, she was thoroughly soaked in chlorinated water and a tirade of four-lettered words rose up through the spray.

"Wipeout!" she cried jubilantly, then fled back to the house, having no desire to witness her husband's rage when he finally surfaced.

Since Hugh had kicked her out of their bedroom, Caitlin had commandeered one of the smaller guest suites. No way was she going to lower herself to move into the staff quarters. It was pretty enough, shades of pink with lots of lace and an overdose of rosebuds in the decor. But half the size of what she was used to, and a very small, reproduction four-poster bed.

She locked the door behind her, squelched over to her wardrobe and began to peel off her sopping-wet clothes, kicking them in the general direction of the laundry basket in the bathroom. She was down to her underwear when someone slammed violently against the door. Then, more genteelly, tried the lock.

To her consternation the door opened.

"Open sesame!" snapped Hugh, dangling a pass key before her eyes.

"Get out of my bedroom, you murdering bastard!"

"My room, my house, my hotel." And he shut and locked the door behind him.

Caitlin ran over to the window and flung it open. She was unsure whether she intended to jump, or simply scream for help, but regardlessly Hugh wrenched her back, almost breaking her arm. He lifted her off her feet and threw her roughly onto the bed. The cold-blooded rage in his eyes was terrifying.

Caitlin stared up at him in horror. "Lay one finger on me and I'll scream the house down!"

"I've never raped a woman in my life. I do not intend to start now." He hesitated, and for a moment Caitlin thought she glimpsed a strangely bleak expression in his dark eyes. "You really thought I would hurt you?"

She sat up. "You've done it before." Her hands were still quivering so she shoved them under her thighs. "You've even tried to kill me – Amanda died instead."

"Poor cow."

Caitlin had to steel herself to ask, "Did you love her?"

Hugh's face was unreadable. "I've never loved anyone. Saves a lot of trouble."

"You're telling me." She shivered.

"Are you cold?" As he handed her the white lace wrap hanging over the back of her dressing-table chair; he accidentally touched her fingers.

Caitlin snatched her hand away and wrapped the dressinggown firmly around her.

His hand dropped to his side. "I take it you don't want a bonk for old times' sake?"

"*No, thank you.*" She watched him leave, without

saying another word and, realising she was still shaken, reached under her bed for her bottle of brandy. She had just taken a hefty swig as Jack put his head around the open door. Too late, she shoved the uncorked bottle beneath the pillow, where it leaked all over the bedsheets.

"Stewart Granger's downstairs," said Jack disapprovingly. "Says he's come to take you on a picnic."

* * *

Caitlin was aware that Marc had gone to a lot of trouble for their first date and was determined not to disappoint him. Though all she really felt like was curling up in bed and going to sleep. She took a lot of care deciding upon an appropriate outfit from the clothes her mother had bought, eventually choosing jeans and a cropped top. Just the thing for playing about on rivers with very handsome men. She just hoped Marc wouldn't make her wear a life jacket.

Marc had hired a red wooden dinghy from a fisherman at Calahurst Quay. It had cost £30 for the afternoon. He had the feeling he might have been had, but didn't trust one of Hugh's punts as far as he could throw it.

He collected Caitlin from Mistletoe House, aware the hotel staff were watching through the windows, and drove the short distance down to the quay. The local 'salts' watched with mounting amusement as he helped Caitlin clamber aboard, then jumped in afterwards, violently rocking the boat.

Caitlin, oblivious of their critical audience, noticed a large wicker hamper stuffed under one of the seats. She could also see a trickle of river water sliding up and down the bottom of the boat.

"Take no notice of the water," said Marc carelessly, apparently reading her mind. "It's not going to sink. According to the guy I rented it from, it's supposed to be lucky."

"For whom?" asked Caitlin, not entirely convinced. She gingerly sat down and wondered on the wisdom of entrusting a boat to a 'landlubber'. Personally she would much rather have taken a punt. She could have reclined elegantly against a pile of silk cushions and trailed her hand languidly in the water. The dinghy was not designed to recline elegantly. She had to sit, bolt upright, on one of the hard wooden seats, which was merely a plank of wood stretched from one side to the other.

Marc remembered to cast off and sat down facing her. Ensuring the oars were safely tucked into the rowlocks, he began to row upstream with long, sweeping strokes. Caitlin was impressed. He had never seemed particularly interested in the rowing machine at the gym.

"I thought we'd go up country," he said, as he got into the rhythm. The oars plink-plinked into the water, casting tiny ripples towards the shore. "Far away from the tourists."

"Fine." Caitlin felt a little thrill run through her. "It should be nice and peaceful."

She leant forward for better balance, unwittingly giving Marc a nice view of her bra-less cleavage, and watched the woods zip past. They had moved swiftly through the gardens of Mistletoe House and into the area owned by the Forestry Commission, easily recognisable as the trees grew neatly in rows. There was the towering Corsican pine, then the Scots pine with its coppery trunks and lastly the vivid green of the Norway spruce, which always mysteriously vanished around Christmas.

Caitlin felt hot, hungover and slightly seasick. She tugged her baseball cap from the back pocket of her jeans and pulled it onto her head. From her front pocket she eased out Jack's paint-splattered sunglasses and perched them on the end of her nose, feeling as though she was in disguise. It was a beautiful day, the temperature was heading towards the nineties. She should have worn shorts but her legs needed shaving.

"You can talk to me, you know," smiled Marc, beads of sweat gathering on his forehead from the unaccustomed exercise. The oars did not miss a beat.

Caitlin was furious with herself to find her thoughts elsewhere when she was alone on a boat with a ravishing man. She was equally furious to realise she couldn't think of anything to say.

"Did you enjoy the launch party?" she enquired at last, if only to be polite.

"I'd have enjoyed it more if you hadn't disappeared. You really are exactly like Cinderella."

Caitlin regarded him cynically over the top of her sunglasses. "With a mother that's married to a millionaire?"

"Cinderella Rockerfella."

"You keep saying that. What does it mean?"

He laughed. "It's a song! Didn't you know? About a poor little rich girl."

Just like Hugh. He was only interested in her mother's money. Caitlin turned away, following the flight of an emerald and gold dragonfly streaking in and out the bays carved into the banks of the river, hovering over the still water. It was joined by another, sapphire and black. For a brief moment they resembled fairies from a children's picture-book.

"I don't think my mother's that rich," she replied slowly. "And it's not really her money. It's her husband's."

"Her seventh husband."

"So what? Elizabeth Taylor married eight times, twice to the same person."

"It must have been something, having six stepfathers? Which one was your Dad?"

"Number one."

"Did he have a title too?"

"No. My father was a penniless Irish artist. He drank a lot of whisky, was very friendly with the Rolling Stones in the Seventies and then died suddenly while touring in the Australian outback."

"What was he doing there?"

"Painting kangaroos, I suppose," shrugged Caitlin. "I was only four at the time."

"Very young." Taking her sarcasm as a hint his questions were becoming too personal, Marc rowed a bit further in silence. The river narrowed and began to curve lazily through open fields, fluorescent with yellow rape. "We have something in common," he said eventually. "Losing parents when we were young. Did it affect you very much?"

Caitlin pushed her sunglasses further onto her nose and huddled into the corner of the dinghy. "No, I didn't really understand. It was more upsetting to be on the move all the time. Just as I would get used to a new town, or country for that matter, Mother would get divorced and we'd be on the move again. I spent my entire life in hotel suites and guest bedrooms."

"You should be sick of hotels."

"It's the only thing I know," she said sadly.

"You were once a singer and dancer."

"I wasn't very good. I can dance but my singing is dreadful!"

"Sing something for me."

The sensuality in those navy eyes made her catch her breath. "You're crazy!" She laughed to hide her embarrassment and looked out across the fields, stretching into infinity, shimmering in the heat. "All we need now is for Pavarotti to glide past with a monster ice cream."

"Are you taking the piss?"

"Yes." Caitlin found her gaze dropping to his mouth. She wondered what it would feel like to have those lips moving relentlessly over her body.

The brandy she had consumed earlier was still capering through her bloodstream. At least, that's how she explained her next action to her conscience, as she slipped off one plimsoll and gently stroked her bare foot up, and then down, his lower leg.

Marc abruptly dropped the oars and, grabbing her foot, caught hold of her big toe and tweaked it. "This little piggy went to market . . ."

Caitlin screamed with laughter, desperately trying to pull her foot from his grasp. "Watch out," she cried breathlessly, "you're rocking the boat."

"Cue for a song," he said and opened his mouth.

"Oh no, you don't!" She tugged her foot back as the boat swayed alarmingly. One loose oar slipped through the rowlock and slid effortlessly into the water. "Bollocks!" she said, and peered overboard.

"I think you mean, 'rowlocks'."

"I thought they were supposed to float!"

"They do." He pointed towards the bank. "There it goes."

Caitlin stared in dismay at the oar, bobbing about on the river, being slowly dragged away by the current. "Oh God, I'm sorry! Will you be able to get it back?"

"Sure," he said and, standing up, dived neatly into the water, barely causing a ripple.

"Oh hell," muttered Caitlin and, sliding off her sunglasses to get a better view, leant over the side of the boat, anxiously waiting for him to reappear. The water, which had seemed so clear only moments ago, now appeared dark and sinister. The seconds ticked past.

"Marc?" she called anxiously, leaning further over.

The boat tipped up and she overbalanced, going headfirst into the water. She just managed a shriek as the water closed over her head, the current whipping off her baseball cap. A dark shape moved rapidly through the water towards her, then she felt Marc's arms around her helping her reach the shallows.

They scrambled up the muddy bank, then Marc went back for the boat. She watched enviously as he moved effortlessly through the water. He reached up into the boat, grabbed the mooring rope and swam back to shore. She sat down on a grassy hummock, pretending she had not been paying attention. Her jeans were sopping wet, and felt very uncomfortable, but she had no intention of taking them off, even if she did look like a prude.

Marc dumped the picnic hamper on the ground and pulled out a large tartan rug to spread over the grass. Tugging his T-shirt off over his head, he wrung it out over the river, then tossed it back into the boat. He left his jeans on.

Perhaps he was a prude too, thought Caitlin, trying not to let her gaze linger on his honey-toned skin. She watched him pour out a bottle of cola into two blue plastic beakers. They had pictures of fat yellow fish on the side. He handed one to her.

"Sorry I've only brought soft drinks," he added, "but I don't think water and alcohol mix."

Caitlin remembered the brandy she had consumed and felt guilty. She was turning into an alcoholic. The first thing she was going to do when she got home, she decided, was to tip that bottle down the sink.

Beside her, Marc was unstacking Tupperware dishes. "Wing or leg?"

"Sorry?"

"Chicken wing or leg?"

"Oh, leg, please."

He piled her plate high and passed it to her. It had a tartan design matching the rug. "My grandmother's picnic set," he explained, rather shamefaced. "Circa 1960."

"It's cute," said Caitlin, watching him unpack the remaining food. The hamper appeared to be moonlighting as the Tardis. Bowls of salad, French sticks, cheeses that were all individually wrapped and sealed in coolbags, slabs of ham, lumps of chicken . . . he'd make someone a wonderful wife. "Are you expecting a lot a people?"

He grinned. "No, just us." He popped a small stick of carrot in her mouth. "But after your disparaging comments regarding modern-day picnics, I really thought I ought to make an effort."

Caitlin picked up another carrot stick and stuck it into a dip. She licked it carefully, attempting to guess the flavour. Cream cheese, garlic and chives? She hesitated, then saw Marc do the same. It didn't matter if they both stank of garlic.

"Try this one," suggested Marc, holding out a small dish. "It's tzatziki – Greek yoghurt and cucumber."

Caitlin dipped in a stick of celery. "It's very refreshing," she agreed. "Did you make it yourself?"

"It's handmade," he replied solemnly. Then laughed. "By the local Co-op!"

Without thinking, Caitlin playfully slapped him. He caught her hand and turned it over, kissing the palm. Oh yes, thought Caitlin, closing her eyes and letting the desire flood through her. Yes, please!

He put her little finger in his mouth and playfully bit it. Caitlin tried to remember when she had last cleaned her nails and hoped a false one would not drop off into his mouth. It was no good. She was not made for spontaneous passion. She was the sort of person that liked to have a bath, shave her legs and clean her teeth before settling down to wanton abandonment.

Marc had other ideas. He took her finger from his mouth, draped her arm about his neck, did the same with her other, and pulled her backwards onto the rug. She fell on top of him and they narrowly missed landing in the potato salad. As they hit the ground their teeth clashed but, before she could move away and apologise, he had caught his fingers in her hair and pressed her lips against his, parting them with his tongue. Caitlin succumbed to temptation and relaxed into him.

He moved one hand behind the back of her head and the other to her waist and then rolled her over, trapping her beneath him. She opened her eyes and stared silently into his, seeing herself reflected back. He began to kiss her again, his tongue teasing her. She closed her eyes in rapture. The controlled passion exhilarated her. After five years with Hugh, repenting at leisure, it was brilliant to find a man who truly desired her.

Without considering the consequences, she slid her hands down his back, following the line of his spine, towards the top of his jeans. She hesitated, but only for a moment, before sliding her fingers beneath the belt.

Marc's iron control finally deserted him. His mouth moved hungrily on hers, needing, wanting, taking. She could hardly keep up with his passion, her lips crushed against the force of his mouth, almost as though he felt she might run away. She cried out as his teeth caught on her lip and he suddenly stopped.

"Oh hell, I'm sorry," he said, sounding slightly dazed. "I didn't meant to hurt you." Then, as she could not find the words to reply, added roughly, "Are you sure you want to do this? If you think it's too soon, you don't have to. We can wait. I won't be offended."

She blearily opened her eyes, trying desperately to come back to earth. He had to *ask*? She paused. Did that mean he thought her promiscuous? Maybe – but she was past caring. He looked so deliciously rumpled, his face worried, his hair ruffled up on end. The sun was already turning his skin a beautiful tawny brown. How could she resist him?

She smiled wickedly. "Come here," she said, "and kiss me."

And then, of course, it was too late. He was undoing the buttons on the front of her top, his chin was grazing her skin as his lips moved down to her breasts, his hands smoothing over her stomach, now taut from all those wretched step classes.

Her clothes were unceremoniously disposed of and

she was suddenly aware of the scratchy blanket beneath her, and the breeze wavering along the bank of the river, so deliciously cool against her naked skin.

Marc slid off his jeans, pausing only for a moment before sliding joyfully into her, burying his face in her neck, his hips moving in time to hers. And as her heart and mind exploded and she quivered in the most blissful ecstasy, she heard his breathing, raw and ragged in her ear, his heart pounding against hers, holding her so tightly she thought he might crack a rib.

"Sorry," he muttered, kissing her gently. "Sorry, the next time will be more romantic, I promise."

Wasn't the countryside romance enough? Did he want moonlight and roses as well? Overwhelmed by the love and affection surging through her, she gazed into navy-blue eyes that stared so tenderly into hers and she wanted to weep. Do you love me as much as I love you? she wondered.

But she was too afraid to ask.

Chapter Seventeen

When Caitlin returned to Mistletoe House at eight o'clock that evening, Hugh was waiting for her in her room, lying stretched out on the bed. Beside him, an ashtray overflowed with half-smoked stubs and a cloud of cloying cigarette smoke still lingered in the air. Although he appeared to have been waiting some time, he did not look at all pleased to see her.

Perversely Caitlin felt smug. "What's the matter, Hugh? Isn't life after death as much fun as you'd thought it would be?"

He sat up, flicking the last cigarette butt into the ashtray without bothering to extinguish it first. His dark saturnine gaze, which she still hadn't grown accustomed to, regarded her stonily. "Where the *hell* have you been?"

Caitlin felt far too exhilarated to be intimidated. "Out," she replied, throwing her bag on a chair and barely glancing towards him. Let him stew. All those wasted years, when she had waited for him to come home at two or three in the morning, reeking of cigarette smoke, women's perfume, sex. Some nights he hadn't even come home at all. So let him torture himself as he imagined her with another lover, jealousy tearing out his insides. Let the bastard *suffer*.

"Out where?" He spoke as though spewing broken teeth.

She strung him out a bit longer. "I've been on a picnic."

"A *picnic*? With bloody Yogi Bear, I presume?"

"It's none of your business – we're not married any more." Unable to look in his direction in case she burst out laughing, Caitlin went to the chest of drawers by the window and took out a navy sweater. As the sun slowly set, in an explosion of pink and orange, the air had become chilly.

Pulling the sweater over her head, she failed to catch the dangerous glint in his eye. "I'm Calahurst's very own merry widow. What I get up to is my own affair."

"So it was a man."

Caitlin did not deign to answer. She pulled her last two bottles of brandy from under the bed and went to tip them down the bathroom sink. Bubbling over with her new-found confidence, she felt she no longer needed the alcohol as a crutch.

Baffled, Hugh followed her, giving a howl of outrage as he saw the brandy swirl around the sink and down the plughole. "What the hell are you doing?" He snatched up the bottle. "That's fucking expensive!

If you want to disinfect the bathroom use bleach like everyone else!"

She shrugged. "You want the brandy, you have it. I'm going on the wagon."

"*You?*" He began to laugh. "*You?* Stop drinking? That'll be the day!"

Why did everyone talk in song lyrics, thought Caitlin distractedly, returning to her bedroom.

Hugh screwed the lid back onto the brandy. By looking into the mirror above the sink he could see Caitlin picking up a jar of instant coffee, spooning some into a mug and switching on the kettle. His fingers tightened over the neck of the bottle and it was only as the rough metal on the edge of the lid bit into his fingers that his gaze returned to his own reflection. Sickened by the rabid fury apparent in his expression, he struggled to regain control, abruptly dropping the brandy bottle into the bin as he returned to the bedroom.

Caitlin was flopped in front of the TV, one leg hooked casually over the arm of her chair, eating Häagan-Dazs ice cream straight from the tub, apparently watching a romantic comedy on one of the movie channels. "Shut the door on your way out," she said.

Hugh was irritated by her sanguine self-assurance. "So, our marriage is over?"

"It was your idea." She began to channel-hop, pausing on some guts-and-gore action-flick with Bruce Willis dripping blood all over the screen.

The sound of gunfire drilled right into his head.

Caitlin turned up the volume. "I'm afraid the police have got your little black book. It's helping them with their enquiries. But there's always the telephone directory. You might think you've slept with all the women in Calahurst but there's bound to be someone you missed out."

She was not that indifferent then. Hugh opened his mouth to bite a retort; Caitlin turned up the sound again so he slammed the door as he left.

* * *

Jack was back behind the reception desk. When Caitlin had employed a receptionist he thought his days of servitude were over but the wretched girl kept going sick and apparently he was the only person available to cover. This left no time for painting. Feeling very hard done by, he had even resorted to complaining to Leo.

Unfortunately, Leo, stomping down the stairway in an extremely bad temper, had pointed out that in the three months Jack had resided in Mistletoe House he had not so much as picked up a paintbrush. And not through lack of opportunity.

"But I can't find anything to paint!" grumbled Jack.

"Bollocks, you're not trying. This is one of the most beautiful areas of the country."

"It's not like taking polaroids. I have to have inspiration –"

"Inspiration, my arse. Just get on with it. Why not

stick a dead sheep in a glass case?" he goaded. "There's bound to be one lying about in a field. Concept art, isn't it?"

"It's been done!" snarled Jack. "Besides, I'm an artist not a taxidermist."

Leo shrugged. "Please yourself! Find yourself work as an artist and I'll employ another receptionist. It's about time you started earning your keep. I'm not a fucking charity." And he stalked off through the front entrance.

Comic relief arrived in the form of Lord Richmond, banging the brass bell on the counter when he could plainly see Jack sitting behind it, half-heartedly watching *Die Hard* on TV and doodling a set of gallows attached to a rope around Leo's neck.

"I want to see that painter chappie," boomed Lord Richmond, making Jack start, his pencil skidding across the paper, neatly decapitating the caricature of Leo.

Jack gazed in fascination at the fleshy jowls, swaying from side to side, as Lord Richmond's rubbery lips opened and closed, revealing large, crooked yellow teeth like one of the forest ponies.

"Well?" demanded Lord Richmond.

Jack shoved his sketchbook aside. "That's me."

"You?" Lord Richmond took in the dreadlocks, patchy eyebrows, hooped earring and paint-splattered clothes. "You're the painter?"

The guy was obviously one brain cell up from a mollusc. Jack pointed to a large splash of 'crimson sunset' over his heart. "See," he said gravely. "Paint."

"I meant an artist not a decorator."

Jack lifted his sketch pad and pointed to the gallows. "Drawings," he said, then, pointing to himself. "Artist."

Sarcasm was wasted on Lord Richmond. He flicked through the pad, paused and gave a howl of outrage. "That's my daughter!"

"Where?" Jack craned his head round to look. Perhaps Lord Richmond was getting mixed up with the sketch of wild boar. But there on the page was Belinda, in all her glory, reclining amongst the sand-dunes, with Calahurst Quay as a romantic backdrop. A rather earthy-looking water nymph.

"She's your daughter?" Jack was incredulous. Maybe Belinda was conceived in a test-tube. Then, when he noticed Lord Richmond's florid colour starting to tinge purple, he added imperiously, "You can trust me. I'm an artist."

"Hmm." Lord Richmond regarded him stonily, then flicked through a few more pages. "I suppose they're all right. If you like that sort of thing."

Jack restrained an overwhelming impulse to punch this pompous twit right across the room. He had the idea that Caitlin would not approve, although it would certainly make him feel better.

"I want you to paint my daughter for her eighteenth birthday," said Lord Richmond at last, fixing Jack with a beady glare. "None of this nuddy stuff though. My wife has commissioned a couture gown from some flash London designer and you can paint her wearing that and her grandmother's pearls. I trust you charge a reasonable rate?"

"Twenty thousand pounds," said Jack, who had absolutely no desire to work for Lord Richmond and his sex-crazed daughter.

"Done. I'll leave it to you to arrange the sitting. It will have to fit in with my daughter's leisure pursuits."

"What?" The bugger had actually *agreed*!

Lord Richmond eyed him curiously. "The usual occupations for a young lady – ballet, riding . . ."

Jack wanted to ask, "Horses or men?" but didn't have the guts. He thought he'd wait until he had the twenty grand stashed away in some nice Swiss bank account before he reverted to type. He shook Lord Richmond's hand. "You have yourself a deal, Mr Richmond."

"Lord."

"Sorry, Mr Richmond-Lord."

Aware that a guest was hovering in the background, Lord Richmond let it pass. He handed Jack back his sketch pad and waddled off towards the bar.

Hardly had he turned his back then Jack began rubbing his hands with glee, muttering, "20K, 20K . . ."

Marc Granger regarded him in amusement. "Won the lottery?"

"Bloody good as!" Jack ensured Lord Richmond had left. "As my mother would say, 'A husband and his money are soon parted'."

"That's true," agreed Marc, "But, as my grandmother used to say, 'Don't count your cheques before they're cashed'."

"You think I should have asked for a deposit?" He

did a double take. "Hey, you're that Stewart Granger my sister is crazy about."

"I do hope so," grinned Marc.

"Did you want to see her?"

"Is she working?"

"Ha, I'm the only one fool enough to work around here! Caitlin's in her room. I'll call her." He picked up the telephone.

"No need. I'll surprise her. Which room?"

"Number ten. It's up two flights of stairs, turn right and go along the corridor, past the staff quarters, to the far end of the house. It's the last door on the right. It's called the Rose Suite and overlooks the garden."

Marc found Caitlin's new suite easily. All the guest rooms and suites had brass plaques on the door stating their name, usually after flowers or trees, in black Gothic lettering. The door was not locked so, as there was no reply to his loud knock, he walked straight in, praying he had the right room. But there was Caitlin's pink checked top and jeans, screwed up on the floor, and husky singing coming from the bathroom. He followed the steam.

Caitlin was having a shower. He knocked politely on the open door of the bathroom. She peered around the frosted glass of the shower and shrieked.

"Sorry, did I startle you?"

"A bit!" She smoothed back her hair from her forehead, to prevent the soap running into her eyes. "What are you doing here?"

She was so pleased to see him it almost broke his

heart. He was such a bastard – could she not see what he was doing? He should tell her the truth – but he'd lose his job and hurt her badly. And, after all she had been through, Caitlin did not deserve to be hurt again.

"I came to see you," he replied, his eyes surreptitiously following the length of her body, clearly silhouetted against the glass door. "I didn't mean to walk in unannounced but you didn't answer my knock."

"Sorry?" She looked confused. "I can't hear you over the water."

He stepped into the steamy bathroom, careful not to slip on the puddles, and walked slowly towards her. Her shower gel smelt distinctly of brandy. It was amazing what fragrances The Body Shop could concoct.

"I came to see you," he repeated as he drew level with her. The shower was constructed on a tiled platform above the floor so he had to tilt his head to look up at her. The water glistening on her cheeks resembled tears, giving her a vulnerable air. He felt his stomach contract.

She looked delighted. "How sweet!"

He tried hard not to stare at her right breast, squashed up against the glass. She was absolutely gorgeous, those huge green eyes filled with love. His willpower failed him and, taking a deep breath, he slid off his shoes and stepped up into the shower, pulling the door shut behind him. The water hit him square on the chest. It was the second soaking he had had that day. He was going to be really clean.

"But we had a date for *tomorrow* night," she said, smiling up at him.

"I know." He relieved her of the soap she was still clutching and tossed it out into the bathroom. "But patience never was my strong point."

* * *

Hugh sat on an old stone bench by the rose garden, surrounded by the flowers' delicate fragrance, infuriated that the scent reminded him of Caitlin. He could see her bedroom window from where he sat and watched as she and Marc came out of the steaming bathroom, both utterly drenched, and somehow managed to fall onto the four-poster bed without untangling from their passionate embrace.

A sudden stabbing agony made him glance down at his hand. The empty wine glass he had been toying with was crushed. Silver fragments of glass littered his lap and one jagged edge protruded from his thumb. He plucked it out and hurled it into the rose garden, pressing his bloody thumb to his mouth to stem the flow.

After a moment he re-examined it. Bright red blood oozed from a nasty jagged gash. Hugh shook the glass from his trousers and walked across the lawn towards the terrace without glancing at Caitlin's window again.

The French windows leading to the wine bar were open, loud pop music and assorted customers spilling out onto the terrace. As Hugh turned sideways to force himself through, he caught a glimpse of Jack outrageously chatting up Annelise Fitzpatrick, oblivious to her fuming father, Lord Richmond, not two foot away. Hugh grinned. Any moment now the old duffer was going to reach for his elephant gun.

God save him from impecunious relations, thought Hugh, finally reaching the blissful solitude of reception. Both Jack and Elena were taking up suites that could be earning a tidy sum if occupied by paying guests, Elena in particular was charging a fortune to room service and it wasn't as though she couldn't afford to stump up the cash herself. And as for that wastrel of a brother-in-law . . .

Hugh couldn't understand what women actually saw in Jack. It must be the novelty value of that awful hair, he decided. And those moth-eaten eyebrows. Did he have to wear sunglasses *all* the time? Hugh was sure Georgia had been such a disappointment in bed purely because she fancied Jack.

Hugh took a plaster from the First Aid box in reception and stuck it on his thumb. Returning to the bar, he stood menacingly behind his brother-in-law. "I hate to spoil your fun, dear boy," he drawled, "but the phone on the reception desk has been ringing non-stop."

Jack shrugged, not taking his gaze from Annelise. "I can't hear it."

"Then perhaps you should return to your post. You'll hear it more clearly."

Perhaps realising Hugh was in a foul temper, Jack

smiled ruefully at Annelise. "See you," he said and left.

Hugh moved to the stool he had vacated. Annelise did not seem to notice the changeover. She was wearing a clinging scarlet dress, which started mid-breast and finished mid-thigh, no stockings on her tanned legs but black, over-the-knee suede boots instead. With her thick auburn fringe, Gucci leather jacket and lashings of black eyeliner, she looked more like a rock chick than the wife of a respected MP.

Without even asking, the barman plonked down an opened bottle of Krug between them. It was Hugh's favourite – but Hugh had a basic ache no amount of fine champagne could cure.

"Hello," said Annelise in her deep rasping voice, which always sounded as though she had smoked sixty cigarettes before breakfast and then gargled with broken glass. She blatantly eyed him up and down and smiled slyly. "You must be Leo. You look very much like your brother. Twins in fact."

"There's no likeness at all," dismissed Hugh, fear of discovery making him sound disagreeable. "I'm five years younger, my eyes are brown . . ." he trailed off, realising he was protesting too much. Annelise had once known him more intimately than even his own wife. Perhaps blatantly sitting right next to her had been a rather stupid idea. He should make his excuses and leave now. He should, of course, but he wasn't going to.

"Ah yes, the eyes," mocked Annelise. "The windows of the soul."

Hugh deliberately trailed his finger along her bare arm. "And what can you see in mine?"

"Very little."

Old cow. Did she think she was being funny? Hugh took a long drink of his champagne, feeling its tranquillising warmth flood through him, and began to poke the bowl of peanuts on the bar with a discarded cocktail-stick.

Annelise regarded him speculatively and poured herself a drink from his bottle.

"That's 1982 Krug," he said frigidly, "not house white."

"I know," she smiled. "Your brother used to drink it too."

He stared at her, suddenly cold. It had only been a matter of months since they had shared a bed. If anyone could recognise him behind this plastic face then it would be Annelise.

"Your father was a wine buff?" added Annelise innocently.

He relaxed. She hadn't the slightest idea. He shouldn't be so paranoid. "That's right," he said, adding bitterly, "While the house fell down around our ears, he spent all our money on specialist champagnes and wines that no one was allowed to drink."

"Lucky alcohol keeps." She raised her glass in silent toast.

"A popular misconception." Hugh declined to clink glasses; it was a habit he deplored. He watched her sip the champagne. Their eyes met. She was starting to look her age, he noticed. Her roots needed touching up; tiny lines from her eyes creased into her hairline and there were more above her upper lip, giving her a discontented expression.

He had always been madly in lust with Annelise and would probably have married her if William Fitzpatrick had not beaten him to it. She oozed sex appeal with her thick mane of red hair, her green-blue eyes, her long legs and voluptuous, if rather freckly, breasts. She made love like a tiger – and he had the scars to prove it. She was the only woman to ever wear him out. He had to have her now. But was it really worth the risk? Surely Annelise would never betray him . . . would she?

Like Oscar Wilde, Hugh could resist anything but temptation. He took her glass away from her and carefully placed it on the bar.

"Let's go for a walk in the garden," he said, staring at her with hungry eyes. "The roses smell lovely."

Annelise hid a smile and pointedly took another sip from her glass. "I know, I can smell them from here."

Bitch – *she* hadn't changed. "Have you seen our new outdoor pool?"

"I swam in it this afternoon."

Hugh dropped the pretence. "Stop playing so fucking hard to get."

Her eyes were suddenly frosty. "What's that supposed to mean? Just because I'm friendly, polite, sociable – does not mean I'm more easily fuckable."

"You're not being easy. You're being bloody

difficult." *And was it really worth his effort?* He cast his chocolate-brown gaze around the bar to see if there was any other talent. But there were only two other suitable targets and they were both with other men. He took another swig of his drink and wondered whether to cut his losses and take himself off to Raj's club. Plenty of eager young girls there.

Then Annelise put her hand on his arm. "You were going to show me your new outdoor pool?"

He did not even look in her direction. Just finished his drink and picked up his jacket. "I thought you'd seen it?"

"Three times but it would be much nicer to have a personal tour."

His eyes narrowed. He knew Annelise of old. She was up to something. But it could be as harmless as wanting to be up to him.

"All right. Come on then." He strode off through the French windows and onto the terrace, Annelise following unsteadily.

It was so warm outside they could have been abroad. The night air had a sultry feel, full of Eastern promise. Hugh cast a sideways glance at Annelise but she had turned away to breathe the scent of the rose garden. She attempted to pluck a crimson bud but it refused to part from its stem and she had to bend over to bite it with her teeth. Her dress rode up, and up, and still he couldn't see any knickers. Hugh felt a sudden streak of desire burn through him.

Annelise tucked the rosebud down the front of her

dress. It looked ridiculous but who was he to criticise? He cast a look back at the house as he ducked beneath the fat bunches of wisteria blossom draped over the stone archway leading to the pool. Caitlin's room was in darkness.

Annelise was now fingering the amber petals of a honeysuckle which clambered over the surrounding brick wall.

Unable to erase the memory of his wife from his mind, Hugh attempted to concentrate on the woman in hand. "You might leave me some garden," he derided.

Annelise let the flower spring back and hurriedly teetered after him. Hugh felt mollified. He did like a woman who came on command. Then he cracked his head on a hanging basket of flowers, crammed with white pansies, petunias and trailing lobelia. He rubbed his forehead irritably. There were hundreds of the damn things – the place was starting to look like fucking Kew Gardens.

Hugh switched on the floodlights, careful to avoid falling over the large terracotta pots, overstuffed with white geraniums and sad little citrus-trees. Even the surrounding garden had been restocked with clambering roses, wisteria and honeysuckle, running rampantly out of control. Much like my wife, he thought sourly.

Annelise walked across the rustic terracotta pathway towards the edge of the pool. The water was like glass, every emerald and sapphire mosaic tile magnified. She leant forward and trailed a hand across the water; ripples circled forever outwards. She peeled off her boots, hitched up her dress and sat down, dangling her long brown legs in the pool. Hugh felt in desperate need of a cigarette.

"We could swim?" suggested Annelise. "I haven't been skinny-dipping since school."

If she had thrown a bucket of cold water over him it could not have been more effective. Hugh saw Amanda lying face down in the swimming-pool, a cloud of red smudging the water, her long hair swirling like ribbons of seaweed. Except he had thought she was Caitlin.

He turned to retch silently into the bushes. His legs were shaking. He stumbled across to the nearest sun-lounger and collapsed onto it. There was a large splash. It took a while for his eyes to focus. Annelise had apparently taken her dress off, leaving her rosebud wilting on the terracotta tiles, and dived in. Hugh watched her swim relentlessly through the water, effortlessly up and down, obviously expecting him to join her.

The only difference between Annelise and a prostitute, thought Hugh distastefully, was that a prostitute was more honest about payment. Most of his mother's jewellery had disappeared into her greedy little hands. What would she ask for tonight?

Bored of waiting, Annelise climbed elegantly from the pool. Her smooth, tanned skin was so perfect she could have been spray-painted. She wore no bra but her breasts showed no signs of drooping and her stomach remained flat despite having had three children. Uncharacteristically, she still had her knickers on, a black lace thong with flashy gold embroidery.

"Why didn't you join me?" she asked, not in the least embarrassed by her nakedness. "The water's lovely."

"And cold," said Hugh disparagingly, regarding her goose-bumps and loganberry nipples.

She laughed and sat on his lap. He was not impressed. She was over 5'10" and, although not at all fat, quite well-covered. She was also dripping chlorinated pool water all over his suit. He was about to tip her off and skulk back to the bar for the rest of his champagne, when she put her arm around his neck. Her right breast was about an inch from his mouth.

Hugh picked her up and dropped her into the jacuzzi. She sat up, shrieking, to find he had jumped in after her, disappearing beneath the azure water. Less than a minute later he exploded to the surface, her lace thong between his teeth.

She burst out laughing. "Well done!" she clapped delightedly. "I see you haven't lost your touch."

Hugh regarded her silently. So she had known all the time.

Bang went another evening of pleasure.

Chapter Eighteen

Georgia had set her alarm for midnight (shift work all over again) but found she was unable to sleep. She was far too excited. So she switched off the alarm ten minutes before it was due to ring and clambered out of bed. She had not changed from the jeans and shirt she had worn earlier in the evening, but wore her deck shoes instead of her usual clumpy mules.

Amanda's old room was only a few doors down from her own but Georgia had to creep past Leo's suite to get there – over old, warped floorboards which creaked and squeaked at every step. Georgia was terrified Leo might suddenly stick his head around his door and catch her. Judging her by his own alley-cat morals, he would assume she was bed-hopping. She was not worried about the security staff – they were more concerned with people breaking in from the outside.

Georgia did not need to switch on any lights; the moon shining through the corridor windows provided enough illumination. She paused outside staff bedroom seven, hoping she had got the right one. Amanda's room had been sealed the day her murder was discovered. When the hotel had been redecorated, Caitlin, deciding the blue and white sellotape was an eyesore, had peeled it away, taking most of the paintwork off too.

The bedroom door was locked. Only the police had keys – but it would take more than a locked door to keep Georgia out. She took a piece of metal wire from her pocket and inserted it in the lock. A couple of sharp twists and *voila!* There were certainly benefits to helping out at the Juvenile Offenders' Rehabilitation Workshops on Saturday mornings.

The door opened noiselessly. She entered and quickly drew the curtains in case anyone was outside, before flicking on her torch. For added security, she threw a couple of cushions against the crack under the bottom of the door. That was the trouble with these old houses. Everything was lopsided and nothing fitted.

Slowly Georgia swung the white beam of the torch around the room. *God, what a mess!* She picked her way through the discarded clothing littering the floor. Her sister had never been tidy, but this?

Amanda's room was decorated in the same airy-fairy style as her room at home and overlooked the drive. Spookily, the bed was still immaculately made but Amanda's leather suitcases were sticking carelessly out from underneath. The wardrobe doors were swinging open, the clothing scattered across the floor. Amanda's rather bizarre underwear was still draped over the chest of drawers, as though she had left not a moment previously. The underwear led a trail to the window, which had a thin layer of dust over the sill. Or had the Scenes of Crime officers left it behind when dusting for fingerprints?

Then Georgia realised something more sinister. The clothing was viciously slashed and torn and stained with lipsticked graffiti. She balanced the torch on the dressingtable and, her hands shaking, picked up a discarded pale-pink, satin shirt. Two round holes had been neatly cut over the bust. And above, in bright red lipstick, was written the slogan, "Hello Boys!"

Georgia leant over the sink but could only retch. The nausea overwhelmed her. She forgot she was a policewoman. Reality burst back with a vengeance.

She stared at the reflection of her face, gleaming Hallowe'en white from the light of the torch. "Caitlin," she said, the sound of her own voice bringing back some of her confidence. "Caitlin did this."

Forcing a self-assurance she did not feel, Georgia moved around the bedroom executing a lengthy and thorough search. Resisting the temptation to tidy up, she was careful to replace everything correctly; she could find no additional evidence. Amanda's belongings remained scattered around the room but there were still large holes in her life. Any personal effects such as diaries, notebooks, photos, must have been taken for examination. Valuables items, such as Amanda's camera and portable TV/VCR had been returned to her father. There were lighter patches in the dust where they had been. Georgia was left with the crap that no one wanted yet was loath to throw away.

Georgia began to fume. It was over three months since her sister's death; all this stuff should have been bagged up and placed in the police station property store in case it was needed as evidence in Court. What were Calahurst CID playing at? Did they want to keep the place as a shrine? She felt like wrecking the room in her frustration yet her police training slammed the brakes on her emotions.

She glanced at her watch; almost one thirty. Time enough. She had blown it. There was nothing to be gained from staying and everything to lose if she remained and was caught. Leo Kirkwood already had his suspicions. She would hate to have to submit to his pawings again.

She picked up the pink satin blouse and shoved it down the front of her denim shirt, the bagginess disguising her contraband effectively. She locked the door behind her and tiptoed down the passage.

It was as she moved towards the stairwell that she drew level with the window overlooking the garden. A flash of light streaked through the window ahead of her. *A thunderstorm? Get real.* She pressed her nose against the glass, misting it up. She had to wait almost five minutes but there it was again. The jerky movement of a thin beam of light. There was someone else with a torch, messing about by the outside pool, which was still floodlit. At half past one in the morning?

Adrenaline flowing, Georgia ran down the stairs,

jumping the last few steps and swinging round the banisters, then skidding through the wine bar towards the French windows. They were unlocked. It didn't occur to her to call security. She just plunged straight out onto the terrace and collided with a man loitering in the dark.

Georgia put out one hand to the balustrade to steady herself. "Shit, Fabian! Are you trying to give me a heart attack!"

"Sorry," he replied mournfully.

Without thinking, she flicked the beam of her torch onto his face. Fabian squinted and held up his hand to shield his eyes.

"Sorry, Fabe," she said, and quickly clicked the dimmer-switch. "What are you doing out here alone?"

"I promised Mr Simpson, the caretaker, I'd wash down the poolside and turn off the floodlights when the last guest had left. It's his wife's birthday and he would have been in trouble if he'd been late home."

"But it's almost two in the morning! You're not telling me someone's still in the pool?"

Fabian nodded. "If I'd have known I'd be out here this late I would never have agreed."

"Chuck them out!" said Georgia. "You've got to learn to be more assertive. Sometimes you can be such a doormat, Fabian. It's a wonder you don't wear a T-shirt with 'Please wipe your feet here' written on it."

"I can't chuck them out," muttered Fabian defensively. "It's Mr Kirkwood."

Georgia was not impressed. "Make him switch off his own bloody floodlights."

"I tried that. He told me to get lost. Or words to that effect."

"That man is such a prat."

"I think he's got other things on his mind."

"Such as?"

Fabian smiled wryly. "Mrs Fitzpatrick on his lap."

Georgia blinked. "You're kidding me! He's a fast worker."

"You mean she's a tart," said Fabian. "Rick and Hugh had her at the same time once – now she's in the jacuzzi with Leo. And the last time I looked, she didn't have her swimming costume on."

"And Leo?"

"I couldn't see for all the bubbles."

"Perhaps he was giving her mouth-to-mouth resuscitation?" Georgia said dryly.

Fabian grinned and the lines of tension disappeared. "You could call it that. But it wasn't her mouth he was kissing."

"Spare me the gruesome details. What about Caitlin? Have you told her? She won't want the hotel to get a worse reputation than the one it's already got."

"No, I didn't like to bother her. She's got a new boyfriend, Stewart somebody, and he's staying the night. I could hardly barge in. I might have caught them at it." Fabian looked bleak. "Everybody in this place is getting their end away except me."

"I thought you were dating our local celebrity, Marina Grey?"

"She seems to be going off me. I think she fancies

Jack. All the girls here fancy Jack – he's so full of Irish blarney. He was supposed to be duty manager tonight but he sloped off with Belinda Richmond. He said he was painting her portrait. Does he think I'm stupid?"

"Not your night, is it, Fabe? Tell you what, let's make an executive decision. *I'll* wash down the poolside and switch off the floodlights for you. How's that?"

"It has to be done tonight," warned Fabian. "Not tomorrow morning. Some of the guests get up really early to have a swim before breakfast."

Georgia patted his shoulder. "No problem. You can leave it to me."

"Make sure you leave the safety lights on." Fabian yawned and stood up, his knees cracking where he had been sitting hunched up for so long.

Georgia watched him stretch like a cat and admired his muscle-tone, set off to advantage in his Chemical Brothers T-shirt. Marina didn't know what she was missing. Even if Fabian did have the IQ of a Brussels sprout, trade him in for skinny Jack Sprat? Marina must be mad.

"Thanks," Fabian sighed. "You're a real friend."

"I know. Now beat it and get your beauty sleep."

He didn't need telling twice. Georgia watched him leave, then waited ten minutes to be doubly sure. She switched off her torch, leant on the balustrade and looked back at the house. Some of the guest rooms still had lights on but their curtains were tightly closed. Caitlin's room, at the end of the house, was in darkness.

Georgia curled her lip. Silly cow must be exhausted by all that passion.

Georgia shoved the torch into the front of her jeans and padded silently across the lawn, hoping she wouldn't tread in anything. Dogs were banned from the hotel but foxes would steal in from the woods to forage around the kitchen bins.

In the dark, the swimming-pool shone out like a beacon. It had been built in what had been a walled garden to afford it some privacy, although the surrounding brickwork was ornamental and had decorative holes, like massive portholes, with wisteria, honeysuckle and roses tumbling across them. Georgia attempted to peer through the nearest one but the shrubbery on the other side was far too overgrown, although the gardener had recently pruned it back. She had to resort to tiptoeing round the entrance, up the tiled brick steps, moving softly in her deck shoes.

The floodlights hurt her eyes. She paused for a moment to let her eyes adjust, then peered through the leaves of a hibiscus. The whitewashed changing rooms, with their green 'stable' doors, appeared deserted. The pool was still, the lights underwater revealing it was completely empty. The jacuzzi at the far end was deserted too.

"Mr Kirkwood!" she called, her voice echoing eerily back to her. "I have a telephone message for you!" As though anyone would phone at this hour.

Silence. She stepped under the floodlights and walked along the poolside, wary in case anyone sprang out at her. It must be her police training that made her so paranoid. She shivered, feeling as though a hundred eyes were watching her from the bushes. Although the security camera, high up on the poolside bar, was not active. Leo Kirkwood obviously had no wish for witnesses to his romantic tryst with Annelise.

As Georgia circled the pool, she tested the door on each changing cubicle, her heart virtually flossing her teeth as she rattled each one. They were all locked from the outside. She then backtracked to the jacuzzi. The area surrounding it was wet but the bubbles were still and she leant over, peering down to the bottom, hoping they had not drowned in the heat of their passion. But the jacuzzi was deserted too.

She sighed, disheartened. Leo and Annelise had been here earlier but there was no certainly no trace of them now. It was almost disappointing. Georgia was no voyeur but she felt that she might have learnt something to her advantage.

Georgia cast one lonely look around the pool garden before turning off the lights at the mains. And then, just as her fingers closed over the switch, something caught her eye. Gold and sparkling, it twinkled from the lower branches of a buddleia, like a decoration left over from Christmas. Georgia went to investigate. The item was the bottom half of a bikini, or perhaps a thong to be worn as underwear, as the garment was more lace and string than lycra. Georgia fished it out and regarded it distastefully. If Annelise Fitzpatrick made a habit of leaving her clothes scattered around Calahurst, it was amazing her husband had not wised to her years ago.

In the distance, Georgia heard a car door slam and the sound of wheels scrunching up the drive. Well, that answered her question, Annelise must be returning home after her night of passion.

Feeling somewhat foolish, Georgia abruptly performed a U-turn. She was wasting her time. There was nothing here. What on earth had she expected to find? Annelise and Leo having nookie in the jacuzzi? Embarrassing or what? She should get a grip. Adultery wasn't a crime.

Not for the first time, Georgia wished she hadn't read quite so many Enid Blyton books as a kid. She'd be drinking ginger beer next. If the entire force murder squad hadn't found her sister's killer in over four months, what on earth made her think she could just waltz in here and catch her – or him – instantaneously?

She stifled a yawn. God, it was almost three in the morning, and she had to be up at five thirty, ready to take the 'early bird' body conditioning class at seven.

Overwhelmingly depressed, Georgia dropped the offending knickers into the nearest rubbish bin, switched off the lights and stumbled back to the house.

Chapter Nineteen

Marc walked down the corridor towards the Detective Superintendent's office, humming the chorus of 'Love Is All Around', because that was all he knew. He was almost sent flying by Seb Hunter, storming out of Paul's office just as Marc was about to knock on the door.

"Why are you so cheerful?" snapped Seb. "Did you get laid or something?"

Marc, although slightly taken aback, did not reply. He had realised long ago that Seb didn't like him and so he merely smiled politely and walked through the open door. Detective Superintendent de Havilland was sitting rigidly at his immaculately tidy desk, his hands clenched so tightly together the knuckles had turned blue.

Marc hid a smile. The guy took 'chilling out' to an art form. "Hello, sir," he said cheerfully, booting the door shut with his foot. The slam reverberated around the office, causing the forest of potted plants to tremble.

"Is it OK for me to debrief you on the Kirkwood case?"

"You can wipe that smirk off your face, Granger," said Paul frostily. "Annelise Fitzpatrick was found dead in her BMW convertible this morning. At Calahurst Quay – six foot under water."

"Annelise Fitzpatrick?" *Hell, she'd been in the bar at Mistletoe House only the night before . . .* Marc sat abruptly on one of the easy chairs as the floor seemed to shift beneath him. Perhaps the Detective Superintendent had made a mistake? After all, Lord Richmond had so many daughters . . ." The MP's wife? Sexy redhead with predilection for miniskirts? I don't believe it – unless, was it suicide?"

Paul regarded him over the top of half-moon, gold-rimmed spectacles. "No," he replied firmly. "She was wearing a seatbelt. She was not, however, wearing underwear. Suicides are usually particular about the way they are dressed."

"Could it have been an accident? Maybe her brakes failed going down the hill?"

"Unlikely. Annelise is local and that part of the quay has been pedestrianised for the past ten years. Besides, even a drunken tourist could not fail to notice the olde worlde paving slabs and bollards."

With the return of his usual sarcasm, it was clear the Detective Superintendent was beginning to thaw out. Marc wondered why he was so uptight. It was almost as though he was taking Annelise's death personally

"You can imagine how the press are lapping it up," Paul added scathingly. "I've had reporters virtually camped out on my doorstep. The Chief Constable has cancelled his holiday in Bermuda and Detective Chief Superintendent Nicholson phones me up every fifteen minutes to see if I've got a lead. He seems to have conveniently forgotten Detective Superintendent Drysdale's in charge."

"This might not be connected with the Kirkwood case. Three deaths do not make a serial killer."

"They do if you're the editor of a tabloid newspaper."

Marc hid a smile. "Do we know how long Mrs Fitzpatrick was in the water?"

"No. The postmortem is not until this afternoon. Her husband last saw her at seven thirty yesterday evening. She was on her way to Mistletoe House to meet up with friends for a drink in their bar."

"And her body was found this morning?"

"Yes, just off the quayside. An angler caught his line on her car. Anyone else would have given it up but no, our hero dives into the river to go and investigate. He's now giving interviews to the press at £50 a time. I'm only surprised he hasn't phoned Max Clifford."

"Does DCI Hunter have any leads?"

"Just the health club connection. How are you getting on there? You said you've got a report?"

Marc leant forward and placed the file on the Detective Superintendent's desk. He felt his news had been pre-empted somewhat. "Mrs Kirkwood took a loan from her wealthy mother, the Marchesa del Lisle de Monterez, to make the refurbishments. I don't have the exact total but the final bill is near to £800,000."

"We knew that already." Paul flipped the file into his pending tray, hardly bothering to hide his disinterest. He picked up his biro, dug into his in-tray as though it was a lucky dip, and took out a handful of expense claims.

Marc frowned. It was distracting to observe his boss signing forms when he was attempting to brief him. "Hugh Kirkwood's younger brother, Leo, has turned up to claim his inheritance. He fell out with Hugh shortly after his marriage to Caitlin and went to live in America, where he earned his living as a professional show-jumper and occasional polo player."

"Knew that." Paul began to stamp the forms.

Is that all he did all day?

"Mrs Kirkwood had a miscarriage nearly two months ago," said Marc, "followed by a nervous breakdown, which was hushed up. She refused all psychiatric treatment but at one stage was hooked on prescription drugs. She's clean now though."

"Knew that too. Did *she* tell you?"

"No, but buy Fabian, the fitness instructor, a couple of drinks and he'll tell you anything. He can't hold his liquor."

"Fascinating." Paul dropped the claim forms into his out-tray and started on the invoices in his in-tray. Anything he did not like the look of was highlighted with a gaudy fluorescent pen. "DI Reynolds found out the same information from the hospital, without having to claim on expenses. Anything else?"

"Just that Mrs Kirkwood did not murder Mrs Fitzpatrick. She has an alibi."

"For all night?"

"Yes. She was with a man."

Paul paused, highlighter in mid-air. "That was quick work. Is he willing to make a statement to that effect?"

"It was me."

The highlighter flipped onto the floor. "You were with her all night?"

Although Paul's voice remained perfectly calm, Marc was in no doubt of his fury. "Yes, sir."

"And I can assume you were not playing table tennis?"

"Er, no."

"I think you've overstepped your brief, Detective Sergeant. You're off the case. You were due to take over from DS Moody when you were originally posted here from Special Branch. I think it's time you took up the job."

Although he knew this was coming, Marc still had to ask, "Who will take over from me?"

"Seb Hunter is in charge of the murder squad. It's up to him to place an officer undercover if he so wishes. And incidentally, Granger, you'll have to give up your membership of the health club." He paused. "Unless you wish to pay for it yourself. It is a free country after all."

Marc looked up. A glimmer of hope?

Paul returned to his paperwork and Marc knew he had been dismissed. Depression weighed low as he headed for the CID general office and checked when DI Reynolds expected him to be on duty. Two 'til ten.

Goodbye to all enchanted evenings. And no more romantic picnics for him.

* * *

Following her extra-curricular activities the night before, Georgia slept in until lunchtime. No one noticed. So much for the 'early bird' class. She had a headache to rival her most successful hangover, took a couple of paracetamol, shoved on a pair of dark glasses and staggered down to the dining-room where she was able to cadge some leftover breakfast.

The staff had their meals in a small room adjacent to the main dining-room. All the better to rub their noses in it. Both rooms were painted pale green with large unframed mirrors and Monet reproductions on the walls, plastic foliage throughout but the guest's dining-room had a little ornamental fountain bubbling softly in one corner. The paintings of Hugh's ancestors, some of which had hung on the walls for over a century, had been consigned to the attic.

Caitlin, Leo and Jack always ate in the main dining-room with the guests, which usually infuriated the socialist-inclined Georgia, but today she was grateful to be alone. She sneaked a spare copy of *The Independent* from reception and settled down to half a pink grapefruit and assorted crispbreads – the downside to living in a health spa.

Her headache was just starting to recede when Fabian sat next to her, his luncheon tray laden with three times his official entitlement. He was wearing his running gear and a bright perky grin. Inwardly she groaned. With all the attention she had paid him over the last couple of days he probably thought she was his new best friend.

"Hi, Georgia!" He lowered his voice to a conspiratorial tone, "You'll never guess what?"

"You're right," she agreed, wearily massaging her forehead. "It would take me forever. So why don't you put me out of my misery?"

"They found a body in the water at the quay."

"Another drunken tourist?" Georgia picked up her coffee. "Why doesn't the council put up proper railings?"

Fabian seemed disappointed by her lack of enthusiasm. "But it wasn't a tourist. It was Annelise Fitzpatrick."

"What?" Her coffee crashed to the floor, the scalding liquid streaming away across the bare boards. She hurriedly dumped a pile of paper napkins on top, hoping to soak up the worst of it. "Oh fucking, fucking hell . . ." It was barely lunchtime and already her day was freewheeling out of control.

"Shh! Mr Kirkwood's in the next room!"

"Oh my God! You think he did it?"

"Annelise was here last night. Mr Kirkwood must have been the last one to see her alive."

Georgia stared incredulously at him. The boy was brighter than he looked. Damn this headache! *She* was supposed to be the police officer. Why hadn't she worked it out?

"I'm going to phone the police," said Fabian, "and tell them I saw him with Annelise last night."

"*No!* I mean, don't rush into anything. You could be making a horrible mistake." Georgia massaged her forehead again, attempting to think rationally. "After all, why would Mr Kirkwood want to murder Mrs Fitzpatrick? He's probably very capable and undoubtedly had the opportunity – but there's no motive. Do you know how she died?"

"She drove her car right off the quayside and into the river."

"Maybe it was suicide – or just a horrible accident?"

"Bum! I didn't think of that."

Georgia thoughtfully drank Fabian's black coffee but he was too polite to point it out. He moved his tray further out of reach in case she began on his tropical fruit salad.

"But then, Annelise was not the suicide type," mused Georgia, replacing the cup on Fabian's tray. "She loved herself too much. People like that don't try to kill themselves in case they get hurt."

"So you do think it was murder?" Fabian's blue eyes gleamed.

"I didn't say that!"

Fabian remained silent as Kimmie and one of the beauticians walked past their table, giggling behind their frosted pink nails. "You were *thinking* it though," he hissed.

Georgia glared at him. "*Thinking* something will not result in being sued for slander. So don't mention this conversation to anyone – especially not Mr Kirkwood."

"Absolutely!" agreed Fabian. "I mean, I know we've all got to go sometime – but I'd rather it wasn't in a jacuzzi."

* * *

Marc returned to Mistletoe House just after lunch. He wanted to explain to Caitlin why he was standing her up tonight. He knew he was a bastard, but he hoped he was an ethical bastard. Unfortunately, according to that smarmy brother-in-law of hers, Caitlin was out. So Marc had to be content with leaving a message, although somehow he knew Caitlin would never get it. Ten years of dealing with villains convinced him Leo Kirkwood was a devious son of a bitch. But what could Leo hope to gain?

As Marc sipped an orange juice on the terrace, hoping Caitlin might still turn up, he noticed Georgia de Havilland sneaking furtively through the shrubbery and into the garden surrounding the outdoor pool. Now what was the silly girl up to? Marc put his glass down on one of the little round tables and followed her.

He found Georgia surreptitiously filling test tubes with water from both the pool and the jacuzzi. Nancy Drew! He almost burst out laughing. Didn't she have anything better to do?

"Novel way to test the chemical balance," he said, after creeping up behind her.

Georgia shrieked and dropped one of the test tubes.

He caught it, without spilling any, and handed it back.

"I'm checking for evidence," she squeaked. "I think Annelise was drowned in either the jacuzzi or the pool and moved to the quayside by her murderer."

"You're wasting your time," he said, completely unfazed. He was used to Georgia. Once she got a notion into her head there was no stopping her. Still, he had to admire her tenacity. "Both the water in the pool and the jacuzzi is constantly pumped through filters and the chlorine will kill anything stone dead."

"Piss," said Georgia, up-ending the test tubes into a terracotta pot.

Marc grinned. "That too."

"What about the postmortem? Did Annelise have chlorine in her lungs?"

"You're a bit quick off the mark, George. The postmortem hasn't been done yet."

"Well, will you ask them to check?"

Her persistence was beginning to exasperate him. "No point, chlorine disperses almost immediately. And the only way to find out if Annelise *was* murdered is to check her body for cuts and bruises synonymous with a struggle – which are also pretty much the same as could be received during a car crash." Marc patted her shoulder. "Sorry, George. Even if you are right it would be impossible to prove."

Disheartened, Georgia sat on the jacuzzi steps. "Damn, where's Sherlock Holmes when you need him? This time I really thought I was on the right track."

"Don't get comfortable," said Marc. "You're not a member. Technically you're trespassing. And if Caitlin should catch you you'll be in even bigger trouble than you are now. She doesn't think very highly of the police at present."

"Actually, I work here," said Georgia, and somewhat smugly waved an ID card in the air.

Marc, thinking it was fake, had to admire her bravado. "What as? Pool attendant?"

"Fitness instructor. I originally trained in aerobics to pay my way through college. As soon as I heard they were hiring additional staff I sent in my CV and was hired by Leo Kirkwood himself."

He studied her open expression. It sounded plausible, but still . . . "I can't believe you've thrown away your career in the police just to be an aerobics teacher."

"I'm *undercover*. You remember? The careering-out-of-control-break?"

"Does your father know you're here?"

"Are you kidding?"

At least that figured. Marc regarded her consideringly. "How did you know that Mrs Fitzpatrick had died? It hasn't been officially released to the Press – although they know a body has been found."

Her blue-grey eyes did not quite meet his. "This is a one-horse town. You've only got to sneeze and everyone knows about it."

He was not going to let her off the hook that easily. "What makes you think Annelise came to an unfortunate end in this whirlpool? Your father is convinced she lost her knickers as a trophy to her murderer. Not that she accidentally left them here after a spot of skinny-dipping."

"Say again?" Georgia turned pale.

"Which bit?"

"About Annelise's knickers . . . didn't she have any on?"

"No."

Georgia's next action was to run across to the large refuse bin located between the jacuzzi and the flower-bed and to start rummaging.

Marc watched her with amusement. "What are you looking for?"

"Nothing," came the muffled reply, as drinks cans and fruit peel were jettisoned across the tiles.

He decided to let the very obvious falsehood pass and patiently waited for her to emerge. At least no one could doubt her enthusiasm to catch the murderer.

When she did finally stand up straight, kick the bin, and come grumpily back to him, he realised the significance of her new, very short, mousy, hairstyle.

"You're in disguise too," he teased. "And I bet the Kirkwoods are too dumb to recognise you as Amanda's sister!"

Georgia looked sheepish. "I call myself Georgia Kelly – I thought the Irish surname would appeal. They've no idea who I really am. They'd hardly have hired me otherwise – particularly as I'm a police officer. You won't tell Dad, will you?" Georgia seemed to realise she had been a bit too free with her information.

"No. But if you hurt Caitlin in any way –"

"Fancy her, do you?" teased Georgia. "Join the queue. Since her supposedly beloved Hugh copped it, Caitlin's had dozens of men falling over themselves to date the glamorous black widow. Suckers."

"A string of men?" echoed Marc in disbelief.

"Yup, and top of the list is a wimp called Stewart."

Marc tried hard not to laugh. "How do you know he's a wimp?"

"With a name like Stewart, he's hardly going to be built like Rambo, is he?"

* * *

Despite what he had promised Georgia, Fabian could not resisting telling Caitlin. After all, the man was her brother-in-law – she deserved to know he was as big a rat as her depraved late husband. Fabian, however, was astonished at how badly she took his news and would have been totally nonplussed to see her frenziedly hurling her belongings into an inadequately sized suitcase not five minutes after he left.

Caitlin, who was not much good at packing at the best of times, wrenched out the drawers of clothes, tipping them into bin-liners she had just filched from the cleaner's cupboard down the hall. Then she scooped up her ornaments, toiletries and make-up, dropping them on top. Some did not survive the experience.

Hugh, hearing the commotion from the bed in the

adjoining guest suite, clambered over the blonde beside him, pulled on his clothes and sprinted down the corridor. Remembering the last time he had barged into her bedroom, he had the presence of mind to knock first. It also gave him the time to tuck in his shirt.

"Come in," sobbed Caitlin, thinking it was Marc.

Hugh was beside her in a second, enfolding her into his arms. "Caitlin, darling, what on earth's the matter?"

"Keep away from me!" she screamed, instinctively taking two steps back.

Hugh shrugged: a vulnerable gesture of defeat. "What have I done now?"

"You killed Annelise!"

"I did *what*?"

"You murdered Annelise Fitzpatrick," said Caitlin, her sobs coming out in great gulps. "The police found her body at the bottom of the river."

"And you think I'm responsible?"

"Witnesses saw you with her last night."

He laughed. "If, by 'witnesses', you mean Fabian, than you are quite correct. But she also had a drink with her father in the bar. And she arrived with two men, neither of whom were her husband. She probably had a whole regiment of fellows lined up after me. I ask you, what sort of woman turns up at a health club wearing an indecently short dress, backless lace knickers and thigh-high boots?"

"How the hell would you know what her knickers looked like?"

"I had the pleasure of taking them off."

For a moment Caitlin didn't believe she had heard him correctly. "You have no conscience, do you?" she whispered. "That poor woman is dead and you couldn't care less. Well, I have no intention of being next. I'm leaving."

He frowned. "Where will you go? You have no money."

"My mother has gone to visit her friends in London. I'll join her."

"Going home to Mother? How unoriginal. But I suppose it makes a change from Mother coming home to us."

She raised her hand to his face but he caught it and bent it behind her back.

"Unpack," he said softly.

"No way! I'm leaving you." She twisted, trying to get free, and he released her so suddenly she had to catch hold of the bedpost to steady herself. "I should have left a long time ago," she added bitterly, "when I caught you in bed with Rick."

He shrugged nonchalantly. "You could have joined in. We did offer."

"Pervert!"

Hugh slapped her, quite casually, yet with such force the blow caught her temple and sent her staggering against the bed. The bin-liners crammed with her stuff cascaded onto the floor.

"I thought you'd be pleased to see me go." She blinked away the tears, determined not to let him witness the pain he'd caused.

"I've changed my mind. I think we ought to give this marriage another try." He turned away so that she could no longer read his expression. "No one in my family has ever been divorced before."

"We don't have to get a divorce. You're dead!"

"Thank you for reminding me." He kicked a bin-liner under the bed and helped her to her feet, his fingernails digging cruelly into her hand. Slowly he raised it to his lips but she could see no love in his eyes, just cold, bitter hatred. "We'll just have to get married all over again, won't we?"

Chapter Twenty

July

Caitlin grimly thudded along the treadmill in the Fitness Studio, Jack's Aswad CD playing in her personal stereo. If she turned her head slightly to the right she could gaze across the lawn to the park and the forest beyond. She had already run three miles but was pondering on the logic. Here she was, living in one of the most beautiful areas in the country, running on a machine in a sweaty gym. At least it took her mind off Marc.

She sighed and increased the speed of the treadmill. Next to her, Marina clambered on the step machine and was soon springing up and down. Her black glossy curls were bouncing, her breasts swinging rhythmically from left to right, despite a sports bra underneath her pink leotard. Three men loitering by the bench-press opposite had not moved since she started.

"Say, Caitlin," beamed Marina, pausing for breath, "I thought I'd tell you – that new female aerobics instructor – Georgia – is wonderful. I've lost nearly a stone since I've been doing her classes."

For some reason this did not make Caitlin feel any happier. "I thought Fabian was considered the aerobics god around here?" she grumbled.

"Fabian's great too, all those muscles and flowing blond hair! But when he's jumping around on that stage, in those tight lycra shorts – well, I never know which way to look!"

Rick, standing in the corner of the gym, caught Caitlin's attention. He was explaining a warm-up routine to a new member, a pert little brunette. "If you stand with your legs wide apart," he was saying, "bend one leg and *lean* into the stretch, you should be able to feel it *here*." And, as he smoothed one hand over the girl's inner thigh, he caught Caitlin's reflection glaring at him in the mirror and turned beetroot.

He was almost knocked flying as Marc abruptly entered the gym, still wearing his outdoor clothes, and strode straight over to Caitlin, incandescent with rage.

"If you want to dump me," he said, his voice quiet but distinctly icy, "why don't you have the guts to tell me, face to face? Instead of getting your brother-in-law to keep telling me you're out?"

Caitlin was taken aback. "But you're the one who stood *me* up."

Aware that Rick and Marina were enthralled by their altercation, Marc switched off the treadmill and, taking a firm hold of Caitlin's arm, steered her out to the deserted corridor.

"Once," he hissed, "just *once*, I stood you up. Yet I've phoned, I've written, I sent you a beautiful bouquet of pink roses – but I suppose you get so many –"

"I didn't receive any flowers –"

"I left messages with your brother-in-law –"

She laughed brittly. "My very own message service. Believe me, he said nothing."

"Why not? Why would he want to jeopardise our relationship? Is he in love with you?"

The truth hovered uncomfortably on Caitlin's lips. "The opposite," she admitted miserably. "Legally the hotel is his but, because of the money my mother has put in, he has found it very difficult to get rid of me. And he would *really* like to get rid of me."

"Move in with me," suggested Marc. "No strings – you can sleep in my spare room. I only live five minutes' drive away. You'd hardly know you'd moved out."

Oh *heaven*. She was tempted, so very tempted. But Marc still had not said he loved her. She had rushed into marriage with Hugh. No way was she going to make the same mistake again.

"I'd really like to," sighed Caitlin, "but I don't want to give Leo the slightest advantage."

At once she realised she had chosen the wrong words. As his eyes darkened she realised Marc now thought she preferred the hotel to him.

"A fight to the death?" he sneered.

Caitlin shivered. Could it come to that?

"Sorry," said Marc. "I guess I'm just Mr Tact and Diplomacy." He put his arm around her. "Come on. Let me take you away from all this. We need to talk. Are you busy this evening? Can you come out to dinner?"

Caitlin conveniently forgot the large box of chocolates she had miserably consumed earlier. And the minute salad waiting as punishment. "Yes, please," she said. "I'd love to. Just give me a few minutes to change."

As they walked through reception twenty minutes later, they passed Hugh chatting up a teenage redhead from Caitlin's step class. Marc strode up to him and delivered a punch that sent Hugh flying into a flower arrangement. Water, petals and spongy green oasis splattered in a five-foot radius.

Hugh sat up amongst the debris, nursing a bloody nose. "What the fuck was that for?"

"You don't interfere with my life," said Marc blithely, "and I won't interfere with yours."

* * *

Marc drove through the Forest and down to the sea. They stopped at a little village called Port Rell, an old fisherman's harbour, now modernised with yuppie flats and designer boutiques. It was quaint, in its way, but had none of the original charm of Calahurst. Caitlin would not have chosen to come here but she had the idea that Marc wanted to put as much distance between them and Mistletoe House as possible.

He parked the Mondeo on the quayside. It was high tide and they paused to lean over the adjacent railings, looking on the grey water churning below. A sudden high wave smacked against the wall, sending salty spray over them.

Caitlin breathed the sea air deep into her lungs, so happy she could burst. Marc smiled at her, cuddling her close as they wandered around the edge of the harbour, admiring the millionaires' yachts. As the sky grew darker, they browsed through the old shops along the winding cobblestoned streets, mostly boutiques, trinket and souvenir shops all cold-heartedly aimed at the tourists.

As the air became chilly, Marc's humour began to fade. Caitlin caught him staring at her, searchingly, and wondered what she had done wrong. Surely he wasn't still upset that she had refused to move in with him? She steered him away from the expensive boutiques, in case he thought she was angling for a gift, and attempted to keep the humour flowing – but it was hard work. Although Marc had never had the terminally cheerful bounce of Fabian, he was not usually so quiet.

He cheered up as they chose the restaurant for their dinner, a seventeenth-century coaching inn, renamed The Smugglers' Inn for the benefit of the tourists. It was a quaint building, with an uneven roof, located on the corner of the road and painted white. The inside was rather like Marina's cottage with exposed brickwork and beams, and large bay windows that looked out over the harbour lights.

Marc chose an empty table by the window. It was tucked away in a romantically darkened corner, just across from the alcove containing the fireplace, all herringbone brickwork and blackened grate. The seats and tables were constructed from the local oak and there was a tired-looking yellow rosebud thrust into a small vase between the ashtray and the salt and pepper.

The restaurant's speciality was fish. Caitlin had dined here before, with Marina, and so picked her favourite – salmon poached in wine. Marc decided on swordfish in a Mediterranean sauce. He also ordered a whole bottle of wine for Caitlin and a mineral water for himself because he was driving. As he splashed liberal amounts of wine into Caitlin's glass she realised she had forgotten to tell him she had given up alcohol.

After their food had arrived and the waiters had left them alone, Marc settled back in his chair and asked, "Why don't you want to move in with me? Is it too soon after Hugh? Are you worried what people might think?"

Caitlin squirmed in her seat. "Yes and no."

He took a sip of his mineral water. "It would help if you could elaborate."

"Can't we change the subject?"

"Yes, if you like. It depends on how far you want our relationship to progress."

She took a swig of her wine, unconsciously mirroring him, just to delay the agony of having to confess the truth. Or rather, remember the pack of lies.

He smiled encouragingly. "Look, I understand about Hugh, and I know I'm rushing you – but I do think you care something for me. Am I right?"

If he only knew! She nodded dumbly.

"So what's the problem?"

Caitlin tried desperately to think of a reply. It was worse than her interview at the police station. Any minute now he was going to switch on a tape recorder and read out a Caution. How could she possibly tell him the truth?

"Would you like to know why I stood you up?"

Caitlin had not liked to ask, unwilling to antagonise him. Five years married to Hugh and she was growing weary of confrontations. "It doesn't matter," she replied evasively, and pretended to focus on the perils of de-boning fish by candlelight.

"It does to me," he said shortly. "I hate breaking promises."

Caitlin gave up with the fish, fiddled with her napkin, realised it made her look nervous and picked up her drink, swilling it around unenthusiastically.

He took it from her hand and firmly returned it to the table. "Come on, Caitlin. You can talk to me."

It seemed there was no choice. He was never going to let the topic drop. She took a deep breath.

"Yes, I loved my husband," she replied, staring fixedly at the wilting rosebud, unable to meet his eyes.

He smiled tenderly. "Most women do."

The only sound was the quiet buzz of genial conversation around them. She began to clench at the napkin again. Then, because she could bear the silence no longer, she nervously gabbled on, desperately hoping he would understand.

"When I first met Hugh I was the fitness instructor and he was my boss. He was so glamorous, so handsome, always cracking jokes, I fell in love with him. But I never expected him to want to marry me. He always had some sophisticate on his arm, usually Annelise. I couldn't believe he loved *me*. I'd never had a dream come true in such a spectacular fashion."

"So when did it start to go wrong?" asked Marc quietly.

"My wedding day. I caught him in bed with the gym instructor."

"Oh dear."

She couldn't bear to look up, could only guess at his emotions. Disgust probably and she hadn't even told him the half of it.

"I'm talking about Rick here . . ." she added.

"Jesus," he whistled. "Hugh was in bed with *Rick*?"

Did he think she was making it up? Her gaze sunk even further, about level with the scratched oak table, so that her hair half-fell over her face, giving her something substantial to hide behind.

"Uh huh. Hugh even suggested I join them."

"Bastard! Why didn't you leave?"

"Where would I go?" Her eyes flew to his face. She knew he would never understand. "I would have had no job, no home. I'd rowed with Jack and my mother that very day. They had seen through Hugh in two seconds flat. They tried to warn me. *I* told them I never wanted to see them again."

He took her hands in his, holding them tightly. "You

don't have to tell me any more. I'm sorry, I should not have brought the subject up."

She didn't hear him, ducking her face from his scrutiny, focusing on the little stone fireplace opposite. Staring into the flickering flames, she almost felt she had returned to the past, seeing herself, making those same idiotic mistakes all over again.

"Stupidly I stuck with Hugh," she sighed. "I was convinced our marriage would get better. But of course it didn't. You can't change people. Hugh was never foolish enough to get caught like that again but I knew he was unfaithful to me. So I concentrated on getting pregnant."

She glanced back at Marc. He was listening intently. "I was desperate to have a baby. I wanted someone to love. Someone that would love me back. But the years passed and nothing happened; Hugh said it was my fault. The hotel was failing; he drank more; I drank more. We would row and then he would hit me."

Marc's hand tightly gripped hers. His expression was unreadable.

"I went to all these clinics," she continued, "had hundreds of tests, but they could find nothing wrong with me. 'Perhaps your husband has a low sperm count,' they said. But of course Hugh always denied there was anything wrong with him." She paused and took a deep breath. "And then I found a letter from his doctor, hidden away in his briefcase. It said . . . it said that although it was not 'impossible' for Hugh to have a child, it was 'extremely unlikely'."

Marc frowned. "So how did you –"

"The Immaculate Conception?" she derided. She already disgusted him; she could see it in his eyes. One more confession would not make any difference. "Well, I fiddled the hotel accounts to get some cash and took myself off to a private fertility clinic. Artificial Insemination by Donor. Romantic, eh?"

He stared at her incredulously. "And Hugh thought the baby was his?"

"Of course. Why wouldn't he?" She withdrew her hands from his, before he moved first. "Then, after Hugh died I . . . I lost the baby." She dragged her eyes back to his face to gauge his reaction.

Marc sat back, stunned. "I don't know what to say."

She dropped her gaze, unable to look at him. She could not bear to see the condemnation in his eyes. He wouldn't want her now. She should make it easy for him and just leave. *Fool!* she cursed herself silently.

Marc realised she had left her dinner, having just moved it aimlessly around her plate. "Didn't you like your meal?" he asked. "I'm sure they could cook you something else."

Startled, her eyes darted up. How could he possibly think of *food* at a time like this? Tears blurring her vision, she abruptly shoved back her chair to escape, knocking over the wine glass in her hurry.

He caught her wrist. "Where are you going?"

"This was a mistake, I –"

"Sit down!" He pushed her back into her seat.

"Is anything wrong, sir?" interrupted the waiter.

Marc was forced to make his voice sound normal. "No, everything is *fine*."

"Would you like to see the dessert menu?"

"No, thank you." Marc turned his back on him. "Now listen, Caitlin –"

"Perhaps some coffee, sir?"

"Fuck off and leave us alone!" howled Marc.

The waiter, as white as his dress shirt, fled back to the comparative sanctuary of the kitchens.

Then Marc saw Caitlin's shocked face and took her hands in his. "I'm sorry, so sorry. Don't go. Please don't leave me."

Caitlin stared at him uneasily. For just a brief moment, it was as though Hugh was sitting opposite her. Arrogant, wilful Hugh, who had never cared whom he hurt, provided life went the way he desired.

Then she noticed the dark shadows beneath Marc's eyes. He looked so tired, strained. Perhaps things were going badly for him at work? Then she had to dump all her problems on him. Why hadn't she kept her big mouth shut?

He took hold of her hands and held them tightly. "I don't care about the past. Your past or my past. It's gone. All I know is that I love you. I can't let you go."

Marc's eyes were so dark with longing they were almost black. Slowly, tenderly, he moved his thumb against the inside of her wrist. She closed her eyes. She had never felt this way about Hugh.

"Let's go," he commanded. "We can have coffee back at my cottage. We need to talk." He signalled for the bill.

Talk? Hadn't she talked enough tonight? Caitlin felt that prickle of fear return. Unless – unless he was going to – ask her to *marry* him. But then she would have to tell Marc that Hugh was still alive . . . *Oh what a tangled web we weave* . . . well, her web of lies had more knots in it than even the keenest boy scout could cope with. It would take forever to unravel them all. Caitlin decided to keep quiet. She had made quite enough confessions tonight already.

They walked down the staircase and into the street, hand in hand. Marc's black Mondeo was parked outside, on the opposite side of the road, next to the railings that divided the pavement from the harbour. Marc unlocked the door, his arm still draped about her waist. She leant into him, tucking her fingers into the belt loops of his jeans, and snuggled against him. She felt so happy, just being with him. What would happen when he learnt the truth about her? About what she had done?

Marc lifted her chin and kissed her. She could feel the warmth of his body through her thin cotton shift dress and relaxed into him.

As he lifted his head she cuddled into his shoulder and sighed contentedly. "What a beautiful sunset," she said, looking at the orange sky above The Smugglers' Inn.

"Mmm," agreed Marc and then opened his eyes. There was no sun. It was half past ten and the sky was royal blue. Slowly he turned to gaze in her direction. "That is not the sun setting."

"Of course it is," said Caitlin. "What else would make the sky turn orange?"

A fire engine clanged along the seafront and disappeared up the hill to join the main road to Calahurst.

Marc leapt into the car, starting it up and jamming his foot on the accelerator, almost before Caitlin had joined him. She had to grip onto her seat as they swung violently around the narrow bends towards Calahurst. And as her fingernails dug deeper into the upholstery, she realised she was muttering a prayer, over and over again.

"Please God, don't let it be Mistletoe House . . ."

The orange glow filled the horizon as they approached the village and the bitter scent of smoke percolated through the air-conditioning of the car. As the cars in front began to slow down, Caitlin could actually see the flames leaping into the air between the houses and the smoke hovering threateningly in a solid mass above. For a moment she thought it was the police station ablaze but then, as the traffic came to a standstill in front of them, she realised it was The Stables pub.

The police had blocked off the road into the village and a crowd had gathered to watch the drama. As well as fire crews from Calahurst and Port Rell, there was an engine from Norchester. Thank God the fire was not in the woods. After the recent hot weather, the whole Forest would have gone up.

With the road blocked off and no alternative diversion unless they drove all the way back to Port

Rell, they had to join the back of a long queue of traffic. Marc, out of habit, swung up onto the pavement, bumped along on the inside – to the intense fury of the other drivers in the queue – and drove into the police station yard.

Caitlin eyed the neighbouring patrol cars. "Is it all right to leave your car here?"

"Oh yes," replied Marc, who thought she was referring to the fire. "We're perfectly safe."

Caitlin, relieved that neither her hotel nor the Forest were in danger of burning down, wanted to leave and could not understand why Marc was so interested in the fire. She felt like a ghoul, particularly as an ambulance screamed up behind them, blocking them in, and two men in fluorescent vests jumped out and ran across to the burning building.

"Oh God! Do you think someone's been injured?"

Marc swung his long legs out of the car. "I'll find out."

"Marc! Come back!"

But Marc had seen his colleagues from the station helping the fire crews and his police training was causing a shut-down of his brain. "Stay there," he said. "You'll be quite safe, so long as you don't move."

Caitlin watched him step over a thick yellow hose trailing across the yard and disappear behind a fire engine parked on the pavement. Her heart began to thud. She fumbled with the door handle. No way was she going to sit here and watch him barbecued just because he wanted to be a hero.

She clambered out of the car and ran across the police station yard. Even though the pub was on the other side of the road, she could feel the heat and the flames crackled like pistol shot. Where the hell had he gone? He was so tall, he should be easy to spot – but then, so were the firefighters.

She watched as two firefighters staggered out of the pub, across the car park and into the road, carrying a man between them. They passed him on to a paramedic and ducked back into the building. Frantic that Marc might have been hurt, she hurried over but as she drew closer she could see the victim was shorter and not so broad in the shoulder.

She peered at the man's smoke-streaked face. "*Hugh?*"

"*Caitlin?*" he mimicked. He ran his fingers through his hair, dislodging a cloud of ash. "Bad luck just seems to follow you around, darling."

Why did he always make her feel like a gauche sixteen-year-old? Knowing it would be a complete waste of time to enquire after his health – he would only subject her to more sarcasm – she said, "I didn't realise The Stables was one of your haunts."

He grimaced. "It was Georgia's choice. She likes the fruit wines."

"Georgia? You've been dating *Georgia*? The new fitness instructor?"

"Mmm," said Hugh. "I don't know what it is with me and fitness instructors. Perhaps I should see a psychiatrist, break the habit."

But Caitlin was not listening. As Hugh broke into a coughing fit, she watched Marc stagger out of the burning building and across the road, with Georgia leaning against his arm.

"I'm perfectly all right," Georgia was saying, as she abruptly sat on the pavement outside the police station, wheezing and gasping for breath.

Marc rubbed her back. "I think you should go to hospital and be checked over. Smoke inhalation can be dangerous."

"I tell you I'm *fine*!"

Hugh, showing a complete disregard for his date, was still staring, thin-lipped, at Caitlin. "Does your boyfriend make a habit of rescuing other men's damsels in distress?"

Caitlin, her stomach knotted with jealousy, couldn't reply.

With a sigh, the pub finally collapsed, showering sparks and small lumps of burning wood across the road. Hugh and Georgia were forced to leap up, out of the way. They all retreated into the police station yard, watching as the flames ate into the debris, climbing triumphantly higher, the heat scorching their clothes even from this distance.

"Is everyone all right?" asked DCI Hunter, appearing through the smoke. He patted Marc on the shoulder. "Excellent work, Sergeant Granger. I didn't realise you were on duty tonight."

Sergeant? Caitlin felt the familiar panic rush through her.

Marc's eyes met hers. His mask of fabrication did not come down quick enough.

Marc was a police sergeant . . .

It was as though one of the burning beams had just clunked her over the head. Why hadn't he told her – unless he had been sent to interrogate her about Hugh's murder? The police undoubtedly still thought her to be the prime suspect. She was so stupid. Why hadn't she seen through his lies? Thinking about his behaviour, it was so obvious. After all, what normal man would want her, with all her emotional baggage? He didn't love her; he probably despised her. And she had slept with him. Told him about the baby. Told him *everything* . . . oh God, she wished she were dead.

Caitlin turned away and ran off down the road, ducking under the blue and white tape. As she hit the crossroads she checked over her shoulder to see if she was being followed, just as Marc grabbed her arm and swung her round to face him.

She struggled ineffectively. "Let me go, you bastard!"

"Caitlin, you've got to listen to me –"

"You just wanted information," she cried. "You lied to me!"

"I was going to tell you – that's why I wanted to talk tonight."

"You'd tell me anything, whatever you thought I wanted to hear. Is that what tonight was about? Were you recording every word I said?"

"Listen to what I'm trying to say!" he pleaded. "I *know* you didn't kill your husband –"

"Of course I didn't!"

"Caitlin, please!" His arms were sliding around her waist in that familiar way. He was attempting to calm her down, make her see his point of view but Caitlin didn't want to hear it. There was no way he could make everything all right. They were way beyond a lover's tiff. He had lied to her, betrayed her trust. Nothing would heal the raw agony burning inside her.

She pushed him away, seeing him stagger, caught off-balance, a fleeting glimpse of pain in his eyes. He was good. The perfect portrait of suffering. He was wasted on the police, she thought. The bastard ought to be in the movies.

And for a brief moment she felt powerful, felt her strength to hurt, even though, deep down, she knew he didn't really care for her. It was all an act. But as she searched for that pithy one-liner, the icy put-down which would *really* wound him, she realised she was too late. The tears had already started down her cheeks.

So she turned before he could witness them and ran, ran faster than she had ever run in her life, leaving him in no doubt that this time she did not want to be caught. Did not want to listen to his feeble apologies, unconvincing lies, pathetic protestations of innocence.

But there was something she could not fail to hear. Just before she moved away, just before she began to run, she heard him say, softly, brokenly,

"I love you, Caitlin . . ."

Chapter Twenty-one

"I have witnessed bigger fuck-ups in my long career," said Detective Superintendent de Havilland, "although this one would be pretty hard to beat."

Marc stared at the purple orchid on the desk. He knew every petal intimately. Seb Hunter, also failing to meet his boss's eyes, settled for his tie instead.

"Mrs Kirkwood has filed a complaint," continued Paul de Havilland. "She has good reason to complain and has every chance of winning the case. Our only hope is to wrap this up, once and for all, and the resulting publicity should overshadow the less-than-finer aspects. Perhaps we should try working together as a team," he added sarcastically, "rather than the 'death or glory' approach?"

"Sir," began Seb Hunter testily, "if I had known DS Granger was working, undercover –"

"Sorry," said Paul, "that was my fault. I had the idea we might learn more if Granger joined the leisure club incognito. I was not expecting him to be quite so, er, enthusiastic about it."

"I'll resign," said Marc.

"There is no need for that," said Paul irritably. "Mrs Kirkwood is no longer under investigation. Our problem is an arsonist with a predilection for country barns."

"I have some new information on that, sir," said Seb Hunter. "DI Reynolds has been centring an investigation around an arsonist released from prison in February. Apparently other police forces have reported mysterious farm fires since that date."

"Bloody hell! Clive Reynolds actually making himself useful. He'll be Chief Constable before we know it."

"What about Annelise?" interrupted Marc. "She was drowned."

"Suicide," shrugged Seb.

"Bollocks," said Marc.

"Perhaps Granger can rejoin your squad, Seb?" suggested Paul blithely. "It might help to have a fresh perspective on the case?"

"Yes, sir," said Seb Hunter, his eyes staring straight ahead. "I'm sure you're quite right."

* * *

Marc moved his belongings from the CID general office into the incident room and spent the next few days wading through the statements and reports accumulated on the case. There was a lot of waffle, circumstantial evidence and theorising but no hard proof. The worst offender was Detective Inspector Clive Reynolds, with his suggestion linking a recently released arsonist with the two fires. Clive's evidence was so insubstantial he could have been working on *The X-Files*.

Marc made two cups of black, sugarless coffee, took them into DCI Hunter's office and closed the door.

Seb Hunter regarded him over the top of his reading-glasses. "Are you trying to curry favour, Detective Sergeant?" He took off his spectacles and laid them carefully on his leather blotter. "Or have you solved the case?"

Marc bit back the retort that sprang to his lips and glanced down at his notes instead. "According to the Fire Investigation Unit, the blaze and subsequent explosion at the hotel pool house was started by someone deliberately stuffing paper around various chemical containers and setting it alight."

"Yes," Seb made no attempt to disguise his indifference. "Nice to see you've done your homework."

"The Fire Investigation Unit also believe the blaze was started using a cigarette-lighter, mainly because one was found at the scene. Inside the barn around the time of the fire, according to various witnesses, were Caitlin Kirkwood, Hugh Kirkwood, Amanda de Havilland and Belinda Richmond."

"Your point being?"

"I've read the statement Caitlin gave you. Hugh

and Amanda are unfortunately not in a position to volunteer information. And I am unable to find any evidence that anyone spoke to, or any statement was taken from, Belinda Richmond."

"She's the daughter of the Lord Lieutenant," replied Seb, replacing his spectacles and shuffling his paperwork.

"What has that got to do with it?"

Seb regarded him with ill-disguised dislike. "Detective Chief Superintendent Nicholson indicated that he did not want anyone putting pressure on Miss Richmond. Apparently she suffered a breakdown following the fire and has not been completely right in the head since. Annelise's death appears to have sent her into a parallel universe."

Marc couldn't believe what he was hearing. "We're talking about a murder investigation and you're pussy-footing –"

"Granger, trust me on this. Leave Belinda Richmond alone. The girl is utterly crackers. You won't get anything out of her, except grief from her extremely influential father. Now, is there anything else you've found out? Anything *important*?"

OK, thought Marc grimly. Time to throw in the grenade . . . "The cigarette-lighter found at the scene."

"Yes?"

"Is mine."

He finally had Seb Hunter's concentrated attention. "Is that a joke?"

"At the time of the fire I was assigned to Special Branch. I was on protection duty that night, baby-sitting Princess Victoria. Mrs Kirkwood was having problems starting the firework display. I lent her my cigarette-lighter."

It was apparent Seb was not as well-informed as he would have liked. He picked up his coffee, swilled it around then, abruptly replaced it on the desk without drinking from it. "Did Detective Superintendent de Havilland know the cigarette-lighter was yours?"

"Why else did he send me to Kirkwood Manor undercover?"

It was difficult to ascertain exactly what was going through Seb's mind as he studied Marc's deliberately open expression for a few moments before asking, "Do *you* think Mrs Kirkwood killed her husband?"

"I don't believe so. She had the motive, she had the opportunity, maybe she's even capable of killing. But she did not murder Annelise Fitzpatrick because I was with her. I was also with her when The Stables burnt down."

"Perhaps she hired a hitman?"

"Our mysterious arsonist? I've been doing some research. He's a local man, been in and out of prisons since he was a teenager. He was born on a farm, hence his passion for barns and outbuildings. He was released in February and in this area in March. He could have easily set fire to The Stables last night – but he was helping Devon & Cornwall Constabulary with their enquiries when Annelise was killed. Besides, as you know, the MO was different."

"Damn!" Seb sat back in his chair, his arms folding across his chest as he stared out of the window at the tourists meandering down Calahurst High Street. For a moment Marc believed he had convinced him but then, "He could have set fire to the swimming-pool at Kirkwood Manor though."

Back to square one. The words 'clutching' and 'straws' came to mind. It was very tempting to start banging his head against the office wall but Marc forced himself to remain calm. Falling out with Seb Hunter would not achieve anything and might even work against Caitlin's best interest.

"Sir, have you ever been on protection duty? For royalty?"

"I've never worked for Special Branch, no," Seb replied, adding scathingly, "bloody secret squirrels."

"Let me tell you about protection duty, sir. Each member of the immediate Royal Family has their own personal protection officer. In addition, there are local Special Branch officers (like me) providing backup and others checking the building and grounds before an event begins. There's the dog section, searching drains, toilets, every nook and cranny for bombs, plus the firearms unit standing by. Even officers from the local nick are roped in. On the night of Hugh Kirkwood's birthday, there were probably more officers working on site than in the whole of police headquarters."

"That's not difficult," muttered Seb, who had a poor opinion of the upper echelons of the constabulary hierarchy.

"Yet someone suggests that a well-known, local nutter manages to bypass the entire security operation, designed to withstand assassins, kidnappers and terrorist attacks, just to indulge in his hobby of setting fire to barns. He could have burnt down The Stables or even the many farm outbuildings across the river. It would have been a whole lot easier."

"Your point?" enquired Seb wearily, finally raising his cold coffee to his lips.

"Unless our man was on the guest list, the only way he could have got through the gates was if he were James Bond."

"And you have a copy of that guest list?"

Marc opened the file he had wedged beneath his arm and dropped it on the desk in front of Seb. He pointed to the minute sheet on the first page. "Number 1A – Hugh Kirkwood's Fortieth Birthday Party – Guest List.". He flicked through a few pages to 1A. There was a shred of paper clinging to the green paper tag. "But it seems to have gone walkabout."

Seb slammed his fist against his blotter. "I'll kill that admin clerk!"

"Relax," said Marc, good-humouredly. "This is the police. If there is one thing we're proficient at, it's generating paperwork. Everyone from the Chief Constable down would have a hard copy of that guest list."

Seb slid his spectacles up over the bridge of his nose and began to flick through the file. "I want one on my desk by 1700 hours."

"Yes, sir." Marc tried hard not to appear too triumphant.

"And I want a statement from Belinda Richmond – it's up to you how you obtain it."

"No problem."

"Just don't sleep with her," Seb added. "I don't think my nerves could stand the repercussions."

* * *

Marc drove up the narrow winding drive to Ilex House, through a garden with enough azaleas and rhododendrons to rival Exbury. The beautiful pink and white blossoms were falling already and it was difficult not to wince as they were ground into the tarmac by his tyres. He took particular care negotiating the final bend in case one of the many Richmond girls should be belting the opposite way, behind the wheel of a sports car worth the price of a smart terraced house in central Norchester.

An immense white stone edifice, Ilex House boasted an abundance of turrets, spires and domed conservatories, as though it had been designed by the Prince Regent on LSD. Marc parked outside the front door, next to a gleaming Aston Martin DB7 – so clean it looked as though it had only ever been driven indoors. He walked up the short flight of stone steps and was about to ring the bell when Lord Richmond stomped through the door, surrounded by bouncing Labradors. He was wearing tweed breeches and coat, and a cap pulled low over his eyes to disguise his bald head. He also carried a shotgun over his shoulder.

"Who are you?" he grumbled, taking the gun from his shoulder and regarding Marc with rolling eyes. "What do you want? Can't you see I'm busy?"

Marc, having spent his formative years in a British

colony, was unimpressed by the aristocracy. "I'd like to see your daughter, my lord. If she's available?"

"Which one? I've got a house full of damn daughters. All bloody useless."

"Erm, Belinda?"

Lord Richmond raised the shotgun until it was level with Marc's nose. "Why can't you leave the poor girl alone? Don't you think she's suffered enough? Go and find one of the village girls to poke." Then, as Marc didn't move, "Be off with you! Unless you want your backside full of shot!"

Marc pulled his warrant card from his jacket pocket. "I think you misunderstand me. I'm Detective Sergeant Granger from Calahurst Police Station. I would like to interview her about the fire at Kirkwood Manor Hotel last March. It's purely voluntary. I believe Belinda could provide vital information about what happened that night and help us find the murderer."

Lord Richmond sat abruptly on the lower step, dropped the gun beside him and put his head in his hands. "Belinda's gone," he mumbled, his voice choked with emotion. "I don't know where she is. I don't think I can stand it. Not two daughters. Some bloody pervert's murdered her and left her in a ditch. I know he has. And she was my favourite . . ."

Marc felt helpless. He peered through the open door but the hallway was deserted. Where was Jeeves when you needed him most? He rang the bell.

"You're a detective," Lord Richmond was saying. "Can't you find her?"

"When did she go missing?"

"She left the house at ten thirty this morning. She said she was going to visit that artist at Kirkwood Manor – he's painting her portrait don't you know? But when my wife rang to speak with Belinda, that Caitlin creature said no one had seen her."

A butler appeared in the doorway and, seeing his master sitting on the top step in tears, immediately summoned assistance. As two footmen helped Lord Richmond to his feet and back into the house, Marc got into his car and dialled the station on his mobile phone. If they had not heard from him within twenty minutes they were to instigate a search for Belinda Richmond. Then he drove off towards Mistletoe House.

* * *

Marc parked haphazardly next to the fountain and walked up the steps into the dark, gloomy hallway of Mistletoe House. Caitlin was sitting behind the reception desk, surreptitiously watching *Star Trek* repeats on satellite TV. She jumped guiltily when Marc strode in through the door, then paled as she recognised him, sliding off her stool and making a bolt for the sanctuary of the manager's office.

Marc was there before her, blocking her exit. "Do you hate me that much?" he asked softly, watching the colour slowly flood into her cheeks.

"Why can't you just leave me alone?"

"I wish I could."

He had not realised he had spoken aloud until Caitlin sneered, "I'm sure there are plenty of other women who would love to be with you. Some women like a man in uniform."

"I'm CID," he felt obliged to point out. "We're the ones in suits."

"As good as a uniform. You all seem to wear identical designer copies."

Marc gave up trying to be nice and pulled his warrant card from his jacket pocket. "I'm here on business, Mrs Kirkwood. Could you tell me if Belinda Richmond has visited today?"

"She had a sitting with Jack this morning," shrugged Caitlin, "but stood him up. It's very inconvenient. Lord Richmond commissioned Jack to paint Belinda's portrait and he now has to compose the whole thing from memory."

"You won't mind if I look in the visitors' book?"

"Not at all," replied Caitlin, turning it round to face him. She sat down and turned the sound up on the TV. The USS Enterprise engaging the Borg in full-scale warfare did not make it easy for Marc to concentrate on deciphering the guests' handwriting. Eventually, at the bottom of the page, scrawled in childlike writing and heavily illustrated with doodles of daisies, he found Belinda's name.

Feeling bloody-minded, he leant over the reception desk and switched off the TV. "It's an offence to pervert the course of justice, Mrs Kirkwood."

Caitlin regarded him icily. "The way I see it, justice

in this village is perverted enough without any help from me."

"I've found what I was looking for."

"Terrific. I've got a party popper in here somewhere. Let's celebrate."

"Caitlin," he growled, "do you *want* me to arrest you for obstruction?"

"Only if you promise to handcuff me."

Marc took a deep breath. "I want to look round the hotel to see if I can find Miss Richmond. I don't have a warrant but you're welcome to come along too. If you don't let me in, I'll be forced to obtain the authority from a magistrate. And if the tabloids find out, all the public-relations work you've put into this hotel goes to waste. Am I making myself clear?"

"Crystal," said Caitlin. "Where do you want to start?"

"Are the suites all booked out?"

"Yes – all foreigners. Americans, Germans and Japs. Jack's in the Water Lily Suite, painting Kimmie. He's using her as a body double for Belinda."

"Yeah, right." Marc was unable to hide a smile. "OK, we'll start with the public rooms, then outside. I'll leave the bedrooms until last. I don't wish to cause any . . . er . . . inconvenience."

"Sure you don't," grumbled Caitlin under her breath but he pretended he hadn't heard her.

It did not take long to search the ground floor of Mistletoe House, Marc inspected the men's changing rooms, Caitlin checked the women's. They met on the terrace and walked along the side of the house, towards the Elizabethan Garden.

Caitlin struggled with the latch but only succeeded in breaking a fingernail.

"Here, let me," volunteered Marc. "It probably needs oil." For a moment their fingers touched. Her hands were cold. He wanted to enfold them in his own to warm them but she had already pulled away, her face crimson. Perversely, he felt pleased. So she wasn't as indifferent as she pretended.

The gate swung open; Marc stared incredulously across the garden. There was Belinda, totally naked, standing in a flower-bed, curving her body against the statue of Venus. The brilliant sunlight reflected from her alabaster skin, contrasting against the rough, lichen-stained stone, and turning her fair hair almost white. A smile played upon her candy-painted lips yet there was a strangely blank expression in her half-closed eyes. Behind her was Leo Kirkwood, fully clothed but for his trousers, which had slithered down around his ankles. His face too, was curiously devoid of emotion. He had Belinda's voluptuous breasts clasped in each hand and, as the gate creaked open, he had paused in mid-thrust.

It was clear that one glance at the disgust in Marc's face made Leo realise how ridiculous he must look. But he pulled up his trousers lethargically all the same.

Marc picked up Belinda's discarded button-through dress and wrapped it around her. "Come along, Miss Richmond, I'll drive you home. I've been looking everywhere for you. Your father's very worried."

"Why?" enquired Belinda, turning her vacant blue eyes on him. "I'm perfectly all right."

"He didn't know where you were."

"I did tell him I was coming here," said Belinda. She put a hand to her mouth. "Oh, I was supposed to be meeting Jack, wasn't I?"

"I'll tell him you had a headache," said Caitlin, "and that you'll call him to arrange another sitting."

At the catch in her voice Marc turned but Caitlin was concentrating on looking Belinda straight in the eye, although her complexion was ashen. If he hadn't known better Marc would have thought Caitlin was the wronged wife. Not for the first time, he wondered what it was, exactly, that gave between her and Leo Kirkwood.

"Oh, thank you, Caitlin." said Belinda. "Tell Jack I'm really sorry. My memory's hopeless at the moment." She turned to wave at Leo. "Goodbye, Mr Kirkwood. Lunch was lovely; we'll have to do it again sometime. Thank you for having me."

Leo laughed but turned it into a cough when Marc's paint-stripping glare fell upon him. "The pleasure was all mine," he said. And casually dropped a condom into the nearest bin.

Caitlin waited until Marc and Belinda had gone before she turned her venom on Hugh. "Don't you realise," she stormed, "that anyone could have seen you? Look at all those windows, for God's sake!"

"I know," said Hugh blithely scraping the mud from his exquisite Italian loafers before striding off down the path. "That was the point."

Chapter Twenty-two

After letting the station know he had found Belinda, and asking them to inform her father that he was bringing her home, Marc whisked her off to The Parson's Collar for a clandestine interrogation. He should really take her back to the interview room at the station, read out her rights and record every daft and irrelevant thing she said – but he felt he would obtain more success in relaxed surroundings. *Romance the girl a little . . .* derided a tiny voice inside his head.

The Parson's Collar was an ultra-fashionable wine bar right on the edge of the quay. It had been imaginatively decorated like a church, with old pews for seats, and gargoyles growing out of the wall. There were confession-box loos, and stained-glass windows of weary saints gazing out across the street, creating a Picasso-like view of the quay. The alcohol was served from a cut-down Victorian pulpit, beautifully carved from local oak, and the worn stone font was sacrilegiously piled high with snacks. The atmosphere was only slightly spoilt by loud funky music and *Today's Specials* chalked up on the hymn board.

Marc grabbed a table at the back, close to the bar and behind a large plastic aspidistra. He sat next to Belinda, rather than opposite her, so that she could not escape. He was rather disconcerted when she snuggled up to him like a puppy and one of her little cold hands started to stroke up his thigh.

Marc clamped his legs together and, to take his mind off it, wondered why the aspidistra was plastic when they were practically impossible to kill off. He should know. He had one in his hall that his grandmother's cat had pissed on every time it was cut short en route to the kitty litter.

"Annelise used to bring me here," said Belinda suddenly, dipping her finger in the ring her glass of mineral water had left on the wooden table and writing her name. She ran out of moisture by the time she reached 'N'. "But that was before she married William Fitzpatrick."

He could not have wished for a more perfect opening. "Did you get on well with Annelise?"

"Oh yes, recently we shared everything. Especially men." Belinda's hand began to edge further upwards and her little rosebud mouth smiled enticingly. "Why don't we go back to my place? We'd have more privacy there." Her azure eyes sparkled mischievously from beneath mascara-coated lashes. "I've never had a policeman before. Will you handcuff me to the bed?"

Marc firmly removed her hand, hoping Detective

Superintendent de Havilland was not about to pop out from behind the pulpit with his whisky and *Financial Times*. "Were you and Annelise sharing Leo Kirkwood too?"

"I don't know. Annelise never said so." Belinda's face crumpled. "And it's too late to ask her now . . ."

He handed her the glass of mineral water and waited for her to regain her composure before asking gently, "I thought you were dating Jack O'Neill?"

She smiled through her tears. "Jack is sweet but Mummy doesn't approve of him."

"Because he's an artist?"

"She hates Caitlin."

"Yet she likes Leo?"

"Leo owns Kirkwood Manor," replied Belinda with breathtaking simplicity. "Although Hugh was always Mummy's favourite. She thought he might marry Annelise. So did Annelise!"

As Marc watched her go off into peals of uncontrollable giggles, it occurred to Marc that she might be high on something already. Perhaps this was why Lord Richmond was so anxious she should not be interviewed?

"Hugh prefers blondes though," Belinda was saying. "He dithered so long asking Annelise to marry him that she got fed up and ran off with William Fitzpatrick. He's not so rich but he comes from an old county family and he's an MP. Mummy always wanted one in the family." Belinda's forehead crinkled. "Weird how Hugh ended up with Caitlin. I mean, she's nice enough but really she's just Miss Nobody from Nowhere. When Hugh married her out of the blue like that it ruffled a few feathers, I can tell you!"

"Why do you think they married?" asked Marc, curiosity getting the better of him.

"Mummy says he was dazzled by her showbiz background but when Caitlin came to Calahurst she was just an aerobics instructor. Personally I think Hugh married on the rebound from Annelise. He was getting old, all his chums were married. Still, he picked the wrong girl in the end, didn't he? He should have stuck with blondes. He should have waited for me!"

"Didn't you feel that the age gap between you and Hugh was a little excessive?"

Belinda put her head on one side. "You mean, is he too old for me?" The mischievous sparkle was back in her eyes. "Yes, of course he is – but he's a genius in bed. So much more to offer than the shunt and grunt boys from round here."

"What about Amanda de Havilland? I thought she was his mistress?"

Belinda waved her hand dismissively. "That would have fizzled out. She told him she was pregnant, you know, just so that he would divorce Caitlin and marry her. But it was just another lie. She was always in trouble at school for lying." Belinda paused, reflectively staring through the coloured glass windows to the quay beyond. "Our headmistress said Amanda would get her come-uppance one day. I bet even that old witch could not have foreseen this."

Belinda said the words so nonchalantly Marc's fingers tightened around his glass and it was a while before he could bring himself to speak. Amanda's pretty, elfin face danced before his eyes as he remembered that kiss last Christmas, that beautiful stolen kiss. Poor Amanda. She had her faults but she hadn't deserved to die like that. No one deserved to die like that. What a waste of a life.

He forced himself back to the present. So, Amanda had told Hugh she was pregnant? Well, it was one way to trap a commitment-shy spouse. Had Hugh realised she was lying, or did his pride blind him to the truth? Why hadn't the prat worn a condom? Or perhaps she had sworn she was on the pill. Sometimes men could be so stupid.

It occurred to Marc that Amanda's phantom pregnancy now gave Caitlin a very good motive for murder. Was Amanda's one little white lie enough to set off the chain of repercussions that led to her death? *Oh Amanda, you little fool . . .*

Glancing up, he caught Belinda exchanging torrid eye-meets with the barman, evidently bored with his conversation. In the last hour she had had sex with Leo, made a clumsy pass at him and now she was trying to get off with the barman . . .

"You must have been devastated when Hugh was killed?" he said dryly.

Which guaranteed him 100% attention. "Hugh's not dead," she retorted. "We made love in the Elizabethan Garden only this afternoon. You saw him yourself."

Belinda was obviously further gone than he had thought. "That was Leo. Hugh's younger brother."

"They do look alike," conceded Belinda. "But Leo's eyes are brown. Perhaps he went back to America? I haven't seen him since Hugh's orgy." She gave a mocking smile. "Have you ever had group sex? Lots of people doing wonderful things to you? It was heavenly – until Caitlin turned up. That girl is a real party-pooper."

Belinda was back in Never-Never Land again. Marc had to admit defeat. He was getting nowhere faster than a water-skiing hippo. Let Seb Hunter haul her into the station if he thought anything she had said was pertinent to the investigation, because if he didn't take Belinda home soon Lord Richmond was likely to come searching for her – riding shotgun. Marc called across to the barman for the bill.

As Marc began counting out his change he noticed Belinda was counting out tablets on the table beside him. He snatched the bottle from her. "What the fuck are these?"

"They're my marzipan tablets. I'm supposed to take one in the morning and one at night – or is it two at night and none in the morning . . . anyway, I forgot to take any yesterday so I took four for breakfast. That should be OK, shouldn't it?"

Now he understood. Belinda was high on tranquillisers . . . no wonder she was permanently laid-back. "Come on." said Marc firmly. "I think we ought to leave now."

"Just when I was beginning to have fun," pouted

Belinda, putting her hand inside his shirt. "I thought you liked me?"

He extracted her hand just as Detective Inspector Reynolds walked in through the door.

Clive raised his eyebrows. "Half the station is looking for you," he said. "I never thought to find you here."

Of course not, thought Marc resignedly. He knew the rest of the station had him pegged as the last boy scout. Well, his whiter-than-white reputation had certainly got muddied now. A romantic tête à tête with the Lord Lieutenant's daughter. In a wine bar. During working hours.

Belinda took the opportunity to wind her arms around Marc's waist and bury her face in his back. Marc smiled weakly. "It's not how it looks."

Clive appeared amused. "Seb Hunter wants you. Something about a guest list?"

"Oh hell!" Marc realised Belinda was beginning to unbutton his shirt and slapped her hands. "For Christ's sake, Belinda!"

"Would you like me to drive her home?" asked Clive. "I'm only here to buy a bottle of plonk for a dinner party we're having tonight. I'll be passing Ilex House on the way back to Norchester."

"Would you?" muttered Marc in an undertone. "I warn you, she's a liability – high on tranquillisers the doctor gave her. He should have prescribed bromide while he was at it."

"No problem. Come along, dear." Clive held out

his hand as though Belinda was a child. She took it obediently. "Let me take you home."

"Have fun," said Marc and went to pay the barman.

Belinda dubiously followed DI Reynolds outside. His maroon Alfa Romeo Spyder was parked down the street on a double yellow line. He unlocked the doors, moved his briefcase onto the back seat and gave Belinda the bottle of wine to hold. She clamped it between her thighs, did up her seatbelt and the DI pulled smoothly away from the quayside. He drove through Calahurst's one-way system up the hill, past the police station on the corner – and the turning to Mistletoe Lane. Instead he took the 'A' road to Norchester and the car was swallowed into a cool green tunnel of trees.

"This is a nice car," said Belinda, flattened back against the multi-coloured beads covering the passenger seat, as the speedometer hit 100 mph. "I bet you pull all the women. It's dangerously sexy."

"Like me," said DI Reynolds.

Belinda smiled nervously and fiddled with paper wrapped around the wine bottle.

After a couple of miles of silence, he suddenly swerved off down a bumpy farm lane, frightening the chickens loose in the yard, and sending a couple of ramblers into a ditch.

Belinda sat up in her seat. "Where are we going? This isn't the way home. I live in Mistletoe Lane."

"We're just taking a quick detour. A little trip. You like taking trips, don't you, Belinda? You like taking all sorts of things."

317

Belinda thought maybe she had not heard him right but watched the dusty hedgerows flash past with a prickle of unease. He swung though an open gate into an empty ploughed field, juddered along for a few feet and stopped the car.

Belinda dropped the wine bottle, released her seatbelt and struggled with the door catch but it was locked. "Let me out," she demanded. "I've changed my mind. I'll walk home."

He leant over her. She could see every dissipated line, blemish and vein, and his pink scalp gleaming through his thinning blond hair. He was not quite the amiable *Boy's Own* hero at such close proximity.

"Drugged up to the eyeballs?" he mocked, trailing a finger across her lips, and down her throat. "You won't get far."

"I bet I can run faster than you," she said scornfully.

DI Reynolds indicated his police radio, jammed into the glove compartment. "But can you run faster than a patrol car? And Daddy won't be very pleased to hear you've been picked up by us."

"I don't care. It's better than being trapped in here."

"You don't like me?" he said, slowly undoing the little silver buttons on her dress. "I'm heartbroken. I like you an awful lot."

Belinda cringed against the seat as he pulled open her dress and placed his hands over her breasts, his mouth closing over hers like a sink plunger. She squirmed but he had her pinned to the seat. She lifted her hand and raked the side of his face with her long, violet nails.

He hit her. "Bitch," he grunted, "you were far more amenable the last time we did this."

Belinda put a hand up to her throbbing head. "Last time?" she faltered, hypnotised by the blood trickling down the three long scratches on his cheek and dripping onto his crisp white shirt. The shirt probably lovingly ironed by his wife the previous evening.

"Yes, darling. Surely you haven't forgotten Hugh's birthday party? The pool? You have such a delicious body."

Belinda recalled a long-forgotten dream, of fun and laughter, a man in grey kissing her in a swimming pool and a girl with long blonde hair. And then there had been the blood. So much blood . . .

Belinda shook her head, trying to erase the memory. They had promised the nightmares wouldn't come back. All she had to do was take her marzipan tablets and her bad dreams would go away for ever.

DI Reynolds moved closer, taking her chin between forefinger and thumb. "And we had such a *good* time . . ."

She could feel his breath on her mouth, see the salt and pepper stubble of a five-o'clock shadow on his face, his cruel features merging into a grinning, blood-soaked demon. "No!" she whimpered. "Please, no . . ."

He laughed and his mouth closed down on hers, his teeth splitting her lip as he pressed her back in the seat.

Suddenly the driver's door was wrenched open and the DI was grabbed by the scruff of the neck and hauled out of the car. Belinda pressed her fingers to her sore lips and looked up into the face of her saviour – Hugh Kirkwood.

Hugh smashed his fist into the DI's jawbone and, taken by surprise, he fell back against the side of the car and slid down onto the parched furrowed soil.

DI Reynolds opened and closed his jaw experimentally and stared up at Hugh, tears stinging his eyes. "Shit, Hugh, you turn up in the damnedest places."

"I followed you," said Hugh shortly. "Get out of the car, Belinda."

Belinda wrapped her dress firmly around her and slid over the handbrake, clambering out the driver's side of the car. Her heels sank deep into the crusty soil and Hugh had to take her elbow to hold her steady. She would have snuggled gratefully into his chest but he pulled her hands away and pointed to Caitlin's red Mazda, abandoned by the five-bar gate.

"Wait for me over there," he said in a harsh voice. "I won't be long."

Belinda, not daring to look at the Detective Inspector, did as she was told.

Clive Reynolds, realising he was at a disadvantage, quickly got to his feet, watching Belinda staggering across the lumpy ridges of soil towards the gate. "Don't think about hitting me again," he warned Hugh, "or it will be you picking your expensively capped teeth out of the dirt."

Hugh regarded him with dislike. "I'm not stupid. I know I don't stand a chance against you in a fight. Besides, violence is not my style."

"Of course it's not," taunted Clive. "You get other people to do your dirty work."

Hugh narrowed his eyes, his fists clenching impotently by his side. "Did you set fire to The Stables?"

"Don't be ridiculous. After that last cock-up, I haven't even lit a barbecue."

"So who did? I could have been killed."

"Don't be so fucking paranoid," muttered Clive irritably. "Who would want to kill you?"

"My wife for a start," replied Hugh grumpily. "Perhaps it was one of the others? To pay me back for going freelance?"

Clive shrugged. "Unlikely. I think it was just a local nutter. A horrible coincidence, that's all. Look on the bright side. It could help take the pressure off us."

Hugh did not appear entirely convinced. "I'd better go," he sighed, "in case someone sees us together."

"What about her?" Clive thumbed back to Belinda. "I've just rescued her from DS Granger. God knows what she told him."

"You really think he'll believe a word she says? She never made much sense in the first place."

Clive frowned. "Don't let your cock rule your head, Kirkwood. I still haven't forgotten how you went into a mad tailspin after Annelise found you out. I don't want to have to clear up any more of your messy mistakes."

"That was different."

Clive glanced back to Belinda, watching them

nervously from the car. "Hmm," he said, "you think so?"

Hugh followed his gaze. "Just leave the girl alone, Reynolds. She's mine."

"You're old enough to be her grandfather."

"To quote Groucho Marx, 'You're only as old as the woman you feel'. Yesterday I was twenty-three; today I'm seventeen."

"Hooray for plastic surgery," Clive said nastily. "Officially Caitlin is your wife . . ."

"Don't be bloody facetious. If we're doing a head count, you have a wife in Norchester and a mistress in Port Rell."

"You needn't sound so holy. What about that butch aerobics instructor you were telling me about? The one you took to Last Days and fucked in the steam room at Mistletoe House?"

"Makes a change from the jacuzzi," Hugh retorted. "She's just the hired help, not really my type. An interesting way to while away the long summer evenings, yet still leaving my weekends free."

Clive laughed. "Bugger that. You just fancy yourself as the Lord Lieutenant's son-in-law. You cocked up once with Annelise so you're trying again with Belinda."

"Absolutely," mocked Hugh. "And if the daffy Belinda does not come up to scratch, Richmond has three remaining unmarried daughters."

"Fifteen-year-old Tania, Deanna who is ten, and sweet little Rosie who is barely out of nappies. Even you are not that desperate, Hugh."

Hugh shrugged. "If all else fails I can seduce his fat wife. But, to return reluctantly to the point, lay off Belinda."

"So you can lie on her, I suppose?" Clive sighed. "Oh, all right. She wasn't as accommodating as I remember."

Hugh sighed. "I don't understand you. Why fool around when you have a gorgeous baby and a wife who loves you?"

"Same reason as you."

Hugh shook his head. "That's not the same reason at all. I have no children, my mistress is dead and my wife can't stand me."

"Some people," said Clive, "have all the luck."

Chapter Twenty-three

Lord Richmond was extremely pleased with Jack's portrait of Belinda in her birthday gown and wrote out a very large cheque immediately. Lady Richmond was pleased too, until she discovered the alternative version of Belinda in her birthday suit, stuffed in the back of her wardrobe. Jack's cheque was halved, literally, before his eyes. Which left him back where he had started, bored and broke, minus two large canvases and several tubes of paint.

His punishment did not end there. Jack was the only person in Calahurst not invited to Belinda's party.

Sitting mournfully on Caitlin's bed, watching her put the finishing touches to her make-up, he said, "Please take me with you. I'll do anything."

"Of course you will." Caitlin carefully lined the inside of her eyelids with white kohl to make her green eyes appear larger. "You'll be an embarrassment; you'll cause a disturbance; you'll be thrown out. So why don't I save you the indignity and leave you here?"

He flopped back onto her bed. "How can you be so cruel to your only brother? Have you never heard of Romeo and Juliet?"

"Yes – and they came to an extremely sticky end. I'd hate for you to go the same way." She stood up and admired her reflection in the mirror. Her mother had brought her a new gown back from London. It was fuchsia-pink satin, almost fluorescent in its brightness and moulded tightly to her body. She wore matching over-the-elbow satin gloves and high-heeled sandals.

Jack regarded her sourly. "Another couture gown? I bet it cost thousands. Better not get used to them Your next husband might be a farmer."

"Oh, grow up."

"You don't think six foot three is enough?"

Caitlin held open the bedroom door. "Come on. Out. I don't know why you're so upset at being left behind tonight. What did you expect, painting the Lord Lieutenant's daughter in the nude?"

"Money," said Jack bitterly.

"Get real." She hesitated, feeling sorry for him. "You didn't really care for Belinda, did you? She's a complete nympho. She even slept with my late, unlamented husband."

"I know," sighed Jack. "The first time we met she offered me sex on a plate – well, a dinghy if we're going to get picky. I think I'm more upset that she dumped me so quickly – and for that revolting brother-in-law of yours. He must be at least thirty-five, twice her age. What does she see in him?"

"A large country hotel and two thousand acres of parkland."

"Apart from that."

"Jack, stop feeling so sorry for yourself. You want to go to the party? Crash it like you did in the old days. You want to get Belinda back? Cut off those stupid dreadlocks, have a shave, a bath and put on a decent suit. And, if you really want to piss everybody off? Have fun."

* * *

Ilex House had been built in the early nineteenth century for a nobleman whose feckless son subsequently lost it to a wealthy merchant in a game of chance. The merchant, having more to prove, totally remodelled it, basing the design on a chateau he had seen in a painting on someone's wall. His architect, accustomed to designing churches, threw in a few of his favourite Parisian chapels, and the architect's assistant sneaked in a copper-domed conservatory modelled on San Marco in Venice. The result was a glamorous mess.

Although many people privately thought it in extremely bad taste for the Richmonds to throw a party so soon after the death of their eldest daughter, no one declined their invitation. They were far too important to offend.

Caitlin, who would have rather stayed at home, was jollied along by Elena, recently returned from London, who pointed out that the party would be a fabulous opportunity to network. Caitlin did not have a date, although the invitation had stated 'and partner' so she decided to take Fabian, purely to annoy Hugh. Unwittingly, she succeeded in annoying Marina, who had split up with Fabian some weeks earlier and had hoped to have seen the back of him.

Elena, Caitlin and Fabian arrived, slightly squashed, in Marina's Jaguar. Hugh had the honour of having one of the Richmond cars sent for him. They had their coats taken by a real live butler and were ushered into a ballroom three times the size of the one at Mistletoe House. The room was long and wide, painted white with pink granite columns along the sides. Colossal antique mirrors and bits of seriously dead tiger lined one wall. Latticed windows onto the terrace, interspersed with potted palms and stone elephants, lined the other. The ceiling was painted like the canopy of a jungle and from each end hung a crystal chandelier.

Caitlin gaped at the opulent bad taste. Although she had lived in Calahurst for almost six years she had never been invited to Ilex House. If Lady Richmond had her way Caitlin would not have been invited, period, but Belinda had issued invitations to all and sundry. Caitlin edged towards one of the palm trees to check if it was real.

"Wow, look at all these handsome men," gawped Marina, ensuring her tummy was tucked in and her bosom was stuck out.

"And it's not even Christmas," agreed Elena.

Fabian winced and gazed at the floor. Caitlin

squeezed his hand consolingly. She realised it was a bit mean to let him witness Marina's flirting – but too late to do anything about it now.

"I'll start at that end of the ballroom," said Marina, pointing through the guests, "and you can start from here."

"Done," said Elena, her new best friend. They both roared with laughter.

Caitlin cringed and hauled Fabian off to the bar. She ordered a large brandy; her principles were disappearing faster than rabbits at a magicians' convention. She ordered a brandy for Fabian too, in the hope that it would cheer him up, but he knocked it back like cherry cola. She sat on a bar stool and eyed him worriedly. As a fitness fanatic he had always been teetotal.

"Hello," said a voice from two feet above.

Slowly she looked up a black dinner jacket into a pair of crinkling navy-blue eyes. "Who invited you?" she asked disagreeably.

"The Honourable Belinda Richmond," said Marc.

"Not so honourable," said Caitlin. "She's slept with both my brother and my brother-in-law in the space of one week. Thank Christ she's not bisexual."

"Bitch," said Marc and walked away.

"Shit, shit, shit," said Caitlin. Why couldn't she be a nicer person? It was no wonder everyone in Calahurst hated her. Apart from the fact they considered her to be a serial killer, of course.

"Sorry?" said the barman.

"Quadruple brandy," said Caitlin. "No ice, no lemonade, no cherries – in fact, you can dispense with the glass too. Just give me the bottle."

"Ma'am?"

"Oh forget it."

"Let's dance," said Fabian.

In addition to a live band, Lady Richmond had hired a DJ from one of the top London clubs. Calahurst gentry stood around the walls, looking as though they were having their bikini lines waxed, while their teenage children crowded onto the dance floor, moving ecstatically as one to the relentless pulsating beat.

Sandwiched between two sixteen-year-old girls wearing tiny satin slip dresses, Caitlin wondered on the wisdom of her ballgown and felt very old.

Fabian, however, was in his element, his eyes closed, blond locks flowing about his shoulders. He had discarded his jacket and tie and now swivelled his hips, bumping and grinding to the music, Caitlin doing her best to keep up. It was a long time since she had been to a nightclub. Hugh had always sworn he was too old.

She looked for her husband amongst the multitude, wondering if he had the cheek to turn up and, with a shock, saw him staring straight at her through the swarming dance floor. He was wearing Jack's sunglasses and talking politely to Lord and Lady Richmond. Belinda was swinging on his arm, conducting an imaginary orchestra. Caitlin quickly looked away and searched for Marc. He was standing in the shadows, talking animatedly to Paul de Havilland. They appeared to be having a row.

Caitlin glanced back to Fabian and was irritated to find he had danced off with one of the sixteen-year-old nymphets. The French windows beckoned. Ducking through onto the terrace, she sat side-saddle on a weathered stone lion, wondering why she didn't just leave. She really ought to return to the party and network – but it was so hot. Her ballgown was totally inappropriate for the sauna-like conditions on the dance floor.

She could see Fabian dancing with his new friend. Her slip dress was very similar to Caitlin's petticoat. Perhaps it was her father's wild Irish genes battling for supremacy, or the full moon, or most likely the full glass of brandy she had drunk earlier, but Caitlin suddenly had that familiar feeling of recklessness, of crazy abandon that had gotten her into trouble before.

Quickly, uncaring if anyone could see her, she unzipped her dress and wriggled out of it, dumping it carelessly onto the balustrade. Her petticoat was fuchsia pink too, with a long lace section from way above her knees to her ankles and split to the thigh to match the style of her dress. She gathered large folds of lace between her hands and tugged. The fabric came apart with ease.

Caitlin discarded the lace in the bushes and danced a few steps across the paved terrace to experiment. Her new slip dress was extremely short, with far less material than any of those worn inside the ballroom but, provided she did not sit down and reveal her nonmatching, acid-green knickers, she would be fine. She would just have to dance all night.

"I think you ought to stop right there," said a familiar voice. "Else I might have to arrest you for indecent exposure."

Caitlin turned and Marc stepped out from the shadows, lighted cigarette in his hand. "My last girlfriend used to have a thing about taking her clothes off in the great outdoors," he added, conversationally. "What is it with modern women?"

Caitlin had no wish to hear about his girlfriends. Ex or otherwise. "I thought you had given up smoking," she accused, while waiting for her brain to come up with some witty retort which would really put the bastard in his place.

"You give up liquor and I'll give up smoking."

The one-liner was a long time coming, however, and instead she could only drool at the magnificent figure he cut in a dinner jacket. "I've only had one drink," she said defensively, hoping he couldn't read her mind.

His eyes slid unhurriedly over her body. "Really?"

"I was hot!"

"Me too," he smiled tenderly, "but I think I'd get thrown out if I did a striptease. Would you like to dance?"

Caitlin hesitated.

"Yes, I truly am a masochist," he said. "If you can forgive me, I'm willing to start over."

"You lied to me." She could not prevent the anguish creeping into her voice.

331

"No, I just didn't tell you I worked for the police. It's not the sort of job you broadcast. You never know how people are going to react."

"Especially after they've been wrongfully arrested and accused of their husband's murder. If I had known you were a police officer I would never have let you over the threshold – let alone slept with you!" She felt a hot flush flood her body as she remembered that afternoon on the riverbank, the evening in the shower . . . she just wanted to curl up and die of shame. How could she have thrown herself at him like that?

"You tricked me," she whispered. "You just wanted to get information out of me. Sweet-talk me into making a confession." She laughed bitterly. "A honey-trap, isn't that what they call it? I suppose your mates down the station took a vote and chose you as the guy most likely to succeed. The one I would be most likely to fuck." Her tongue tripped over the words, she had so nearly said 'fall in love with'. She bit her lip, before she incriminated herself further, and waited for him to reply. For him to deny everything she had said.

He blew a column of smoke towards the stars, his eyes never leaving her face. "I do care about you, Caitlin. I never lied about that."

"And the rest?" Her voice trembled. *Tell me it's not true, damn you!*

His silence was killing her. Then he shrugged.

"Well, bully for you," she spat, rage flowing through her veins, giving her courage more effectively than a dozen bottles of brandy. "I hope you enjoyed your fun while it lasted. I despise you. I always thought the police stood for honour, justice, integrity –"

"Caitlin!" he caught her hand just as she raised it to slap his face. "It wasn't like that. I give you my word. I admit some of what you say is the truth. But my feelings for you were real. I never lied about that."

He almost sounded upset. He was good. She'd give him that.

Caitlin wrenched her wrist away from him. "Let me go," she hissed. "Let me go or I'll scream so loudly they'll hear me in Port Rell. I'll tell everyone what you did. How you took me to bed purely to screw a confession out of me. Your brilliant police career will turn to ashes. That's all you really care about isn't it? Your career."

"You know that's not true!"

"Isn't it?"

He stared at her aghast. "You really hate me that much?"

"Yes," she said flatly. "I do."

Who was she trying to kid? She only had to look into those dark hooded eyes to realise just how much she wanted him. She clutched at the stone lion to steady her trembling limbs and to ensure that she did not cause a major embarrassment by flinging herself into Marc's arms and begging to be ravished like one of Marina's sex-starved heroines.

Marc took another drag on his cigarette. The ash glowed. If only he put his arms around her, held her close, showed her how much he loved her, she would melt into a pool of gunk. Words meant nothing.

"Perhaps you had better put your dress back on." He dropped the cigarette and ground it into the paving slabs.

Like my heart, realised Caitlin miserably, and her hopes crashed in bitter disappointment.

"I can see I'm wasting my time," he said and abruptly turned back to the ballroom.

Don't look back, thought Caitlin in anguish. Please don't see me crying.

She felt stupid, standing in her petticoat. She should never have come to this dreadful party. She was way out of her depth with all these lords, ladies and *nouveaux riches*. She was just a nice middle-class girl, who would have been happy just to dance her way through life. At least, she used to be. Before her social-climbing mother, womanising husband and the spiteful machinations of fate had all ganged up against her.

She had turned towards the steps that would eventually lead to the road, with the intention of thumbing a lift back to Mistletoe House, when Fabian materialised beside her.

"I've been looking everywhere for you," he accused. "Why did you run out on me like that?"

She had to admire his cheek. "You went off with someone else!"

"That's how people dance – in one big happy group."

"Well, I wasn't happy and I'm not into groups."

He frowned. "What happened to your dress? I thought it was longer than that?"

Caitlin carelessly pushed her despised couture gown over the edge of the balustrade and into the shrubbery and hoped to never see it again. Taking Fabian's arm, she sighed, "Let's dance."

The ballroom was much as they had left it. Caitlin stepped behind the gigantic speakers and sidled over to the DJ. As she whispered in his ear he pulled a face but nodded. She moved back onto the dance floor towards Fabian; the techno rock faded and a soft, melodious beat filled the ballroom. The teenagers slowed in confusion, losing the beat along with the relentless bass rhythm.

"Now," said Caitlin, taking Fabian's arm and placing it around her waist then taking his other hand in her own. "We are going to dance – strictly ballroom, Fabe."

As they danced to The Platters' 'Smoke Gets In Your Eyes', a hush fell over the dance floor. The teenagers, parting to give Fabian and Caitlin more space, stared incredulously. The older generation, realising the significance of the song, watched tight-lipped.

"Caitlin," said Fabian, as they moved in perfect synchronisation, "why does that boyfriend of yours look as though he wants to punch my lights out."

"You have an over-vivid imagination. Tell me, can you see Mr Kirkwood?"

"Yes."

"And how does he look?"

"Like someone's just stuck a firework up his bottom."

"Goody," said Caitlin.

"'Scuse us, Fabe," said Marc, suddenly appearing beside them. He caught hold of Caitlin's wrist and dragged her off the dance floor.

"Let go of me," pleaded Caitlin, twisting and struggling to be free, all her earlier bravado vanishing like pixie-dust. "People are staring." She cringed as they passed Lady Richmond. "Hell, I'll never be able to look her in the eye again."

Marc did not reply, merely pulled her down the terrace steps and into the garden.

"My wrist is hurting!" She attempted to prise away his fingers but they were walking so quickly across the soft, velvet lawns it was all she could do to remain upright. The party was now merely a hum in the distance. She began to feel cold. "Where are we going?"

"You're going home," said Marc abruptly. "Whatever possessed you to request that record? Considering your husband has just died in a fire, don't you think it was totally tasteless? Do you have a social death wish?"

"It was on the tip of my tongue to ask for 'Great Balls Of Fire'," she retorted, "but it's not so easy to dance to. I'm way past caring what anyone thinks. It doesn't matter if I act like Shirley Temple or the bitch from hell. Everyone hates me. I feel about as welcome as a pork sausage at a bar mitzvah. I did think about going home I admit – but not now. I'm having a great laugh winding the bastards up. Or at least I was having fun until you went into your caveman routine."

As the shrubbery loomed, dark and forbidding, he stopped abruptly and turned her round to face him. The moon cast shadows on his face; he looked hard and unforgiving.

"You might be having fun but don't you realise you're just getting everyone's back up? This sort of behaviour is not the way to make friends and influence people."

"I'm twenty-four years old. Don't talk to me as though I were a child." Her eyes sparked furiously. "Your average Mills & Boon fan might fall for this macho behaviour, Mr Darcy, but not me. Besides, who are you to tell me what to do? It's not like you give a shit."

He released her, his harsh face now sad and vulnerable in the moonlight. He stared at her silently before saying, "I just hate to see you make a fool of yourself in front of all these people."

She felt herself weaken. "I'm not making a fool of myself. I'm showing people I don't care what they think about me. You don't know what it's like, living in a village where everyone hates you, where everyone thinks you murdered your husband for his money."

"Does it really matter to you what they think?" Marc sounded thoroughly exasperated. "Who are 'they', for Christ's sake? A few prats with inherited titles and inherited wealth. They're just living in the glory of their ancestors' pasts. Who's worried what 'they' think?"

"Me." Caitlin sat on a tree stump, defeated. It was

damp, and would probably leave a green mouldy patch on her slip, but she did not care. "You wouldn't understand. This is an English thing and you're Canadian."

"Actually, I'm English and, technically, you are Irish."

Caitlin glowered at him. "Are you always right?"

"Always," grinned Marc. "I'm a police officer."

She didn't laugh. "Ah yes. A police officer." She stared at her feet.

Marc knelt beside her. "Do you want to go home? Or back to the party?"

She had overdone the 'macho' speech. Was he now incapable of making a decision? She tried to recall just how much she had hated him. But the hate seemed to feel very much like love and all she really wanted was for him to take her into his arms and kiss her.

"I don't know," she muttered.

He took one of her hands in both of his and she stared into those navy-blue eyes, now almost black. Did he really love her or was he still trying to obtain information? If she leant forward, would he kiss her? If she ran away, would he chase after her and carry her away to his cottage in the woods? Did she want him to?

"We can just sit here if you'd rather," he added. "I'm sure if I try real hard I'll remember some poetry about moonlight."

Finally she laughed, a happy, gurgling laugh which bubbled out of her mouth and floated off towards the stars before she could stop it.

The relief on his face was perceptible. "Does that mean you've forgiven me?"

She regarded him through half-closed eyes. "Maybe. Grovel a bit more."

He moved closer, tenderly brushing one stray curl from her cheek, then tentatively kissing where it had lain.

She sighed softly. "Do you love me?"

"Always," he said and began to kiss her.

Hugh, romping in the rhododendrons with a dishevelled Belinda, watched Marc pick Caitlin up in his arms and disappear amongst the large fragrant blooms of the carpenteria bushes.

Hugh turned his head away. "Belinda," he said bleakly.

"Mmm?" said Belinda, who had always been told it was rude to speak with her mouth full.

Hugh hauled her up. "Belinda, would you like to get married?"

"To whom?"

"Me!"

"Oh." Belinda thought for a moment. "Oh, all right."

Hugh sighed. When he had asked Caitlin to marry him, five years ago, *she* had said 'Yes, please!'

Chapter Twenty-four

Georgia had not been invited to Belinda's birthday ball. But she had no need of fairy godmothers, pumpkins or glass slippers. All she required was a paper knife to break into Leo Kirkwood's bedroom to make her evening complete. After all, if she ever failed to hack it as a police officer, she could always make a living as a burglar.

Now was her only opportunity to find Annelise's knickers, if Leo had been fool enough to keep them as a trophy. He must realise they were evidence or he would not have crept back to the poolside to retrieve them from the bin. If he had any degree of intelligence he would have destroyed them. But then these blue-blooded, upper-class types weren't known for their great intellect. Perhaps he had tucked them under his mattress or a loose floorboard? Georgia was so excited at the thought of solving her sister's murder single-handedly she hardly knew where to start.

She tried to remember her secondment to the drug

squad as a young probationer. Drug dealers always knew the very best hiding-places, whereas it never occurred to fraudsters that they might be caught. As for burglars, they were usually too thick to even think of a more exotic place to hide their ill-gotten gains than under their own bed.

Georgia started to tap, tap, tap, around the panelling. There was one place it sounded hollow, then she realised she was next to the light switch. The electrician had to put the wiring somewhere. Secret panels? What was she thinking of? Too much Enid Blyton again. To keep a grip on reality, Georgia fast-tracked to the bathroom instead.

She checked the toilet cistern, the druggies' favourite, and then behind the cast-iron bath. It was the old fashioned sort, standing on four dusty lions' feet. She disturbed an army of earwigs and a very large spider but that was all. Like Old Mother Hubbard, Leo's cupboards were bare, apart from his complete range of Ralph Lauren's Polo Sport and his contact-lens solutions. She had not realised he was short-sighted.

Georgia returned to the bedroom and searched through the wardrobes, marvelling at the rows of expensive designer suits, then his bedside cupboard, discovering a whole library of porn. There was nothing under the bed, apart from a little round piece of plastic, like a contact lens but tinted brown. She peeled up the carpet – zilch – rifled through all the books in the bookcase in case they were false, they weren't, and took all the videos out of their cases.

Dispiritedly, Georgia wandered into the sitting-room and, by the time she had completed a thorough search, it was almost midnight. She had found absolutely nothing. She sat on the window seat and drummed her heels against the wall. She ached with disappointment. At least her search had been careful. The suite did not look as though it had been disturbed, although it was a lot less dusty than it had been – most of it was over her.

She was about to leave when she noticed the panelling inside the window on her right was far more worn than on the left. On closer examination, she found a crack running around one of the panels. She pressed against the wood and it sprang open. She put her hand in the space behind and found a video tape.

"Eu-bloody-reka!"

Without bothering to close the panel, she sprang off the window seat and ran back into the bedroom to the video recorder. Slamming in the tape, she settled back to watch.

* * *

Marina wandered through the maze of corridors in Ilex House trying to find a bathroom. As the house reputably had twenty-seven that should not have been a problem. But Marina had been at the champagne cocktails and would have had trouble finding her own feet. So far she had discovered Lord Richmond in bed with the wife of the local MFH, both of them wearing nothing but riding boots; Elena in the conservatory entwined with William Fitzpatrick; and Tania Richmond in the library with Jane Austen, a comatose Fabian at her feet. Marina grinned. Any more alcohol and she'd be seeing Colonel Mustard in the kitchen with Professor Plum.

She opened another door and switched on the light. Instead of Turner and Constable on the walls she found posters of boy bands and an enormous four-poster hung with lace. Belinda's bedroom. Hoping to find an en-suite bathroom, Marina walked tentatively inside and closed the door behind her.

Belinda's bedroom, that which was not covered with posters, was painted pink, with a white fluffy carpet. The *chaise longue* at the end of the bed was covered in white leather and sequinned scatter cushions – with soppy slogans such as 'I Need A Hug'. Even Marina, Queen of Kitsch, wanted to throw up.

The bathroom was pink marble with gold fittings, there was a sunken bath and more candles than the Brompton Oratory. Marina managed to wash her hands without knocking any over and was just about to leave when there was an almighty crash and a man fell through the open window.

Marina screamed and he threw himself on top of her. Marina opened her mouth to scream again but he was very good-looking and he did seem rather familiar.

He clapped a paint-splattered hand over her mouth. "Shh, Marina, it's me!"

Marina bit it. "You're squashing me!" she complained, and pushed him off.

He raised his face up out of the dust. "You don't recognise me?"

Marina stalled for time. "Of course I do," she snapped, standing up and smoothing the creases from her gown.

"So who am I?"

Marina gazed into his large jade eyes, fringed with thick black lashes. There were only two people she knew with eyes that beautiful. Caitlin and –"Bloody hell, Jack, you've cut your hair!"

Jack grinned. "That's the first time I've ever heard you swear. I must have made an impression."

"What are you doing climbing in through the window? I thought you were a burglar."

He shrugged. "I'm gatecrashing. Lady Richmond does not approve of me dating her daughter Belinda."

"I'm not surprised. Is that why you've cut your hair?"

"Do you like it?"

Marina regarded him doubtfully. "It's a bit short." Fascinated, Marina stooped to stroke his head. His hair was a sleek as an otter, yet the dreadlocks had always given the impression that his hair was appallingly out of condition.

"*Now* you tell me." He scrambled to his feet. "It took years to grow those dreadlocks."

"The style is fine," lied Marina, anxious to soothe his feelings. "It's just a bit lopsided. Did you do it yourself?"

He eyed her balefully. "If I were you, I'd quit while I was ahead."

They glared at each other. Marina realised he was wearing a suit and recognised it. "Wow, *Armani*," she breathed. "You must have earned lots of money for your painting of Belinda?"

"Lots," lied Jack solemnly, having stolen the suit from Leo's wardrobe not thirty minutes earlier. He offered her his arm. "Come on, take me to the party and show me a good time."

* * *

Georgia stared at the TV screen as the picture flickered and then shot into focus. It was black and white but very clear, the date and time clicking past in the corner. At first Georgia could not understand what she was looking at and then she realised it was one end of a large swimming-pool. The water was still and the surrounding area deserted.

Then there was a disturbance at the edge of the screen and two young women jumped into the water. They were both blonde, their hair floating around their shoulders like mermaids. Georgia could see them laughing and giggling, and splashing each other, although there was no sound. Neither of them wore swimsuits.

A man dived in, fully clothed. He had grey hair and middle-age spread. He lifted one girl up onto the side and began to kiss her breasts. With horror Georgia recognised her sister and abruptly switched off the tape.

She was watching the security video from the hotel pool. The pool inside the barn which had burned down. The man was Hugh Kirkwood and the other girl must be Belinda Richmond. Georgia stared at the blank screen, seeing her own frightened reflection. *Get a grip, George!* She took a deep breath and slowly pressed 'play'.

* * *

When Marina and Jack entered the ballroom, the dance-floor was so crowded they could not see anyone they recognised. It was impossible to get near the bar, so they half-heartedly danced with each other. Marina was well aware that Jack was wishing he was with Belinda. When they sashayed past Lady Richmond, Jack maliciously forced Marina to introduce him. As Lady Richmond beamed it was clear she had not the slightest idea who he was. Marina dragged him away before he could cause any trouble.

"Where the hell's Belinda?" he muttered, scanning the crowd from his vantage of six-foot-three.

Marina, wrestling with her conscience, replied, "The last time I saw her she was with Leo." She felt she owed it to Caitlin to ensure Jack did not make a fool of himself but had always been hopeless at lying.

Jack's face darkened. "Where?"

"I think they went for a walk in the garden."

Jack abruptly turned and stalked off through the French windows, leaving Marina, feeling miserable and decidedly second-best, alone on the dance floor. She was even more upset when William Fitzpatrick, spotting she was alone, moved in for the kill.

Jack strode out onto the terrace to search for Belinda. It was difficult to know where to begin. As far as the eye could see there were, what could politely be termed, courting couples. And most of the men were tall and dark and the women slight and blonde. Casually he meandered up to each couple and attempted to check their identity. One woman called him 'a bloody pervert' and pierced his foot with a four-inch stiletto. A few minutes later he had to duck as a well-known captain of industry threw a punch at him, landing right on target.

Rubbing his tender jaw, Jack wandered down into the garden and through the shrubbery. There was an awful lot of rustling going on. Tentatively he parted the leaves.

And found Leo and Belinda making love in a rhododendron bush.

* * *

Georgia watched in horrified fascination as Hugh Kirkwood made love to first Belinda then Amanda. Her finger itched to press 'fast-forward' and so spare her embarrassment but knew she could not afford to overlook any evidence, no matter how painful.

Someone else moved into the picture, a man very like Hugh but younger and more handsome. Leo

Kirkwood? At this distance it was difficult to be sure. After a brief conversation with Hugh he tore off his clothes and jumped into the pool, sliding his arms around a willing Amanda. Georgia turned from the screen, sickened. How could her sister degrade herself like that?

Like she herself had done, a little voice reminded her. A proper police officer obtained results by painstaking research and hard graft. Not by sleeping with the suspects. She was kidding herself. She'd never make CID. Not when the only way she could get results was by prostituting herself.

Through eyes blinded by tears she looked back at the television. And then hit the freeze frame. Amanda and the man she thought was Leo were floating motionless in the water. And Belinda Richmond had vanished.

* * *

Jack stormed back into Ilex House. He found Marina propping up the bar, chatting up a small gingery man who was excitedly leering down the front of her dress. Without the slightest apology, Jack grabbed her wrist and hauled her back onto the dance-floor.

Marina was surprised. She had never realised he liked dancing so much. It wasn't as though he was any good at it either. The most she could hope for was that he tired himself out quickly.

"It is customary to ask a lady first," she reproved, forgetting she had resolved not to speak to him.

"What?" Jack was not paying attention, concentrating on dancing frenziedly to the latest hip-hop beat, his long arms whirling around his head like a stoned octopus.

Marina glared at him. "I was in the middle of a very interesting conversation."

"With William Fitzpatrick?" he derided. "Of course you were."

"He's going to help me with the research for my next book," she lied, jigging furiously up and down to try to keep up with him, and hoping her strapless Marks & Sparks bra was up to the job. "*A Minister For Love.*"

"You need *help* with one of those trashy romances?" Again, he dragged her off, away from the dance floor and into the hall, pushing her up against the door to a little salon, currently being used as a cloakroom. "Allow me."

As he buried his face in her neck Marina could only freeze incredulously. It was as though the family tabby had suddenly transformed into Shere Khan. His hands moved familiarly over her body; the grazing of stubble on his chin was scraping her collarbone, taking off the top layer of her skin. Still smarting at the 'trashy romances' remark, she opened her mouth to protest, and found it swamped by his – brutal and relentless, not at all like gentle Fabian or even the heroes in her novels. Then, just as suddenly, he released her.

"If you get writer's block again," he said, "call me." And he turned towards the front door, fully intending to stomp off into the night and get pissed at The Parson's Collar.

So this was what being weak at the knees actually felt like, thought Marina in a daze. She caught his arm and pulled him firmly back against her, before he could escape.

"I don't think I can wait that long," she breathed, before pressing her fuchsia lips against his.

Jack, falling forwards, put out his hands to avoid squashing her and the salon door flew open. They crashed into the darkness, landing on a pile of coats, which had slipped from their hangers. Marina hardly paused for breath. She wrapped her arms around his neck and kicked the door shut behind them.

* * *

Lord Richmond stood on a chair, and chinked a fork against his wine glass. "Ladies and gentlemen, I wish to make an announcement," he beamed, and wobbled slightly. "Tonight is the eighteenth birthday of my daughter, Belinda. A very special time for a young woman. And tonight is even more special. I am very pleased to announce the engagement of the Honourable Belinda Richmond to Mr Leo Kirkwood."

There was a stunned silence then the guests burst into applause. Hugh made a short, witty speech – the same one he had given on his engagement to Caitlin.

Then as the music resumed, Hugh whispered to his future father-in-law, "With your Lordship's permission,

I would like to take Belinda back to Kirkwood Manor for a nightcap. I have something special I would like to give her. Something which belonged to my mother."

Lord Richmond beamed and patted him on the back. "Of course, dear boy, of course. I will send for the car."

* * *

Georgia watched Hugh sitting alone on the side of the pool, still wearing his white shirt but naked from the waist down. He was talking to someone, off camera, who gradually walked into view, swinging a large hammer from his fingertips. Tantalising, his face remained out of shot.

He was wearing a pale suit. As he half-turned, pointing towards the camera, Georgia got a clear shot of a flamboyant tie before he stepped out of the picture. Hugh obediently stood up and walked off towards the staff office. A few moments later the screen fizzled and went blank.

"Damn," cried Georgia, kicking the bed in frustration. "Damn, damn, damn!"

* * *

As Lord Richmond's Jaguar swept up the drive towards Mistletoe House, Hugh realised Belinda had fallen asleep on his shoulder. Irritably he pushed her off before she got lipstick all over his shirt. Her head hit the side window with a clunk and she abruptly woke up.

"Are we there?" she asked, bewildered.

"Yes." Hugh motioned to the driver to stop by the fountain and pushed Belinda out of the car.

She tottered up the steps, giggling. "Ooh, I think I've had too much to drink. Are you going to carry me over the threshold?"

And risk putting his back out? "It's unlucky before the wedding, darling."

She skipped into reception. "Where is everybody?"

"In bed. It's past midnight."

"Let's do it here, on the desk. I've never done it in a hotel lobby before. Wouldn't it be funny if someone walked in and caught us?"

I'm getting too old for this, thought Hugh wearily. All I want to do is go to bed and *sleep*.

"Have you bought me a present?" asked Belinda, still dancing around him.

Christ, where did she get the energy? "It's a surprise," replied Hugh, steering her towards the staircase.

"Is it jewellery?"

"Why don't you wait and see?"

Belinda got halfway up the stairs and decided to slide down the banister. She did it quite successfully too, despite the ballgown. Keeping a tight hold of his temper, Hugh walked back downstairs and caught hold of her hand.

"Am I a naughty girl?" she giggled.

"Yes," he muttered, between gritted teeth. "And if you don't behave I shall spank you."

"Yummy," said Belinda, wrapping her arms around his neck and planting her mouth firmly on his. "I can't wait."

* * *

Slowly Georgia rewound the tape on picture search and froze the shot of the tie. The boffins at Technical Services could probably zoom in to see each thread in clarity. Georgia was reduced to squinting at the screen, moving the video forward, frame by frame, until she had the clearest shot possible. She recognised the cartoon character of Sylvester the cat, who was dancing across the tie – which she knew was red even though the video was in black and white.

How did she know the tie was red?

She had seen it before.

* * *

"Is this your room?" asked Belinda, about to walk into the cleaner's broom cupboard.

Hugh, dragging her down the corridor before she woke up any of his staff, attempted to open the door to his bedroom and found it locked. Shit, if he had to leave Belinda on her own while he returned to reception for a pass key there was no telling where she might end up. He rattled it in exasperation.

* * *

Georgia almost shot through the ceiling. She hit the power switch on the TV and pressed the eject button on the VCR. The machine began to whirr and click. What was taking it so long? She stuck her fingers through the flap and attempted to prise it out.

"Eject, you bastard!" she said frantically. "Eject!"

* * *

Hugh tried the next door along, his private sitting-room, which opened out into the bedroom. No problem. He pushed Belinda over the threshold and closed the door behind them.

Belinda snuggled into his chest. "Are you going to kiss me? You haven't kissed me for five whole minutes. Don't you love me any more?"

Hugh kissed her. She tasted of toothpaste and bubblegum. It was oddly erotic. He kissed her again, then picked her up and carried her into the bedroom, dropping her onto the bed.

She regarded him with big blue eyes. "Am I going to get my present now?"

"Oh yes," said Hugh and began to unbutton his shirt. "Right now."

Underneath the bed, oblivious to the creaking springs not two inches from the top of her head, Georgia finally remembered when she had seen the red tie before.

She had given it to Marc for Christmas.

Chapter Twenty-five

Marc and Caitlin walked hand in hand though the woods to his cottage. He led her firmly up the stairs, which creaked at every step, ducking under the blackened beams and into the little bedroom. There was no carpet, just the polished floorboards reflecting, in little silver pools, the moonlight streaming through the bay window.

Without bothering to either switch on the light or draw the curtains, Marc slowly undressed her, tenderly kissing her, before tugging the duvet off the bed and throwing it on the floor.

One day, thought Caitlin irrelevantly, as the floorboards began to squeak alarmingly beneath them, I might actually make love in a bed.

* * *

Marina woke up and realised in panicky horror that she

had no idea where she was. It was dark, she was lying on something soft and warm, and when she tried to sit up, it grumbled and wound two strong arms around her waist.

Normally Marina would have been quite chuffed to find such a hunk in her bed, but still she could not quell that sense of unease. There was definitely something not right. This wasn't a room in her cottage. Why was it so dark? Where was the bed? Fighting claustrophobia, she pulled away from that delectable male embrace and, fumbling around, eventually found a light switch.

"Fucking hell, Marina, turn that damn light off! Do you want to blind me?"

She stared incredulously at the handsome rogue shielding his eyes, reclining on what appeared to be animal skins spread over across the floor of this small sitting-room. She had always admired Elinor Glyn it was true, but this was taking idolisation too far . . .

The man smiled encouragingly but it was a while before she recognised him. Of course, the dreadlocks . . .

"Jack! What are you doing here? Er, wherever here is."

Jack took his hand from his eyes and regarded her quizzically. "You're not going to try and tell me you've forgotten about last night? Have you've been drinking pina coladas again?"

Marina put her hand to her head. Her memory was playing cat and mouse, nothing made sense.

She forced herself to remain calm. "Jack, where are we?"

"The crimson salon – Richmond's pad." Jack began to rummage through the furs, presumably to find his clothes. "They were using it as a cloakroom, do you remember? Beats me why no one bothered to collect their coats – although, come to think of it, there don't seem to be so many here as there were when we started . . ."

Marina groaned and buried her face in her hands. "Oh great. That's really *great*. You mean, while we were at it last night, everyone was trooping in and out to get their coats? What will they think of me?"

"Not a lot," Jack squinted at his watch. "They're probably asleep. It's five o'clock in the morning."

"At least I won't have to face anyone. Perhaps I'll spend the rest of the year with my cousins in Greece and when I come home everyone will have forgotten all about it." Marina unlocked the door and peered out into the darkened hallway. "I'll write Lady Richmond a note when I get home. I'm sure she won't mind that I didn't thank her in person."

Jack appeared amused. "Er, Marina, where are you going?"

She regarded him balefully. Stupid question! "Home. Before anyone else sees me. Don't you realise, I'm never going to be able to live this down?"

He laughed. "Well, although you look absolutely terrific as you are, I really think you ought to put your dress back on first . . ."

* * *

Marc grumpily drove Caitlin back to Mistletoe House at five o'clock in the morning, unable to understand her need to temporarily keep up appearances. She also forced him to drop her off at the end of the drive, which meant she had a long walk back to the house.

As the main entrance was locked (Hugh being spiteful again?), she had to break in through the bar entrance, by smashing one of the panes in the French windows with a rock from the garden. The alarm went off but no one appeared to notice, even though it took her five minutes to silence it. So much for the security guards.

Caitlin staggered upstairs and fell asleep on top of her bed, utterly exhausted.

* * *

Marina dropped Jack off at Mistletoe House and was in the middle of a thirty-three point turn around the fountain when he solemnly tapped on the driver's window.

"I've been locked out."

Marina regarded him suspiciously. Was this a line? "Can't you shin up a drainpipe or something?"

"And set off the intruder alarm? Knowing my sister, she probably has everything linked up to the SAS. In twenty seconds a helicopter full of gun-toting thugs will appear over the horizon like extras from *Apocalypse Now*."

"Get in the car," sighed Marina. "You can sleep on my sofa."

She drove the short distance down Mistletoe Lane to her cottage. The trip wasn't nearly long enough for her to wrestle out a solution with her conscience. All she could think about was Jack and the way his beautiful green eyes kept flicking over her body when he thought she wasn't looking. It was a long time since anyone had looked at her like that – *had* anyone ever looked at her like that?

It must be the effect of all that alcohol, she realised miserably. But she hadn't seen him drink anything. And, if he had, surely the effect would have worn off now?

She parked the car outside the garage and switched off the engine. For a moment she waited, just in case he felt like leaning over and kissing her. He didn't move. Marina decided she didn't want to look too obvious and, fumbling with the door handle, almost fell out of the car in her haste to get away.

Jack watched her progress with lazy amusement as she tripped up the step and dropped her keys onto the flagstones.

"Oh, I'll never find them now!" she wailed.

Jack slid out of the car and casually scooped up the keys, which were glinting in the early morning light. Instead of dropping them into her outstretched hand, he unlocked the door himself, holding it wide open for her.

"Marina," he said, watching her stumble over the threshold and boomerang off the chintzy furniture, "relax. Stop pratting about."

"Oh but I –" Miserably Marina shut up and dug her

nails into an old oak dresser to stop her legs giving way from what felt suspiciously like love. "Would you like coffee? Er, I mean tea – breakfast – anything?"

"Anything?" he teased.

Marina smiled weakly. She had walked straight into that one. "Are you very hungry?" she asked. "I can do you a fried breakfast, or cereal, or –"

Jack kissed her to shut her up. "Which way to the bedroom, Marina?"

"The – the bedroom?" repeated Marina faintly, torn between ecstasy and wondering if she'd just stepped into one of her own frightful books. "Well . . ."

"Never mind," said Jack and, picking her up, he carried her towards the stairs. "I'm sure I can work it out."

* * *

When Caitlin woke the next morning she had no hangover, unpleasant flashbacks or a mouth that tasted like a kitty-litter. She just felt extremely smug. She sauntered down to breakfast, feeling exactly like the Cheshire Cat, and was informed by a rather disapproving receptionist that her ballgown had arrived from Ilex House at eight o'clock that morning. Caitlin was not so pleased when she found out both Fabian and Georgia had conveniently disappeared and she would have to take the early step class. Goodness knows where Georgia was but Fabian was probably still asleep in the library at Ilex House.

The step class seemed to take forever. She developed a thumping headache, had to keep stopping to take a rest and, when it was over, she was suddenly overcome by nausea and spent ten minutes throwing up her breakfast in the changing-room loos.

She staggered upstairs to her room and groped in the bathroom cupboard for some paracetamol, only to send a cascade of brightly coloured boxes to the floor. Tampons. Trying not to throw up again, she bent to pick them up and replaced them in the cupboard, stacked one on top of the other, then paused. They were covered in dust.

Nausea, faintness, no periods. No prizes for guessing what was wrong with her. It must have been the day of the picnic. But Marc had worn a condom – hadn't he? Of course, she had not actually checked . . .

How could she have been so stupid as to have had unprotected sex?

Caitlin gave a small cry and sat down on the tiled bathroom floor. She was having a baby and had only herself to blame. What would Marc say? Getting pregnant was notoriously the age-old way to hook an uninterested man. It was also notoriously unsuccessful. The man was just as liable to run in the opposite direction.

Yet a little voice from deep within was whispering delightedly, "I'm having a baby . . ."

* * *

Caitlin drove down to the chemist in Calahurst and

attempted to purchase a pregnancy-testing kit without anyone she knew witnessing it. She had not realised there were so many types to choose from. The chemist, being an imaginative sort, had piled up the kits into a mini Coliseum, surrounded by fluffy toy rabbits. Eventually, Caitlin grabbed the nearest, from the top of the pile, anything to get out before she was seen. Unfortunately she dislodged the entire display and it crashed dramatically around her ankles, like the fall of Rome.

The chemist, who had held a grudge against Caitlin ever since she started selling toiletries with the crest of Mistletoe House, made her pile each packet back up again, during which time almost every villager came in to make a purchase. If she was hoping to keep her condition a secret she had failed spectacularly. Miserably she tramped back to the hotel, completely forgetting about her brand-new Mazda MX5 abandoned on the double yellow lines outside the pharmacy and found a note waiting for her at reception.

Dear Caitlin, it said, *You will be <u>delighted</u> to learn that I have announced my engagement to the Honourable Belinda Richmond. I shall be requiring my mother's engagement ring back. Please place it in an envelope and leave it in the office safe. Thank you. Leo Kirkwood.*

Caitlin furiously crumpled the note into a tiny ball and threw it at the portrait of Hugh's father, hanging above the fireplace. "Bastard!"

The receptionist, a pale brunette of sensitive disposition, visibly cringed.

"Wasps," muttered Caitlin, embarrassed, sidling

towards the staircase. "Better call Rentokill. They can get rid of the rat at the same time."

* * *

As Marc was already up and dressed, after dropping Caitlin off at the hotel he had decided to drive straight into work. He had to endure some good-natured ribbing from the Uniform officers on the night shift but he made himself a cup of coffee, piled up all the relevant paperwork on the murders and settled down at his desk to read. Four hours later he was still despondently wading through the large case file in front of him, wondering if there was something, glaringly obvious, that he had missed.

The words began to blur into each other and the headache he had been able to ignore until now started to pound. He took a break, sipping at his second stone-cold black coffee, and stared through the tinted windows at the charred ruins of The Stables pub, still roped off with fluorescent orange tape. He couldn't go on like this. But if he didn't find out who had murdered Hugh, Amanda and Annelise, Caitlin would be tainted by the allegations for the rest of her life.

He was just wondering whether to ask the admin officer if she had any paracetamol she could lend him, when Clive materialised like a malevolent genie and sat uninvited on the corner of his desk.

Marc pretended to be engrossed in the case file and hoped he would go away.

"Congratulations," said Clive.

Marc, presuming Clive was being sarcastic about his return to the squad, murmured, "Thank you," and wished he would piss off.

"Your girlfriend is pregnant."

Well, he'd certainly got his attention. "Which one?" sighed Marc, awaiting the inevitable punchline.

"Caitlin Kirkwood. De Havilland is going to go crazy."

Wearily Marc glanced up at Clive's sneering face. The Detective Inspector was not known for his flashes of humour. He was only a couple of years older than Marc but with his blotchy complexion and lines of dissipation it could have been decades. It was hard to believe they had once been close friends during their time in Special Branch.

"Have you been drinking?" asked Marc politely, only half-joking.

"So she *hasn't* told you yet?"

Marc returned to his paperwork. "Fuck off, Reynolds, I'm not in the mood."

"So she hasn't told you," repeated Clive slowly. "I wonder why? Unless she doesn't want you to know."

Around the incident room the other officers were seemingly engrossed in their paperwork. In the adjoining room Seb Hunter had paused in his dictation, tape recorder still in the air, and was watching the two of them intently. Marc, furious that he was providing entertainment for all and sundry, pushed his file to one side and resisted the temptation to smash Clive's head into the wall.

364

"Do you have something you wish to get off your chest, Reynolds?" he enquired sarcastically, in a fair imitation of Paul de Havilland. It was the only way to keep a hold on his temper.

Clive, oblivious to Marc's vibes, continued self-importantly. "Ironic, really. Hugh and Caitlin tried for years to have a baby. She had to have all sorts of tests. And then when she had the miscarriage . . ."

Marc, growing tired of the game, said curtly, "You've been misinformed. I can assure you, Caitlin is not pregnant."

"But she is, Granger. Just ask the chemist in the High Street. You seem surprised? Perhaps she told you she was infertile? It was Hugh that had the non-existent sperm count. There was nothing wrong with her. Perhaps she mentioned the test-tube baby?" He smiled insolently. "It must have been a dream come true for Mrs Kirkwood, meeting someone like you. A normal man. Someone with enough sperm to fertilise the whole of Europe every time he came. And for free."

Marc stood up. His chair crashed onto the floor, the metal clang reverberating around the office.

Clive realised that perhaps he had gone too far. Warily he took a step backwards. "You don't like to hear the truth?"

"The truth doesn't appear to be coming into this conversation. So why don't you shut up, asshole."

"You think you're so clever." Clive dropped the mask, his hatred and envy unequivocal. "All this time you were attempting to seduce a confession out of Mrs

Kirkwood, she was using you too. Can't you see? It's all she ever wanted you for. Another baby. And you're a walking sperm bank."

Marc punched him so hard Clive's feet lifted off the ground and he smashed into a filing cabinet. The top shelf of box files creaked, swayed, then crashed down. Clive put up his hands but was too late. By the time the cabinet collapsed he was already unconscious.

Seb's long, elegant fingers dug painfully into Marc's shoulder. "Come with me."

"I'll save you the trouble," said Marc, and handed over his warrant card. "I quit."

* * *

It was rather an anticlimax after ten years in the force, thought Marc sadly, getting into his car and driving back to his cottage via The Parson's Collar. But, ever the police officer, he only drank orange juice. He did not bother to take any of his belongings, other than his briefcase. He had no wish to remain in the station longer than necessary. The admin officer could post his things back to him. Or dump them. He didn't really care.

The sky, which had been a perfect cobalt blue early that morning, was now slate grey. As he swung into Mistletoe Lane, lethargic droplets of rain started to dot his dirty windscreen. He waited until he could no longer see, then clicked on his wipers, smearing the grime in a dirty rainbow across the glass.

He parked his car in the ramshackle garage which his grandfather had tacked, half-heartedly, onto the side of the cottage. Marc had always meant to repair it but had never had the time. He had plenty of time now. Thank God he had savings; at least he wouldn't starve.

He grabbed his briefcase and made a run for the front door; the summer rain had become quite a torrent. With his head down and his jacket pulled up over his head he did not see someone waiting for him on the doorstep until they had almost collided. His heart danced an extra step of its own but it was not Caitlin. It was Paul de Havilland.

"Jesus!" exclaimed Marc irritably. "You almost gave me a heart attack."

Paul gave his usual thin-lipped smile. "I have been called many things in my career but until now I have never been mistaken for the Messiah."

Wrong-footed, Marc could only regard him in confusion.

"Aren't you going to invite me in?" enquired Paul. "I'm getting wet." He looked pointedly up at the hole in the porch, through which the rain tumbled like Niagara Falls.

"I've resigned," said Marc helplessly.

"Fascinating," said Paul. "But I'm still getting wet." He moved to one side and looked at the door.

Marc fumbled for his keys, took forever to find the right one, then tripped over the free newspapers as he stepped over the threshold, forgetting to politely let Paul in first. As Paul entered the hall the alarm went off.

"Oh shit," muttered Marc, hurling himself onto the control panel.

"I'll wait in the sitting-room," said Paul.

Marc grudgingly made coffee but left the biscuit tin in the cupboard.

Paul smiled as he was handed a chipped Nescafé mug. "I understand congratulations are in order?"

Marc scowled, his face as black as the sky outside.

"Feel free to punch me," said Paul. "I'm no longer your senior officer."

"Why are you here?" asked Marc, finding Paul's sarcasm hard going.

Paul looked at his coffee. The skin of the milk was already collecting around the sides. "It would have been nice," he said eventually, "to have concluded your investigation before storming off into the sunset."

"What's the point? The DCI thinks he has it all sewn up. Now, with me out of the way, he'll be free to arrest that crazy arsonist."

"Thanks to the detection work of Clive 'The Wonder Boy' Reynolds? Case solved, promotions all round, much back-slapping, etc, etc?"

"That was not why I hit him."

"No, Clive never was the most tactful individual."

Marc studied him thoughtfully. "I left the station just over thirty minutes ago. Are you psychic or was the incident room bugged?"

"Please," protested Paul. "The ACC Operations would have my head for a golf tee. Let's just say I have my contacts."

"Let me guess? The admin staff?"

"The cleaner," admitted Paul. "Wonderful creatures, cleaners. It's like having your own private MI5."

Marc drained his coffee and abandoned his mug on the windowsill. "If you want me to withdraw my resignation you're wasting your time. I've just about had it up to here with the police."

"Because you can't have your own way? It gets better as you move up the ranks."

"I've spent ten years in the police and I've only just scraped sergeant. I've worked for Uniform, Traffic, CID and Special Branch. The only thing I haven't done is fly the damn spotter plane and I'm sure that would have been only a matter of time."

Paul smiled although it did not reach his eyes. Despite the jokes and relentless sarcasm, it never did.

"Yeah, I know," admitted Marc, reading his mind. "I have an attitude problem."

"Why do you think I chose you for this job?"

"I never did work that out."

"If I had wanted an easy conviction, commendations from the Chief, my five minutes of glory on local TV, I would have selected Clive."

Marc began to feel uneasy. "What are you saying?"

"I want you to come back."

"I don't think DCI Hunter will have me."

"Seb wants to get a Superintendent's pension before his thirty years are up. He makes a lot of self-righteous noise but usually does as he is told."

"Does everyone do as they are told?" Marc picked

at the peeling skin on his knuckles, grazed from where they had made contact with DI Reynolds's receding chin. "Why join the Freemasons when you can have your own Mafia?"

Paul ignored him.

Marc sighed. "Caitlin was to be the easy conviction, right?"

"She was one option," agreed Paul, sipping his coffee then returning it firmly to the table.

"Clive's ex-con?"

"Number two."

Marc was incredulous. "Are you telling me you *know* who did it?"

"You're the detective," said Paul blithely. "You work it out."

* * *

The shower blew away as suddenly as it had begun and, at Mistletoe House, Caitlin decided to play truant on one of the sun-loungers next to the pool before attempting to work out a course of action. Yes, she loved Marc, and would adore to move into his cottage – while continuing to work at the hotel. But she had the impression that Hugh, despite his supposed engagement to Belinda, would not let her go so easily.

And if she did not move in with Marc, he would think she was not serious about him and dump her. And sometime, of course, she would have to tell him she was pregnant. With hindsight, her confession at The Smugglers' Inn had been a horrible mistake.

Wearily she pulled her T-shirt off over her head and sat down on a sun-lounger. She was wearing a tangerine one-piece costume, Jack's Sidestreet Raybans and her black baseball cap. Smearing her body with factor 8, she picked up her glossy magazine and settled down to read. That way she did not have to think. Unfortunately she was also unable to concentrate.

Another bloody day in paradise, she thought gloomily, watching a middle-aged woman zip up and down the pool in her sensible black swimsuit, bearing a distinct resemblance to Jaws. Caitlin sipped on her St Clements and returned to the fashion article in front of her. The words swam into each other. Realising she had read the same piece three times, she irritably hurled it into a terracotta pot, decapitating the resident geranium.

The woman in the pool clambered out, swathed herself in one of the white hotel towels and waddled back to the house. Caitlin sighed. At eight months pregnant she would be far fatter than that. It was a depressing thought. Especially as she had only just slimmed down.

Caitlin took a bottle of gold nail-polish from her handbag and began half-heartedly to paint her toenails. Little flies, attracted by the scent, dive-bombed her feet and became irretrievably stuck. Now she would have to walk around all day with their tiny bodies embedded in the gold, like pre-historic mosquitoes in amber. Perhaps one day, billions of years hence, someone would find one of her toenail clippings and extract the creature's DNA.

Pregnancy was obviously beginning to affect her brain. Caitlin smeared the varnish off before it set with the T-shirt she was using as a pillow. She lay back on the lounger and closed her eyes. The sun went in. She sat up and found Hugh blocking the light.

"Oh it's you," she said and lay back down.

He seized her wrist and yanked her up. "Someone has been in my room."

She tried to pull herself free. "You don't usually complain."

"Something's missing."

"Then phone the police," she replied, growing irritated. The smell of his aftershave was making her feel sick. "Give them another excuse to case the joint. They're here so often I'm thinking of inviting them to the Christmas Party."

He dragged her off the sun-lounger. "You stupid bitch, don't you realise what you've done?"

Her sunglasses flipped onto the terracotta tiles, bounced and plopped into the pool. She started to feel afraid. There was absolute murder in his eyes – and, curiously, desperation too. What on earth was he getting so worked up about?

"Let go of my arm, Hugh! You're hurting me!"

He hit her, taking her by surprise, his signet ring grazing the side of her face, beneath her eye. She was sent flying, smashing back against the sun-lounger which collapsed. He was already walking away.

"If that tape is not back in my room by the end of today," he rasped, "you're dead, Caitlin."

Chapter Twenty-six

Georgia woke up. Hell, her alarm had not gone off. But the room was still in darkness. What time was it? She raised her head to check her clock radio and hit it on the underneath of Leo Kirkwood's bed. She groaned. She had woken up in strange beds many times but never actually underneath one.

She looked at her watch. Twelve thirty. She had missed her step class again; Caitlin would kill her. Unless she had stayed out all night with that new boyfriend of hers? I'm not that lucky, Georgia thought ruefully.

She crawled out from under the bed. Her body felt as though it had been run over by a truck. She sat up slowly in case the bed was occupied but the suite appeared to be empty. The events of last night came back to her.

The tape! She dived back under the bed, her nose scooting through the dust. Emerging triumphantly with the videotape, she kissed it. Now she had the evidence, all she had to do was prove the identity of the murderer . . .

* * *

Caitlin lay on her bed with an ice pack over her eye. In the summer heat it did not take long for the ice to melt. She discarded the pack on the floor (where it leaked all over the carpet) and staggered over to the mirror, her vision distinctly blurred.

Her stomach turned over at the sight of her reflection. She looked as though she'd gone a couple of rounds with Lennox Lewis. It had taken no time at all for her face to swell, despite the ice, and her eye was just a narrow, bloodshot crack. The red emphasised the green of her eyes, making her look like a vampire. The flesh around the eye had darkened – it should be a beautiful purple-black by tomorrow – and, to finish it off, there was a little cut from Hugh's signet ring in the corner.

"Yuck," said Caitlin and quickly put on the sunglasses she had retrieved from the pool. She sat on the dressingtable stool and surveyed her reflection. "Mirror, mirror, on the wall, who's the ugliest of them all?"

It was time to make a decision. Marc and the baby or Hugh and the hotel.

It was no contest really. Caitlin slipped on a pale pink shift dress, slid sandals onto her feet and, without even bothering to take her handbag, walked out of the bedroom, closing the door behind her.

* * *

Georgia, wearing khaki chinos and an olive-green vest, in the hope that she would blend in with the forest, crept through Marc's garden feeling faintly ridiculous. She had seen him jog off down Mistletoe Lane five minutes earlier, but had waited to be sure. She had been surprised to find him at home. Thank goodness she had not arrived earlier. Imagine breaking into his cottage and finding him sitting watching TV.

She was going to climb onto his garage roof and in through the bathroom window. She knew the catch was broken from the time she had lived with him. And, knowing Marc, it was unlikely he had fixed it, or changed the code on the burglar alarm. Then she had twenty seconds to charge downstairs to the hall, to key the code into the alarm before it went off, alerting half of Calahurst – particularly the police station.

It was easier than Georgia imagined. The garage was covered in wisteria, the fat purple bunches of blossom only now beginning to fade. The stem of the plant was like thick rope, tangled all up the walls and over the roof tiles. It was easy to hook her Reeboks amongst the branches and clamber up the side of the house. She plucked at the casement window, got her fingers underneath the frame and slid her hand through the gap to unhook the catch. The window swung wide, banging back against the wall. Georgia scrabbled up the side of the wall, levered herself over the windowsill and landed in the bath. The alarm sensor high up over the bathroom cabinet began to wink furiously. She fell out of the bath, wrenched open the door to the corridor, skidded on the landing rug, and ran for the stairs, sliding down the banister into the hall.

She looked for the alarm panel. It was just above her, over the top of a little bookcase. Every red light was flashing furiously, including the yellow bulb under 'Arm'. She took a long stride towards the bookcase, the rug beneath her rucked up and she went flat on her back. The alarm went off.

And then went silent.

"Can I help you?" enquired Marc.

"Oh shit," said Georgia.

* * *

Caitlin was forced to walk down Mistletoe Lane to Marc's cottage as she could not find her car anywhere. Hugh must have borrowed it again. He could keep it. She wanted nothing that would remind her of him or his wretched hotel.

Slowly she opened the rotted, wooden gate to Marc's cottage. Haphazardly hung, it creaked loudly and scraped reluctantly across the path, leaving behind a deep groove in the old stones. She glanced up at the sitting-room window expecting Marc's face to appear. It did not.

As Caitlin walked down the garden path, the

brambles snagging at her pink dress and scratching her bare legs, she realised she had not decided how she was going to tell him about the baby, or if she even should.

She should certainly not come straight out with it – that smacked of desperation. Or try the simpering approach, as though she could not think how it had happened, which would merely irritate him. She could announce it after sex, which would make him feel trapped. Or perhaps she shouldn't say anything at all.

And hope he did not notice.

* * *

"Most people enter through the front door," said Marc, his hands on his hips, staring down at Georgia in amusement. "And knock first."

Georgia felt at a disadvantage on the floor so she stood up. "I thought you were out."

Marc waved a key ring. "And I thought I'd forgotten to set the alarm," he said. "Amazing coincidence. This is the first time I've been burgled too."

"Sorry."

"Are you going to explain?"

"No," said Georgia, rubbing the base of her spine, which felt distinctly bruised. It was much safer to let him think her completely crackers rather than admit that she suspected him of murder. In fact, the more she considered it, despite the evidence of the security video, perhaps she was insane to even contemplate such a thing. Marc, a cold-blooded killer? Get real!

Georgia ran her hand across her eyes in shame. She had let her imagination and enthusiasm run away with her again. "Stupid, stupid, stupid," she cursed under her breath, banging her fist against her forehead, quite forgetting she had an audience. CID? Ha! She might as well sign up for Traffic right now.

Marc's navy-blue eyes regard her speculatively but he merely said, "I thought I returned all your love letters and compromising photos?"

She glanced up indignantly. "There weren't any compromising photos!" Then she realised he was offering her a cop-out and hung her head.

"Well, is it Granny's silver you're after?"

"And what would I want with your grandmother's silver?"

"Beats me," shrugged Marc good-humouredly. "To clean it perhaps? You really ought to offer to do it in penitence."

"Stop winding me up!" Georgia paused. It was no good. She had to drop the pretence. She had to know the truth, even if it cost their friendship. "Marc, do you own a red tie?"

"A red tie?" he repeated in amazement. "Is *that* why you broke in?"

"Yes," replied Georgia, hoping she looked suitably stupid. "I need to borrow a red tie. It's for a theme night at Mistletoe House. Vicars and Tarts. Erm, I mean, St Trinian's."

It was plain he did not believe a word of it but still he did not offer up one word of censure. "Follow me," he sighed, and started up the stairs.

Marc's ties should have been neatly hung up on a special rack inside his wardrobe. Mostly they were screwed up at the bottom. A couple were flung over a chair. Another was stuck beneath a bookcase to stop it wobbling. They were nearly all black. One, immaculately pressed and still in its cellophane, was a clip-on tie. Georgia regarded it disdainfully.

Marc smiled. "That's all that remains of the uniform I had as a young PC. It's so that a thug couldn't strangle me with it."

"Why bother to strangle you when he could slash your throat or shoot you instead," said Georgia cynically.

"This was ten years ago." He flipped through his collection. "Hmm, I thought I had a red one here somewhere. It was my grandfather's, very old-fashioned, almost a kipper tie in red-orange. I think I gave it to Oxfam."

Georgia's heart was clambering up her throat. "Didn't you have one with a cat on it? One that I bought you?"

Marc laughed. "God, yes! I'd forgotten about that. You bought it back from the States. It was red silk. But I have to wear subdued colours for work. I don't want to look like a target."

She was hurt. "I thought you liked it. You're not at work all the time."

"It was a nice colour but it had a cartoon cat on it – I am a bit old for that sort of thing, George."

"They're the *fashion*." God, why did she bother? Dragging Marc, kicking and screaming, into the twenty-first century was like persuading the Queen to have her tongue pierced. "It was Sylvester – the cat that kept trying to eat Tweetie Pie."

"You know I hate cats," protested Marc. "Next door's tabby is always crapping on my lawn."

"What lawn?" scorned Georgia. "It looks like a hayfield."

Marc was rummaging through his wardrobe. "You know, I think I remember what happened to it."

Georgia folded her arms. Marc's filing system was legendary. "Sure you do."

"You remember the Valentine's Day Ball? I donated it to the raffle for Police Widows and Orphans."

"You *gave* my present *away*?" Georgia spat out each word like a red-hot chilli pepper.

"We had split up!"

"We might have got back together!" Who was she trying to kid? "Anyway, I never gave any of *your* presents away."

His forehead furrowed. "Did I give you any?"

It was comforting to realise how meaningful their relationship had been to him. "A single red rose and some perfume for Christmas," she retorted. "I've used up all the perfume but I pressed the rose and stuck it in the pages of last year's diary," she added, twisting the metaphoric knife. "It meant a lot to me . . ." Significant pause. ". . . at the time . . ."

He smiled kindly. "What a romantic you are!"

"Which is more than can be said for you!" Did he think she was after sympathy? So what if she hadn't been the love of his life. Big deal. Who cared? But still her voice did not sound as cool and detached as she would have liked. "Tell me, Marc, *darling*. Do you happen to remember which sucker won my present?"

"I haven't a clue." He regarded her suspiciously. "You're not going to try and get it back are you? Because I can tell you right now, I'm not going to wear it!"

There was a knock at the door.

"Hell!" Georgia nearly screamed from the frustration. "Immaculate timing!"

"I won't be long," said Marc and shot down the stairs.

* * *

As the door opened Caitlin looked up and wished she had had the foresight to drink a glass of brandy. This is the man I love, she told herself firmly, avoiding the temptation to turn and run like a 'Trick or Treater'. Instead she smiled up at him. Beguilingly, she hoped.

"Hi," said Marc, kissing her lightly on the cheek. "Why are you wearing sunglasses? It's raining."

He didn't seem particularly pleased to see her. Caitlin blinked away those easy tears. It was only self-pity, she told herself firmly. Get a grip! But although the sunglasses hid her bruises they could not disguise the tears; they just trickled underneath. As Marc lifted his hand towards her face, she flinched away. She had no wish to complicate matters further by having him misunderstand her reasons for coming to him.

Firmly he removed the sunglasses. "Shit! How did you get that?"

What did it matter? "I walked into a door."

"Sure you did. And it got its revenge by punching your lights out. Pull the other one, Caitlin. Your damn brother-in-law did it."

"How did you know?" She sighed. "Don't tell me. You're a police officer."

"I'll kill him. I'll fucking kill him." Marc turned sharply on his heel.

Caitlin, hoping he had not gone in search of a blunt instrument, nervously followed him into the hall just as Georgia came breezily down the staircase.

"What's the matter, Marc?" called Georgia, in blithe ignorance of Caitlin waiting by the door. "Who is it? Tell them to sod off."

Georgia Kelly? Caitlin started to wonder if she had drunk that glass of brandy after all.

Marc reappeared, car keys in his hand.

Caitlin turned on him. "What is *she* doing here?"

Georgia paused on the stairs. "Oops," she said and flushed bright red. "Sorry about that, thought you were a salesman." She made an effort to smile brightly, aware she was supposed to have been taking a step class fifteen minutes ago. "Don't worry about me, Mrs Kirkwood. I'm just going."

"Too right you're just going," snarled Caitlin.

"You're just going straight back to the Employment Office."

Marc stepped between them. "What's the hell's the matter?" he hissed. "George only came round to borrow a tie."

"A tie?" Caitlin, unable to trust her tongue, turned and walked out. Marc grabbed her before she could theatrically slam the door on him. Aware she had an attentive audience, she let herself be hauled back into the cottage but refused to look him in the eye and, fuming silently, stared at the cracks between the floorboards instead.

Georgia, realising she was *de trop*, took the opportunity to sidle past them. "I'll see you guys later," she murmured. "Or maybe not."

Marc led Caitlin into the sitting-room and, without releasing her, lifted her chin so that she was forced to look at him. "You think I'm having an affair with her? Is that it?"

She could only nod miserably.

He regarded her kindly. "Just because your late husband was a complete bastard does not mean every man is."

She wished she could just come out with some glib comment, toss out a witty retort, pretend he meant nothing to her and leave while she still had her pride. But he was standing between her and the door, and at this moment her brain was fogged with wretchedness and her voice not even capable of reeling off her name and address. Not that she had an address any more. *Oh God, what was she going to do?*

"I *knew* you and Georgia had something going," she began slowly, to break the awful silence. "The night of the fire at The Stables. I'm not stupid, I can tell when a couple are having an illicit affair – I do work in a hotel." She broke off, aware her voice was rising hysterically.

"OK," he shrugged, "we had a relationship, I admit it. So what?"

So what? She stared at him. He sounded so unfeeling, so callous. He could not even be bothered to think up a lie. He also sounded exactly like Hugh.

"Any more skeletons about to come waltzing out of your closet?" she asked bitterly.

"Did it ever occur to you that I delayed tedious explanations purely because I knew you would react this way?"

It could have been Hugh standing in front of her; only the accent was different. She closed her eyes. It was like stepping into a time warp.

"It was before I met you," said Marc. "My relationship with George finished just after Christmas. We tried living together; it didn't work out, George went back to her family and that was it. She only came round to borrow a tie – for a costume party."

She shrugged. "It's original. I'll give you that."

"Don't be like this," he said. His performance was so good he actually sounded upset.

"Like what? Like myself? Mean, moody, and seriously pissed off? I'm nobody's Stepford Wife, Marc. Sleeping Beauty just woke up."

"Caitlin, you're being unreasonable."

Guilt transference, she thought numbly. Very Hugh. Yet perhaps all men were like this. Her hand slid down across her tummy. And she still hadn't told him about the baby. *Should* she tell him? Why not move back in with her mother? Forget the past five years ever happened. *Because you're twenty-four years old*, she told herself firmly. *Grow up!* And the baby had a right to know its father.

"OK," she said flatly. "I believe you." Like she had believed Hugh. Hell, she was stuck on a carousel. The same old excuses, the same old lies, and here she was, forgiving but not forgetting into eternity. What was that old nursery rhyme? Oh yes, *Here we go round the mulberry bush* . . . again and again and again.

"I don't want you to see Georgia again," she said. "Promise me."

She saw his eyes narrow like a cornered wolf. "Why not?" he said. "Don't you trust me?"

"I don't trust *her*. She's only worked for me a few weeks and already she's been out on dates with my brother *and* my brother-in-law. She's a fast mover. And I'm not talking about bloody aerobics."

"How can I avoid seeing George when she works at the hotel?"

"So I'll fire her."

"You can't do that. It's unfair."

"Of course it's bloody unfair. I'm sick of aerobics instructors moving in on my men."

"I can assure you, George is not the slightest bit interested in me."

"I bet."

They stared at each other, battle lines drawn.

He shrugged, helplessly, and held out his arms. "I love you. What do you want me to say? That I won't see her again? You know that's impossible. Her father lives right here in the village. Even if you fire her I could still meet her in a pub or one of the shops. I can't believe we're arguing about something so trivial. We're supposed to be on the same team." He sighed. "That was the trouble with George. She always wanted to pick a fight."

Caitlin seized a cushion from the settee and threw it at him. It hit him square in the chest. "Don't compare me to her!"

"You have more in common than you realise." He picked up the cushion and held on to it, almost as though it was a shield.

He looked defeated, vulnerable. Caitlin felt herself weaken. "I don't want to pick a fight."

"You're going the right way about it. Are all women like this? Aren't you happy unless you've having an argument?"

"Stop trying to put the blame on *me*."

"I'm not apportioning blame, Caitlin, I'm just trying to understand why you're so upset?"

"You can't *understand*? Which bit don't you *understand*? God, Marc, I come here and find Georgia Kelly sauntering down from your bedroom –"

"You have no reason to be jealous of George. She's in the past. I'm sorry I misled you over my relationship with her, but what would you have me do? Write you out a list of all the women I've slept with? I'm thirty-two for Christ's sake, not a teenage virgin."

He tossed the cushion in the direction of the settee. It missed and knocked over a half-drunk cup of coffee and a pile of cigarette-butts. They cascaded onto the floor, the coffee seeping into the Persian rug.

Marc did not even appear to notice. "I think you'd better go," he said. "We'll discuss this more rationally when we've both calmed down."

It was all going hideously wrong. "Marc, I'm pregnant." She stared at him aghast, unable to believe she had said it. And so bluntly.

The shutters came down. "Who's the father?"

"W . . . what?" The weirdest thing was, she realised later, was that he didn't even seem surprised.

His face was grim. "You heard me."

"I don't understand . . ."

"We had protected sex, Caitlin. Didn't you notice? So I repeat, who's the father? Leo Kirkwood?" He stretched out his hand and stroked her cheek. There was no tenderness. "Is that why he beat you up? Rather odd behaviour for a man who supposedly doesn't give a damn about you. Or did he reject you? Is that why you came to me? I'm second choice over that fucking hotel."

Caitlin could not believe what she was hearing. "Condoms can rip," her words somersaulted over each other. "They're not 100% safe – read the packet."

"They're safe enough for me. Hell, you have a nerve. You come here accusing me of having an affair with

Georgia . . . and all the time . . ." He shook his head.
"You make me want to puke. I can't believe I've been
so stupid. I felt guilty for deceiving *you*." He held open
the door. "Get out."

She took a step backwards. Away from the
murderous rage in his eyes. "But Marc –"

"Do you want me to throw you out?"

She pushed past him and fumbled with the catch on
the front door, her eyes blinded by tears. He silently
pushed it open for her but she did not even glance in his
direction, for fear he should see the pain and
desperation mirrored in her eyes.

And as she ran down the overgrown path towards
the road she did not look back.

There *was* no turning back.

Chapter Twenty-seven

Clive was unimpressed by Hugh's panic and, after shooing his curious wife out of his study, returned to his laptop computer, serenely typing out two more paragraphs before telling Hugh, "You'll have to leave the country. Any more dead bodies and we'll be on *Crimewatch UK*."

Exasperated, Hugh snapped down the lid of the laptop, almost severing Clive's fingers. "And where would I go? Even banana republics have extradition treaties."

"I'm sure I can find some remaining pink bit to send you to." Clive mimicked Hugh's public school accent perfectly. "You'll hardly know you've left dear old Blighty. And look on the bright side – it will only be until everything calms down."

"You said that last time."

"Well, it's your own fault. You haven't exactly kept a low profile since your return. Getting engaged to the

Lord Lieutenant's daughter, I ask you! I'm surprised you didn't pick one of Princess Victoria's relations."

Hugh began to pace the study. Two strides and he nearly collided with the MFI bookcase. What a horrid little house Clive lived in; the police must pay peanuts. Hugh managed three paces in the opposite direction and stared through the secondary double glazing, across the dirt and the noise and the grime of industrial Norchester to the electricity pylons beyond. Ugh! He bet the tourists never ventured into these back streets. It was like gazing on a Lowry painting, except today's working-class were now far too porked-out on chips, burgers and Sky TV to resemble anything like matchstick men.

Clive had returned to his laptop and was blithely tap, tap tapping away. As he surfed the net, some tart wearing only the bottom half of a bikini flashed onto the screen. Cyber-porn. Hugh curled his lip. Why couldn't Clive have the *Erotic Review* delivered like everyone else. Not only was the man a sleaze, he was an ignorant sleaze too.

"Your friends charging my wife with my murder didn't exactly help matters," said Hugh caustically. "Whose bright idea was that? Caitlin may be a little tart but she's not a mass murderer. A woman who spends half an hour trying to help a spider climb out of the bath, rather than washing it down the plug-hole, is hardly likely to have the makings of a serial killer."

Clive switched off his laptop and began to wind up the lead to the telephone socket. If only he had taken as much care in other areas of his life, thought Hugh sourly, they wouldn't be in this mess now. For the first time Hugh noticed the discoloration around Clive's eye-socket, despite his best efforts to disguise it with his wife's concealer stick. It seemed he wasn't the only person Clive had irritated today.

"If everything had gone according to plan," Clive was saying, as he packed the laptop away in its travel case, "the hotel fire would have looked like a horrible accident. Picture the headlines – *'Wealthy Hotelier And Wife Die In Fire – Inferno caused by faulty electrics'*. You do remember the plan, don't you, Hugh? The infallible plan. The one which couldn't go wrong?"

Hugh glared at him. "I don't see why I should be taking the credit for the monumental cock-up. You were the one brandishing the cigarette-lighter as though you were at some U2 concert."

"I couldn't get the fucking wiring to spark –"

"And you're the one who couldn't tell the difference between a blonde and a brunette."

"And it was *you* I caught having sex with a couple of schoolgirls instead of his wife. *As per the plan.* Did you think I was going to ask the girl for ID before smacking her over the head with a hammer?"

Touché! Hugh grimaced. "I wonder if Lord Lucan had this much trouble?"

Clive regarded him coldly. "Lord Lucan never came back."

"Is that a threat?"

"Return to your wife, Hugh," sighed Clive, reaching

for the telephone, "while I sort out this god-awful mess you've got us into. I think you'll find that she's going to tell you she's pregnant."

* * *

Hugh found his wife in her suite, sobbing her heart out on the bed, a half-packed suitcase spread-eagled on the floor. For a moment he felt sorry for her. But only for a moment.

"God, you look a state," he said in disgust. How on earth had he ever found her attractive? A snivelling Irish *aerobics instructor* – when he could have had his choice from the many daughters of an English peer?

Caitlin raised her head. Her bruises were just beginning to show through her red swollen face, which was zigzagged with scratches. Her hair stood on end, her make-up was streaked, her eyes were puffy with crying. "Come to admire your handiwork?" she mocked and reached out for the wineglass beside her bed.

Hugh dashed it from her hand. It dropped softly to the floor, dark brown liquid splashing violently across the carpet. "Not now you're drinking for two, darling."

Caitlin buried her head in the pillow. "That was diet cola. And it's going to be hell to get out of the carpet." She was silent for a moment, then her muffled voice asked, "How did you find out about the baby?"

Damn Clive, he was telling the truth. "Calahurst, as our dear Georgia is so fond of saying, is a one-horse town. And you know how horses like to grass. That was a joke," he added pointedly, as Caitlin continued to soak her pillow. "Where's your sense of humour?"

Caitlin raised her head. "It's a bit late in the day to be playing happy families."

"You're right," said Hugh. "Particularly as I'm not the father."

"Funny, Marc thinks it's yours – or rather, 'Leo's'."

Hugh tried to keep a grip on reality. Reality according to Caitlin. "Why the fuck did you tell him that? Were you trying to make him jealous?"

"No, he worked it out for himself. So much for the great detective. *And* he's been seeing Georgia behind my back."

"Bloody tart." If there was one thing Hugh absolutely hated, it was sharing his women – unless he was allowed to join in. Thank Christ Marc never had the opportunity to fuck Annelise.

"So I fired her."

"Congratulations," said Hugh nastily. "Who's going to take her classes?"

"You can bloody take them for all I care." And she placed the pillow over her head.

It was difficult to argue with someone who couldn't give a damn. After gazing helplessly at her back for several moments, Hugh snarled, "Don't forget what I said about that tape," then left, slamming the door behind him. He hoped to God she hadn't passed it on to her police-sergeant boyfriend, or even worse, the editor of one of those down-market tabloid newspapers.

He found himself breaking into a cold sweat just thinking about it. Caitlin thought she was being clever; the stupid bitch had no idea of the demons she was about to unleash.

Slowly he returned downstairs. He cadged an entire jug of Pimms from the bar and took it out to the swimming-pool to await the call from Clive. As he walked through the garden he caught sight of Ilex House in the distance, the spires rising triumphantly above the forest. There was no way he was going to give that up. But even if he made it back from Outer Mongolia (or wherever it was Clive intended sending him this time), what if the Richmonds found out about Caitlin's baby? Belinda would be shipped off in a chastity belt to some maiden aunt in Scotland and he would find himself mysteriously dropped from every social occasion south of Oxford. Rumour did not wait for blood tests.

Hugh sat on one of the sun-loungers and peeled off his blue polo shirt. He had been invited to tea at Ilex House. But it was only three o'clock. No doubt at four a butler and maid would set the table on the terrace overlooking the wooded valley. There would be little cucumber sandwiches, with the crusts cut off, like Nanny used to make, with silver cutlery and linen napkins. And an enormous pot of tea, served in the best china.

Four o'clock. An hour yet. What was he going to do until then? He had to do something to take his mind off that bitch.

His chest was starting to look pink already. Belinda should be here to rub suntan lotion on him, instead of endlessly discussing the wedding with her perfectly dreadful mother. She was growing complacent, taking him for granted in just the same way that Caitlin had done. And Caitlin had learnt her lesson fast enough when he had produced some competition.

Hugh rolled onto his stomach and took another swig of Pimms. He could see through the porthole in the wall towards the hotel and stared up at Caitlin's room despite himself. So, she was finally pregnant – by another man. He felt his insides behind devoured by an irrational rabid envy. Although it wasn't very macho to admit it, he had always wanted a family. Briefly he thought about Amanda and just as quickly pushed her to the back of her mind. If he allowed himself to think what might have been he would go crazy.

If he could be bothered to put all his energies into it, he was sure he could win Caitlin back. Of course, she would have to have an abortion. There was no way he would bring up another man's child as his own. He remembered the first time they had made love. How pathetically grateful she had been. How wide-eyed and eager to learn what pleased him. And now she was putting that knowledge to use on pleasing someone else. *Bitch.*

A sudden movement caught his eye. Across the lawn weaved Tania Richmond, Belinda's little sister, her head buried in a book as usual, her spectacles sliding from her nose. He watched her progress with amusement. How could she read and walk at the same time, yet not fall flat on her face?

Tania did not have the obvious beauty of her sisters. She was taller and skinnier, her hair the natural mouse that theirs had originally been, scraped back unbecomingly into a lank ponytail. But there was definitely something about her, decided Hugh, something quite enchanting, her large myopic eyes reminding him of one of the fawns in the park. And if he made a false move, she would undoubtedly scamper off into the forest.

As she walked up the steps towards him, he noticed she was wearing a bikini and perked up. It was a very small one, yet still too big for her. It emphasised her long slim torso and little tip-tilted breasts. As she drew closer Hugh recognised the pink gingham and *broderie anglaise* of one of Belinda's favourites. She had a red baseball cap on her head and, threatening to drop off at any moment, was a dark-blue towel hooked carelessly over her prominent hip-bones.

He grinned as she nearly walked into the pool. And sat up to watch her disappear into the changing rooms. Unaware she was being observed, he saw her drop the book on the floor, flip her hat onto a hook and start to undo her top. He had a quick glimpse of lily-white breast before she kicked the door shut. But not quite shut.

Hugh smiled. It was about time he had some fun. With a quick glance back at the house, to ensure the coast was clear, he heaved himself off the sun-lounger and picked up his Pimms.

The possibilities of what use he could put the fruit to were infinite.

* * *

After ignoring the incessant ringing of his doorbell for several minutes, Marc furiously wrenched open the door, almost snapping it off the hinges. Instead of Caitlin, as he had secretly hoped, he found Georgia, leaning forlornly against the wall, lethargically tugging at the rusting bell pull.

"We've got to talk," she said.

"Talk away," said Marc, abruptly returning to his sitting-room, leaving the door open. "But don't expect me to listen."

Georgia hovered uncertainly on the threshold, then followed him, carefully closing the door behind her. She found him stretched out on his settee, his trainers dropping dried mud all over the chintz, smoking and staring out the window at the jungle he called a back garden.

Georgia, remembering her training course on 'domestics', went to put the kettle on. "What's the matter with you?" she asked, emerging at length from the kitchen with two chipped Nescafé mugs filled with steaming black coffee. "What happened to 'love's young dream'?"

Marc, already on his fourth cigarette, to count from the fresh butts littering the carpet, did not even turn his head. "Caitlin's pregnant," he said flatly.

Georgia nearly tipped the coffee into his lap. "Bloody hell! Haven't you guys heard of condoms?"

Marc regarded her through a haze of smoke. "Fuck you."

"Don't take it out on me. You're the one that made the mistake."

Marc turned his gaze back towards the window. "Not my mistake. Leo Kirkwood is the happy father."

Georgia burst out laughing.

Marc drew deeply on his cigarette. "Your unfailing ability to read a sensitive situation never ceases to astound me, George."

"You sound just like my father," she said, handing him his coffee. "You've been working with him too long." She looked sombre. "That's what I've come to see you about."

"Oh, go away and leave me alone. I haven't the stomach for heart-to-hearts."

"This is work."

"Fuck work. I've resigned."

"Why?" she asked, perfectly calmly. This was nothing new. Marc had been threatening to quit for years. She could never understand why he had signed up in the first place.

"I haven't the stomach for that either. There's more criminals in the police than every prison in England."

She perched on the arm of the settee. "A teensy exaggeration, don't you think?"

He eyed her balefully, navy eyes crinkling against the cigarette smoke, gathered like a storm cloud above the settee. "Georgia, I'd really like to be left alone."

He really did look terrible, realised Georgia in growing amazement. He had never looked this devastated following one of *their* rows. Had the macho lover-boy really fallen in love with the whingeing, whining Mrs Kirkwood? Georgia grinned. There *was* a God . . .

Surprised she did not feel in the slightest bit jealous, Georgia decided to play Claire Raynor instead. "You vant to be alone?" she said, mimicking Garbo brilliantly. "Why? So you can smoke yourself to death? Stop feeling so full of self-pity and try to look at this objectively. Precisely when did Caitlin tell you she was pregnant?"

"What's it to do with you?"

"Considering you're CID you're very stupid. Was it after she came round this afternoon?"

"Yes."

"Then she's jealous. She found us together and thought we were having an affair. So, to get her own back, she lets you think Leo Kirkwood got her pregnant. Being a bitch has nothing to do with it. She's having a baby and at the mercy of her hormones. Imagine nine months of PMT."

An inch of ash from Marc's cigarette dropped onto the blue Persian rug. "So you don't think Leo slept with her?" he said hopefully.

Georgia shuddered, remembering her own encounter with the depraved Mr Kirkwood. "Not unless she's a complete masochist. They hate each other. Haven't you ever picked up on the vibes?"

"It could be sexual attraction."

She grimaced. "I don't think so. Leo Kirkwood is actually Hugh."

There was silence while she waited for the bombshell to hit home. For a moment his dark-blue eyes stared uncomprehendingly into hers. Then a reluctant smile lifted the corner of his mouth as he waited for the punchline. "Say again?"

He actually thought she was *joking!* "Hugh staged his own death," she explained earnestly. "He's alive and well and living it up at Mistletoe House."

He dismissed her words almost as soon as they had left her lips. "That's impossible! There was a body – your father identified it. He was satisfied the corpse was Hugh and he knew the Kirkwoods from way back."

"Then he made a mistake," retorted Georgia. "It happens! Hugh and Leo *were* brothers after all."

Marc was still turning the information over in his head. "Caitlin would know the truth. She was married to Hugh for five years. If anyone would recognise him it would be her. Which would mean," he added bleakly, "that the Kirkwoods are in this together."

Sometimes, thought Georgia, Marc could be very stupid. "If you thought your husband had killed his own brother *and* two ex-girlfriends wouldn't you keep quiet in case you were next on the list?"

"She could have told *me*."

"You're the last person she would have told. You're a police officer."

"Not any more." Marc stubbed the cigarette out on the arm of the settee.

Georgia winced and watched as he flicked the butt onto the floor with the others. It had taken years for his grandmother to save up for that three-piece suite. Marc lit another cigarette but his hand was shaking.

Georgia gently laid her hand on his shoulder. "If you love her, why fight it? Is it so impossible for you guys to get it together? What's your problem?"

"You mean, apart from Caitlin murdering her husband and being pregnant by another man? There's no problem, no problem at all!"

"Is that all that's stopping you? Listen, pop quiz: Leo is dead. Hugh has a zero sperm count. Caitlin is pregnant. Who's the father?"

Marc sat bolt upright. "Jesus!"

"Now you're being blasphemous."

"Can't you be serious for just one minute?" He moved abruptly from the settee and began to hunt around the sitting-room for his car keys.

Georgia extracted the keys from a bowl of rotting fruit and waved them above her head. "Before you go charging off into the sunset searching for the obligatory happy ending, I want you to take at look at a videotape for me."

"Are you crazy?" asked Marc, thoroughly exasperated. "Don't you think I have better things to do than watch damn videos?"

He made a grab for the keys so Georgia dropped them down her cleavage. He was about to plunge his hand down the front of her shirt when he caught a frosty glint in her eye, reminiscent of her father, and thought better of it.

Georgia pushed him back onto the settee. "This isn't just any 'damn video'. It's the recording from the CCTV cameras in the indoor pool at Mistletoe House the night Hugh supposedly died."

"Fuck!" Marc snatched the tape from her, his cigarette dropping down behind one of the cushions.

Georgia hastily retrieved his cigarette before the settee caught fire and, after juggling with it for a few moments, dropped it into his coffee mug.

"Why the hell didn't you give me this earlier?" he demanded.

"Ha! Like, in the middle of whingeing about your love life, you were going to draw breath long enough for me to tell you about it!"

"Where did you get it?" asked Marc wearily.

"I found it behind a secret panel in Hugh's bedroom." She looked smug. "Just call me Enid Blyton."

"Hugh's bedroom?" Marc balked. "For God's sake don't tell your father. Tell him an informant gave it to you."

"Do you think I'm an idiot?"

She watched him squat in front of his video recorder and tried not to wince as he roughly shoved her precious tape in. "Careful!"

"This had better be good, George, and not one of your wild flights of fantasy."

Georgia bit her tongue as the TV screen flickered into life and Marc sat back on the sofa to watch with her. All they needed was a takeaway pizza and a couple of beers and it would be quite like old times, she thought wistfully. She also had to work hard to prevent herself sliding her arm along the back of the sofa and tickling the back of his neck.

The swimming pool suddenly came into focus, with surprising clarity for a black and white picture. For a moment the pool was deserted then two young women appeared from nowhere to run along the tiled edge and jump in. Amanda de Havilland and Belinda Richmond. Georgia felt her heart drop. How many times had she replayed this scene in her head. Her sister seemed so happy, so carefree, and in just a few minutes she'd be dead, floating in her own blood.

She watched as Hugh Kirkwood lifted Amanda onto the side of the pool and began to kiss her breasts. Belinda, jealous, remonstrated with him. Laughing, he abandoned Amanda and smoothed his hands over Belinda's bottom, lifting one of her legs and curling it around his back, his hands holding her firmly at the waist as he pulled her onto him. Then, as Belinda's eyes closed in ecstasy, Amanda, at Hugh's prompting, moved behind, her hands closing over Belinda's breasts.

Marc looked sideways at Georgia and noticed her how pale she'd gone, her fingers digging bloodlessly into the sofa cushions. "We can fast-forward this bit if you like?" he suggested. "It's not relevant."

"It is," Georgia replied harshly. "See who's just popped up in the far corner of the screen? Caitlin."

Marc frowned and lent forward to squint at the TV. "Are you sure?" He used the palm of his hand to wipe away some of the dust on the screen, leaving greasy smears instead. "The figure is so tiny."

"She's wearing a wedding dress so it must be her." retorted Georgia. "I don't know if Hugh was expecting her to turn up, but she sure wasn't expecting to find him. Look at the way she's waving her arms about, screaming at him. She's furious."

They watched Caitlin stalk out the door but the three in the pool hardly paused with their frenzied sex, just took the opportunity to exchange places. Before they could reconvene, someone else walked through the door and right up to the deeper end of the pool, where the fun and games were taking place.

"Leo Kirkwood?" exclaimed Marc. "But he was supposed to have been in America."

"Yeah, and he can't wait to jump in the pool and join in. Stupid bugger thinks it's Christmas all over again. And all the time he's shagging my sister, the clock in the corner of the screen is ticking away the rest of their lives."

Marc, thoroughly uncomfortable, both with the events on screen, and Georgia's strange, set expression, reached for the remote control to speed things up a bit, but Georgia catching hold of his arm, stopped him.

"Look, in the shadows," she muttered, "there's someone watching, waiting. We didn't see *him* come in – unless he was there already?

Marc studied the screen. "Hugh must have been expecting him, and Leo for that matter, or else he would have locked the door to keep the spectators out."

"Ha, the guy is such an exhibitionist, I'm surprised he didn't fit a turnstile to that door. All these people trooping in and out!" She dug her fingers into his arm again: "See how our murderer keeps his back to the camera? I don't think he realises it's there at first. Or if he does, perhaps he doesn't realise it's switched on – or doesn't care! He must have come from the direction of the office. We ought to take a look at the plans of the pool house. Wasn't there a fire exit on that side?"

Marc shrugged, "I don't remember. I don't think so. I think that was the way to the storerooms in the attic."

"Where the fire started!" Delightedly, Georgia slapped him on the back. "I think we've cracked it, Sherlock."

Although he had no wish to dampen her enthusiasm for catching her sister's murderer, Marc still had to say: "He couldn't have lit the fire. It's too early."

"No, but he could have set everything up ready. Don't you see what's happening? Your evidence is right there on the screen! Hugh sees the murderer come in but *ignores him*. Belinda sees the murderer but *doesn't react*, even when he bends down and kisses her 'hello'. While she doesn't exactly encourage him, she's not fighting him off either. *Belinda knows the murderer*."

Marc attempted to calm her down. "You can't read too much into this, George. Don't go looking for clues where they don't exist."

Georgia, still theorising, wasn't listening, "Perhaps Belinda has met him before and is frightened of him, too frightened to fight him off, so she lets him kiss her. Look, he's moving away now, and Belinda is taking the opportunity to grab her clothes and leave. There you go, she knows he's a *murderer*."

"Picking that moment to leave certainly saved her life," muttered Marc. "But it doesn't necessarily follow that she knew what he was about to – *Oh shit*, look what he's got in his hand . . . *a hammer!*"

Georgia buried her face in one of the cushions. "'Scuse me, if I don't watch this bit," she croaked.

Which was quite understandable. Even Marc felt the bottom drop out of his stomach as he watched the murderer casually lift the hammer and drop it onto Leo's skull.

The black and white picture could not disguise the horror. Amanda, finally realising something untoward was happening, opened her eyes, tried to escape. The murderer slammed the hammer into her face.

"Jesus Christ," muttered Marc, the bile rising in his throat, the tears blistering his eyes. He grabbed at the remote control, to switch the fucking thing off, but knocked it under the couch. He was forced to witness Amanda's desperate struggle to live, while Hugh, who had done nothing when the murderer killed his brother, half-swam, half-waded to help her – but it was too late.

Amanda was lying motionless, the water around her black with her own blood.

Marc, frozen, could not reply when Georgia asked, "Is it over? Is it OK to look now?"

As she didn't get an answer, Georgia tentatively lowered the cushion. "Why do you think Hugh is so upset?" she asked, as they watched Hugh climb out of the water and sit on the edge of the pool, his head in his hands. "When he was obviously in on the whole thing?"

"Because he's just seen his favourite mistress murdered, instead of his wife," ground out Marc. "How the hell do I know the way the bastard's mind works? Can we switch the fucking thing off now please?"

"In a minute," said Georgia. "There's just a bit more."

Marc watched the killer walk over to Hugh, still swinging the hammer from his fingertips. If only he would bring the blessed thing down on Hugh's head, swiftly despatching him to hell. Of all the people in the pool that night, Hugh was the only one who had really deserved to die. Perverted, evil bastard.

"The murderer has realised he's on camera," Georgia was saying, "that's why you only ever see the back of his head. He's yelling at Hugh for having the camera switched on in the first place, which means the whole business *was* pre-meditated. Hugh's now going to switch off the CCTV camera. He looks quite upset. I didn't know the unfeeling bastard had it in him!"

"Now will you switch the bloody thing off?" enquired Marc.

Georgia was still grumbling under her breath. "If only the murderer would turn his head, just slightly. Once he realises he's on candid camera, he pointedly looks in the opposite direction. But see his tie? It's flipped over his shoulder slightly. It's the same one I gave you."

"How can you tell?" asked Marc, as the screen finally went blank. "There must be millions of ties like that."

"Yeah, in the States, where I bought it – but not here in the UK. It's the same tie. *I know it is!* All we have to do is find out who won the tie in the raffle and we have the murderer!"

"I'll speak to the secretary of the Sports & Social Club," said Marc. "Perhaps he'll remember. In the meantime, we know the guy has light-coloured hair, perhaps blond or grey, and he was wearing a pale suit. We've certainly got enough to arrest Hugh Kirkwood."

"For accessory?"

"It's a start," agreed Marc. "And who knows, once he sees life imprisonment looming, maybe he'll tell us who killed Amanda and Leo."

"Can I come?" asked Georgia eagerly. "I want to see his face when he finds out he's been rumbled."

"No," Marc replied shortly. "I want you to take the tape to your father. Tell him everything."

"Huh, you get all the fun jobs." She paused. "Hang on a minute. How can you arrest Hugh for accessory to murder when you're no longer a police officer?"

The suspicion of a smirk briefly hovered over Marc's lips. "Technically I can't – but he doesn't know that!"

Chapter Twenty-eight

Georgia returned to the police station, tried Paul's office without success, then the canteen, although he rarely ate there, preferring Mrs Barnaby's chicken and mayonnaise sandwiches. So she went downstairs to the duty sergeant's room and looked on the destinations board. In big green letters was written 'office'. She groaned.

"Are you looking for the Detective Superintendent?" chirped up the teenage communications operator, who was filing her long nails over the top of the switchboard.

"Yes, have you seen him?"

"He went out. His car's still outside," she gestured through the window onto the station yard, "so he can't have gone far. His phone has been going crazy this morning."

Georgia frowned. "Dad's briefcase is still in his office. He usually takes it everywhere – he keeps his whole life in that thing."

The communications operator had lost interest. "If I see Mr de Havilland, I'll tell him you're looking for him. Unless you want me to page him?"

"Yes, please. Tell him to return to his office as soon as possible – we've solved the hotel murders." Before the girl had the opportunity to comment, she added, "Is DCI Hunter around?"

"He's in Devon, not due back until tomorrow."

"Detective Superintendent Drysdale?"

"On leave."

"Damn. Well, if you can't get hold of the Detective Superintendent, contact DI Reynolds." She paused. "This might sound like a funny question, but do you remember someone winning a red tie at the Police Valentine's Day Ball? A red tie with a picture of a cartoon cat on it?"

"You think I'd be seen dead at a Police Social? I went to the Hunt Ball."

There was no answer to that. "I think I'll go back upstairs," murmured Georgia, "to wait for the Detective Superintendent."

Georgia returned to her father's office, feeling as though she could scream with frustration. She sat in one of the easy chairs, fidgeted about, then tried out Paul's executive leather chair; her feet barely touched the floor. She felt dwarfed behind the colossal oak desk – but also felt a pleasurable prickle of power. How far would she make it up the police hierarchy?

Resisting the temptation to rifle through her father's in-tray (he was the Detective Superintendent after all), she picked up a copy of *Police Review* magazine and began to half-heartedly leaf through it. After less than five minutes she grew bored and walked over to the window. Where the hell was he?

The plants on the windowsill required watering and there was a large dollop of bird's droppings on the glass, frozen in mid-trickle, but she could not see her father approaching up the High Street. She turned back to his desk and tripped over his briefcase, bashing her knee against the desk and knocking the case open. The contents flew out. Swearing to herself, she rubbed her knee and bent to collect everything up.

Biros, notebooks, the Kirkwood case file, claim forms, a Sebastian Faulks novel and an old-fashioned diary (DCI Hunter had a Psion personal organiser). There were his sandwiches, sadly crumpled and squashed, and today's paper with the crossword incorrectly completed, amidst a lot of crossing out. He usually finished it in five minutes flat. Right at the bottom of the pile, Georgia came across a thick, glossy brochure.

Georgia stuffed everything back into the case but paused over the brochure. It had an expensive matt cover, with a portrait of a golfer on the front, against a background of lush forest. Her father had not told her he was going on holiday. He rarely went abroad and had only had a weekend in Paris at the beginning of June to avoid being sent to the launch of Mistletoe House.

Feeling guilty for being so nosy, Georgia opened the brochure. She had not realised her father played golf. He always seemed to work so hard he had no time for hobbies. Perhaps he was looking to his retirement.

She leafed through the thick vellum pages, admiring the drawings of golfers in mid-swing, elegant ladies sipping cocktails by a vast azure swimming-pool, expensive cars lined up against a backdrop of a Jacobean stately home, which looked just like Mistletoe House. This was one boring holiday he was about to take. Why didn't he go somewhere exciting like the Amazon or the Australian outback? She flicked past a few more pages and came across a housing estate. In a holiday brochure? Backtracking she read some text.

MISTLETOE PARK
An exciting new venture from Greenwood Development.
A Business Park, Village, Leisure Complex and
Conference Centre.

MISTLETOE VILLAGE – *Over two hundred new homes, shops,*
and a pub in a country park setting.

MISTLETOE HOUSE HOTEL – *A restored Victorian mansion*
with incomparable leisure facilities. Available for
international conferences.

MISTLETOE BUSINESS PARK – *already earmarked by a major*
Japanese electronics company for their UK headquarters,
it will have easy access to the new distributor road.

Mistletoe Park
An enviable lifestyle at an affordable price.

She dropped the brochure. It was impossible. An industrial estate in the middle of the King's Forest? A new village with over 200 homes? They would never get planning permission.

And then she remembered the distributor road. Planning permission had been granted for that. The only objectors had been a few New Age travellers, the odd local celebrity and middle-class housewife. Everyone else had welcomed it as the opportunity to expand Calahurst's tourist industry. Lord Richmond was going to cut the ribbon and a brass band was going to march all the way from Norchester to Port Rell.

Mistletoe Park . . . surely it was just a bad dream?

Slowly Georgia turned to the back page. There, in the middle of a map of the King's Forest, was an artist's impression of 'Mistletoe Park'. And underneath it said:

Greenwood Development
Directors:
Mr Raj Patel (Chairman), Mr Sanjay Patel,
The Rt Hon William Fitzpatrick MP,
Mr Paul de Havilland, Mr Hugh Kirkwood.

Her father? But police officers were not allowed to take on directorships. It was against police regulations and could undoubtedly lead to a conflict of interests. 'The law is not above the law', as the Chief was fond of saying. There must be some mistake. Her father was the most honest man she knew. He had once even reported *her* for speeding. Besides, he wouldn't get mixed up with Raj Patel, would he? Or the depraved

Hugh Kirkwood? Why take on a directorship anyway? It was not as though he needed the money.

Or did he? Guiltily, Georgia remembered all that heated correspondence between her father and Lloyds a decade ago. She knew a large part of his fortune was invested through them, but had not been aware he had been one of those to lose money. He had never confided in her. But then, had he ever confided in anyone?

Her hand shook as she carefully closed the brochure and replaced it in her father's briefcase. She fastened the catches, sat it upright and slid it round to park it neatly against the desk. No one would ever guess she had been inside. But she found she could not take her eyes away from it. It was as though she had suddenly developed X-ray vision like Superman. Instead of the case, all she could see was that damn brochure.

The scene from the video flashed into her head, Amanda floating in the pool, the subsequent fire at the hotel; it was all starting to make sense. The last few weeks had been like attempting a jigsaw without a picture. Now it had all become clear.

Hugh Kirkwood had wanted to sell his estate to Greenwood Development. But he already owed hundreds of thousands, so he clumsily set up an insurance scam and staged his own death. Perhaps he meant to burn down Kirkwood Manor? It would make development so much easier without that Victorian monstrosity right in the middle. Maybe Amanda had discovered his plan, so she had to die; Annelise must have recognised him. But why burn The Stables? Was it to throw the police off the scent – or just a coincidence?

The police. Her father . . . Georgia was so shocked she could not even cry. No way was her father a murderer. He was distant, repressed, which was why her mother had left. Sometimes ruthless, but surely not so cold-blooded that he could murder his own daughter?

But Hugh Kirkwood had not worked alone; he had an accomplice – her father? Was that why he was still suffering over his daughter's death, in as much pain as though it had happened yesterday? *Because he had been the one to kill her?*

When DI Reynolds suddenly entered the office, she was so frozen by grief she could not look up or even move.

Although he seemed surprised to see her sitting in the Detective Superintendent's chair, Clive smiled and said, "Trying it out for size?" Then he noticed her tight, wan face. "Are you all right?"

"Yes," said Georgia slowly. "I'm fine." She stared away into space. *Her father, a ruthless killer?* It couldn't be true. *No way.* Her father was a hero. He'd got commendations for bravery. He was the good guy.

"You paged me?" prompted Clive. "About the Kirkwood case?" He looked at her in concern. "Georgia, are you sure you're OK?"

Mentally she shook herself and stared up him. "The murders at Mistletoe House," she said bleakly. "I've solved them."

Clive sat on the corner of the desk, carefully pushing

his boss's precious orchid to one side first. That was wilting too.

He smiled encouragingly. "Care to tell me who you think did it?"

She reached down and slid out the videotape from her bag. "It's all on here." Carefully she placed the tape on her father's desk and stared at it, fully expecting it to burn right through the wood and plop onto the carpet.

His smile vanished. "Where did you get that?"

"Hugh Kirkwood's bedroom."

"You were in his *bedroom?* What the hell – no, don't waste your explanations on me; save them for your father. I don't want to know. I'm more interested in this tape. Is it some kind of home movie?"

"It's from the CCTV unit in the barn that burnt down. It shows the murderer smashing Leo Kirkwood's head in with a hammer. Hugh Kirkwood is alive and well and living it up at Mistletoe House. That's why you couldn't find his murderer. Because he was never actually murdered."

"Let me have a look," Clive held out his hand. "Give me the tape."

Georgia pushed it towards him. Let someone else take over the responsibility. She couldn't handle it. Not any more.

"Is it genuine?"

"Of course it is! You think I'm going to edit together a few episodes of *Prime Suspect* just to look big on the *Six O'clock News?*"

Clive, ignoring the sarcasm, regarded her curiously.

"And you say the tape definitely shows the murder being committed?"

Finally someone was showing interest. "Every single blow, every drop of blood, every last moment of my sister's life is recorded on this tape."

"You actually see the murderer?" persisted Clive. "He's recognisable? Have we got enough to make an arrest?"

"You can't see the murderer's actual face, just his body and the back of his head. He's wearing a pale suit, probably grey, and a silly tie with a cartoon cat on the front. Sylvester, you know, from *Loony Tunes*? I thought it was Marc, at first, but he says he gave the tie to a charity raffle. I don't suppose you went to the Police Valentine's Day Ball, did you?"

Clive wasn't paying attention. "Are you aware that Marc resigned today? An admission of guilt, perhaps?"

Georgia remembered that she'd never really liked Clive. "Maybe we should show the tape to DCI Hunter," she said. "After all, it's his murder enquiry. We can play it on the video in the rest room. It would save going to Technical Services up at headquarters."

"DCI Hunter is out," said Clive. "Gone off on a jolly to interview that arsonist Devon and Cornwall have got in custody. And the video recorder in the rest room has been commandeered by the administrative officer. She's showing a training film to the civvies."

"I think this is far more important than a training film!"

"It's never wise to upset the civvies," smiled Clive.

417

He dropped the videotape into his briefcase. "Come on, let's go."

"Go?" repeated Georgia blankly. "Go where?"

"Mistletoe House. To arrest Hugh Kirkwood."

Excellent idea, thought Georgia. Too bad Marc has already beaten you to it. Again she felt that irrational wave of intense dislike for the man standing in front of her. While she and Marc had done all the work, perhaps putting their own lives on the line, this prat was willing to step in and take all the credit.

"What for?" she stalled. No way did she want him turning up at the hotel to find Marc in the middle of arresting Hugh. Not when Marc was technically no longer in the force. Another police officer might overlook this, call it a 'Citizen's Arrest', just pleased to have Hugh in custody. But not Clive.

He was looking at her as though she was an idiot. "Suspicion of murder."

"We've got no evidence. That's how we became unstuck before – when we arrested Mrs Kirkwood." When *he* had arrested Mrs Kirkwood. Georgia turned crimson.

He did not appear to notice her gaffe. "We've got the tape," he shrugged. "What else do we need?"

"You haven't seen the tape," pointed out Georgia. "And besides, it doesn't show that Hugh was involved, just that he was present. What's to stop him swearing that someone was forcing him, at gunpoint perhaps, to take part?"

Clive began to appear irritated. "I thought you'd be pleased to be in at the kill."

Not when the suspect was her father. "Officially it's nothing to do with me," she said airily. "I'm supposed to be on a career break."

"We can't waste any more time," snapped Clive. "It won't take long for Hugh Kirkwood to realise you have got his tape." Clive held open the office door. "After you."

Georgia stared at him. He was leaving her with very little choice. If she prevaricated any longer he would realise something was up. But if she went with him she might be able to stall him long enough for Marc to have Hugh halfway to Calahurst Police Station by the time they arrived at the hotel.

"Thanks," she murmured and walked calmly through the door.

Clive suggested taking his car; she didn't argue. Men could be boring about their status symbols. He guided her through the station car park, with one hand on her shoulder, towards a rather nifty Alfa Romeo Spyder. Georgia who had a weakness for fast cars and fast men, was impressed.

As Clive twisted round to throw his briefcase into the back, she was alarmed to catch a glimpse of a Smith & Wesson handgun beneath his jacket, in a holster under his arm.

"Do the firearms department know you have that?" she asked, without thinking.

"Yes, I've just returned from another operation where we thought we might run into trouble."

"So shouldn't you check it back in?"

"We don't have time," said Clive testily.

Georgia slid down in the seat, crimson at the rebuke. Never criticise a senior officer. But still she felt uneasy. Why would a CID officer be assigned a firearm, just because he thought he 'might run into trouble'? This was England. The police did not carry guns as routine. If there was an incident that required their use they would be assigned to either the Immediate Response officers or the Tactical Firearms Team. The only plainclothes police officers to carry guns were Special Branch officers. And Clive was *ex*-Special Branch. He must be lying. *But why?*

"Um, is this really a good idea?" she mumbled. "I'm not criticising you, of course, sir, but technically I'm on a career break. I don't have my warrant card – and shouldn't we have backup?"

"We can always dial treble 9."

Georgia reddened at his obvious sarcasm and slid further into her seat. This didn't feel right. She must be mad to have agreed to come with him. While Clive was busy arresting Hugh, she should phone the station to get some backup, or page her father again. Or call out the bloody SAS.

Georgia wondered why every instinct in her body was willing her to jump out of the car and keep on running.

Chapter Twenty-nine

Considering it was the height of the holiday season, Mistletoe House appeared deserted when Marc arrived. He parked his car beside the fountain and strolled towards the front entrance, hoping Hugh was going to be easy to track down; it was unlikely he would come quietly. Marc was also hoping to see Caitlin, although he had some serious apologising to do before she was likely to take him back.

Before Marc had the opportunity to walk into reception, he heard screams coming from the outdoor pool. He sprinted around the side of the house and across the lawn but instead of finding Caitlin about to be brutally murdered by her reincarnated husband, he found Hugh with Tania Richmond – who wasn't screaming in horror but with laughter.

For a moment Marc could only stare at them incredulously. These days it was not unusual to interrupt Hugh/Leo making love to a teenage girl – but

Tania? Hugh was supposed to be marrying Belinda – and Tania was only fifteen.

As he watched Hugh lower his head to kiss Tania's breasts, Marc felt the nausea overwhelm him. It was as though he were watching a technicolour replay of the tape he'd seen not twenty minutes earlier – Hugh kissing Amanda – and then her skull being callously smashed in.

A red mist seemed to come down in front of Marc's eyes. He wasn't aware of Hugh hauling himself out of the water until a punch was thrown at him. Marc instinctively ducked.

"You perverted bastard!" swore Hugh. "You're always spying on me. Is that the only way you can get it up? By watching other people?"

Marc was speechless. Hugh accusing *him* of being a pervert? He was not the one shagging teenage nymphets.

Marc saw another blow coming towards him, neatly stepped aside and returned it, his fist connecting with the side of Hugh's jaw, knocking him off his feet and into the swimming pool. Hugh, his arms flailing wildly, pulled Marc in too.

They surfaced, their faces inches from each other, both virtually spitting with rage. Hugh reacted first, gripping Marc's shoulders and shoving his head under the pool surface. Marc, who had been expecting another punch, was taken by surprise. He took a gulp of air and found he was choking on chlorinated water.

Marc tried to grab Hugh's forearms and force him to

release his grip but, as that had no effect, he swung his feet up and wedged them against Hugh's stomach, pushing back with all the force he could muster. His release was instant. As he exploded back into light and air, his eardrums roared and he puked up the water he had swallowed.

Hugh was a few feet away, gasping for breath. "Bastard!"

Marc hit him again and he disappeared under the water. As Marc had no desire to drown him, he hauled him up.

"I haven't got time for this crap," spluttered Hugh. "I'm supposed to be at Ilex House this afternoon, arranging my wedding."

The arrogance of the man! Did he truly believe Belinda would marry him after she found out he had been making love to her little sister? And she was going to find out. Marc would see to that. He was not going to stand by and witness another woman ruin her life by marrying this wanker.

"Without a bride?" Marc took his handcuffs from his back pocket before Hugh could realise what was happening. "Besides, where you're heading, you'll have all the time in the world."

* * *

Unknown to either of them, Tania, thinking Hugh was being attacked by a madman, had dialled treble 9 on her mobile telephone and the local patrol car arrived, sirens blaring, just as Marc hauled Hugh out of the pool. The two constables, who were expecting to discover that another poor bugger had come to a sticky end at Mistletoe House, were rather surprised to find Marc had already made an arrest, particularly as he wasn't actually a police officer any more. But they were quite happy to take over, re-arrest Hugh for the murders of Amanda, Leo and Annelise, and bundle him into their patrol car.

Hugh was taken to Calahurst Police Station and dropped off at the cell block – volubly protesting his innocence and demanding to see both his solicitor and his 'old friend', the Chief Constable.

Marc went home to change into dry clothes but still had to return to the station to make a statement. He tried to find Georgia to tell her the good news about Hugh's arrest – but she had vanished. She hadn't been at the hotel, she wasn't at home – nor did she appear to be anywhere in the police station.

Feeling more irritated with her by the moment, Marc wandered into the duty sergeant's office to ask, "Has anyone seen Georgia de Havilland?"

"She's upstairs," muttered the civilian communications operator, not even glancing up, "visiting her father."

"She isn't." Marc, suddenly feeling tired, sat in the only available chair. "I've checked already." Was he going to have to hang around until Georgia decided to make an appearance? As Hugh was safely locked up in the cells, all Marc wanted to was return to Mistletoe House to make up with Caitlin. Instead he could visualise remaining at the station to see this whole business through to its bitter conclusion.

"Have you tried her mobile?" enquired the Station Sergeant, taking pity on him.

"She doesn't have one."

"Her home number?"

"She's not there."

"Never mind, I'm sure she'll turn up. You know Georgia, late for everything. Can I get you a coffee while you wait for her?"

"Yes, please," replied Marc, who had no desire to head towards the CID office and wait for Georgia there. "Black, no sugar, thanks. Is it OK if I borrow your phone and a copy of the force directory? I'd like to make a few calls."

"Help yourself," said the sergeant and went off to the station kitchen.

Marc was relieved. He wasn't in the mood for polite conversation and, as everyone knew he and Georgia had once enjoyed a torrid affair, it was only a matter of time before someone starting winding him up, wanting to know why he was in such a hurry to find her.

Marc pulled the Sergeant's grubby telephone over to his side of the desk and pulled the slim, dog-eared copy of the force directory from beneath it. He flipped through until he found the number for the Sports & Social Club secretary, a Chief Inspector who worked at Norchester police station, and swiftly dialled the number.

"Can I speak to John Ivar please?" he asked politely, as some minion on the other end picked up.

"He transferred weeks ago," replied the disinterested voice.

"Where to?" asked Marc.

"Couldn't tell you."

"Thanks," muttered Marc, dropping the phone onto its cradle. "For nothing."

"Have you got a problem?" asked the communications operator.

He regarded her consideringly for a moment. While hating everyone knowing his business, if a communications operator couldn't locate a contact number what hope did he have? "I'm trying to track down Chief Inspector John Ivar," he admitted. "It's to do with a case I'm – I used to be working on." Fool, he cursed himself inwardly. Why did he have to remind her he wasn't a police officer any more. Now she wasn't obliged to tell him anything.

"Oh, him," said the communications operator breezily. "He's helping to set up a new unit at HQ to train Special Branch how to protect visiting Royals." She paused, obviously unable to resist a taunt. "I'm surprised you didn't know that – you being an ex-protection officer yourself."

Keep calm, thought Marc, gritting his teeth. He wasn't going to get anywhere by upsetting the civvies. "Do you have his telephone number?"

"Sure," she said. "But it won't do you any good dialling it – he's gone off to the States for a couple of months; to see how they do things over there."

"Shit," said Marc and thumped the desk.

He startled the Station Sergeant, who had returned with a tray containing three huge mugs of coffee and a plate of chocolate biscuits, and was just about to place them on the desk.

"Sorry," muttered Marc. "Don't mind me. I'm having a bad day."

"So I heard," smiled the Station Sergeant, putting the tray on the desk and pushing over one of the coffees. "You've resigned, haven't you?"

"Yes," replied Marc, having no wish to discuss it further. He was already regretting his hasty action and had suffered a lengthy lecture from the Custody Sergeant following his illegal apprehension of Hugh.

"I hear you punched Clive Reynolds into the middle of next week?"

"Er, yes."

"Have a KitKat on me," said the Station Sergeant and grinned.

Marc took the biscuit, unwrapped the red paper, and slid his thumbnail along the silver foil to break off a finger. Chocolate was a rather inadequate substitute for a cigarette, which he'd quite happily kill for right now but, as the station was a non-smoking zone, he'd have to make do with dunking the KitKat into his coffee for a double fix of caffeine.

"What's the problem?" asked the Station Sergeant, picking up a coffee mug the size of a soup bowl with a picture of *The Simpsons* on it.

Marc's mug was decorated with characters from *South Park*. Right up his street. "I don't suppose you know who won the red silk tie in the raffle at the Police Valentine's Day Ball?" he asked wearily.

"That's funny," interrupted the communications operator. "Georgia de Havilland was in here earlier asking just the same question."

Marc perked up. "What did you tell her?"

The girl smirked as she delivered her punchline. "That I went to the Hunt Ball instead!"

God save him from smart-ass civvies. Marc's KitKat snapped in half and landed with a 'plop' into his coffee.

The Station Sergeant, however, had stopped slurping his coffee and was looking at Marc with interest. "Would that be the one with Sylvester embroidered on it?"

"Yes! Do you know who won it?"

"Sure I do," replied the Station Sergeant. "Your old friend, Clive Reynolds."

* * *

Marc burst into Paul de Havilland's office without bothering to knock.

Paul casually glanced up from his desk. "I presume you have discovered the identity of our murderer?"

Marc seized him by the lapels of his Armani suit and punched him across the room. "You knew! You fucking knew!" He threw a small plastic bag onto Paul's chest. It was tied with an orange property label. "This is not *my* cigarette-lighter – it's not even real silver – it's *Fabian's* cigarette-lighter. I took it out of the bag to look at properly and could see it's even got his bloody name on it! You blackmailed me into playing your stupid power games over a worthless piece of tin."

Paul sat up and pressed his fingers to his lips to check if they were bleeding. They were. A thin trickle of crimson trailed down his chin. He pulled a silk handkerchief from his pocket to stem the blood.

"How did you find out the truth?"

"I've got the CCTV video from the night of the fire. It was Clive Reynolds who murdered Amanda and Leo Kirkwood – with a sledge-hammer – which means he's a fucking psychopath – what the hell's he still doing in the police force?"

Paul smiled thinly. "Technically, I think you'll find he's perfectly sane –"

"He killed Amanda. You know he did it. What are we doing, still discussing it four months after the event? Why the fuck didn't you arrest him at the time if you knew he was guilty?"

"Fear," Paul replied, "unlikely as it may sound to you." He hauled himself up, walking slowly back to his desk. "The fact that I outrank Clive counts for nothing. He's in the pay of Raj Patel. If I had betrayed Clive, or Hugh for that matter, Raj would have arranged Georgia's death in revenge. It was safer to remain silent."

Marc stared at him incredulously. "Raj? Raj Patel is behind this? The fire, the deaths? I don't get it. There's no sense to it, no motive."

Paul wearily lowered himself into his executive

chair; now it seemed to dwarf him. "One of Raj's companies, Greenwood Development, wanted to buy the Kirkwood Manor estate. It is not officially part of the King's Forest so he was going to seek planning permission to build a business park and up-market housing estate, using the hotel as the core for a leisure complex. Raj asked me to become a director – which was perfect timing because the Chief thinks I'm too old and wants me to retire. I knew some of Raj's business dealings were a little on the murky side but the development of the Kirkwood estate was above board, well thought out. I was convinced it couldn't fail."

"Quit with the self-justification and get to the point."

"Hugh suggested the land could be used more economically if the hotel was not slap bang in the middle. We agreed to let it 'accidentally' burn down and build a new leisure complex from scratch, using all the latest design technology. The finance would be raised from the housing development but, I have to admit, I did think Raj might be overreaching himself.

"The fire was supposed to start in the barn, during the firework display, and spread to the house. That way, everyone would be outdoors and no one would get hurt. The blaze could be blamed on a stray firework. But it had been raining – and of course Clive and Hugh were not exactly experts in pyrotechnics. The barn burnt to the ground in a matter of minutes – but failed to spread to the house. Then the Fire Investigation Unit found Fabian's cigarette-lighter at the scene. Right idea, *wrong* cigarette-lighter. Caitlin must have dropped them both when she found Hugh and my daughter together in the pool. Clive found yours and used it to start the blaze. He didn't realise a second lighter had been dropped at the scene. He just thought that if things went wrong he could always put the blame on Caitlin. He knew the lighter would have her fingerprints all over it so he kept it for security."

"Or he could blame me," said Marc dryly. "My fingerprints are probably all over it too. Tell me about Leo Kirkwood. He lived in America, he and Hugh were estranged – why was he at the hotel on that particular night?"

"Leo was lured over from the States by the promise of a share of the sale of the estate. You see, Hugh had an ulterior motive for suggesting that the hotel was destroyed. He wanted to fake his own death, claim on the insurance, use that to pay off his debts then sell off the estate at a huge profit. So he killed Leo to provide a corpse and a new ID for himself – and became the main beneficiary of his own life insurance and, of course, the estate. Clive, who is on Raj's payroll, was roped in to help, but confused Amanda for Caitlin and killed the wrong woman.

"I knew nothing of this. I only found out the truth when I went to interview the pathologist the morning after the fire. I have known the Kirkwood family for years and arranged to identify 'Hugh's' corpse to save Caitlin from further distress. I recognised Leo's body immediately."

"And still let everyone believe it was Hugh?" derided Marc. "So, basically you go along with Hugh's deception, then effectively help him and Clive get away with the murder of your own daughter? What kind of a father are you?"

"To lose a child . . ." Paul's voice cracked, "under any circumstances . . . but to know it's . . . your own fault . . ." Tears began to seep down the lines around his eyes but he made no effort to wipe them away. "I wanted to tell everyone the truth but I couldn't. Not just because I was involved, but because I feared for the safety of Georgia. The only way I could see around the problem was to get someone else to solve the case for me. Seb Hunter is fundamentally honest – but vain and silly. But you, you're different. You're honourable and trustworthy. You don't give a shit about promotion or people pulling rank. You just want to do the right thing – save the heroine and slam the bad guy in jail. Your boy-scout mentality made you perfect."

"The perfect patsy," said Marc bitterly. "You set me up just as Raj set you up. Why the fuck didn't you tell me all this at the beginning? We could have worked together to get the bastards that killed Amanda. We could have done something to prevent Annelise dying. OK, I understand you were frightened that Hugh and Clive might have hurt Georgia in retaliation – but what could they do from behind bars?"

"You haven't been listening," Paul's voice was tired, "Hugh is a nobody. He's unimportant. Clive, however, is in the pay of Raj – and Raj is *untouchable*."

"Untouchable?" Marc laughed in disbelief. "No one is untouchable!"

Paul shook his head sadly. "Considering you've spent ten years in the police, you are incredibly naïve."

There was a brief knock on the door before DCI Hunter waltzed in, blithely dumping an overnight bag on one of the easy chairs. "I got here as quickly as I could," he said, beaming at them. "What excellent news!"

Marc and Paul stared warily at him, surprised and confused.

"What?" muttered Seb, looking from one to the other. "What is it? Have I barged in on some private discussion?"

"Which excellent news are you referring to, Seb?" enquired Paul.

"The Kirkwood case. The communications operator rang me on my mobile and passed on Georgia's message; so I dumped the arsonist and came straight back. You must be very proud of her, sir, solving the murders single-handedly. I assume she and Clive are on their way to make an arrest? I passed them on the main road earlier, going hell for leather. So, don't keep me in suspense, who did it?"

"Shit!" exclaimed Marc. "Georgia's shown Clive the tape." He caught hold of Seb's arm. "Which way were they going?"

"I saw them turn off into Mistletoe Lane. I assumed they were heading towards the hotel. What's the matter? Is there a problem?"

Marc released him and headed for the door. "Clive's our murderer," he said abruptly. "Georgia doesn't know it but she will soon. Put a call out. Get everyone round to Mistletoe House – now!"

As Marc wrenched open the door, Seb looked to Paul for confirmation.

"It's true," Paul nodded. "Wait!" he called to Marc. "I'm coming too. It'll take time to mobilise everyone. You'll need all the help you can get."

But, as he reached the door, he found Marc had deliberately let it swing back in his face.

* * *

Caitlin attempted to creep along the second-floor corridor past Hugh's suite with the minimum of noise, not easy with two huge suitcases crammed with family antiques. She had just reached the top of the staircase when she almost collided with Georgia coming up.

Caitlin frowned. "I thought I'd given you the sack?" Then, as she spied DI Reynolds following close behind, the frown became a scowl. "I hope you're not trespassing on my property without a warrant?"

DI Reynolds took his hand from his jacket and lifted his gun so that it was two inches from her nose. "Who needs a warrant?"

Chapter Thirty

DI Reynolds paced Hugh's bedroom like a mangy tabby cat with delusions of being a caged tiger. Caitlin watched him nervously. Suddenly everything was beginning to make sense. There was no way Hugh could have killed Leo and Amanda on his own. For all his threats Hugh had always been a blustering coward. But why was Georgia here? Was she another accomplice?

DI Reynolds had paused by the huge oak wardrobe. Turning the key, he rummaged through the row of Hugh's identical designer suits and pulled out a handful of beautiful silk ties. He handed two to Caitlin.

"Tie Georgia's wrists behind her back," he said. "Then tie her ankles together."

As he had the gun Caitlin didn't argue. Georgia sat resignedly on the floor while Caitlin bound her feet together, then tied Georgia's wrists as she had been instructed.

At first Caitlin fastened the knots loosely, but Georgia shook her head. "It's not worth antagonising him," she whispered. "Don't worry. I'll get us out of this. I'm an undercover police officer."

The way her day was going, Caitlin wouldn't have been surprised if Georgia had admitted to being one of the Spice Girls. She shrugged and glanced across at DI Reynolds to see if he had overheard their exchange, but he was on the other side of the room, staring out of the window at the garden below, almost as though he was on the lookout for someone.

Caitlin debated whether it was safe to make a run for it but DI Reynolds abruptly turned from the window and stalked back towards them. The first thing he did was squat on the floor to check that the tie around Georgia's wrists was tight.

Caitlin held her breath.

But he stood up again, seemingly satisfied. "OK, Mrs Kirkwood," he said, "lie face-down on the floor."

She did as he asked, resting her cheek against the cold, hard boards. He took her hands firmly in his own, crossing them behind her back and tightly wrapped one of Hugh's flamboyant silk ties around her wrists. She could feel his skin, warm against hers, his breath against her hair and smell the scent of his expensive aftershave.

For one brief moment, after checking the knots were secure, he paused, gently smoothing a stray curl from her cheek. Caitlin closed her eyes to hide her fear, her heart providing a bass rhythm for her jerkily incoherent thoughts. Was he going to rape her? Shoot her? Put a bullet in the back of her head like in a Quentin Tarrantino movie?

Suddenly he moved away. Almost faint from relief, Caitlin opened her eyes a millimetre and covertly observed him as he took a little silver box from his breast pocket. A cigarette-lighter. It was even engraved – just like the one she had borrowed from Marc – the one she had dropped in the pool house, after discovering Hugh and Amanda making love.

DI Reynolds walked through the connecting door into Hugh's sitting-room, checked the door to the corridor was locked, then flicked open the cigarette-lighter. A tiny yellow flame danced briefly in the air before he set the heavy, velvet curtains ablaze.

With a sudden rush the fire tore into the ancient fabric, devouring it, then began to lick up the oak panelling. And as he smiled, with a certain amount of satisfaction, the flames consumed everything in their path. Paintings blackened, curling into a crisp; the glass in the many silver-framed photographs of Hugh's rich and influential friends shattered, one after the other; the heavy Victorian furniture began to spit and crackle as the fire tore into it. Caitlin felt a lump in her throat as she watched everything that was familiar from her life with Hugh go up in flames.

Dark, ominous smoke gathered against the sitting-room ceiling and poured unchecked into the bedroom. DI Reynolds covered his nose and mouth with a handkerchief and walked back through Hugh's bedroom, past the women on the floor, opening the other door to the corridor.

Georgia swallowed. "You're not going to leave us here?"

DI Reynolds turned to look at them, one last time. Then he was gone.

Georgia rolled over to the door between the sitting-room and bedroom and brutally kicked it shut with her feet. "That should give us a few more minutes," she coughed. "Now, what can I use to cut these bloody ties off?"

"Razor blades?" suggested Caitlin, nodding towards the bathroom.

Georgia regarded her with open disdain. "I'm talking about cutting off silk ties here, not fingers."

"Um, you could smash the glass in the window and rub your wrists up against a broken pane –"

"And I thought I was the Enid Blyton freak," sighed Georgia. "I was thinking more in the line *of scissors*. Have you got *any scissors*, Caitlin?"

"Well, there's the nail scissors in the dressing-table and the ones Hugh keeps in the bathroom to trim his ear and nasal hair and – I know! There was a large pair in the little chest of drawers beside his bed. I used them to slash his suits on the night of his birthday party. With any luck they're still there."

More likely they were in a plastic bag, tied with an orange property label, sitting in a dark corner of Calahurst Police Station awaiting their day in court, thought Georgia darkly, remembering what other use

Caitlin's scissors had been put to that night. Still, this was no time to recall old grudges.

"Right," she said feigning a confidence she did not feel, "see if you can open the window. Let's get some fresh air in here, before we suffocate. Screaming for help would be good too."

"OK," said Caitlin, pleased a professional was taking charge.

Georgia rolled over to the bed, managed to wriggle into a kneeling position, then heaved herself up onto her feet. Bending slightly, she backed up against the little bedside cupboard and yanked the top drawer out. Keeping a firm hold of the handle, she tipped it onto the bed. So far, so good. She turned around to see what she'd got. Holey socks, mainly. Plus boxer shorts, cigarettes, condoms, loose change and a pair of pink rubber gloves. Kinky.

Georgia stared at the motley collection in despair. If the scissors weren't in Hugh's bedside table where were they? The dressing-table? The wardrobe? She hadn't got time for an extensive search. And, come to think of it, why would anyone keep a large pair of scissors in their bedroom anyway? Or did the Kirkwoods make a habit of slashing each other's clothes?

Caitlin, smashing several panes of the window with the edge of the dressing-table stool, made Georgia jump with fright.

"Sorry," said Caitlin. "The catch was too fiddly to operate with my hands behind my back."

"At least it might attract someone's attention," sighed Georgia, abruptly sitting on the bed. *Because that was the only way they were going to get out of here . . .*

The thick, black smoke was still pouring relentlessly into the bedroom, under the crack in the adjoining door and beneath the gappy floorboards. Georgia's throat and lungs felt raw; the constant coughing made it worse. She lay down, closing her eyes. Strangely, she didn't feel afraid. Giving up didn't seem so bad any more. Perhaps dying from smoke inhalation would be quick and painless. Just like falling asleep.

Vaguely, she became aware of Caitlin screaming, "Marc! Marc!"

"Marc?" Groggily, Georgia raised her head and, opening her eyes, saw that Caitlin was yelling through the broken window. "Marc's here?"

"I saw his car on the drive but he's gone round to the front! He couldn't hear me!" Caitlin sat abruptly on the window seat, weeping tears of hopelessness and frustration. "Fuck, shit and bugger it!"

Marc's here, thought Georgia, her spirits rousing. Perhaps there was hope after all!

She tried to stand again, swinging her legs onto the floor, sending a pile of socks over the edge too. Something clattered onto the bare wooden boards. She looked down, almost casually, then saw it: red plastic; a long thin oval shape, with a white cross painted on it. Georgia began to laugh, hysterically. Boys and their toys . . .

It was a Swiss Army penknife!

* * *

Marc had driven at a steady 15 mph down the drive towards Mistletoe House, keeping a watchful eye out for Georgia and Clive, until he rounded the first lot of rhododendrons and saw the smoke billowing from the blown-out windows of the second floor.

Caitlin! Pressing his foot hard on the accelerator, he had completed the remainder at 90 mph, straight across the park and over the flower-beds. The guests and staff (including Fabian and Rick) were standing around the fountain, not quite sure what to do. There was no sign of Caitlin or her brother Jack. Hugh, of course, was cooling his heels in the police cells.

Marc screeched to a halt, threw open the car door and sprinted across the gravel drive, taking the stone steps to reception in one stride. As he ran through the hall, he met Clive Reynolds walking brazenly down the staircase, swinging a police-issue firearm from his finger-tips like Wyatt Earp.

Marc dived for cover behind the reception desk – but not quickly enough. Clive calmly lifted his gun and fired three times. A bullet ripped into Marc's thigh, taking a large portion of jeans and flesh with it and splattering blood across the polished wooden floor. Clive then disappeared in the direction of the gym, presumably to leave via the French windows and across the terrace, thus avoiding the crowd of prospective witnesses gathered around the fountain.

Marc risked a glance down at his thigh and was forced to swallow the bile that rose in this throat. Shredded denim, skin, muscle. Not pretty.

Using the desk for support, he dragged himself up and managed to take a few halting steps along the corridor after Clive before gravity took over and he fell back against the panelled wall, biting heavily on his lower lip to prevent himself from crying out. To hell with chasing after Clive, he had to find Caitlin. If Clive had freaked out – Marc swiftly put this thought firmly from his mind and, pushing away from the wall with one elbow, attempted to stand again and promptly hit the deck.

For a moment he lay on his back, feeling faint and sick, aware of a distinct ringing in his ears. The fire alarm? Directly above him was one of the sprinklers. If it launched into action now, it would make his day complete. So he rolled onto his stomach and watched Clive walking into the gym at the end of the corridor and, more sinisterly, the heat shimmering above the burnished oak floor as smoke began streaming through the air-conditioning.

Marc patted his pockets, searching for his mobile phone. *Shit*, he must have left it in the car. He noticed the varnish on the panel beside him begin to blister. Big, fat bubbles, popping like bubblegum.. He rested his head on his forearms, trying to summon the strength to battle his way back up the staircase. He had to find Caitlin and Georgia. He had to save them.

He remembered Paul's mocking words – 'The last Boy Scout' . . .

* * *

Georgia seized the penknife and, flipping out the main blade, slid it between her wrists and Hugh's silk tie and began sawing. She felt a sharp sting, as the blade cut into her skin but in the next second the tie loosened and finally fell away. She brought her hands forward onto her lap, rubbing her numb wrists. Blood was pouring from a nasty gash across the fleshy part of her palm but that was the least of her problems. She slashed the ties around her ankles, then pulling the bedsheets from the bed, stumbled across the bedroom towards the window, where Caitlin was still slumped on the window seat.

"Caitlin!" Georgia shook her. "Are you OK? Speak to me!"

Caitlin opened her eyes. "I'm fine. Just get me out of here!"

Georgia slit the ties that bound her, then releasing the catch on the bedroom window, pushed it open as wide as it would go, feeling the pure, fresh air against her face. Brushing away the broken glass still littering the sill with her sleeve, she half-pushed Caitlin through the window onto the tiny ornamental balcony outside, then jumped after her, bundling the bedsheets along too, just as an explosion rocked the building.

* * *

There was a deafening crash as the corridor ceiling collapsed behind Marc. He covered his head as masonry rained down, the clouds of smoke and dust clogging his lungs. As it cleared, he was almost surprised to find himself still breathing.

There was no way he would be able to return to reception and the staircase to the upper floor. The only way out was through the French windows in the dining-room, the gym or the bar, and onto the terrace. The same route Clive had taken. He'd have to find another way to rescue Caitlin and Georgia.

He struggled from beneath the rubble and began to drag himself down the corridor. As he reached the open door of the gym he tried standing again, levering his shoulder up the panelling. The wood felt warm. He risked a glance around the doorway to check if the room was clear and a vicious upper cut sent him on a collision course with the corridor wall.

As he lay on the floor in agony, he became aware of Clive standing over him, gripping a dumbbell in his left hand, the gun now shoved into the front pocket of his suit trousers. "You think you're so smart," he spat, "but you're fucking useless." And lifting the dumbbell above his head, he casually dropped it on Marc's face.

* * *

As Mistletoe House shook to its very foundations, Caitlin braced herself against the wall. "What the hell was that?"

"It sounds like Hugh's sitting-room just dropped through the Water Lily Suite," said Georgia calmly. "I brought you out here to prevent you joining it."

Caitlin forced herself to focus on her. "And what are *you* doing?"

"I'm making a rope out of bedsheets," said Georgia. "It's the only way we can get down to the terrace. Unless you want to spend the rest of your life on this balcony?"

Georgia looped one end of the 'rope' around the balustrade, then dropped the other over the edge towards the terrace. It was not quite long enough but it was adequate. Georgia tugged on it, experimentally.

"Do you think it will hold?" asked Caitlin nervously.

"I do hope so." Georgia offered her the end of the rope. "Do you want to go first? Women and children and all that?"

"No, thanks," said Caitlin. "After you."

Georgia shrugged and began to slowly let herself down. She had to jump the remaining distance but landed lightly on the terrace below.

"Come on, Caitlin. *You* do it. It's easy!"

Caitlin tugged doubtfully on the bedsheets and sat so that both legs dangled over the edge of the balustrade. It wasn't that far, really. Only a matter of feet. She could probably jump the distance without a rope. Yet – and it was the weirdest thing – she found she couldn't let go of the balustrade.

Georgia was pacing the terrace below. "Hurry up!"

Caitlin looked down. She could hardly see the ground, or even Georgia, for all the smoke. It swirled around her, like a silken scarf, the toxic fumes choking her.

She pushed herself back against the side of the house. "I can't do it!"

Georgia's voice wavered scathingly from below. "Of course you can. You're supposed to be a fitness instructor."

"I'm a *pregnant* fitness instructor. What if I fall?"

"So you break a leg, spend a few months in traction. Big deal. It's that or burn? Which do you prefer?"

"But I might lose the baby."

"No, you won't."

"I'm not stupid, Georgia. If I fall from here I lose the baby. I don't have to be an expert in physics to work that out."

Georgia's voice began to sound frayed. *"Slide down the rope . . ."*

Caitlin put her head in her hands. "I can't," she whispered, her voice choked by sobs. "I killed the other baby. I can't kill this one too."

"But . . . you had a miscarriage?"

"The doctor told me to rest," Caitlin was aware her voice was rising hysterically. "To stay in bed. And what did I do? I took aerobics classes. I lost my baby because I didn't want to lose the hotel."

For a moment Georgia was silent, then she said kindly, "Would you like me to come back up?"

Caitlin sat down onto the balustrade before her legs collapsed under her. "No," she replied, her voice sounding almost normal. "I think I'll wait for the fire brigade."

"Don't be stupid. They might take forever and the

building is going to collapse any minute. Stay there. I'm coming back."

The girl was bloody Tarzan. Somehow it made Caitlin feel worse. Still, there was no sense the two of them dying up here just because she was a coward. The *three* of them . . . Rubbing the tears from her eyes with the back of her hand, Caitlin quickly pulled up the bedsheets.

"What the hell do you think you're doing?" squawked Georgia furiously, making an ineffectual grab for the rope as it slithered up, over the window panes and out of reach. "Are you *nuts*?"

Caitlin didn't answer.

* * *

Instinctively Marc rolled over and the weight clanged onto the floor. He dived past Clive and grabbed the nearest barbell to the door, using all his strength to swing it up against Clive. It smashed into his hipbone. Clive went flying and his gun fell from his pocket, bounced harmlessly off the floor and went spinning beneath the pec deck.

"I guess that makes us even," commented Marc, struggling to his feet. Unable to grab the gun himself, he was forced to kick it away to prevent Clive seizing it. The weapon skidded across the gym, flew through the French windows and out onto the terrace.

"Bastard," grunted Clive, grabbing Marc's ankle.

Marc, already unsteady on his feet, toppled over,

making one last lunge at the weight-rack to steady himself. The rack wavered, then fell. A 10 kg dumbbell struck Clive's head, knocking him out.

There was a sickening crunch and large portions of the ceiling began to tear away, crashing towards the floor, sending showers of sparks across them both. As the supporting wall between the gym and the aerobics studio crumpled, Marc grabbed the unconscious Clive by the scruff of the neck and dragged him outside.

* * *

Caitlin sat on the balustrade, staring at the ground. It shimmered like a mirage. *God, it was so far away.*

Where were the fire engines? The police? Georgia was long gone, presumably to fetch help. Caitlin peered again at the ground. It appeared distant but very solid. If she fell from here she would definitely break something – but she had no choice. She had to save herself and, more importantly, Marc's baby.

Tentatively, Caitlin dropped the rope back over the side, then rolled onto her tummy and began to lower herself over the edge. The weight of her body pulled at her arms and she completely failed to get a grip with her feet. Unlike Georgia, she slithered clumsily down, until she reached the end of the rope – and found she was still several feet from the ground.

"I've got you," said a male voice. "Just let go."

She took a deep breath and dropped into a firm warm embrace.

"You can open your eyes now."

"Marc!" She wound her arms tightly around his neck. "Oh Marc!"

Slowly he let her feet slide to the ground but still held her close against his body. "You do realise," he said softly, "that, now I've got you, I'm never going to let you go?"

Chapter Thirty-one

December

It was a long time before Caitlin could bring herself to go back to Mistletoe House but she wanted to put the past behind her and start the New Year afresh. She chose a cold, bleak day, which seemed to match her mood. There was just the faintest dusting of a fine powdery snow. The chestnut trees in the park rose harshly against a colourless sky; the winter sun was just a vague pearly gleam above the horizon.

Caitlin and Marc stood on the gravel drive, now churned up by a fleet of fire engines, and surveyed the grim remainder of a once-beautiful house. The fire had greedily devoured the building and nothing had endured except its blackened shell. Its heart, its life, had gone forever.

A large 'For Sale' sign was hung over the door, forlornly swinging from just one nail, creaking eerily in the bitter wind.

Unable to look upon it any longer, Caitlin turned to the gardens but somehow that was worse. The once velvet lawns were brown and scorched, the flower-beds overgrown, her beautiful deer had fled deep into the Forest.

It was likely that the land would now be sold. Defence lawyers were expensive and Hugh needed every penny he could get. Caitlin had not bothered to add her request for alimony to his list of creditors. She felt she had really had enough of other people's money.

She was currently living off her meagre savings, as Marc was living from his. The Chief Constable had refused Marc's resignation but it was agreed that he could take a long career break until he recovered from his injuries and was able to make a decision about his future. Caitlin knew he was sick of his job, but what alternative was there for an ex-police officer? Security guard?

Caitlin shivered and Marc took her hand, as they walked around the ruins, past the rose garden and the shrubbery. For six years that house was my life, realised Caitlin. Now it's been destroyed I'm finally free.

As they returned to the fountain, now drained and full of weeds, Marc squeezed her fingers. "Are you all right?"

"Big mistake coming back," she replied gruffly, kicking up the shingle drive. "I need a stiff drink."

He raised his eyebrows.

Playfully she punched him. "I meant a stiff cola. One with all the sugar, caffeine and addictive E numbers left in. I'm depressed, deflated and actually rather bored. I need some hyperactivity to inject excitement into my life."

"As I'm obviously not excitement enough, I shall take you to The Parson's Collar," said Marc, "but you can buy your own drink!"

And as they finally drove away, she didn't look back.

* * *

Marc parked his car at the end of the quay and, as they walked along the cobblestones towards the wine bar, Caitlin asked, "How's Georgia? Is she very upset about her father going to prison?"

"Devastated," sighed Marc. "He was her hero. No other man came close."

"How did her Discipline Hearing go?"

"As she said herself, she couldn't be reduced a rank. So they just gave her a severe bollocking, like they gave me, and a very large fine. I think she realises that the CID is not really for her. She's quite enjoying herself in Traffic, belting up and down the motorway after speeding sales reps. I think she's only disappointed that she can't use her MGF to keep up with the Porsches."

"Oh look," said Caitlin, stopping suddenly outside Last Days and pointing up at the 'Lease for Sale' sign. "Where's Raj's nightclub gone?"

"Vice squad got together with licensing and closed him down," replied Marc. "Raj would have appealed but he had more pressing matters on his mind. Like bankruptcy and a jail sentence."

Caitlin wasn't listening. She appeared to have gone

into a trance. "It'd make a terrific dance studio," she sighed dreamily.

Marc waved his hand in front of her eyes. "Dance studio? For whom? The average age of this village is 75."

"What about all those teenagers and twenty-somethings that used to flock here from Norchester?"

"That was when it was a *nightclub*, in a pretty setting. There are plenty of aerobics studios in Norchester. And you'd have to charge customers a fortune to recapture the exorbitant rent on this place."

But Caitlin had walked up the steps and was rattling a chain linking through the door handles. "Damn," she muttered. "It's got a padlock on it."

"I thought you wanted a drink?" said Marc pointedly.

"I do but –" Discontentedly, Caitlin gave the padlock a final tug – and it fell open.

Marc's mouth dropped open. "How the hell did you do that?"

"Wishful thinking?" she grinned. "Actually, I think some idiot hadn't snapped it shut." Caitlin slid the chain from the double doors and gently pushed one open.

"That's breaking and entering," said Marc, disapprovingly.

"Did you see me break anything?" And she plunged into the dark building.

Marc nervously scanned the street, then quickly ducked through after her, closing the door behind him.

Caitlin had found the fuse box and suddenly the

lights blazed on, making him blink and giving him just enough time to see her vanish through the swing doors on the other side of reception. He had a brief impression of jungle murals, with a cloakroom designed like a straw hut, before he hurried after her onto the main dance floor.

"Caitlin, what the hell do you think you're doing? If we're caught –"

She laughed at his serious face. "You're such a wimp."

"Wimp? *Wimp*?"

"Look at all this space," she beamed, swinging her arms out and spinning round. "Isn't it glorious? Perfect for aerobics and step classes – we could hire Fabian until I'm fit. The poor thing still hasn't found another job."

"So long as we don't have to adopt him," said Marc grimly. "He and Elena spend enough time in our house as it is. At least Jack moved in with Marina."

"We could do dance classes, ballet, even tap-dancing." She began to jive across the floor. "There's already a stage for the instructor and a built-in sound system . . ."

"Be careful," pleaded Marc. "Don't dance around like that. You don't want to give birth. Not here, not now."

Gleefully she ran up the stairs, two at a time, pausing to thumb disparagingly towards the fibre-glass lake and waterfall. "But that can go."

Marc followed behind, watching with alarm as she sped along the balcony, hurtling past little round tables, with chairs balanced on top by the cleaner. Merrily, she knocked them all onto the floor, one after the other, like synchronised swimmers diving into a pool. Marc tried to intercept but the crashes reverberated around the building.

How am I going to explain *this* to the Chief Constable, thought Marc, glancing worriedly towards the door. Surely they could hear the racket right down the quayside?

Caitlin was now conga-ing around the debris. "Don't you think it's terrific? Just think, there's so much room, we can even have a gym up here."

Marc stopped dead. "We? What's with the 'we'?"

"And a sauna, and a steam room and a jacuzzi."

"Not a jacuzzi," said Marc, catching up with her and pulling her round to face him. "It might leak."

"OK, we'll have that downstairs. There's plenty of room; we could even have a pool."

"No pool," said Marc firmly.

"A small pool?"

"Not even a puddle."

"But you admit it's a terrific location? We'd hardly have to make any changes."

"We?" he teased. "Why do you keep saying 'we'?"

"This time I'll do it properly. I'll get a bank loan like a normal businesswoman, not go crying to Mummy for help."

He became serious. "For a bank loan on this scale you'll need security."

"I'll sell my car."

"I think you'll need to do a bit more than that."

"Money," said Caitlin bitterly. "Why does everything boil down to money?"

Marc stared at her. "If you really want it that much, I'll help you. I can get out of the force on a medical pension. We can use my cottage as security and live off the pension until the place is up and running."

"I don't want your money," she scowled. "I don't want anyone's money. I want to do it by *myself*."

"We'll do it by *ourselves*," said Marc quietly. "We're getting married together, we're having a child together, why can't we run a business together? Equal partners."

She smiled. "I hate to say it, Marc, but what do you know about aerobics?"

"About as much as you know about making money! You can be in charge of aerobics. I shall be in charge of finance."

"My own personal financial advisor?" she teased. "Does that mean you'll want to suck my toes?"

"Yes," said Marc seriously. "And anything else which comes to mind."

She put out her hand. "OK, Mr Granger, you have yourself a deal. Although I think I get the better half of the bargain."

He gathered her into his arms. "Not really – you see, I get to have you."

"Fool!" She giggled and held up her face to be kissed. "Love really is blind!"

"That's what happens when your heart's on fire. The smoke gets in your eyes . . ."

THE END